INTRODUCTION TO INFORMATION PROCESSING

FOURTH EDITION

BERYL ROBICHAUD, PH.D.

Consultant and Former Senior Vice President
Management Information Services
McGraw-Hill, Inc.
New York, New York

Research Scholar
Center for Coastal and Environmental Studies
Rutgers University
New Brunswick, New Jersey

EUGENE J. MUSCAT, ED.D.

Professor of Information Systems
McLaren College of Business
University of San Francisco
San Francisco, California

ALIX-MARIE HALL, M.B.A.

Manager, Information and Communications Industry Group
Coopers & Lybrand Management Consulting Services Division
New York, New York

Member, Executive Committee
Database and Publishing Division
Information Industry Association
Washington, D.C.

GLENCOE

Macmillan/McGraw-Hill

Lake Forest, Illinois
Columbus, Ohio
Mission Hills, California
Peoria, Illinois

Sponsoring Editor: Mel J. Hecker
Editing Supervisor: Ira C. Roberts
Design and Art Supervisor/Interior Design:
 Annette Mastrolia-Tynan
Production Supervisor: Mirabel P. Flores

Cover Designer: Sulpizio Association
Cover Illustration: Gregg Purdon

Library of Congress Cataloging-in-Publication Data

Robichaud, Beryl.
    Introduction to information processing/Beryl Robichaud, Eugene
J. Muscat, Alix-Marie Hall.—4th ed.
        p. cm.
    Rev. ed. of: Introduction to data processing. 3rd ed. 1983.
    Includes index.
    ISBN 0-07-053211-7:
    1. Electronic data processing.   2. Business-Data processing.
I. Muscat, Eugene J., date.   II. Hall, Alix-Marie, date.   III. Robichaud,
Beryl. Introduction to data processing.   IV. Title.
HF5548.2.R6 1989   87-31674
651.8—dc19   CIP

Introduction to Information Processing, Fourth Edition

Imprint 1991

Formerly published under the title *Introduction to Data Processing*.

3 4 5 6 7 8 9 10 11 12 13 14 15 VH 00 99 98 97 96 95 94 93 92 91

ISBN 0-07-053211-7

CONTENTS

Virtually all people involved in business activities today process data in some form in their jobs. Office workers may spend their entire day doing a variety of data processing tasks, but even sales people, factory workers, researchers, and farmers spend part of their time doing paperwork, another name for information processing. Young people ready to enter the job market, as well as those already in it who would like to advance their careers, find that knowledge of information processing and computers is a skill in great demand.

Introduction to Information Processing, Fourth Edition, explores the field of information processing: its meaning, its methods and equipment, and its needs for human resources. The textbook presents the basics of modern methods of processing data, while assuming little or no familiarity with information processing on the part of the instructor or the student. This new edition also provides an understanding of such key topics as new software developments, microcomputers, telecommunications, and networking in the business environment. Computer information processing is emphasized because of its ever-increasing importance to modern business. The textbook traces the development of computer technology and examines computer hardware, programming, and software development. The use of computers for problem solving in business and for meeting personal needs for information is also covered.

Introduction to Information Processing, Fourth Edition, is designed to meet the needs of students who will pursue a business information processing career. In addition, all students who should be computer literate can use the fundamental concepts described in this book.

The discussions and illustrations of various jobs throughout the textbook enable students to picture a variety of business employees interacting on the job, to understand the flow of data from one worker to the next, and to appreciate the need for planning, accuracy, and good communication.

Components of the Program

The fourth edition of *Introduction to Information Processing* includes a textbook, a work kit with actual business forms, and microcomputer applications on disk for popular microcomputer models, and a source book and key that includes tests and transparency masters for duplication.

Textbook. The textbook is divided into six parts that cover the following areas: information processing concepts, computer hardware, computer information systems, computer programming and software, career opportunities, and the future of information processing. These parts are divided into chapters that begin with performance goals. The chapters are subdivided into short, readable topics. Each topic contains exercises that reinforce the concepts that have been presented. At the end of each chapter there are Review Questions; discussion questions; and Information Processing Activities, which summarize the work assignments found in the work kit. At the end of each part you will find a Software Project that will better help the student understand how word processing, spreadsheet, database, graphing, and integrated software actually work. Short lessons in BASIC are included at the end of the book for those teachers who wish to teach their students the basis of a programming language in the course. The BASIC Projects offer students the opportunity to develop a conceptual, or hands-on, awareness of computer programming. In addition, a glossary to aid students in the development of information processing vocabulary has been included as an appendix.

Part 1, Concepts of Information Processing and Computers, introduces students to the concept of information processing, to the operations that make up an information processing cycle, and to the development of modern business information processing. Students are exposed to the wide variety of business equipment now used in modern offices for data input, processing, storage, and output. A chapter on the history of information processing equipment covers the evolution of computing machinery and word processing.

Part 2, Computer Hardware, describes the different input, processing, storage, and output equipment that make up a computer. This section builds student understanding of computers: how computers operate and in what ways they differ from other machines. The functions performed by different units of hardware are described, the major types of computer systems are differentiated, and new technology in the areas of data communications and networking are explained.

Part 3, Computer Information Systems, explains what information systems are in the context of business, specialized industries, and personal home use. This section describes how the work of people and machines is organized into systems and procedures that produce the information required to run a business. The student is taken step by step through the process of developing information systems: systems analysis, system design, system implementation, and system evaluation and maintenance. These stages are defined and then illustrated by using a case study of a common system.

Part 4, Computer Programming and Software, presents concepts of computer programming and software applications packages. The use of programming languages is defined and illustrations of the most popular languages are provided. Special attention is given to the differences between operating software, applications software, and software utilities. Detailed explanations of word processing, telecommunications, accounting and business management, database management, and spreadsheet software are all included.

Part 5, Opportunities in Information Processing, describes the trend toward a service economy and what that means in relation to an employee's need for a background in information processing. Some of the personal characteristics and general aptitudes that lead to success in an information processing career are discussed in relation to existing opportunities in the area. New areas of expanding opportunities are also explored. The student will learn about the differences between working in a centralized computing environment as opposed to a decentralized environment, and will be given an overview of career opportunities in business and government.

Part 6, The Future, examines the key trends in computer technology and suggests ways in which these changes will shape the world in which we work and live. Such issues as computer technology and employment opportunities and individual privacy and criminal activities are all examined.

Appendix 1, BASIC Projects, contains nine BASIC exercises through which the student can learn the fundamentals of the BASIC programming language. All the elementary commands are covered, and the student actually completes a program with each of the exercises.

Appendix 2, Glossary, contains definitions of all the fundamental concepts covered in the text.

Information Processing Work Kit. This self-contained packet of activities consists of an instruction manual, a booklet of business forms and working papers, and a flowcharting template. Although the kit may be used independently of the textbook, the 14 sets of activities correlate with the 14 chapters of the textbook.

The purpose of the work kit is to teach students information processing job skills. Each section of the instruction manual contains a statement of skills-directed performance goals. The activities that the manual directs students to perform are set in realistically described job environments. The students thus become familiar with the types of assignments they will face in employer-sponsored training programs and on the job. No equipment beyond that provided in the kit is necessary, although it is suggested that computer equipment be made available to students.

Information Processing Source Book and Key. The source book and key contains teaching suggestions for both the textbook and the work kit. Included are sample answers for the end-of-chapter discussion questions and suggested classroom activities, scheduling options for courses of varying length, and suggested methods to evaluate students' work. Also included are references to a variety of transparencies, films, books, and magazines that are useful in expanding discussions of textbook topics in ways relevant to local business needs. There is a section containing microcomputer applications that introduce the assignments that the student will find on the optional program disk. The source book and key also contains a test for each chapter of the textbook and a mid-term and a final.

Information Processing Microcomputer Applications. An optional set of interactive exercises, coordinated with topics discussed in the text and the related work kit chapters, is also available. These projects allow students to get a feel for problem solving in the area of information processing, and give them actual experience working with the computer.

Acknowledgments

The authors would like to thank the many instructors and business persons who have helped make the fourth edition of *Introduction to Information Processing* both relevant to today's student and useful to tomorrow's business worker. The authors are especially grateful to the following educators for their thoughtful review and helpful suggestions: Joseph D. Albillar, Apollo High School, Glendale, Arizona; Pamela C. Ergler, Altoona Area High School, Altoona, Pennsylvania; Eileen Jason, Kane Business Institute, Cherry Hill, New Jersey; Carolyn P. Ott, Walton Comprehensive High School, Marietta, Georgia; Gary L. Schepf, Nimitz High School, Irving, Texas; and Myra W. Ward, Milton High School, Milton, Florida.

The authors would also like to thank the following people for their technical review of the manuscript: Rosemary Fruehling, Software Technology Center, Minneapolis, Minnesota; Michael Gilbertson, Inventure, Minneapolis, Minnesota; and Brian Kiteley, City University of New York, New York, New York.

Beryl Robichaud
Eugene J. Muscat
Alix-Marie Hall

PART 1

CONCEPTS OF INFORMATION PROCESSING AND COMPUTERS

CHAPTER

1 | INFORMATION PROCESSING CONCEPTS

Information Processing Terminology

Information
Data
Information processing
Data processing
Electronic data processing
Input
Output

Information processing cycle
Hard copy
Source document
Classifying and coding data
Alphanumeric code
Summarizing data

Sorting data
Storing data
Retrieving data
Reporting data
Copying data
Communicating data
Microcomputer

Performance Goals

☐ Define the terms *information, data, information processing, data processing,* and *electronic data processing.*

☐ Describe three needs for information within every business.

☐ Define *input, output,* and *information processing cycle.*

☐ Name and describe the four groups of activities involved in information processing.

☐ Describe three advantages of using computers for information processing.

☐ Explain why microcomputers are important to business.

Information processing is a modern term for an activity that is as old as recorded history. **Information** means facts organized in a meaningful way, and the purpose of information processing is to produce useful information from unorganized facts. Ancient societies processed information about their business and government affairs. Sales records, inventories, and taxes levied on individuals were recorded on clay tablets, and as far back as 2000 years ago the abacus was used to compute business profits and costs of government programs. Today, the same type of facts are recorded on magnetic disks, and computers produce information about profits and costs.

Modern information processing starts with a collection of **data**—facts represented by numeric and alphabetic characters and special symbols such as $, %, or @ signs. This raw data is changed into information. The varied activities performed to convert data into useful information are known as **information processing.** The older term *data processing* has the same meaning but points out a change in focus. Early processing of business related facts by computer was called **electronic data processing.** Now the preferred term is *information processing,* as it emphasizes the production of information—the result of the processing activity. To most people, information processing also means using computers to produce information from data.

Prior to this century, most information had to be produced by hand. Today, millions of people are using computers in offices

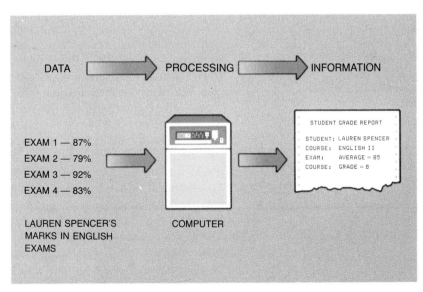

INFORMATION PROCESSING. Computers are used to produce information from data.

and at home to produce useful information about all aspects of business, government activities, and personal affairs. Although computers are used in almost every field, from scientific investigation to sports, in this book we will concentrate on the use of computers in the more typical information processing activities found in modern business and government operations.

WHY BUSINESS NEEDS INFORMATION PROCESSING

In order to succeed, businesses must ask themselves many questions, such as these: How much money did we earn this year? Do we have enough inventory to supply our customer needs? What is the average pay of our computer programmers? These are the types of questions that are more and more being answered by reports generated by information processing activities.

No matter how large or small a business is, it requires information to satisfy the following three functions:

1. *To operate a business.* To keep itself running efficiently from day to day, a business must process information. For example, data about hours worked must be processed so that employees can be paid; data about customers' orders must be handled so that the products ordered can be shipped and the customers billed for the goods sent to them.

2. *To satisfy outside needs for information.* Businesses must satisfy a variety of outside demands for information. Stockholders want detailed information about earnings from companies whose stock they own. The Treasury Department of the U.S. government requires every company to file quarterly reports on taxes withheld from employees' pay. Another federal agency, the Department of Labor, reviews employment data to ensure that minorities and women are not discriminated against in job opportunities. Businesses must file tax returns reporting business profits with state governments as well as the federal government and must keep track of local sales taxes.

3. *To make business plans.* To make plans about future business activities, managers need specific information about past performance and results. Managers must know, for example, both the volume and costs of products sold. By studying this information, managers can make plans for the future manufacture of products and establish prices at which these items should be offered for sale. In business, as in any activity, information increases understanding and helps people make better decisions.

The particular items of information required to fulfill these three needs vary with each business. Banks must record daily the amounts deposited and withdrawn by each customer. Each day airlines must process data to reserve passenger seats on thousands of flights. Manufacturing plants must handle data about production, research, and operating costs. Department stores must keep track of their inventory and sales to customers. Doctors must have information on hand about their patients' medical histories. Schools need records of student attendance and grades.

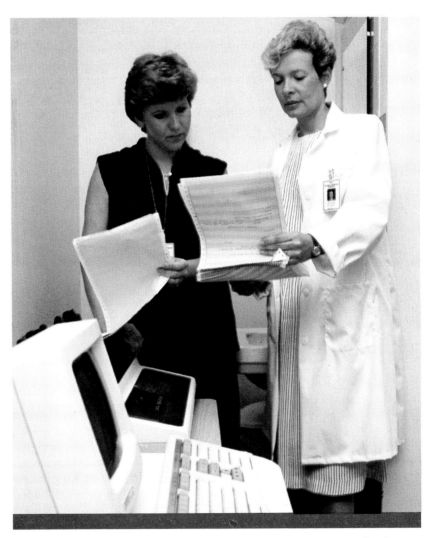

BUSINESS INFORMATION PROCESSING. Vital information, such as results of a patient's tests, is required to recommend treatment. *Courtesy Chedoke, McMaster Hospital.*

Though each company may have its own information requirements, the type of processing operations and the equipment used to produce useful information from raw data are similar, from business to business.

CHECK YOURSELF

Supply the missing words.

1. Information is needed in any business simply to __?__ the business, to satisfy __?__ demands for information, and to make __?__ for future business activities.

2. Facts organized in a meaningful way are called __?__, and unorganized facts are referred to as __?__.

3. The term *information processing* has the same meaning as the term __?__ *processing*.

4. The term __?__ processing means using computers to convert data to information.

5. Data is recorded in three forms: __?__ characters, __?__ characters, and special __?__.

Answers: (1) operate, outside, plans; (2) information, data; (3) data; (4) information; (5) alphabetic, numeric, symbols.

WHAT IS DONE TO CONVERT DATA INTO INFORMATION

Whether done by computer or by hand, information processing consists of four groups of activities:

1. Input preparation
2. Processing operations
3. Storage and retrieval
4. Output reporting and communication

These four activities linked together may be viewed as a cycle in which data is converted into useful information.

The starting point of the cycle is a collection of raw data, called **input.** At the end of the cycle is useful information, called **output.** The term **information processing cycle** refers to all the operations that occur from the collection of input data to getting output into the hands of those who need it.

From start to finish, an information processing cycle may have a few or a very large number of steps, depending upon the complexity of the information required. However, all information processing includes some type of input, processing, storage and retrieval, and output operations.

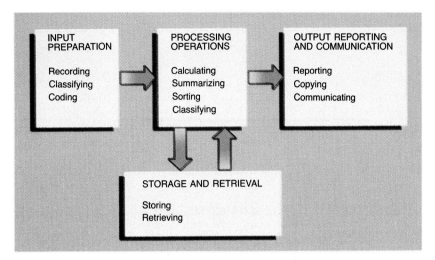

INFORMATION PROCESSING CYCLE. Information processing requires data input, processing, and storage and retrieval operations in order to produce output information.

INPUT PREPARATION

The first step in any information processing activity is input preparation, which refers to the tasks of collecting, recording, and classifying the data needed to produce the required information. The source of the data varies, depending upon the particular information activity. If payroll checks are to be prepared as output, data about the number of hours worked by each employee must be collected. Schools require data on test scores and class performance to prepare students' academic reports. For diagnosis of a patient's ailment, a doctor must assemble data from patient interviews, from tests given the patient, and from any previous treatments already reported.

Recording Data. To collect and record input data in a form that can be processed may involve the writing of data by hand or the keying of data on a machine. Such a recording operation takes place when a sales clerk prepares a sales slip or when a bank teller validates a savings deposit form made out by you. Factory machinists record the quantities of parts produced. Filling station attendants use a credit card to imprint a customer's name and address on a charge ticket for gasoline and oil. To reserve space for a passenger, airline reservations clerks enter input data on a keyboard connected to a TV-like screen called a *video display terminal* (VDT) or a *cathode ray tube* (CRT). All these actions are examples of recording business data.

If data is recorded in a printed form readable by human beings, the recording operation is said to produce **hard copy.** Hard copy can be prepared in several ways. A document such as a customer bill can be prepared by hand, by typewriter, or by a

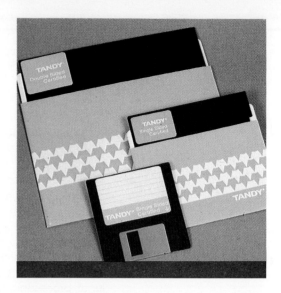

NONREADABLE COPY. Magnetic disks contain data in a form readable by a computer. *Courtesy 3M Corporation.*

computer printer. Data is not always recorded in a form readable by people. Data is now more often recorded as magnetized spots on magnetic disks. These spots are meant to be read by a computer.

Recording, as the first operation in the information processing cycle, is of special importance. An error in recording will result in errors in other operations. An error in recording one amount on a sales slip will mean the summarizing and reporting of wrong totals on the final sales report. Business forms on which data is recorded as the starting operation in an information processing cycle are sometimes called **source documents.** Obviously, it is essential that all data recorded on source documents be accurate.

Sometimes information produced as output from a previous information processing activity may be used as input data to satisfy additional information needs. For example, the number of hamburgers ordered by a customer of a popular food chain is recorded and first used to calculate the charges for the food. Later, the same data will be used to update automatically the restaurant's inventory of hamburger supplies and the sales records. Reuse of verified data already recorded in machine-readable form makes it much easier to ensure accuracy in information processing activities.

Classifying and Coding Input Data. Often it is necessary to include a classifying and coding operation as part of data preparation. **Classifying and coding** is the task of identifying one kind of data and distinguishing it from another kind by means of code numbers or letters. The use of codes speeds up processing of data whether processing is done by hand or by machine.

Data may be classified and coded so that it identifies a particular person or item, such as a customer, an employee, or a product. For example, a purchase order comes from a particular customer who must be identified. Often the purchase order names the salesperson who is to receive credit for the sale, and it must always identify the product ordered.

Data also may be classified to identify groups of similar people or items. For example, all customers of a company may be classified by geographic locations: the Northwest, the Southwest, the Midwest, the Northeast, or the Southeast. Students in school are classified by the grade they are in, such as tenth grade, eleventh grade, or twelfth grade.

Our own names are an example of a classification system. A last name identifies a family group, and a first name identifies a particular person in that family group. Your home telephone number is a code number. A telephone number usually consists of ten numbers. The first three numbers stand for all telephones within a specific geographic area, such as a state or a section of a state. The next three digits stand for all telephones within a specific city or part of a city or town. The last four numbers distinguish a particular telephone.

A good example of classifying business data by code numbers is the use of social security numbers. The federal government gives each person a unique nine-digit code number for identification purposes because it is easier to identify people by number than by name. Not only is the social security number usually shorter than a person's name but it also provides more precise identification of the person. No two people have the same social security number, but many people have the same name. For instance, in just one city, there are over 3500 Smiths, 2500 Cohens, and 1800 Rodriguezes—a number of whom may have the same first names.

A coding system may consist of numeric characters (numbers), alphabetic characters (letters), or both. A coding system that is made up of both numeric and alphabetic characters is called an **alphanumeric code system.** Of the three types of codes, numeric codes are the most common because they are the simplest to use in computer information processing.

A good example of a completely numeric code system is the post office ZIP Code that should appear as part of the address on all mail. The ZIP Code starts with a five-digit number identifying the particular post office responsible for delivering the mail to the correct address. New Jersey, for example, is divided into many postal areas, each of which has a different ZIP Code number. The ZIP Code for Hightstown, New Jersey, is 08520; the city of Freehold, which is 20 miles (approximately 32 kilometers) away, has the ZIP Code 07728. An additional four digits are used in some large cities to identify an individual organiza-

EXAMPLES OF CODES
Names
Phone numbers
Social security numbers
ZIP Codes
Account numbers

EXAMPLES OF STATE CODES	
CA	CALIFORNIA
CO	COLORADO
FL	FLORIDA
IL	ILLINOIS
MA	MASSACHUSETTS
NY	NEW YORK
OK	OKLAHOMA
TX	TEXAS

CLASSIFYING. Codes on credit cards permit easy identification of customers. *Courtesy Mobil Oil, Interbank Card Association, and VISA U.S.A. Inc.*

tion. The University of San Francisco, for example, has its own nine-digit ZIP Code, 94117-1080.

The post office has established another code that is alphabetic; it is used to identify the name of each state.

An alphanumeric code system is used by some state motor vehicle bureaus for the identification of automobiles owned by residents of the state. These codes are recorded in the motor vehicle files and appear on automobile license plates.

The classifying operation is time-consuming if not done by computer. That is why every effort is made to classify data before it is used—that is, to classify data even before it is recorded. Banks identify customers by printing the customer account number on each customer's blank checks. Gasoline companies and department stores identify customers by issuing them credit cards showing customer numbers. Supermarkets identify different items of merchandise by labeling them with identifying symbols for categories such as meat, produce, and dairy products.

PROCESSING OPERATIONS

In some cases a few and in other situations many different types of processing operations may be required to convert input data into output information. This depends upon the complexity of the company's or individual's information requirements. Calculating, summarizing, and sorting of data are the most common types of operations performed in business information processing. Also, the operation of classifying, when done by computer, is part of the processing activity. (As described earlier, manual classifying and coding are steps in input preparation.)

Calculating. Usually some calculating operations are needed to produce useful information. Much of business information processing, however, can be done with the simple arithmetic operations of addition, subtraction, multiplication, and division. Scientific work involves more complex mathematical manipulations of data, for example, the use of square roots.

Summarizing. The operation of **summarizing** is performed to reduce a large volume of data into a smaller volume of information. There are several reasons for summarizing business data. The first is to make information more usable. Factory managers, for example, must keep informed about the total number of overtime hours worked in their plant so that they can decide whether additional staffing is needed. A long list of the daily overtime hours of each employee would be confusing to the plant manager. Instead, employee overtime hours can be summarized into weekly totals by factory departments to make the information more concise and usable for decision making.

A second reason for a summarizing operation is to simplify further processing of data. Often daily sales data is summarized each week into weekly totals so that there is a smaller volume of data to be processed for monthly totals of sales. When data is summarized throughout the month, information about results for the whole month can be made available sooner.

Sorting. To make information more usable, data must be arranged in a desired sequence (or order). Data **sorting** is the process of arranging paper documents or data records on magnetic disks or tapes in the desired sequence. There are two types of sorting sequences: numeric and alphabetic.

A numeric sequence is the arrangement of documents or data records by numbers. The numbers may be arranged in *ascending* (from the lowest to the highest) or *descending* (from the highest to the lowest) order. Look at the illustration below showing data listed in ascending order by social security number. Arrangement in numeric sequence also includes sorting data by groups of numbers. For example, accounts receivable

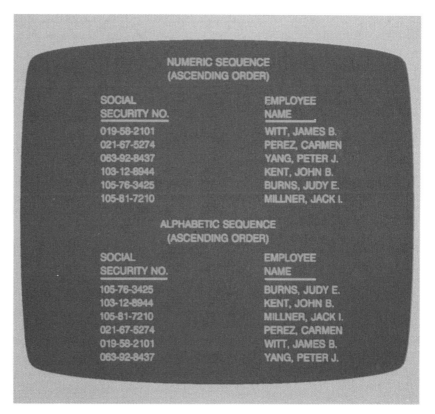

SORTING. Data shown here is first sequenced by numeric ascending order, then by alphabetic ascending order.

(customers who owe money to a business) are often grouped by the number of days the account balance is overdue—1 to 30 days, 31 to 60 days, 61 to 90 days, and 91 days and over.

An alphabetic sequence is the arrangement of data from A to Z or Z to A. The data illustrated above, which was listed earlier in numeric sequence (by social security number), is shown re-sorted and listed in alphabetic sequence (by name).

Data records on magnetic disks may be sorted very quickly by computer, whereas machine sorting of physical documents (such as bank checks) takes longer. Even so, by comparison, sorting of documents by hand is a very slow operation. The sorting required in the delivery of mail is the largest document-sorting activity in the United States, and much of it is still done using hand sorting methods.

Numeric sorting, whether it is done by hand or by machine, can be done faster than alphabetic sorting. This is why we use ZIP Code numbers to ensure fast delivery of mail. Numeric code numbers also make the daily task of sorting millions of bank checks much easier for machines. The code numbers recorded on each check not only provide an abbreviated identification of a particular customer but they can also specify the particular branch bank at which the customer's account is located and the type of account the customer has. However, the fewer the numbers or letters in the code, the faster the sorting operation, whether done by hand or by machine.

STORING AND RETRIEVING DATA

The saving of data for future use in information processing is called **storing data.** Data placed in storage may remain there less than a second or for many months before it is used again. When computers are used for information processing, data is stored on magnetic disks or tapes. A huge amount of data may be stored in magnetic form in a very small space. For instance, a typical floppy disk for a minicomputer can hold the equivalent of 70 pages of information.

Paper documents are also stored (or filed) in modern offices for future use. For example, a bill may be kept (stored) until the date on which it must be paid. After it has been paid, records of proof of payment may be kept for months or even years. Other items of data such as payroll records must be kept in storage many years for audit and tax purposes.

The operation of searching for and finding data that is stored is referred to as **retrieving data.** When stored paper documents are needed, files must be manually searched to retrieve the data that is needed. Using computers and magnetic storage devices, many businesses are now able to retrieve information electronically. For instance, an engineer using a computer can now retrieve a drawing that has been stored on magnetic disk or tape so that she or he can update the drawing or get a print of it. This is extremely important because in almost all types of business information processing data is worked on, stored for a short time, and used or reprocessed at a later date. Data retrieval may require a good deal of time if it is done manually. On the other hand, data retrieval may take less than a second if it is done electronically. To illustrate this concept, think of looking up a telephone number. Looking it up in a telephone book is time-consuming and tedious. Information operators who work for phone companies have computerized phone books that greatly speed up the process of finding a number.

OUTPUT REPORTING AND COMMUNICATION

The final activity in the information processing cycle is to produce the needed information and to get it distributed to the right people. Output **reporting** is the operation of making the output results available to those who need them. The information that comes out of the processing cycle may be reported in many different forms, depending upon how the results are to be used. Some output information is printed on report forms with column headings. Other results may be reported on specially designed forms such as customer invoices or checks. In modern information processing, much of the information produced by a computer does not have to be printed in hard-copy form. Instead, it may simply be recorded on magnetic disks or tapes for

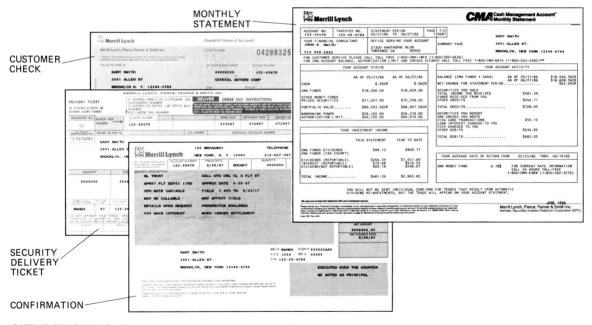

OUTPUT REPORTING. Documents shown are typical financial business documents prepared by a computer. *Courtesy Merrill Lynch.*

future reference. Information stored in this manner can then be visually displayed on a terminal screen for the user. Another form of output is the reporting of information in a physically reduced form, such as microfilm.

Output information is usually needed by more than one individual in an organization and must be copied or reproduced. Often, a copying operation is done by hand on a photocopying machine to make a few copies of a report or other paper document.

Sometimes only selected items of data need to be reproduced. For instance, just the account number and the amount from a check may need to be copied. Whatever the degree of reproduction, the operation is referred to as **copying data.** A copying operation does not always produce a hard-copy document. Information can be copied into a machine-readable form such as magnetic disks or tapes that can then be distributed to individuals who need the output. For example, Standard and Poors, a financial publishing company, allows subscribers to download files that contain the latest information on stock market transactions on a daily basis.

Communicating means the distribution of information (or data) from one person or place to another. Business information may be exchanged orally, either face-to-face or by telephone. Business communications also involve the physical transportation of documents by messenger, by mechanical equipment such as conveyers, and by the U.S. Postal Service and private mail delivery services.

Before the 1950s, selected items of information could be communicated by wire transmission only at relatively slow speeds. Today there are many electronic means for high-speed communication of business data and information. Input data and output information can be transferred quickly from desk to desk, from office to warehouse, from production line to office, or from a travel agency office to an airline reservation computer thousands of miles away. With modern communications methods, reproductions of entire documents can be transmitted across the country in a few minutes using special devices called *FAX machines.* Computers can easily communicate with each other, over the telephone lines, if the computers on both ends of the line use a computer device called a modem.

EXAMPLE OF
AN INFORMATION
PROCESSING
CYCLE

In the illustration on page 15 you can trace operations through a simplified information processing cycle. The example shows input preparation, processing, storage and retrieval, and output reporting and communication activities that are performed to produce sales information for a large automobile manufacturer.

All companies encourage salespersons to sell more of their products. Many, like automobile manufacturers, give special bonuses to those who make the most sales. For this reason, managers need information about sales performance. The information processing cycle illustrated here shows, in simplified form, some of the activities that may be performed to provide this information.

INPUT PREPARATION ACTIVITIES

TERMINAL IN
AGENCY OFFICE

The GF auto manufacturer has about 3,000 sales people located in 453 sales agencies throughout the country.

1. Each month a data entry operator in each sales agency keys into a terminal the following data about each salesperson in the agency:

> Salesperson code number
> Number of automobiles sold in the current month

2. The input data is transmitted electronically to a computer in the central office of the automobile manufacturer.

INPUT DATA

PROCESSING, STORAGE, AND RETRIEVAL OPERATIONS

The input data on the current month's automobile sales from all sales agencies is combined on magnetic disk for processing.

CENTRAL COMPUTER

1. The sales code numbers are used as identification to retrieve from magnetic disk storage information about the automobile sales made by each salesperson as of the end of the previous month. The full name of the salesperson and sales agency is retrieved from storage in the same operation.

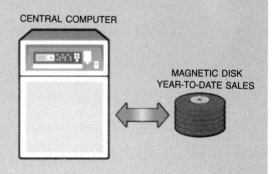

MAGNETIC DISK
YEAR-TO-DATE SALES

2. The auto sales for the current month are added to the previous year-to-date total sales to get a new year-to-date sales figure for each salesperson.

3. The sales records are sorted by year-to-date sales figures to sequence the salespeople in descending order (highest to lowest) of the number of automobiles sold for the year.

4. The new current year-to-date sales total for each salesperson is stored on magnetic disk for use in next month's processing cycle.

OUTPUT REPORTING AND COMMUNICATION

1. A report is printed for management showing the top one hundred sales performers year-to-date who are to be awarded special bonuses.

2. Copies of the report are made and distributed to each agency office.

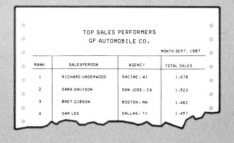

EXAMPLE OF AN INFORMATION PROCESSING CYCLE.

Match each term with the word or phrase that best defines it.

1. Searching for and locating data that is stored.
2. Post Office ZIP Code.
3. First step in any information processing activity.
4. Identifying and distinguishing one kind of data from another.
5. Code system made up of numeric and alphabetic characters.
6. Reducing a large volume of data into a more compact form.
7. Saving data for future use.
8. Calculating, summarizing, and sorting activities.
9. Distribution of information from one place to another.
10. Arranging data in a desired sequence.

a. Alphabetic code
b. Storing
c. Summarizing
d. Input preparation
e. Retrieval of data
f. Sorting
g. Processing operations
h. Alphanumeric code
i. Classifying and coding
j. Calculating
k. Communicating
l. Numeric code

Answers: (1) e; (2) l; (3) d; (4) i; (5) h; (6) c; (7) b; (8) g; (9) k; (10) f.

WHY COMPUTERS ARE USED FOR INFORMATION PROCESSING

Banks, insurance companies, utilities, magazine publishers, and the Social Security Administration are just a few of the organizations in which customer files of millions of records must be kept up to date daily. To do the daily updates may mean that billions of processing operations must be performed each day. Although the number of customer and business transactions is much smaller in a small enterprise, data still has to be processed to produce the information necessary to operate the business. A small gift shop, for example, must keep track of its supplies of merchandise so that it can satisfy customer demands. It also must keep accurate records of amounts paid out for goods, supplies, and services and report its net profit to the government for tax purposes. For all business activities, regardless of size, computers have three advantages over other types of office equipment that process information—computers are:

- Faster
- More accurate
- More economical

FAST INFORMATION PROCESSING

MEASUREMENTS OF COMPUTER PROCESSING TIME

Time	Parts of a Second
Millisecond	One thousandth
Microsecond	One millionth
Nanosecond	One billionth
Picosecond	One trillionth

Until the computer was available, the fastest machines for processing data were punched-card processing machines. The computer by far outperforms every punched-card machine. For example, a punched-card calculator can perform and record in punched-card form several thousand calculations an hour. By comparison, large computers can perform one billion calculations a second.

Operating speeds of smaller computers are being measured in microseconds (millionths of a second) and nanoseconds (billionths of a second). Larger computers even execute instructions in picoseconds (trillionths of a second). The very fast speeds of computers come from the use of electrical impulses to represent data. These impulses travel almost at the speed of light through computer circuitry.

High-speed information processing is essential in businesses faced with large numbers of customers and transactions, as are banks and insurance companies. It also is important to owners of small businesses who must ensure that employees are paid on time and customers are billed correctly.

ACCURATE INFORMATION PROCESSING

Computers not only process data faster, they produce more accurate results than other office equipment does, as long as they are properly instructed. Computers are also efficient: they can work around the clock every day of the year without even a coffee break. The accuracy of computer processing is improved by having the machine check its own work. Special programs are written to help the computer do this. Errors found in the results of processing usually come from errors in either the computer program or the input data to be processed.

Accurate processing is as important as speed in business information processing. Reliability in processing patient medical histories or in processing traffic control data for busy airports can result in the saving of lives.

ECONOMICAL INFORMATION PROCESSING

Compared with other office equipment, computers are not cheap. Still, a business usually realizes savings from computer processing of information. This is because information processing by computer requires much less expensive human effort than does any mechanical means of information processing. Computer processing is more automatic because of the computer's ability to:

■ Accept and store a set of instructions in advance of its work.
■ Handle data stored electronically.

Following instructions just like a robot, the computer performs processing operations in the order specified by the oper-

COMPUTERS. Computers provide faster, more accurate, and more economical information processing. *Will Faller.*

ating instructions. The ability to perform a large number of different operations with little help from the operator is not possible in other information processing methods.

The handling of data in electronic form also makes computer processing more automatic than is the case when other types of processing are used. Imagine what a problem it has been for large companies to handle millions of customer records on ledger cards or even on punched cards.

In computer processing, data is usually stored in electronic form such as magnetized spots on different types of magnetic material (or media). Magnetic disks are most commonly used. On a single 8-inch (20.3-centimeter) disk, millions of characters of data can be stored. The manuscript for this book could probably fit on one 8-inch disk. Smaller diskettes of 5¼ and 3½ inches (13.34 and 8.89 centimeters) are also available. Because data is compressed in such a small space in computer files, there are enormous savings in human effort in handling the files.

Even though computers provide more automatic information processing and require less human effort than do manual or mechanical processing methods, they have created many new job opportunities. Millions of people are involved every day in computerized information processing activities. Many workers prepare the input data for the computers or operate computer equipment. Others are involved in the design of computer systems, and some in the manufacture of equipment. Computers have eliminated many of the boring, repetitive processing tasks involved in converting raw data into information. Accountants no longer have to add up hundreds of numbers and do hundreds of calculations to figure out the taxes due for a business. The computer does all the calculating or information processing. The accountant can spend his or her time advising the company on how to save money or how to improve the profitability of the business. Secretaries need type a letter only once; by using special software, they can send that letter, with each different person's name on it, to as many people as necessary, without retyping the entire letter each time.

The larger the business and the greater its volume of transactions, the more economical computer use is likely to be. However, recent equipment developments have brought computers well within the reach of the smallest businesses and the pocketbooks of individuals who process data at home.

THE SPECIAL IMPORTANCE OF MICROCOMPUTERS

The first computers brought into business offices in this country were very expensive and were used solely by the largest corporations. Only in the 1970s did the availability of less expensive computers make it possible for many smaller companies to afford computers. The development of microcomputers has been of special importance. **Microcomputer** is the name given to a small, low-cost computer system. Though small in physical size, a microcomputer can perform input, processing, storage and retrieval, and output operations rapidly, accurately, automatically, and economically. The IBM PC, the Apple Macintosh, and the Compaq computer are all examples of microcomputers.

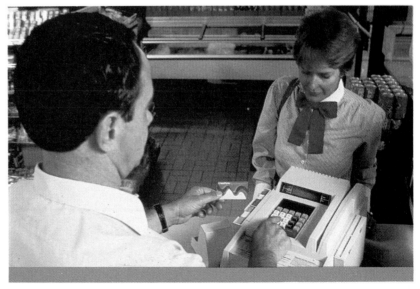

COMPUTERIZED INFORMATION PROCESSING. Sales clerks can easily check a customer's credit using electronic equipment. *Courtesy Mobil Oil Corporation.*

MICROCOMPUTERS. Microcomputers can be used to operate small businesses at home. *Bob Rogers.*

The availability of microcomputers has given an opportunity to almost every type of business activity, regardless of the size or nature of its operation, to realize the advantages of computerized information processing. Today microcomputers are used by individuals in business offices, government agencies, and educational and health institutions. Many microcomputers are also used in the home. Whether located in an office, laboratory, or home, a microcomputer performs the same function as a larger computer system—it produces useful information from unorganized facts (data).

CHECK YOURSELF

Supply the missing words.

1. Three advantages of computer processing over other methods are these: computers have greater speed, provide more accurate processing, and are less __?__ to operate.
2. A nanosecond is one- __?__ of a second.
3. Data is often recorded in the form of __?__ spots in order to reduce a large volume of business records to a small space.
4. To produce accurate results, computers must be properly instructed and have __?__ input.

Answers: (1) expensive (or costly); (2) billionth; (3) magnetized; (4) accurate.

REVIEW QUESTIONS

1. Define the terms *information, data,* and *information processing.*
2. Businesses have three primary needs for processing business data. Name them and give an example of each.
3. Define the terms *input, output,* and *information processing cycle.*
4. Name and describe the four groups of activities in an information processing cycle.
5. Explain the purpose of classifying and coding input data.
6. Name three common types of processing operations.
7. Describe why and how data may be stored in information processing.
8. Name three ways in which output information may be reported.
9. Describe three advantages of using computers for information processing.
10. Explain why the development of microcomputers is of special importance.

COMPARING IDEAS

The questions below are to help you think about what you have learned in this chapter. They are thought questions. There is no one correct answer.

1. Give an example of an information processing cycle that you would expect to find in a school, a bank, or an airline office. Identify some of the items of data input, one or more of the processing operations, and the information output produced in the cycle.
2. Name situations in which you have seen individuals in business using computer terminals for data input.

INFORMATION PROCESSING ACTIVITIES

Now you can perform a few of the information processing activities that business workers perform. Below is a summary of the tasks you will complete. You will find the actual data and business forms you need in your *Information Processing Work Kit.*

1. As an assistant to the sales manager you will complete a quarterly sales report to determine the top salesperson in a local Computer Shack store.
2. You will help a systems analyst at Computer Shack verify the accuracy of a computer output report. You will also review credit card slips for completeness.

CHAPTER 2

HISTORY OF INFORMATION PROCESSING EQUIPMENT

Information Processing Terminology

Information Revolution
Abacus
Electromechanical machines
Control panel
Analytical engine
Stored program
Integrated circuits
Minicomputers

Large-scale integrated circuits
Very large-scale integrated circuits
Microprocessor
Microcomputer
Computer programming

Information processing
Word processing
Word processor
Dedicated word processor
Automation
Office automation

Who's Who in Information Processing

Blaise Pascal
Gottfried Leibniz
Charles Thomas de Colmar
Joseph Jacquard
Herman Hollerith
Thomas J. Watson Sr.

Charles Babbage
Lady Ada Lovelace
Howard Aiken
John Vincent Atanasoff
Clifford Berry
J. Presper Eckert
John Mauchly

John von Neumann
Thomas J. Watson Jr.
M.E. Hoff
Steven Jobs
Stephen Wozniak
Grace Hopper

Performance Goals

☐ Explain what the Information Revolution is, its impact on society, and how it differs from the Industrial Revolution.

☐ Describe key steps in the development of calculating equipment from the abacus to modern business calculators.

☐ Describe the concept of punched-card processing.

☐ Describe four important advances made in the development of scientific computers.

☐ List the reasons for developing the first business computer.

☐ Describe the differences in the four generations of business computers.

☐ List the characteristics of a microprocessor.

☐ Define word processing and describe the four types of equipment used for word processing.

☐ Define *automation* and *office automation* and explain what has made it possible to automate office functions.

Although information has been processed for thousands of years, before 1900 most information processing was done by hand. Even typewriters and simple calculating machines were not common in business offices until this century. Today, millions of computers are used to process data for business. Before 1950 there were none; nor were there any of the hand-held electronic calculators now so common.

Because such enormous changes have occurred in information processing in recent decades, some say that we are living in the age of the **Information Revolution.** Almost every day improvements are made in the ways we record, process, store, report, and communicate information. In the industrial revolution in the nineteenth century, many improvements were made in manufacturing methods. As a result of the extensive use of new machinery in factories, products could be made faster and less expensively. Similarly, the information revolution is making it possible to produce faster and more cheaply the huge amount of information needed to operate our much more complex business and government operations. If used properly, computers can also make our individual lives more productive and rewarding, and offer many benefits to society. For example, medical diagnostic services and educational opportunities can be extended to individuals living in remote areas who do not have such services available in their communities.

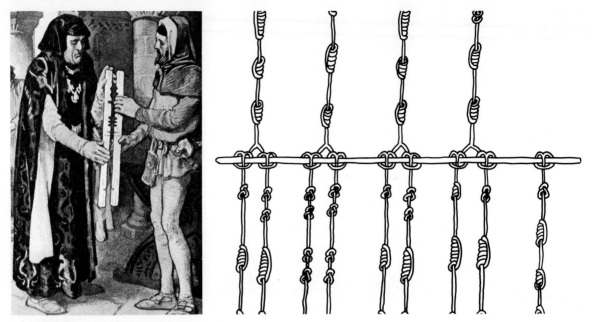

OLD METHODS OF RECORDING DATA. Tally sticks (shown at left) were used in England and other countries to record debts and payments. Matching sticks verified that an account was paid. Knotted strings, called *quipu* (shown at right), were used by the Incas for recording data. *Courtesy the Bettmann Archive.*

Modern information processing equipment has its origin in the simple devices used many years ago to record, process, and store data. The invention of paper was a great advance for data input and storage. Think how difficult it must have been to record data on clay or stone tablets. Recording data on paper is also easier and less bulky than tying knots in certain places on strings or carving notches of various sizes in wood sticks. The Incas of South America used a complex system of knotted strings to record data about the contents of their storehouses. Notched wood sticks (tally sticks) were used by the British government to record debts and payments from the thirteenth to the nineteenth centuries. In 1834, officials tried to destroy old wood tally records by burning them in a stove. But in doing so, they accidentally set fire to the two British Houses of Parliament and both buildings burned to the ground.

The history of information processing is full of interesting anecdotes; however, knowledge of early equipment used for processing data is also useful, because it makes it easier to understand how computers came to be developed and why they work as they do.

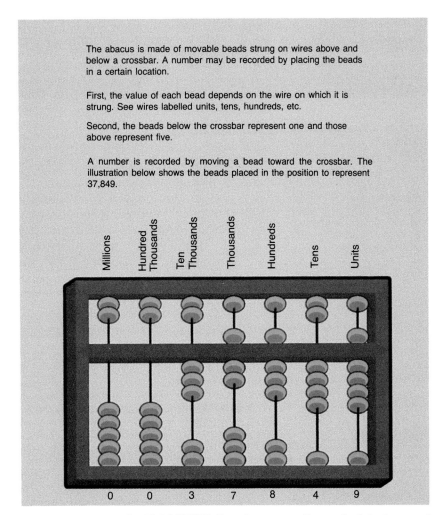

The abacus is made of movable beads strung on wires above and below a crossbar. A number may be recorded by placing the beads in a certain location.

First, the value of each bead depends on the wire on which it is strung. See wires labelled units, tens, hundreds, etc.

Second, the beads below the crossbar represent one and those above represent five.

A number is recorded by moving a bead toward the crossbar. The illustration below shows the beads placed in the position to represent 37,849.

Millions | Hundred Thousands | Ten Thousands | Thousands | Hundreds | Tens | Units

0   0   3   7   8   4   9

MANUAL INFORMATION PROCESSING. The abacus was the earliest device used to calculate. *Courtesy IBM Historical Archive.*

PRECOMPUTER AGE OF EQUIPMENT

From the beginning, people have searched for aids to make calculating operations easier. The **abacus** was one of the earliest of these aids. It was invented over 2000 years ago by Asian merchants to speed up calculation, and it is still used today in China and other parts of the world. However, as shown in the illustration above, the abacus is simply a hand device for recording numbers as one is performing a calculation. It was not until the 1600s that people began to design machines that could actually perform arithmetic. Two equipment developments were particularly important for information processing in the precomputer age:

- The invention of calculating machines.
- The development of punched-card information processing equipment.

CALCULATING MACHINES

After the first calculating machine was built in 1642, numerous equipment improvements were made. There have been five milestones in the evolution of improved calculating machines:

1. The invention of a machine that could add and subtract.
2. The invention of a machine that could multiply and divide as well as add and subtract.
3. The development of production techniques and materials that made it possible to produce on a mass basis inexpensive copies of new calculating equipment.
4. The use of electricity to operate calculators that previously had to be hand cranked. These are called **electromechanical machines.**
5. The incorporation of electronic components in calculators, which made them faster, more reliable, and smaller.

Individuals who made important contributions to the development of improved calculators are identified in the illustrations on page 27.

PUNCHED-CARD INFORMATION PROCESSING EQUIPMENT

The concept of using punched cards for information processing has a curious origin. It came from an invention by a French weaver named *Joseph Jacquard.* In 1801 Jacquard made a machine (a loom) that would automatically weave patterned cloth. A set of prepunched cards controlled the operation of the loom. Holes placed in the cards determined which colored threads were to be used in specified places on the cloth being woven. The cards could be reused many times to make exact copies of the woven material.

The Jacquard concept of recording data in the form of holes punched in cards was used in the design of punched-card information processing equipment. A second lesson learned from Jacquard was that work can be performed automatically if a set of instructions can be given to a machine to direct it in its operation. The latter concept was fundamental for the development of computers.

Dr. *Herman Hollerith,* who worked for the U.S. Bureau of Census, was the first person to suggest that punched cards be used for information processing. Every ten years the government takes a count of all people living in the country (a census) and produces counts of individuals by age, sex, and residence location, along with other information. The counts had always been done by hand, and in 1880 the manual work took more than seven years to complete. Because the country's population

1642

Blaise Pascal. *Courtesy IBM HIstorical Archive.*

Pascal Machine. *Courtesy IBM Historical Archive.*

Blaise Pascal, a Frenchman, was only 19 years old when he built a workable calculating machine that could perform additions and subtractions. Pascal tired of adding long columns of numbers by hand when helping his father, a tax collector, and invented a machine to do the task. The Pascal Machine was about the size of a shoebox and had eight dials. Numbers were entered by turning the dials as in a telephone instrument. The results of calculations were displayed in register windows above the dials.

1673

Gottfried Leibniz. *Courtesy IBM Historical Archive.*

Gottfried Leibniz, a German diplomat and philosopher, built the first calculating machine that could multiply and divide as well as add and subtract.
The Leibniz Calculator, though laborious to operate, gave accurate results and many of its principles are still used in mechanical calculators.

Leibniz Calculator. *Courtesy of UNISYS Corporation.*

1820

Thomas's Arithmometer. *Courtesy IBM Historical Archive.*

Charles Xavier Thomas invented (in France) the first reliable calculator that was available for commercial use. Combining the basic Leibniz machine design with newer engineering techniques, he produced a machine called an arithmometer. About fifteen hundred of these machines were constructed.

1872

Frank S. Baldwin developed the first mechanical calculator produced in the United States. Improving on the Leibniz design, Baldwin made a much smaller and lighter calculator. Thousands were sold by the early 1900s. (Not shown.)

1886

William S. Burroughs. *Courtesy IBM Historical Archive.*

William Seward Burroughs, an American bank clerk, invented the first commercially available calculator that was both a calculating and listing machine. The inventor later founded the Burroughs Corporation, now the UNISYS corporation.

Joseph Jacquard. *Courtesy IBM Historical Archive.*

Herman Hollerith. *Courtesy IBM Historical Archive.*

Thomas J. Watson, Sr. *Courtesy The Bettmann Archive.*

Jacquard Loom. *Courtesy IBM Historical Archive.*

Hollerith Tabulator. *Courtesy IBM Historical Archive.*

THE DEVELOPMENT OF PUNCHED-CARD INFORMATION PROCESSING EQUIPMENT.

was growing so quickly, government officials became concerned that the 1890 census data could not be compiled before it was time to start work on the 1900 census. Hollerith suggested that the census data be recorded on punched cards that would be put in specially designed electric tabulating machines for automatic counting. His suggestion was adopted for the 1890 census work. With the help of the Hollerith punched-card tabulators, the 1890 population counts were completed in five years.

Dr. Hollerith went on to establish a company to manufacture and market punched-card tabulating machines for other government agencies and business organizations. In the 1920s, *Thomas J. Watson Sr.* took over the management of Hollerith's organization, which at that time was called the Computing-Tabulating-Recording Company. In 1924, Watson changed the name of the company to International Business Machines (IBM). From the 1920s through the early 1950s, a number of different machines were developed to process data (sort, calculate, and print) recorded on punched cards. IBM was the largest supplier of punched-card equipment.

KEY CONCEPTS OF PUNCHED-CARD PROCESSING

Several concepts used in punched-card information processing have been important to computer designers. Data in punched-card processing is represented by the presence or absence of punched holes in specific places on a specially designed card. In computer processing, data is usually represented by the presence or absence of magnetized spots in specific places on specially designed disks or tapes.

Punched-card processing machines are directed by a **control panel,** also called a plugboard. The control panel tells the machine what to do—which data to read and to process, whether for adding or printing. A control panel is similar to a telephone switchboard. Wires are used to complete electric circuits between parts of the machine. The purpose of the control panel is to allow a single machine to perform in sequence a number of operations. The concept of control panel wiring was used by the designers of early computers, and later stimulated the development of stored computer programs.

CHECK YOURSELF

Supply the missing words.

1. Before the invention of paper, stone and clay tablets, knotted strings, and wood sticks with ___?___ were used for the recording of data.
2. Calculators operated by electricity were called ___?___ machines.
3. The calculator invented by William Burroughs could add, subtract, and ___?___ data.
4. A calculating aid that has been used for over 2000 years is the ___?___.
5. Because of the ___?___ Revolution, information can be produced faster and more cheaply.
6. The person who suggested that punched cards be used to tabulate census data was ___?___ ___?___.

HISTORY OF COMPUTERS

Computers were invented by scientists and engineers looking for a faster and more accurate way to perform complex mathematical calculations. The earliest documented design of a computer was made by a mathematician who lived more than 100 years before the first computer was built.

CHARLES BABBAGE AND THE ANALYTICAL ENGINE

Charles Babbage, an English mathematician born in 1791, was displeased with the number of errors that occurred in the printed tables of mathematical calculations that were supposed to save others the trouble of making the calculations. Babbage wanted a more accurate way to make calculations and a way to print the results. His search led him to design the **analytical engine.** The analytical engine was truly a forerunner of modern computers. If it had ever been built, it would have accepted input data (on punched cards), performed processing operations in "the mill" (an arithmetic unit), and stored the calculated results in "the store" (a memory unit). The machine was also designed to produce output information in printed form. The operations of the machine would have been controlled by instructions contained on punched cards.

LADY ADA LOVELACE

Babbage was unable to raise enough funds to complete construction of his analytical engine. Also, the technology of his time was not advanced enough to build the machine according to the specifications needed for it to work. Fortunately, several friends left descriptions of the machine. One such friend was *Lady Ada Augusta Lovelace,* a daughter of the poet, Lord Byron. Lady Lovelace, born in 1815, provided complete details as to exactly how the analytical engine was to work. She said of Babbage's machine: "It can do whatever one knows how to order it to perform." This can be said of a modern computer too. Because she described some of the key elements of computer programming, she often is called *the world's first computer programmer.* Unfortunately, Lady Lovelace died young, at

Charles Babbage. *Courtesy The Charles Babbage Institute.*

Lady Ada Lovelace. *Courtesy Culver Pictures, Inc.*

Babbage Analytical Engine. *Courtesy The Charles Babbage Institute.*

THE DEVELOPMENT OF THE ANALYTICAL ENGINE.

age 36. Her accomplishments were acknowledged by the name *Ada,* given to a programming language developed for the U.S. Department of Defense.

COMPUTERS FOR SCIENTIFIC WORK

After the death of Babbage in 1871, nothing was done on computers until the 1930s. By then, even the fastest calculator or punched-card processing machine could not perform complex mathematical operations quickly enough to satisfy the needs of some scientists and engineers. A few decided to design new machines that could process their information faster. They started with Babbage's ideas for the analytical engine and copied features from electromechanical calculators and punched-card processors. Four developments are of particular significance:

1. *The Mark I.* The first computer-like machine to be built was called the Mark I, also known as the automatic sequence-controlled calculator. The machine was designed by Professor *Howard Aiken* of Harvard University. Work was begun in 1939, and IBM engineers made the Mark I

The Mark I. *Courtesy The Computer Museum.*

The Atlanasoff-Berry Computer. *Courtesy Iowa State University Library.*

The ENIAC. *Courtesy The Charles Babbage Institute.*

The EDVAC. *Courtesy The Bettmann Archive.*

EARLY SCIENTIFIC COMPUTERS.

operational about 1943. The machine weighed 5 tons and was 50 feet long.

The thousands of mechanical parts in the Mark I were controlled by electricity. Because it had no electronic parts, it is not considered a true computer. Nevertheless, the Mark I could solve a mathematical problem 1000 times faster than existing machines could. It read data from punched cards, made calculations, and punched results in a new set of cards. Its processing instructions were recorded on punched paper tape. The Mark I was an important step in the history of computers because its design was to influence designers of later equipment.

2. *The ABC (Atanasoff-Berry Computer).* The next significant step was to design a computer that used electronic parts instead of operating electromechanically. Professor *John Vincent Atanasoff* of Iowa State College and one of his graduate students, *Clifford Berry,* are given credit for

designing the world's first electronic computing machine. The ABC machine, named after its inventors, had about 300 vacuum tubes, but it was very limited in capacity. (Most typical microcomputers today have the equivalent of 640,000 to one million vacuum tubes, but the vacuum tubes have been replaced by miniature transistors etched on tiny computer chips.) The ABC could only do addition and subtraction, not multiplication or division. Atanasoff and Berry began to build their computer in 1939 and worked on it until 1942. But the ABC machine never became fully operational because in 1942 both designers became involved in military efforts associated with World War II. Nevertheless, the electronic design of the ABC provided a starting point for the next computer development.

3. *The ENIAC (Electronic Numerical Integrator and Calculator).* The first electronic computer to be made fully operational was the ENIAC. This machine was designed and built at the University of Pennsylvania's Electrical Engineering School. *J. Presper Eckert* and *John Mauchly* are the two individuals credited with directing the work. The ENIAC was built for the U.S. Army to perform quickly and accurately the complex calculations that gunners needed to aim their artillery weapons. It was a critical necessity for the war effort.

   When completed, the ENIAC had 18,000 vacuum tubes and measured 100 feet in length. The electronic parts made the machine much faster than the Mark I, and it could perform 5000 additions per second. The ENIAC operated for ten years, from 1946 until 1955, and it is said that during this time the machine did more arithmetic than the whole human race had done prior to 1945. Although the ENIAC was a very useful machine, there was no memory in the machine to store the program of instructions that guided the computer in its work. Instead, using a concept that followed the control panel of punched-card processing machines, instructions were handled by complex internal wiring and switch controls. This meant that every time a new job was processed, the wiring and switch controls had to be changed. Because of its many parts and vacuum tubes, it also required constant maintenance; even then it frequently broke down.

4. *Stored Programs and the EDVAC and EDSAC.* The final step in the development of computers as we know them today was to add to the machine a large internal memory in which the program of instructions to be followed by the machine could be stored and retrieved rapidly. The **stored-program** concept was a major advance in computer tech-

nology because it gave much more flexibility in the use of the machine. Just who invented the concept is a matter of controversy. Credit generally is given to *John von Neumann*, one of the most brilliant mathematicians in the United States. Von Neumann worked with the University of Pennsylvania group to design and build a successor to the ENIAC machine. The new computer, named EDVAC (Electronic Discrete Variable Automatic Computer) was designed so that it would be capable of storing its program of instruction. EDVAC was not completed until 1951. Meanwhile, a group of scientists at Cambridge University in England had learned of the stored-program design for EDVAC and began to build their own machine incorporating the new concept. Their machine, named EDSAC (Electronic Delay Storage Automatic Calculator) was finished in the year 1949. Thus, EDSAC is acknowledged as the world's first operating electronic computer that stored its program of instructions.

COMPUTERS FOR BUSINESS USE

When World War II ended, American businesses expanded to meet a much greater demand for consumer products. The volume of information processing operations also grew enormously. In the late 1940s, punched-card processing was the chief means of handling large amounts of data. It provided the fastest and most reliable method of information processing available. There were many business organizations, particularly banks, insurance companies, utilities, publishers, and large manufacturers, that had customer or product files containing millions of punched cards. These cards had to be moved by hand from machine to machine for processing. It became difficult to handle very large workloads effectively. A new method of information processing was needed.

UNIVAC, the First Business Computer. *J. Presper Eckert* and *John Mauchly,* who had developed the ENIAC for military use, recognized that computers could be used to improve information processing in business organizations. They also understood that business had different requirements for information processing equipment from research scientists. Information processing in business usually involves handling large volumes of input and output but rather simple arithmetic processing. Scientific work, on the other hand, generally involves small volumes of input and output but very complex calculations. Eckert and Mauchly designed a new computer, called UNIVAC 1 (UNIVersal Automatic Computer), to meet the particular needs for information processing in business and government offices.

Eckert and Mauchly combined forces with Remington Rand (later the Sperry Corporation and now UNISYS) to finance the staff and manufacturing facilities to produce the UNIVAC. The first UNIVAC, containing 5000 vacuum tubes, was delivered to the U.S. Census Bureau in the early 1950s. Another went to a General Electric plant to handle payroll processing.

IBM Gets a Late Start. Although IBM had participated in the development of the Mark I, Thomas J. Watson Sr., head of the company, did not believe business organizations needed computers. Only after Remington Rand delivered a few UNIVACs could Watson's son, *Thomas J. Watson Jr.,* convince his father that IBM should also make computers for business. The first commercial IBM computer was called the IBM 701. But it was not until 1956 that IBM caught up with Remington Rand in the number of computers sold. By then, IBM had developed a popular medium-sized business computer, known as the IBM 650. Ever since, IBM has remained the leading computer supplier in the world.

GENERATIONS OF BUSINESS COMPUTERS

Computer professionals often speak of four or more generations of computer development since the early 1950s when the first UNIVAC was introduced. They mean that a completely new kind of machine was developed in each generation. Generation dates and definitions are not universally agreed upon. However, on the basis of vastly improved types of components used in the machines, at least four generations of computers can be identified. The improvements made in each generation over the previous one resulted in faster, smaller, more reliable, and cheaper computers.

Vacuum tube (bottom); Transistor (top). *Alan Forsyth.*

Integrated circuit. *Courtesy AT&T Bell Laboratories.*

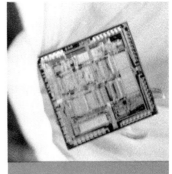

VLSI Chip. *Courtesy NCR Corporation*

EVOLUTION OF COMPUTER COMPONENTS.

FIRST-GENERATION COMPUTERS (1951 TO 1958): VACUUM TUBES

First-generation computers were very large in size and had thousands of vacuum tubes. These tubes produced so much heat that special air-conditioning was required to cool computer rooms. The UNIVAC 1, IBM 701, and IBM 650 are examples of these early business computers. Punched cards were used for input. Output information could be printed or recorded on punched cards. The machines had small memory capacities, and the preparation of the program of instructions was difficult.

SECOND-GENERATION COMPUTERS (1958 TO 1964): TRANSISTORS

In the second generation of computers, tiny, solid-state transistors replaced vacuum tubes. Computers with transistors produced much less heat than those made with vacuum tubes. But more important, the machines were much faster, smaller in size, and much more reliable in operation. Also, the second-generation computers, such as the extensively used IBM 1401, the IBM 7070, the Honeywell 200, and the UNIVAC 1107, had larger memories, from which data could be retrieved more quickly. Data input and output could be recorded on magnetic tape as well as on punched cards. Although the second-generation machines had much greater computing power, they cost less than first-generation machines. Another advantage was that the newer machines were easier to program.

THIRD-GENERATION COMPUTERS (1964 TO 1970): INTEGRATED CIRCUITS

The third generation of computers used **integrated circuits** (ICs) instead of transistors. An IC consists of thousands of small circuits etched on a silicon chip, which in 1965 was about one-quarter of an inch square. The use of integrated circuits meant improvements in computer speed, cost, and storage capacity. Computers could now perform operations in times measured in nanoseconds (billionths of a second).

Third-generation computers included smaller and less expensive machines, called **minicomputers,** such as those made by Digital Equipment Corporation (DEC). For the first time, smaller businesses could use computers. IBM introduced its family of IBM 360 computers of varying sizes with upward compatibility. This meant that a job programmed for a smaller IBM 360 machine would work on a larger IBM 360 computer.

FOURTH-GENERATION COMPUTERS (1970 TO THE PRESENT): LARGER-SCALE INTEGRATED CIRCUITS

Late 1970/early 1971, further improvements in computer design came with the use of **large-scale integrated** (LSI) **circuits** and **very large-scale integrated** (VLSI) **circuits.** This generation of computers compressed more and more microelectronic components into less space. Now hundreds of thousands of integrated circuits, or transistors, could be placed on a single silicon chip. The result was fourth-generation computers that operate 10,000 times faster than first-generation machines.

UNIVAC I, first generation. *Courtesy Sperry Corporation.*

IBM 1401, second generation. *Courtesy IBM Corporation.*

IBM System/360, third generation. *Courtesy IBM Corporation.*

Honeywell DPS-88, fourth generation. *Courtesy Honeywell, Inc.*

FOUR GENERATIONS OF COMPUTERS.

Fourth-generation machines also have larger memories for storage of data and provide faster access to stored data and information.

All major computer manufacturers introduced a fourth generation of equipment that incorporated LSI circuits. Among these computers were the IBM 370, the IBM 4300, the Burroughs 7700, the NCR 8500, the Honeywell DPS-88, and the PDP-11 made by Digital Equipment Corporation. In addition, large-scale integrated circuits were used in a technological innovation—the microprocessor—that changed significantly the future direction of computer development.

Microprocessors. Because development of the microprocessor has caused such substantial changes in the computer industry and in our day-to-day life, it deserves recognition as a major step in technological advance. A **microprocessor** is a complete central processing unit (the brain) of a computer placed on a single LSI chip. A microprocessor is really a com-

MICROPROCESSORS. A microprocessor is a complete central processing unit on an LSI chip.

puter on a chip. In 1969, Dr. *M.E. (Ted) Hoff,* a young engineer employed by the Intel Corporation developed the first microprocessor. His work influenced the future development and use of computer equipment because it made the manufacture of much smaller and cheaper computers possible. A small, inexpensive, and relatively easy-to-use computer that incorporates a microprocessor is called a **microcomputer.** (*micro* means small.)

At first, microprocessors were available only to computer hobbyists, who assembled their own microcomputers the way music lovers develop their own stereo sound systems. Then small manufacturers began to sell fully assembled microcomputer systems. The first commercially available microcomputer was developed in 1977 and was called the Apple II. (Its predecessor, Apple I, was an experimental model.) The Apple computers were developed by a newly organized company called Apple Computer, Inc., founded by *Steven Jobs* and *Stephen Wozniak.* A variety of microcomputers are now made by both the long-established computer manufacturers and newly formed, small computer manufacturers. Chapter 5 describes the features of microprocessors, microcomputers, and larger computer systems. Later chapters will describe the various input, storage, and output devices now used for business information processing.

Many other rapid advances are still being made in computer technology. Manufacturers in both the United States and Japan are competing to build yet another generation of computers. You will read more about recent trends in information technology in Chapter 14. The significant point is that the newer computers will be faster, smarter, and easier to operate.

TRENDS IN COMPUTER PROGRAMMING

Through each successive generation of computer development, the task of preparing instructions for the machine, called **computer programming,** has been simplified. From the develop-

COMPUTER PROGRAM-MING. Rear Admiral Grace Hopper programmed the Mark I and helped develop the computer language COBOL. *Courtesy U.S. Naval Institute.*

ment of the Mark I to the latest generation of computers, one person, in particular, has made a significant contribution toward simplifying the work of computer programming. Dr. *Grace Hopper*, once a mathematics professor, worked with Dr. Howard Aiken on the development of the Mark I. She was one of the first computer programmers in the United States. She worked for Remington Rand on the UNIVAC. Later, Dr. Hopper assisted the U.S. Navy and the Department of Defense in developing a program for the simplification and standardization of programming instructions. She helped develop COBOL, one of the most widely used computer languages. The results of these efforts are described in Chapter 8. In 1986, Rear Admiral Hopper retired as the nation's oldest active officer in the U.S. Navy. At the same time, she vowed to continue her dedication to making computers easier to use.

Check Yourself

Match each term with the word or phrase that best defines it.

1. The so-called world's first computer programmer.
2. Computers made with vacuum tubes.
3. First electronic computer to have a stored program.
4. First computer used to process business data.
5. Central processing unit on a single chip.
6. The forerunner of modern computers.
7. Person credited with the stored-program concept.
8. Computers made with transistors.
9. Designer of the Mark I.
10. Computers made with integrated circuits.
11. The first fully assembled microcomputer.
12. An important contributor to program simplification.
13. Designer of the microprocessor.
14. Computers made with LSI circuits.
15. First electronic computer.

a. EDSAC
b. EDVAC
c. Microprocessor
d. IBM 650
e. Lady Ada Lovelace
f. Fourth-generation computers
g. ABC computer
h. Grace Hopper
i. Mark I
j. Howard Aiken
k. John von Neumann
l. Second-generation computers
m. Third-generation computers
n. Apple II
o. UNIVAC 1
p. M.E. Hoff
q. Analytical engine
r. First-generation computers

Answers: (1) e; (2) r; (3) a; (4) o; (5) c; (6) q; (7) k; (8) l; (9) j; (10) m; (11) n; (12) h; (13) p; (14) f; (15) g.

THE EVOLUTION OF WORD PROCESSING

A distinction is made between information (or data) processing and word processing. As used in business offices, the term **information processing** has been associated with record-keeping and accounting-like activities. It involves primarily the handling of quantitative data and associated alphabetic characters and words that describe the numerical data. In contrast, **word processing** involves the handling of textual data such as letters, reports, manuals, catalogs, or the contents of newspapers, magazines, or books. Today, information processing is done by computers. Word processing may be done by computer-like machines called **word processors,** or by computers using word processing software.

The introduction of typewriters into business offices in the early 1900s led to the development of word processing equipment. While typewriters provided a new means of creating printed letters and reports, it was soon recognized that there was no easy way to revise a typed document once it was completed. Often, a writer wants to improve a typed report by changing terminology, rearranging words in a sentence, or even adding or removing whole paragraphs. Before the development of word processing, such changes usually meant that the whole document had to be retyped.

There are many other business needs for word processing capabilities. The writer of a business letter may wish to send a similar typed letter to many individuals, or perhaps to send a letter with only minor changes from individual to individual. For example, follow-up letters sent to individuals requesting payment of bills may differ only in the name and address used in the heading and the dollar amounts due mentioned in the body of the letter. Before word processing equipment was available, such letters had to be individually typed.

EARLY WORD PROCESSORS

Automatic Typewriters. The prototype to the word processor, the automatic typewriter, was introduced in the 1930s. The automatic typewriter could repetitively type many copies of documents such as form letters, reports, and legal contracts. The operation of the machine was controlled by instructions recorded on a punched paper roller, similar to those found on player pianos, which served as the storage mechanism.

By the 1950s, punched paper tape similar to what was used in early computers was used to control automatic typewriters. The addition of an electromechanical logic mechanism gave much more flexibility to the automatic typewriters. Text to be typed was recorded on punched paper tape, and the automatic typewriter could select text from two different paper tape readers for automatic typing of letters or reports. For instance, one tape could contain names and addresses, while the other could contain the body of a form letter. A personalized letter could be created by combining these two pieces of information.

Magnetic Card and Tape Typewriters. By the early 1960s, the electronic components used in computers were adopted for word processing. The introduction of the IBM Magnetic Tape Selectric Typewriter (MT/ST) in 1964 marks the beginning of the word processing age. Text could be typed, stored on magnetic tape, corrected, or erased. Copies of a stored document could be typed out at 175 words per minute.

The use of magnetic tape as the storage medium for the text that was typed had many advantages over paper tape. Data recorded on magnetic tape could be erased and recorded again; this could not be done with punched paper tape. The storage capacity of magnetic tape was about 20 characters per inch, almost twice that of paper tape. This made it easier to handle and to store the text. Most important, data recorded on magnetic tape could be easily retrieved and revised as needed.

IBM improved its word processing equipment in 1969 when it introduced the IBM Magnetic Card Selectric Typewriter (MC/ST). This machine had as its storage medium a reusable magnetic card that stored the equivalent of a page of text. The IBM MC/ST was a popular machine, and other equipment manufacturers, such as Xerox, Olivetti, Savin, Wang, and Digital Equipment Corporation, began to make competitive equipment. Many new companies also entered the field. Readactron and Vydec were two of these. Vydec was the first to make word processors that stored text on magnetic diskettes.

PRESENT STATUS OF WORD PROCESSING

Computers or computer-like equipment called **dedicated word processors** are now used to perform word processing functions. A dedicated word processor is used exclusively for word processing, while a computer, of course, may be used for many other functions. Increasingly, word processors are being linked to other equipment, including computers, by communications circuits. For this reason, it is good to have knowledge of modern word processing equipment as background for your study of computers.

The varied equipment now used for word processing can be classified in four groups. The first three classes are examples of dedicated word processors.

1. *Stand-Alone Word Processors.* A stand-alone system contains all of the devices needed to perform word processing. A *stand-alone word processor* is self-contained, operates completely independently of other machines, and can usually perform only word processing functions.

The simplest stand-alone word processors are known as electronic typewriters and are generally used by a secretary rather than a word processing center. Although not full-fledged word processors, these machines do have small memories that store a few pages of text. The stored material can be retrieved and edited in a number of ways before it is printed. More advanced systems have larger memories, faster printing capabilities, and some text display device (called a thin window) so that the operator may see the part of the document being worked on.

The newest stand-alone word processors, made with microprocessors, generally include four components. These are:

- A keyboard and visual display screen for text entry and editing
- A microprocessor and main storage unit
- Disk storage systems for text storage
- A high-quality printing device

The keyboard the word processor operator uses to enter data is usually similar to that of an electric typewriter. The video display terminal (VDT), sometimes called a cathode-ray tube (CRT), displays characters and lines of text as they

KEYBOARD FOR WORD PROCESSOR. *Courtesy Richard Hackett.*

STAND-ALONE WORD PROCESSOR WITH LETTER-QUALITY PRINTER. *Courtesy Wang Laboratories.*

are being typed or called up for revision. Most VDTs can display about 24 lines of text at one time; a few VDTs can display much more.

The program of instructions for the word processor is stored in the main storage unit so the instructions are rapidly accessible to the microprocessor. The larger volume storage devices, such as magnetic disks, store the text documents. These documents may be less than one page in length or hundreds of pages long. Flexible, round disks, called floppy disks, are widely used for document storage. Hard disk drives are special storage devices. Like floppy disk drives, they use magnetic disks, but the disk is sealed. Hard disk drives are faster and can hold a lot more information than floppy disk drives can.

The printer used in an advanced word processing system is usually referred to as a *letter-quality printer;* it may print over 600 words per minute. Different type styles are available in interchangeable print mechanisms. One type of widely used printer is called a *daisy wheel printer* because of its pinwheel-like print unit. Printers called *dot matrix printers* are also used, primarily for printing rough drafts and preliminary copies.

2. *Shared-Logic Word Processing Systems.* Where there is a large volume of work to be handled and more than one word processing unit is needed, a shared-logic system is often the most effective equipment for businesses to use.

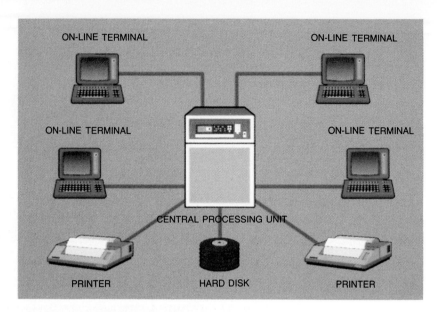

SHARED-LOGIC WORD PROCESSORS.

With this system there can be many, say 12 or more, individual work stations, each with a keyboard and VDT connected by a cable to a large central processing and storage unit. When a central processing unit is shared by work stations, the equipment is called a *shared-logic system.*

The advantage of a shared-logic system is that when the costs are shared among many work stations, a more powerful processing unit and a larger on-line storage capacity can be provided. Also, a faster printer may be shared. This means that the word processing tasks can be accomplished more quickly. For example, a printout can be generated while text is being keyed or edited; usually the two functions cannot be performed simultaneously with stand-alone equipment. Nevertheless, such shared-logic systems have a disadvantage. A malfunction in the central processing unit shuts down all of the work stations connected to that unit.

3. *Shared-Resource Word Processing Systems.* In a shared-resource word processing system, many work stations share such devices as a printer and large storage units. Each work station, however, contains its own processor. This overcomes the disadvantage of the shared-logic systems. A failure in one work station does not affect the others.

4. *Computer Word Processing.* By now you probably recognize many similarities between word processing and infor-

mation processing. In each type of processing you will find input data to be read into the machine, processing operations, storage and retrieval of data, and output operations. The chief difference between the two types of processing is in the details.

Sorting, calculating, summarizing, and classifying are important processing operations in an information processing cycle. Editing of text generally does not involve these operations, so word processors operate with a simpler processing unit and smaller main memory than that needed for information processing. For this reason, information processing work usually cannot be done on dedicated word processors (i.e., equipment used exclusively for word processing). On the other hand, word processing can be done on the general purpose computers used for information processing.

Word processing can be done on computer systems ranging in size from microcomputers to the huge mainframe computers used in business and government offices. All that is needed is a word processing program to direct the computer in its operation. In the early 1960s, IBM introduced the first computer program to handle word processing. Many different computer programs are now available for word processing, and their features are described in Chapter 11.

OFFICE
AUTOMATION

Many other types of equipment are now used in word processing. An optical character scanner can read a typed or printed page and record the data on a magnetic medium for word processing or information processing. Also, dedicated word processors may be linked by special communications devices to computers used for information processing and to other office equipment.

Terms such as the *electronic office,* the *paperless office,* and the *office of the future* are often used to describe the new office technology. A better term is *office automation.* The single word **automation** means performing work without human effort except that of telling a machine what to do and when to do it. **Office automation** is the use of new technology to reduce the human effort involved in performing office functions.

Office automation is made possible by development of new communications technology that makes it possible to transfer data among word processors, computers, copying machines, and laser printers. Equally important is that information stored in these machines can be transferred automatically to the individuals who use the information. Electronic mail lets users of computers correspond with each other via the computer. Chapter 7 describes the new communications technology and how it is used in modern offices.

CHECK YOURSELF

Supply the missing words.

1. The processing of ___?___ material is called word processing, and quantitative material is handled in ___?___ processing.
2. Self-contained equipment that performs word processing is referred to as a ___?___ word processor.
3. A pinwheel-like print unit in a printer is called a ___?___ ___?___.
4. When a central processing unit is shared by many work stations, a word processor is known as a ___?___ word processor.
5. When just a printer is shared among work stations, the system is called a ___?___ word processor.
6. To do word processing on a computer, one needs a ___?___ ___?___ ___?___.
7. A device that reads and records typed data is called an ___?___ ___?___ ___?___.
8. The use of new technology to reduce human effort involved in performing office functions is called ___?___ ___?___.

Answers: (1) text, information; (2) stand-alone; (3) daisy wheel; (4) shared-logic; (5) shared-resource; (6) word processing program; (7) optical character scanner; (8) office automation.

REVIEW QUESTIONS

1. Explain what the Information Revolution is and how it differs from the Industrial Revolution.
2. Before paper was invented, people recorded data in a number of different ways. Describe three of these.
3. List the five important milestones in the development of improved calculating equipment.
4. Describe the origin of the punched-card concept for processing.
5. Give the reason why punched cards were first used by the Census Bureau.
6. For what reason is Babbage's analytical engine considered a forerunner of modern computers?
7. Name four developments in scientific computers and the significance of each.

8. Name the first computer to be used for processing business information. Name its inventors.
9. Describe the four generations of business computers and give the approximate time period for each generation.
10. Define a *microprocessor* and a *microcomputer*.
11. Define *word processing* and *word processor*. List some uses of word processing equipment.
12. Describe the distinctive features of the four types of systems that can be used for word processing.
13. Define *automation* and *office automation*.
14. Explain what has made office automation possible.

COMPARING IDEAS

The questions below are designed to help you think about what you have learned in this chapter. They are "thought" questions. There is no one correct answer.

1. If you were the office manager for an automobile dealer and were given the choice of having either a dedicated word processing machine or a computer, which would you choose? Give reasons for your choice.
2. What suggestions can you make for new equipment that would increase office automation in your school or in a business office in which you have worked?

INFORMATION PROCESSING ACTIVITIES

Now you can perform many of the information processing activities business workers perform. Below is a summary of the tasks you will complete. You will find the actual data and business forms you need in your *Information Processing Work Kit*.

1. As an assistant to the Director of Management Information Systems for Founders Bank you will complete a questionnaire designed to describe the history of computer hardware in banking.
2. You will research the role of men and women in the history of computers and gather data for The Founders Bank Newsletter.

HANDS-ON ACTIVITIES

Write a one-page letter by hand. Then type the same letter using an electric typewriter. Finally, key the same letter using a word processor on a microcomputer. Time yourself and compute how much faster you complete your work using a word processor than by hand or using the electronic typewriter.

CHAPTER

3 COMPUTER CONCEPTS

Performance Goals

☐ Distinguish between digital and analog computers.

☐ Name four types of hardware devices that a computer must have to perform information processing; state the purpose of each.

☐ Explain the distinctions between classes of computer systems and describe the features of microcomputers, minicomputers, mainframes, and supercomputers.

☐ Describe the hardware that might be used for payroll processing, a very common business task. Consider first the hardware that might be used for a large payroll job, and then the type appropriate for a very small payroll job.

In the last chapter you read that a computer is an electronic machine that processes data automatically by following a list of instructions stored in its memory. From this you may have rightly guessed that there are two essential parts to information processing by computer. First, there is the computer, electronic in operation and made up of individual devices that are interconnected. The equipment used for computer information processing is called **computer hardware.** The second essential part is the set of instructions needed to guide the computer in its operation. Professionals refer to these instructions as programs or **computer software** to distinguish them from the equipment.

OVERVIEW OF COMPUTER HARDWARE

The computers discussed so far in this book are known as digital computers; this is by far the most widely used type of computer. Because there is a second kind of computer, an analog computer, it is important to distinguish between the two.

The **digital computer** operates on the basis of counting numbers (digits). The numbers represent quantities or amounts that can be precisely added, subtracted, multiplied, and divided. A digital computer, of course, can also handle alphabetic information. Digital computers are used for processing information in business offices and are used by engineers and scientists to perform complex calculations.

The **analog computer** solves problems by measuring the amounts of change that occur in physical units such as speed, temperature, or pressure. The speedometer of a car and the thermostat in a home are examples of analog devices. The speedometer measures the driveshaft rotations and converts these to a number that represents the speed at which the car is driven. The thermostat measures the amount of room heat and, if the heat is below a specified minimum, instructs the heating unit to turn on. Analog computers are most typically used to control manufacturing processes in industry and in scientific research work. This book focuses on digital computers.

Digital computers must have at least four types of hardware

devices to perform automatically the functions that take place in every information processing cycle, as described in Chapter 1. The four devices perform the following functions:

1. Accept input data and programs into the computer (the input hardware).
2. Control the execution of the processing operations needed to convert the data into the required information (the central processing unit).
3. Store data and permit its retrieval (an auxiliary storage device).
4. Report information in the form needed (the output hardware).

INPUT HARDWARE

Every computer used for information processing needs one or more **input devices,** which read the input data that is to be processed by the computer and the programs of instructions that the computer follows. Many different types of input devices are in use. For example, a typewriter-like keyboard may be used to enter data or program instructions into a computer. Another

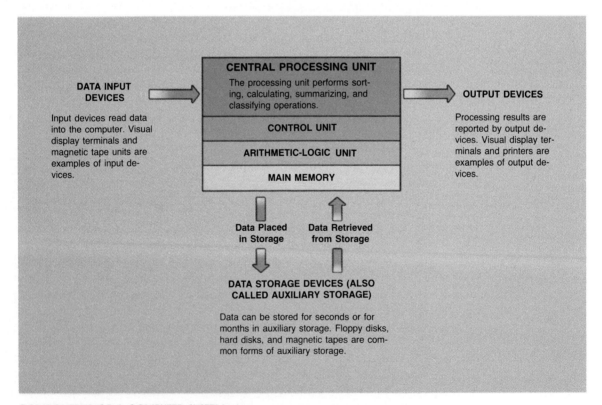

COMPONENTS OF A COMPUTER SYSTEM.

way to input data is to use computer devices that are able to read data and program instructions recorded in magnetic form on floppy or hard disks, reels of magnetic tape, or tape cartridges. Other types of input devices are described in Chapter 4.

CENTRAL PROCESSING UNIT (CPU)

The heart of the computer is a unit called the **central processing unit** (CPU). A computer's CPU controls the execution of the program of instructions and actually handles the processing operations. To perform these functions, a CPU consists of three parts: a control unit, an arithmetic-logic unit, and a storage unit that is generally referred to as the main memory.

The **control unit** acts as manager over all the operations of the computer. It interprets the instructions in the computer program and directs the operation of the computer's other devices in the execution of the program instructions. The control unit also operates as a communications link between the person operating the computer and the machine itself.

The **arithmetic-logic unit** (ALU) of the CPU performs the additions, subtractions, multiplications, divisions, and all other calculating operations called for by a computer program. This unit also performs other processing operations such as sorting and classifying.

Together, a control unit and an arithmetic-logic unit may be referred to as a **processor.** For example, a microprocessor contains all of the electronics components necessary to perform control and arithmetic-logic functions.

The third mechanism in a CPU is the **main memory** or primary storage unit. Different names have been given to this storage unit, the most common of which are *main memory, working storage,* and *primary storage.* One function of the main memory of the processor is to hold the program instructions. The computer retrieves one or more instructions at a time from storage, performs the operations called for, and returns the instructions to the storage unit so that they are available when needed again.

In addition to holding the program instructions, the main memory unit is used to store active input data that is to be processed and the processing results until they are transferred to an output device.

AUXILIARY STORAGE DEVICES

Because the main memory unit is an expensive part of the modern computer, manufacturers have developed other storage devices to supplement the main memory capacity. These additional storage units are called **auxiliary** (*external,* or *secondary*) **storage.** The function of the auxiliary units is to store data that is used less frequently, that does not need to be retrieved immediately, and that, therefore, can be kept outside main storage without significantly affecting machine speed. When the data in auxiliary storage is to be processed, it must be moved to main memory.

Magnetic disks and tape recorders are used most frequently as the auxiliary storage units. As you will see in Chapter 5, auxiliary storage devices differ greatly in their capacity to hold numbers and letters and in the length of time needed to locate the data required and transfer it out of auxiliary storage.

OUTPUT HARDWARE

At minimum, one computer **output device** is needed to report information produced by the processing operations, but there are many different ways of reporting output. For example, processing results may be reported in the form of a voice recording or on microfilm. Much more common, however, are two other types of output reporting. One is to report information in the form of printed copy. This can be done by a variety of printers. A second common way of reporting output is to display information on a screen. This provides a quick and inexpensive way to view the processing results. The computer device that displays information is called a **video display terminal** (VDT), a *video*

VIDEO DISPLAY TERMINAL. Information can be output onto the screen of the video display terminal. *Courtesy Honeywell, Inc.*

display unit (VDU), a *monitor,* or a *cathode-ray tube* (CRT). A VDT can be used interchangeably as an input device or as an output device.

CHECK YOURSELF

Match each phrase with the word or phrase that best defines it.

1. A computer that counts.
2. A storage device to supplement main storage.
3. A type of auxiliary storage medium.
4. Programs of instructions to direct a computer.
5. The heart of a computer.
6. Storage area for a computer program.
7. A device to read data into a computer.
8. The mechanism that acts as manager of computer operations.
9. A common output device.
10. Device that performs calculations and comparisons.

a. Central processing unit
b. Input device
c. Printer
d. Main memory
e. Digital computer
f. Auxiliary storage
g. Computer software
h. Analog computer
i. Control unit
j. Arithmetic-logic unit
k. Magnetic disk

Answers: (1) e; (2) f; (3) k; (4) g; (5) a; (6) d; (7) b; (8) i; (9) c; (10) j.

ALL SIZES OF COMPUTER SYSTEMS

Businesses seeking computer systems to handle their information processing needs and individuals looking for personal computers now have their choice of a wide selection of computer hardware. The purchaser will probably start with the selection of a central processing unit (or processor and main memory unit) and then will want at least one input and output device and some type of auxiliary storage.

Any computer system can be made up of a variety of hardware units, so a buyer can select the particular combination of devices that most effectively perform the work to be done. The selected devices linked together with the central processor become a computer system. This choosing and linking of computer devices is similar to the process of selecting components for a stereo sound system.

Computer systems used for information processing are often categorized by their computing power and cost. Faster and more versatile systems are usually more expensive, and physically larger. Although it is not always easy to distinguish among

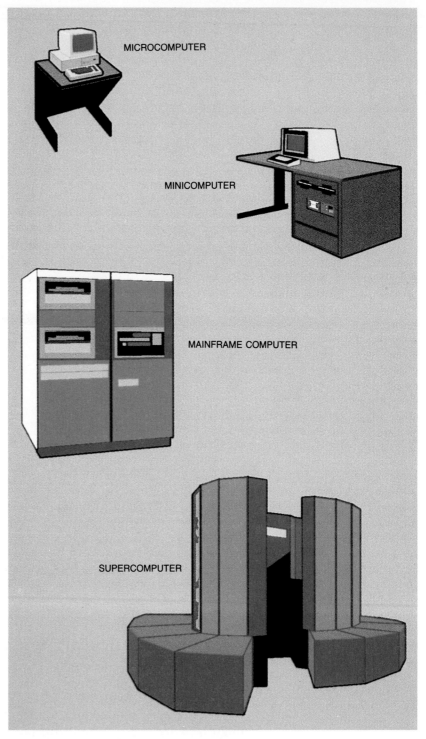

COMPUTERS OF ALL SIZES. Computer systems are categorized by their power and cost.

them, four classes of computer systems exist. From smallest to largest, these are microcomputers, minicomputers, mainframes, and supercomputers.

MICROCOMPUTERS

As you have already learned, the smallest and least expensive computer available for information processing is called the **microcomputer.** These small computers, also called *personal computers,* may be used in an office or at home.

The selection of the hardware for a microcomputer system starts with a microprocessor and a small main memory to store computer program instructions and data being actively worked on. Up to certain limits, a user can also add additional main memory to the computer system.

At minimum, a microcomputer needs a keyboard for keying input data into the machine, but generally it also has a video display terminal that displays the input data as it is keyed. The VDT can also be used as an output device to display processing results.

The main storage device on a microcomputer is seldom large enough to store all the data needed for input to the computer or to store records updated by the computer. The most common forms of auxiliary storage used on microcomputers are magnetic floppy disks (or diskettes), hard disks, and cassette tapes. A **floppy disk** is round, usually 5 1/4 or 3 1/2 inches in size, and looks like a small 45-rpm record. It bends easily and in that way is distinguished from the **hard disk,** which does not bend,

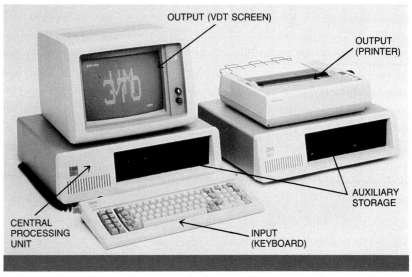

MICROCOMPUTERS. A microcomputer is a small but complete computer system with a CPU microprocessor linked to simple input, storage, and output units. *Courtesy IBM Historical Archive.*

is usually sealed inside of the drive unit, and also is larger in size. **Magnetic-tape cassettes** are similar in appearance to those used for sound recordings on tape.

Almost all business applications and most information processing done at home require some type of printer as an output device to provide hard copy of the work done by the computer. Dot matrix printers, letter-quality printers, and laser printers are all common types of computer printer devices.

The Apple and IBM PC are microcomputers widely used in business offices, classrooms, and at home. Among other popular microcomputers are those made by Tandy, Commodore, and Atari. Many manufacturers, such as Compaq and AT&T, have produced microcomputers on which computer programs written for the IBM PC can be used. Such machines are called *clones* of the PC because they are IBM compatible. This means that software that works with IBM hardware will also run on these computers.

The smallest of microcomputers will fit on your lap, and for this reason they are called **laptop computers.** Laptop com-

LAPTOP COMPUTERS. The portability of laptop computers makes them popular with business travelers. *Courtesy Will Faller.*

puters are portable, so they are popular with business travellers. With a laptop, a sales executive can check inventory balances and forward customer orders to headquarters. You may see one being used by a passenger on an airplane or a train. The typical laptop computer is small and light. For example, the Toshiba T1100 Plus weighs about 10 pounds and measures about 12 by 12 by 3 inches. Inside that tiny package are a complete keyboard, a video display screen, and two disk drives. A printer may be added to the system. Like most laptops, this computer operates with a rechargeable battery. Microcomputers used in offices are **desktop computers,** heavier and larger than the laptops but still small enough to fit on a small desk.

MINICOMPUTERS

Until fully assembled microcomputers became available in 1977, minicomputers were the smallest computers available. Though more expensive than a microcomputer, a *minicomputer* is generally much faster, can perform a wider range of tasks, and can support more input and output devices. A minicomputer is often a stand-alone unit about the size of a small file cabinet, although some models are designed for desktop use.

A minicomputer system can support several input terminals operated at the same time. Many systems provide for input recorded on reels of magnetic tape or on disks. Typically, hard disks are used as the auxiliary storage device and a minicom-

MINICOMPUTERS. Minicomputers are small computers that perform a wide range of information processing applications. *Courtesy Hewlett-Packard Co.*

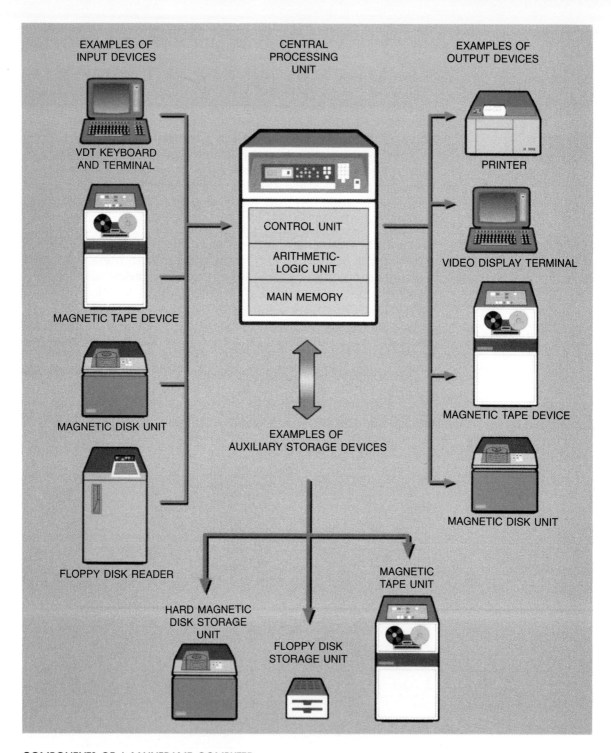

EXAMPLES OF
INPUT DEVICES

CENTRAL
PROCESSING
UNIT

EXAMPLES OF
OUTPUT DEVICES

VDT KEYBOARD
AND TERMINAL

MAGNETIC TAPE DEVICE

MAGNETIC DISK UNIT

FLOPPY DISK READER

CONTROL UNIT

ARITHMETIC-
LOGIC UNIT

MAIN MEMORY

PRINTER

VIDEO DISPLAY TERMINAL

MAGNETIC TAPE DEVICE

MAGNETIC DISK UNIT

EXAMPLES OF
AUXILIARY STORAGE DEVICES

HARD MAGNETIC
DISK STORAGE
UNIT

FLOPPY DISK
STORAGE UNIT

MAGNETIC
TAPE UNIT

COMPONENTS OF A MAINFRAME COMPUTER.

puter will nearly always have a fast printer as well as video display terminals to report processing results.

Because of their cost, few minicomputers have been used in homes as personal computers. They have been very popular, however, in both small and large businesses. In a small business, a minicomputer used by itself offers an effective means of information processing. Larger organizations use minicomputers to supplement the processing capabilities of larger systems.

Digital Equipment Corporation was the first company to make minicomputers and is still a leading manufacturer of these systems. Other manufacturers of well-known minicomputers include IBM, Honeywell, Wang, Data General, Hewlett-Packard, and NCR.

MAINFRAMES

IBM and other manufacturers produce computers that are more powerful than minicomputers. Such machines are commonly called **mainframes** (or mainframe computers). A basic difference between mainframes and smaller computers is that the mainframes have much faster arithmetic and processing units. They also have the capacity to handle at high speed a larger number and greater variety of input and output devices, and they have much larger main memory and auxiliary storage capacities. Mainframe hardware can also support many computer languages simultaneously. For these reasons, many people may use a single mainframe computer at the same time. Some of the users may be in the same building, but in a different room from the computer. Other users may communicate with the computer from a different building, or even from another city. Wherever the data originates from, it is read and processed at much higher speeds than are possible with smaller systems, and the information results are reported faster and in a wider variety of formats and media.

Typically, mainframes have a central processing unit housed in a cabinet about the size of a large desk. Most large systems have a console unit that is connected to the CPU. The console has a keyboard and VDT for communication between the computer operator and the machine. The console provides a means of monitoring and controlling the operation of the computer.

Data entry may be through additional video display terminals located close to or far away from the central processing unit. Large input volumes are usually handled by separate keying operations to record the input data on disks, which then may be used as direct input devices. Another method is to transfer the keyed data on disk to magnetic tape for input into the computer.

The most widely used form of auxiliary storage on large computers is magnetic disk. The disk storage units come in many different forms and capacities, which are described in Chapter 5. In some units billions of characters of data may be stored. Magnetic tape is also a popular means of storing large volumes of data. Data recorded on reels of magnetic tape can be read into the computer, and processing results can be recorded on magnetic tape. For instance, all the data from the 1980 U.S. Census is stored on hundreds of reels of magnetic tape. If you needed to analyze the raw census data, these reels could be read into a computer by a tape reader and analyzed by a statistical analysis program.

A variety of output devices are available for use with mainframes. High-speed printers are almost always used to report output as hard copy. Video display terminals are equally common for displaying output information in text and graphic form.

Mainframe computers are needed by companies and government agencies that have large information processing needs. Even though a system may cost several millions of dollars, it may be less expensive for a business to install one or more mainframe computer systems, rather than a number of smaller

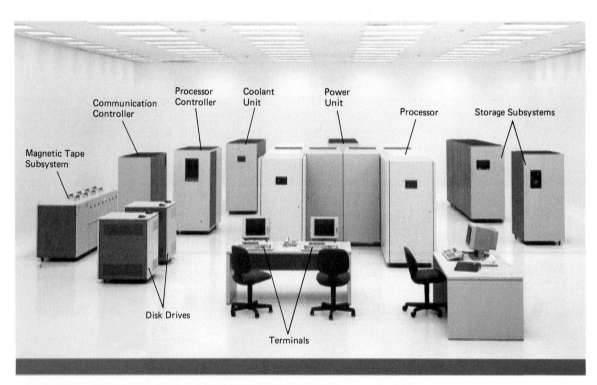

COMPONENTS OF A MAINFRAME COMPUTER. A mainframe is a large computer capable of operating at high speeds and of storing a tremendous amount of data. Shown here is the IBM 3090, Model 400 System. *Courtesy IBM Corporation.*

SUPERCOMPUTERS. A supercomputer, such as the Cray computer shown here, is the largest, fastest, and most expensive type of computer available. *Courtesy of Cray Research, Inc.*

computers. IBM, the largest supplier of these systems in the world, usually provides several models of varying processing capabilities within each new mainframe equipment development. This provides a *family of computers,* which makes it easy to expand computer capacity if a user outgrows a smaller computer. It is a simple task to transfer programs from one model in the family to a larger model. Such upward movement is often called *hardware compatibility* because of the ease with which this transition can be handled. Both IBM's older 370 machines and its newer Sierra series are representative of families of computers.

Within each series there are generally very small, small, large, and very large mainframe computer models. UNISYS, NCR, Control Data Corporation, and Honeywell also make families of mainframe computers. Unfortunately, it is still not easy to convert a program written for one manufacturer's mainframe computer to another company's mainframe computer. In Chapter 10, you will read about industry standards relating to computer hardware and software, particularly with regard to using software on more than one computer system.

SUPERCOMPUTERS

The name **supercomputer** applies to the largest, fastest, and most expensive type of computer available. These machines, capable of performing hundreds of millions of complex scientific calculations per second, operate many times faster than the largest mainframes. One of the latest supercomputers, made by the Cray Research Company, requires only 12.5 nanoseconds (billionths of a second) to execute an operation.

As you might expect, only a few companies, universities, and government agencies have need for such powerful computers. Supercomputers are designed principally for scientific applications that require an enormous number of calculations. Weather forecasting, defense and weapons analyses, and petroleum research are just a few of the applications that can justify the use of these computers. In 1986 the NASA space research laboratory was using the world's most powerful supercomputer. It is capable of 250 million computations per second and is used for aerodynamics research involved in the design of U.S. spacecraft. The few supercomputers manufactured each year come primarily from Cray Research, Control Data Corporation, IBM, and UNISYS.

CHECK YOURSELF

Supply the missing words.

1. From largest to smallest, the four types of computer systems are called __?__, __?__, __?__, and __?__.

2. Before 1977 the smallest computer was the __?__.

3. A round, flexible magnetic disk is called a __?__ __?__.

4. When programs are easily transferred from one computer to another, it reflects hardware __?__.

5. The Apple and the IBM PC are popular models of __?__.

6. The common forms of auxiliary storage used on a microcomputer are __?__ disks, __?__ disks, and cassette tapes.

7. The common forms of auxiliary storage on mainframes are magnetic tapes and __?__ disks.

8. Mainframes usually have a unit called a __?__ which permits communication between the computer operator and the machine.

9. A microcomputer used by an airplane passenger is usually a __?__ computer.

10. A typical microcomputer used in an office is a __?__ computer.

Answers: (1) supercomputers, mainframes, minicomputers, microcomputers; (2) minicomputer; (3) floppy disk; (4) compatibility; (5) microcomputers; (6) floppy, hard; (7) magnetic (or hard); (8) console; (9) laptop; (10) desktop.

AN ILLUSTRATION OF INFORMATION PROCESSING BY COMPUTER

To become familiar with the use of computer hardware and software for business, we will look at a very common and specific business task—the preparation of payroll checks that reimburse employees for time worked. Among the many operations involved in payroll processing are the following important steps:

- Keyboarding employee payroll data such as hours worked and pay rate.
- Calculating the amount of each employee's earnings. This amount, called the gross (total) pay is the sum of his or her regular and overtime earnings.
- Calculating each deduction to be made from the gross pay.
- Computing the net take-home pay (gross pay minus all deductions).
- Printing all the data needed to prepare a paycheck and a statement of earnings and deductions for each employee.

Many repetitive steps must be performed for each employee in each pay period. A computer minimizes the human effort required to get the work done. Computerized payroll processing requires the following:

- Preparing a computer program to instruct the computer how to do the payroll work.
- Making available computer hardware to perform the required processing work.
- Providing human effort each pay period to prepare input data that will be processed by the computer and to operate the computer so that it performs its work.

Each of these requirements will be examined in relation to the payroll tasks so that you can learn better what a computer is supposed to do and how it does it.

PREPARING A COMPUTER PROGRAM

The computer is supposed to accomplish all the payroll tasks without stopping to receive help from an operator. How? Before any of the payroll work can be given to the computer, someone must prepare a list of instructions specifying the work to be done, step by step. This list, a **computer program,** tells the computer what work to perform and how to perform it. The special language used in writing a computer program is known as a **programming language.** Written in English, the program would read something like this.

> Computer, each pay period you will be given input data that records the number of regular and overtime hours each employee has worked. You will also be given a magnetic disk on which the company's master payroll file is recorded. This file contains a record for each employee, including his or her pay rate and pay deduction information.

First, you are to sort the attendance input data by the location (such as plant location) at which the employee works and to sort within each location by employee Social Security number. Then, read the attendance input data for the first employee and match it with the corresponding master employee record, which you can find on the magnetic disk. Select from the master payroll file the pay rate that you need to calculate the earnings for the first employee. Then, multiply the regular rate by the regular hours, and multiply the overtime rate by the overtime hours. Add the two amounts together to get the gross pay. Store the results temporarily.

Next, read from the employee's record the data that tells you his or her withholding-tax rate. Using this information, compute the amount of withholding tax to be deducted from the gross pay. Determine the amounts of all other deductions, and compute the employee's net pay.

Next, computer, retrieve from storage all the results of your computations. Print them and the other reference data in the proper places on the employee's earnings statement and paycheck.

Repeat all these operations for each employee on the payroll. Finally, computer, tell us in writing if you have not been able to balance the hours worked that you read from the attendance input records with the control figure prepared for you. If they have not balanced, prepare an error report. If they have balanced, stop processing.

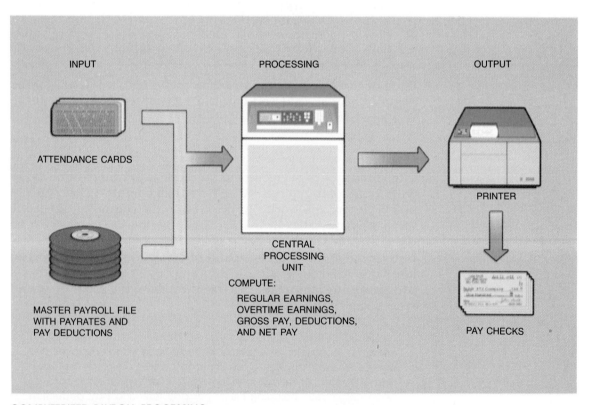

| INPUT | PROCESSING | OUTPUT |

ATTENDANCE CARDS

PRINTER

CENTRAL
PROCESSING
UNIT
COMPUTE:
REGULAR EARNINGS,
OVERTIME EARNINGS,
GROSS PAY, DEDUCTIONS,
AND NET PAY

MASTER PAYROLL FILE
WITH PAYRATES AND
PAY DEDUCTIONS

PAY CHECKS

COMPUTERIZED PAYROLL PROCESSING.

Each of these paragraphs includes several instructions to the computer. The best way to show the step-by-step instructions is with symbols in a diagram called a *program flowchart.* The flowchart summarizes the payroll instructions given to the computer. Once the instructions are in this form, they have to be coded for machine use. **Coding** is the translation of each flowchart instruction into a programming language instruction. There are many programming languages. You will read about some of the most popular ones in Chapter 8.

The person who writes a computer program is usually called a *computer programmer.* First, the programmer writes the program and checks it for diagnostic errors. When the program seems both complete and correct, she or he can test it on the computer. A test run is usually done with sample data representative of the data to be processed.

Once a program has been completely tested for accuracy, it is placed in the *program library,* a file of all the programs needed to perform the computer processing work in a business. When a program is needed for the actual processing of data, it is taken out of the library. It is returned when the processing is completed. For example, a program for payroll work is used for each pay period. Depending on how often employees are paid, this would be every week, two weeks, or month. All programs in the library are recorded in machine-readable form, often in the form of magnetized spots on tapes or disks. Written copies and duplicate magnetic tapes or disks of the program instructions are always maintained in another location for safety and security reasons, in case of vandalism, natural disaster, or fire.

COMPUTER HARDWARE

As you read earlier in this chapter, a computer must have four hardware devices to perform information processing work. In the case of the payroll work, the following computer hardware is needed:

- An input device is needed to read the attendance input data.
- A central processing unit is needed to interpret the payroll program instructions, to direct the operation of the other computer devices, and to perform the sorting and calculating operations.
- An auxiliary storage unit is needed to handle the magnetic disks on which the computer program and the master payroll file information are stored.
- An output device, specifically a printer, is needed to prepare paychecks and earnings statements.

Hardware for a Large Payroll Job. A large company having thousands of employees to be paid every week or even twice a month typically would use a mainframe to do payroll processing work. Of course, the computer system would also be available to handle other processing needs in the company. A large-capacity magnetic-disk storage unit would be needed to handle the stored payroll program and the master payroll file as well as other company data. In addition, a number of keyboards and video display input units would be needed to input data to keep the master payroll file current. Finally, a high-speed printer would be used to prepare the payroll checks and earnings statements as quickly as possible.

Smaller companies may find minicomputers adequate to handle their payroll processing. Video display terminals, disk storage units, and fast printers are also available for these smaller computer systems.

Hardware for a Small Payroll Job. A company having fewer employees can perform payroll processing on a microcomputer equipped with adequate main memory capacity and hard disk storage. Input attendance data for a small payroll can easily be keyed into the computer each pay period. A letter-quality printer of adequate speed would be needed for printing employee payroll checks and earnings statements.

HUMAN EFFORT IN COMPUTER PROCESSING

Computer processing is not completely automatic. Once programs are prepared, people are still needed to prepare the input for each job to be performed by the computer and to operate the computer.

Preparing Input Data. As you know, a computer can perform no work unless it is given input data to process. To do the payroll processing, the number of hours worked by each employee each pay period must be recorded. Also, any employee rate or deduction changes effective during the period must be made in the master payroll file.

The computer must have its input data keyed directly into the machine or recorded in machine-readable form for reading by an input device. Keying of input data directly into a computer or recording of data in machine-readable form is called *data entry*. A data entry operation is always needed for computer processing. Individuals who spend full time on input preparation and the keying of input data are often called *data-entry operators*.

Operating a Computer. Mainframes and many minicomputer systems require full-time trained personnel to ensure effective use of the equipment. A computer operator is responsible for loading and unloading the input and output devices and the auxiliary storage units. In setting up a large computer for

Program preparation. *Courtesy Hewlett-Packard Company.*

Human effort in computer programming.

Data entry. *Courtesy Sperry Corporation.*

Computer operation. *Courtesy Control Data Corporation.*

the payroll work, the operator places the disks with the computer program, the payroll master file, and the attendance records, in the disk storage unit. Blank continuous-form payroll checks and statements are then loaded into a printer.

Once the computer is loaded, the computer operator can start the processing. When the START key is pressed, the computer automatically begins reading the first step of the computer program. The program may include hundreds or even thousands of steps that have to be performed to prepare each employee paycheck. Without any direct human intervention, the computer performs each part of its work assignment.

In one series of steps, for example, the computer performs all the computations necessary to determine an employee's net pay. The results of each of these computations are stored while the next ones are being done. When the computer has finished all the computations for one employee, it retrieves the results from storage and prints them all at once on the employee's earnings statement and paycheck. The steps required to prepare one paycheck may take the computer less than a second. After it finishes one employee's paycheck, it follows all the same steps to prepare a paycheck for every other employee. It continues preparing the paychecks without human intervention until the assignment is completed.

When the computer has printed the paychecks, the operator removes the paychecks and the disks used for payroll processing. Now the computer is ready to be loaded for another information processing job. To complete the payroll work, however, another operator must pass the paychecks and statements through a bursting machine, which separates the forms into individual paychecks that can be distributed to employees.

Setting up a microcomputer for payroll involves many of the same functions. Continuous-form payroll checks must be loaded in the printer. The payroll program and master file on magnetic hard disk or floppy disk must be placed in the auxiliary storage unit. The operator of the microcomputer first directs the computer to load the program into main memory. After this is completed, the payroll attendance data is entered by keyboard or by inserting a floppy disk with the payroll attendance data already recorded. Then the machine can perform its processing operations automatically. The computer requires only occasional attention to monitor its performance.

DATA CODING IN COMPUTER PROCESSING

In our society, people use a system of ten digits to perform arithmetic operations: These are 0, 1, 2, 3, 4, 5, 6, 7, 8, and 9 (the term *digit* refers to any of these ten Arabic numerals). Because this system is based on ten digits rather than some other amount of digits, it is called the **decimal** (or *base-10*) **number system.** Although the decimal number system is now generally used around the world, this was not always the case. Ancient societies used different notations for numbers and, therefore, had different ways of doing calculations.

Modern computers also use number systems that are different from the familiar decimal system. The most important of these for you to know is the binary number system.

BINARY NUMBER SYSTEM

The **binary number system,** also called the *base-2 system*, uses only two digits. The two digits, 0 and 1, are called **bits.** The word *bit* comes from *binary digit*. All the numbers and alphabetic characters that a computer reads as input data are translated into combinations of the two bits, 0 and 1.

Modern computers use the binary number system because it is easier and cheaper to build electronic components that have to represent only a 0 or a 1. The presence or absence of an electronic impulse provides a computer with the capability of distinguishing between the two bits. For example, the absence of a magnetized spot in a specific place on a disk will indicate a 0. The presence of a magnetized spot will indicate a 1. In other words, an *off* electronic condition is a 0, and the *on* position represents a 1.

Obviously, a single bit, representing a 0 or a 1, is not enough to distinguish all the numbers, alphabetic characters, and special symbols that we want a computer to process or to store. Therefore, designers of computers have developed coding systems using groups of bits in different combinations to repre-

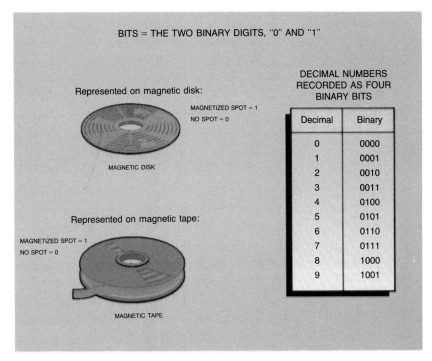

BITS = THE TWO BINARY DIGITS, "0" AND "1"

Represented on magnetic disk:

MAGNETIZED SPOT = 1
NO SPOT = 0

MAGNETIC DISK

Represented on magnetic tape:

MAGNETIZED SPOT = 1
NO SPOT = 0

MAGNETIC TAPE

DECIMAL NUMBERS
RECORDED AS FOUR
BINARY BITS

Decimal	Binary
0	0000
1	0001
2	0010
3	0011
4	0100
5	0101
6	0110
7	0111
8	1000
9	1001

DATA REPRESENTATION IN COMPUTER PROCESSING.

sent the numbers, letters and symbols with which the computers are to work. The two most common coding systems used in modern computers are the EBCDIC system and the ASCII system.

EBCDIC CODE

One of the most commonly used binary code systems in newer models of large computers is known as *EBCDIC* (pronounced "ebb-see-dic"). EBCDIC, which stands for Extended Binary-Coded Decimal Interchange Code, uses eight bits to store a letter of the alphabet, a digit, or a special character. A group of bits used to store a single character is called a **byte.** A byte usually consists of eight bits which the computer handles as a unit. As you depress a key to enter a digit or letter into the computer, the machine translates this into eight bits (combinations of 0's and 1's) and stores it in one byte of storage. Thus, storage of 5000 characters of information takes 5000 bytes of storage. In computer talk, this would be called about 5K of storage, K meaning a thousand. Storage of 5K of information requires the electronics to represent 40,000 bits.

A total of 256 upper and lower case letters, digits (0 through 9) and special characters can be coded using eight positions (or bits) of binary numbers. The EBCDIC codes for numbers and upper case letters is shown in the illustration on page 70. Note

DECIMAL NUMBER OR LETTER	EBCDIC (8 BITS)		ASCII (7 BITS)	
0	1111	0000	011	0000
1	1111	0001	011	0001
2	1111	0010	011	0010
3	1111	0011	011	0011
4	1111	0100	011	0100
5	1111	0101	011	0101
6	1111	0110	011	0110
7	1111	0111	011	0111
8	1111	1000	011	1000
9	1111	1001	011	1001
A	1100	0001	100	0001
B	1100	0010	100	0010
C	1100	0011	100	0011
D	1100	0100	100	0100
E	1100	0101	100	0101
F	1100	0110	100	0110
G	1100	0111	100	0111
H	1100	1000	100	1000
I	1100	1001	100	1001
J	1101	0001	100	1010
K	1101	0010	100	1011
L	1101	0011	100	1100
M	1101	0100	100	1101
N	1101	0101	100	1110
O	1101	0110	100	1111
P	1101	0111	101	0000
Q	1101	1000	101	0001
R	1101	1001	101	0010
S	1110	0010	101	0011
T	1110	0011	101	0100
U	1110	0100	101	0101
V	1110	0101	101	0110
W	1110	0110	101	0111
X	1110	0111	101	1000
Y	1110	1000	101	1001
Z	1110	1001	101	1010

that with the EBCDIC code, each byte is divided into two parts. The zone position has four bits and the numeric position has four bits.

ASCII CODE

A second widely used code system is known as **ASCII** (pronounced "ask-kee"). ASCII, which stands for American Standard Code for Information Interchange, was originally developed for data communications and now is also used as a standard in many microcomputers. ASCII generally is a seven-bit code, which means that seven positions are used to represent the digits (0 to 9), upper- and lower-case alphabetic letters, and special characters. ASCII coding for digits and upper case letters is shown in the illustration on page 70.

The combination of seven bits permits representation of a total of 128 characters. Many manufacturers have added an eighth bit to the ASCII code, which then provides for 256 different characters, the same number as EBCDIC.

OTHER NUMBER SYSTEMS

In addition to the binary number system, some computers use other number systems to represent data. These include the *octal system*, which uses eight digits, 0 through 7, to represent numbers. Thus, the octal system is called a *base-8 number system.*

Perhaps even more confusing is the *hexadecimal system*, a *base-16 number system.* In this system the numbers 0 through 9 are used to represent 0 through 9 as in the decimal system, and the characters A through F are used to represent the numbers 10 through 15. The number 10 is represented by A, 11 by B, . . . , and 15 by F. Fortunately, it is not necessary for most users of hexadecimal computers to learn how to calculate numbers under the base-16 system. The computers translate the results of processing operations back into numbers and letters that we can understand.

CHECK YOURSELF

Match the phrase with the word or phrase that best defines it.

1. The person who writes a series of instructions for the computer.

    a. Hexadecimal system
    b. Decimal system

2. Binary code system used in data transmission and microcomputers.
3. Two binary digits, 0 and 1.
4. Number system based on 16 characters, 0 through 9 and A through F.
5. The person who loads and unloads input devices and monitors the operation of a computer.
6. The best means for illustrating the step-by-step instructions of a computer program.
7. Binary code system of eight bits widely used in large computers.
8. Number system based on ten digits, 0 through 9.
9. Number system based on two digits, 0 and 1.
10. A group of eight bits used to store a single character.

c. Octal system
d. Bits
e. Byte
f. Binary system
g. EBCDIC
h. Program flowchart
i. Computer operator
j. ASCII
k. Data entry operator
l. Computer programmer

Answers: (1) l; (2) j; (3) d; (4) a; (5) i; (6) h; (7) g; (8) b; (9) f; (10) e.

REVIEW QUESTIONS

1. State the difference between analog and digital computers.
2. Distinguish between the terms *computer hardware* and *computer software.*
3. Name the four types of devices common to all business computers and explain the function of each in information processing.
4. Give two examples each of input devices, auxiliary storage units, and output devices.
5. Describe the features of a typical microcomputer.
6. Explain the primary ways in which a minicomputer differs from a microcomputer.
7. Describe the function of a mainframe console unit.
8. Explain what a family of computers is and the meaning of the term *upward compatibility* in hardware.
9. Explain why supercomputers are needed.
10. Define the terms *coding* and *program library.*
11. Describe the purpose of a program flowchart.
12. Name three types of human effort that is required in information processing.
13. Explain the difference between the decimal and the binary number systems.

14. Define a bit and a byte, and explain how they are related.
15. Give the purpose of the EBCDIC (Extended Binary Coded Decimal Interchange Code) and ASCII (American Standard Code for Information Interchange) code systems.

COMPARING IDEAS

The questions below are designed to help you think about what you have learned in this chapter. They are "thought" questions. There is no one correct answer.

1. Describe the components of a specific computer system that you have seen in a school, a business office, or a computer store.
2. Prepare lists of the names of microcomputers that you have actually seen, read about in news accounts, or have seen advertised.

INFORMATION PROCESSING ACTIVITIES

Now you can perform many of the information processing activities business workers perform. Below is a summary of the tasks you will complete. You will find the actual data and business forms you need in your *Information Processing Work Kit.*

1. As a member of the computer operations staff at a large training center, you will assist the Training Director in matching trainees to programs based on their test scores and special skills.
2. You will review four types of computer systems and determine the appropriate hardware to complete a variety of information processing tasks.

HANDS-ON ACTIVITIES

If one page of double-spaced typed material contains about 2 KBytes of information, how many typed pages can be stored on the following devices:

5¼" floppy disk with a 360 KB capacity?
3½" floppy disk with a 720 KB capacity?
5¼" floppy disk with a 1.2 MB capacity? (Hint: a MByte = 1 million bytes)
20 MB hard drive?

SOFTWARE PROJECT

USING WORD PROCESSING: 1

As you learned in Part 1, microcomputers play an important role in helping businesses function. In this and the following software projects you will produce needed business documents under the direction of your supervisor. This activity will be very similar to tasks you might complete in your first information processing job.

The software projects are all based on the needs of the Video-II-Go video tape rental store, a small business that operates in your community. The store has been operating for several years and has been profitable for its owner, the President of the company, Pat Brown. The office procedures used by the owner have been manual up to this time since he has only just recently purchased a personal computer. The Video-II-Go store, being independently operated, does not do a very large volume of business, nor does it require a large staff. For this reason, Pat decided to purchase a microcomputer with 640K of memory, and a monochrome monitor. However, since much of the store's promotional materials will now be created on the computer, he did invest in a good quality laser printer.

The staff is primarily involved with loaning out popular video tapes and collecting the rental fees. Pat is faced with an increasing level of paperwork and hopes that the new computer can help reduce staff hours. You will help the Video-II-Go store by preparing documents to meet a variety of the company's information needs.

Since you will be using some of the files created in these early application projects in a later project, it is suggested that you save all Video-II-Go data files on a single disk. This will make the data transfers as easy as possible and will prevent any duplication of effort.

Each time a person rents a tape from Video-II-Go he or she is encouraged to join the store's Rental Club. This membership allows the person to rent each tape at a discount rate. The membership fees are also a valuable source of income to the owner. If renters do not join at the time they rent their first video tape, they are sent a personal letter outlining the benefits of membership. Pat has found that it is very important to get these letters out as soon as possible after the first rental, since other video stores are doing the same thing. In order to keep up with the competition, he has decided to make this a priority project.

INFORMATION PROCESSING PROBLEM

Video-II-Go needs to produce personalized letters to its customers as rapidly as possible, in order to prevent their customers from joining another company's Rental Club.

INFORMATION PROCESSING SOLUTION

This task can be performed easily using a microcomputer and a word processing software application package. Your supervisor

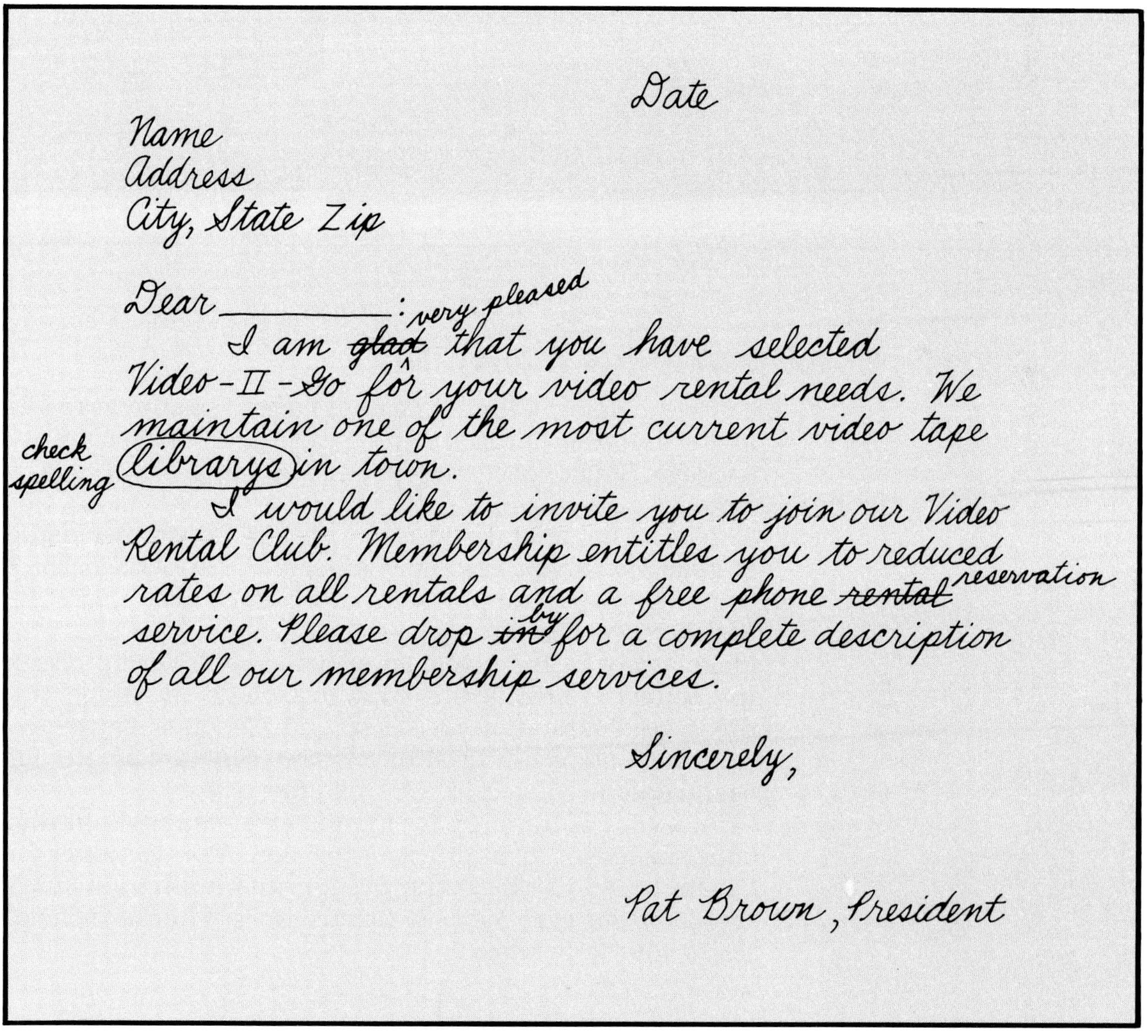

Date

Name
Address
City, State Zip

Dear _____: very pleased

    I am ~~glad~~ that you have selected Video-II-Go for your video rental needs. We maintain one of the most current video tape ⟨librarys⟩ in town.

check spelling

    I would like to invite you to join our Video Rental Club. Membership entitles you to reduced rates on all rentals and a free phone ~~rental~~ reservation service. Please drop ~~in~~ by for a complete description of all our membership services.

              Sincerely,

              Pat Brown, President

will demonstrate a word processing package to you before you begin the keyboarding activities.

The following customers rented video tapes for the first time yesterday. They should each receive a personalized letter as soon as possible.

VIDEO-II-GO			CUSTOMER FILE (NON-MEMBERS)		
Last Name	First Name	Street Address	City	State	Zip
Hastings	Jeff	44 Link	Ft. Worth	TX	76101
Chow	Laura	118 Page St.	Waco	TX	76111
Escobar	Carmen	77a Maple	Ft. Worth	TX	76106
Rashad	Paul	193 B Street	Ft. Worth	TX	76101
Marvin	Rhoda	51 College Way	Ft. Worth	TX	76101
COMPLETED BY	S. M.		DATE	April 6	

KEYBOARDING ACTIVITIES

1. Enter the model letter (shown on page 75) using available microcomputer hardware and a word processing software package. Single space the letter and be sure to enter today's date.
2. Enter the name and address of the first customer using standard business letter format (see your supervisor for a sample). Use a formal salutation, such as "Dear Mr. Smith:."
3. Make a copy of the model letter using your word processing software. Modify this copy to include the name, address, and salutation of the second customer listed. Repeat these steps until you have stored copies of a letter for each customer listed in the Customer File.
4. Print a copy of the letter for Customer #1 and submit it to your supervisor for approval or revision. After the letter for Customer #1 has been approved, print out an individualized letter for each Video-II-Go customer. Submit the copies to your supervisor.

ENRICHMENT ACTIVITIES

1. If your software allows the merging of names and addresses during printing, design your letters to be produced using a single stored letter and a separate address file. Demonstrate this capability to your supervisor.

2. Experiment with the automated production of mailing envelopes. This may include the preparation of mailing labels, printing directly on envelopes, or modifying the letter to be used with window envelopes. Prepare envelopes for the Video-II-Go customers and submit them to your supervisor.

PART 2

2

COMPUTER HARDWARE

CHAPTER

4

COMPUTER INPUT

Information Processing Terminology

Data entry
Batch processing
Transaction processing
On-line inquiry
Interactive processing
Computer-assisted
  instruction
Time sharing
Real-time system
On-line input terminal
Remote terminal
Video display terminal

Cathode-ray tube
Touch sensing
Terminal intelligence
Dumb terminal
Smart terminal
Intelligent terminal
Graphics input terminal
Teleprinter
Off-line input device
Card reader
Key-to-disk input

Key-to-disk shared
  processor system
Magnetic tape drive
Source data automation
Optical character
  recognition
Turnaround document
Universal product code
Magnetic-ink character
  recognition
Data collection device
Speech recognition
  device

Performance Goals

☐ Name three factors considered in the selection of input methods. Give a reason why each is important.

☐ Explain the difference between transaction and batch processing. Give an example of how each is used in business.

☐ Define on-line inquiry processing, interactive processing, and time sharing. Give an example of each.

As you learned in Chapter 1, the first step in any information processing job is input preparation, which is the task of collecting and recording the raw data needed to produce the required information. No work can be performed by a computer unless it is given input data to process.

The source of input data varies, depending upon the particular information activity. To perform the payroll computer processing task described in Chapter 3, data about time worked has to be collected for each employee. To prepare student academic reports, schools must assemble test scores and class performance records from each teacher. Keeping track of your family finances on a personal computer requires you to record data about your expenditures and income.

Input data can be keyed directly into a computer or recorded in machine-readable form for reading by an input device connected to a computer. **Data entry** is the name given to both operations—keying of input data directly into a computer or recording of data in machine-readable form. In the early days of computer processing, all data to be entered into a computer had to be recorded in the form of punched holes either on cards or paper tape. Newer techniques have been developed to simplify the data-entry operation, and many different methods and devices are now available for computer input. Before looking at these, we should understand the objectives that business seeks in its data-entry activities.

DATA-ENTRY OBJECTIVES

In evaluating alternative approaches and equipment to use for data entry, a business usually considers three factors:

1. Accuracy in recording input data.
2. Timeliness by which the input data can be made available for processing.
3. Cost of the data-entry operation.

ACCURACY OF INPUT DATA

The importance of having accurate input data cannot be overemphasized. It is not possible to get reliable and, therefore, useful information out of a computer if inaccurate data has been entered into the system. For example, if in payroll processing an error is made in recording the number of hours worked by a particular employee, the paycheck for that employee will not be correct. The term garbage in, garbage out (GIGO) was coined by early users of computers to highlight the importance of accuracy in input preparation.

To minimize the possibility of input error, every attempt is now made to eliminate the need for manual recording of the same information more than once. In many companies salespeople now key customer order information (such as customer identification and the items ordered) directly into a computer. Formerly, a salesperson recorded sales by writing the order data on a customer order form by hand; this then had to be read by a data-entry clerk. The clerk in a keying operation then recorded the order data for input into a computer. In this case, as in others where input data is recorded more than once, the chance for error is great.

There are many different ways of verifying input data before it is released for computer processing. The use of a video display terminal on an input device allows a data-entry operator to check keyboarded data and make corrections as necessary so that only accurate data is entered into the computer. Another method is the use of precalculated (control) totals to which input data must be balanced. For example, in the payroll processing application described in Chapter 3, the total hours worked were added on a calculating machine to provide a control total to which the input attendance hours as recorded could be balanced.

Still another method of ensuring accuracy of input data is to require verification of keyed data by a second keying operation. The two results are then compared. Any differences in data are checked to determine the correct input. Also, a computer and certain types of input terminals can be programmed to do specified checks on input data to make sure it is reasonable.

TIMELINESS OF DATA INPUT

The amount of time that can be spent on preparing input data varies by type of computer job. The time allowance depends upon when the output information is needed. In the case of payroll processing, paychecks generally must be ready for delivery to employees by a specified number of days following the close of a pay period. This may allow several days for preparation of the input data. In other cases, it may be satisfactory to users of the output information to accumulate the input data for a week or more before processing it. At the other extreme, sometimes data about an event must be processed as the event occurs.

To accommodate these very different time needs for input

preparation, two different approaches to computer processing are used. One is known as batch processing. The second approach is called transaction processing and includes what is known as interactive processing.

Batch Processing. Originally, batch processing was the only way to process data on a computer. In **batch processing,** input data is accumulated as a group (or batch) over a set period of time—daily, weekly, or monthly. Then, all the input is released at one time for processing by the computer. Output information is available only after all of the data has been processed. Applications such as payroll processing continue to be handled effectively by batch processing. The development of modern communication technology and faster processing units, however, has stimulated a rapid growth in systems that record and process transactions as they occur.

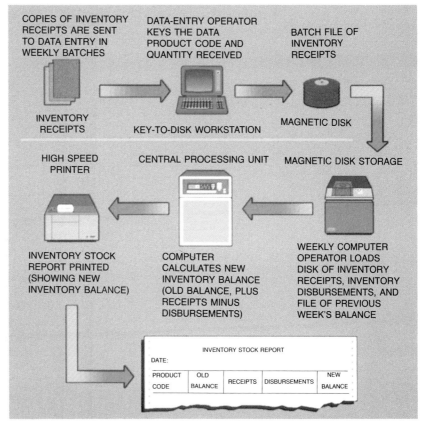

BATCH PROCESSING. In batch processing, data is collected for a specified period and processed on the computer at one time. As an example, inventory receipts are used to update inventory balances on a weekly basis.

Transaction Processing. In **transaction processing,** input data about a particular event is entered into a computer as the event occurs, and the data is immediately processed by the computer. The classic example of transaction processing is the handling of airline reservations. In this application a complete inventory of the seats available on all flights of an airline is kept in a computer storage unit located in one place in the country. Travel or ticket agents throughout the country can communicate by keyboard directly with the main computer to inquire whether or not seat space is available on a particular flight. Within a few seconds, the computer checks its inventory and sends back to the agent a response indicating whether or not the customer can be accommodated. If the customer then approves, the ticket agent presses the input keys to confirm the reservation. With this confirmation, the computer subtracts one seat from its inventory and records the passenger's name. Each day hundreds of thousands of such transactions may be handled by an airline computer.

There are several types of transaction processing. **On-line inquiry** refers to the type of transaction processing in which an individual may directly request information by terminal from a

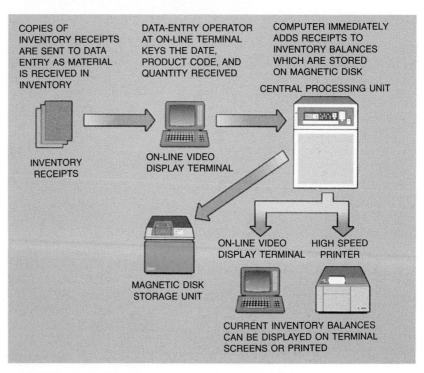

COPIES OF INVENTORY RECEIPTS ARE SENT TO DATA ENTRY AS MATERIAL IS RECEIVED IN INVENTORY

DATA-ENTRY OPERATOR AT ON-LINE TERMINAL KEYS THE DATE, PRODUCT CODE, AND QUANTITY RECEIVED

COMPUTER IMMEDIATELY ADDS RECEIPTS TO INVENTORY BALANCES WHICH ARE STORED ON MAGNETIC DISK

CENTRAL PROCESSING UNIT

INVENTORY RECEIPTS

ON-LINE VIDEO DISPLAY TERMINAL

MAGNETIC DISK STORAGE UNIT

ON-LINE VIDEO DISPLAY TERMINAL

HIGH SPEED PRINTER

CURRENT INVENTORY BALANCES CAN BE DISPLAYED ON TERMINAL SCREENS OR PRINTED

TRANSACTION PROCESSING. In transaction processing, data is processed as an event occurs. As an example, inventory receipts are used to update the inventory balance as soon as the material is received.

computer and receive an immediate answer. Depending upon the particular application, the individual may then direct the computer to update its information. The airline reservation system just described is an example of an on-line inquiry system.

Another term, **interactive processing,** refers to the type of transaction processing in which a user conducts a dialogue (or discussion) with the computer through the keyboard. An example of interactive processing is *computer-assisted instruction* (CAI). A student is aided in a lesson by working at a terminal. He or she receives instructional material on the display screen and is asked to key in answers to questions posed by the computer. The computer then tells the student whether or not the answers are correct.

Another commonly used term is **time sharing,** which simply means that a number of terminal users in transaction processing are sharing the same computer processor at one time. For example, if several students are using minicomputer terminals for CAI at one time, the computer is sharing its processing time among the terminals.

Transaction processing is growing at a very fast pace. More and more doctors are using computers on an inquiry basis to assist them in making medical diagnoses of patients' ailments. Sales people in many retail stores now use on-line inquiry terminals to check a customer's credit status before accepting a request to charge an item. Banks have terminals that permit

COMPUTER-ASSISTED INSTRUCTION. Students are aided in a lesson by working at a terminal, keying in answers to questions posed by the computer. *Courtesy Kay Chernish, The Image Bank.*

customers to check their account balances, and manufacturing plants use transaction processing to keep track of current inventories. A business system that incorporates transaction processing is often referred to as a **real-time system.** In a real-time system, such as the airline reservation system, information is processed quickly enough to produce output immediately usable in an activity.

COST OF INPUT OPERATIONS

You may be wondering why transaction processing is not used for all computer processing, since it has the obvious advantage of producing information faster than batch processing does. The third factor to be considered in the selection of an input method—input costs—answers this question. The hardware used in batch processing is simpler and cheaper than what is required for transaction processing. Because the batch method permits the processing of large amounts of data at one time, it also assures a more efficient use of the computer hardware.

Professionals believe that input preparation usually represents from one-third to one-half of an organization's total costs for processing information by computer. Thus, input can be the largest element of computer costs. For this reason, without sacrificing accuracy, a business normally tries to choose the least expensive method of input preparation that can satisfactorily meet user time schedules for output information.

CHECK YOURSELF

Match each phrase with the word or phrase that best defines it.

1. The type of transaction processing involved in CAI.
2. Accumulation of input data for later processing.
3. The result of inaccurate input data.
4. Processing of input when an event occurs.
5. Many terminals using a computer at the same time.

a. Garbage in, garbage out
b. Transaction processing
c. Interactive processing
d. Time sharing
e. Batch processing

Answers: (1) c; (2) e; (3) a; (4) b; (5) d.

ON-LINE TERMINALS FOR INPUT

Some type of on-line terminal is always used to enter input for transaction processing. An **on-line terminal** is one connected to a computer by cable or by a communications line. On-line terminals also are sometimes used to enter data into computer storage for batch processing at a later date.

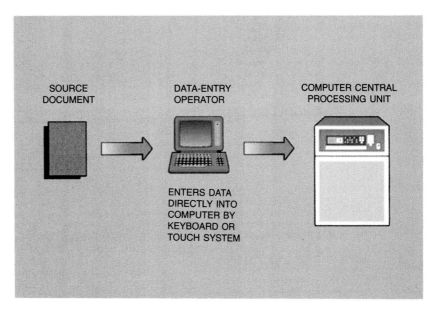

ON-LINE DATA ENTRY.

An on-line terminal that is located at a different site from the computer is called a **remote terminal.** A remote terminal operator gives data to or requests information from a computer using the same type of keyboard as that used by a terminal operator sitting in the same room as the computer. However, telephone lines or special communications networks connect a remote terminal to the computer.

Three types of general purpose terminals are available for on-line input. These are the on-line display terminal, graphics input terminal, and on-line printing terminal.

ON-LINE DISPLAY TERMINAL

The most common device used for on-line input to a computer combines a typewriter-like keyboard and a television-like screen that is called either a **video display terminal** (VDT) or a video display unit (VDU). The keyboard is used to enter numeric and alphabetic data into the computer. The screen is used to display the data that is keyed as input and to display information received back from the computer. The terminal screen itself is often called a **cathode-ray tube** (CRT) or simply a monitor.

On-line display units differ primarily by two characteristics:

- Display screen characteristics
- Degree of intelligence built into the terminal

Display Screen Characteristics. The screens of many VDTs display 25 lines of data at one time with 80 characters on a line, but there are smaller and larger screen capacities available. Early screens displayed white characters on a black back-

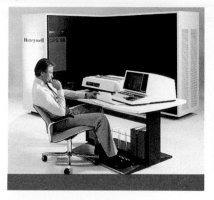

Courtesy Honeywell, Inc.   Courtesy Harris Corporation.

ON-LINE INPUT TERMINALS. Two types of on-line input terminals: an on-line display terminal (at left) and a graphics terminal (at right).

ground, but now most units display either green or amber characters on a black background or black letters on a white background. Screens that can display a number of different colors are also available. Color is especially useful for displaying graphics information, such as charts and drawings. For instance, illustrators using computers can make different parts of a drawing show up in different colors to make the drawing easier to work with.

There are a number of additional features that may be built into a screen to make it easier to use. One, for example, enables an operator to display two page images on one screen. Another feature that is becoming very popular permits entry of data by using touch-sensitive terminal screens. The technique of **touch sensing** permits a user to give the computer a command by using the terminal screen rather than the terminal keyboard. Instead of typing the command, the user simply touches the screen in a predetermined place. The operator chooses the proper command by pointing at a given word, symbol, diagram, or drawing that is displayed on the screen. The computer senses that the particular area of the screen has been touched and accepts the given command.

Touch sensing provides a simple way for a user who is not trained in keyboarding to enter computer commands. While the number of choices that are displayed at any one time on a screen must be limited to ten or less to avoid confusion to a user, the technique still has practical application. It is being used at different types of information stations to give people information about particular facilities and to guide them to requested locations. For example, information stations in the Walt Disney EPCOT entertainment area in Orlando, Florida, are equipped with touch-sensing computer screens. By pressing numbers or letters on the screen, visitors can request information about the types of different exhibits and the locations of particular ones they may want to see. A system has also been

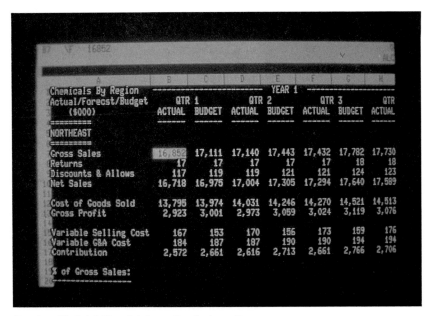

Will Faller.

Courtesy Digital Office & Information Systems Group.

DISPLAY SCREEN CHARACTERISTICS. VDTs have various display characteristics, including the amount of data they can show and the use of color.

TOUCH-SENSITIVE SCREEN. Touch sensing allows the user to give the computer a command by touching the screen in a predetermined place. *Courtesy Hewlett-Packard Company.*

designed to help airline passengers make their own reservations by touch-sensing terminal screens.

In addition to touching a screen directly, there are other ways of entering input data on touch-sensitive screens. A user may use a *light pen* to select a command displayed on a screen or to write on a screen. The light pen, connected by cable to the computer, detects light from the screen; in so doing, it can be used to input a command.

The Apple Macintosh computer introduced the technique of using an interactive device called a *mouse* on touch-sensitive screens. The mouse, about the size of a television remote-control device, is connected by cable to the computer. When the mouse is moved across the desk, an arrow is moved across the terminal screen. The arrow is used to select the particular command that the user wants to give to the computer.

Terminal Intelligence. Although all on-line display terminals enter input data into the computer and permit the display of output, they are built with varying abilities to perform other tasks. For this reason, input devices are often classified with respect to their work ability, which is referred to as **terminal intelligence.** Classed by intelligence, there are three groups of terminals: dumb, smart, and intelligent terminals.

So-called **dumb terminals** are very limited in their work ability. They can be used to key data and enter it into a computer one line at a time, but they have no processing ability. Dumb terminals are no longer commonly used for data input.

Smart terminals are equipped with a microprocessor and a small memory so they can perform a limited number of process-

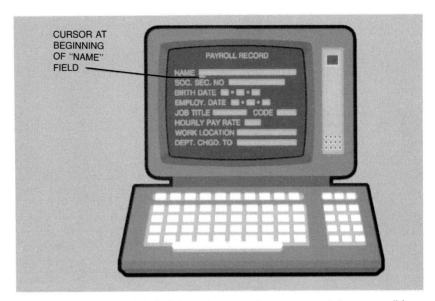

USING A SMART TERMINAL. A data-entry operator can complete a payroll form using a smart terminal. The cursor automatically moves to the first item. The operator keys the data into the highlighted area then presses the return key. The cursor automatically moves to the next field.

ing operations. These terminals can be used to simplify input operations; they prompt an input operator to enter correct data and then they perform an edit (check) to ensure the accuracy of the input before it is given to the computer for processing.

The name **intelligent terminal** is given to an input device that can be programmed and has substantial processing capabilities. It includes a disk and a small central processor in addition to the keyboard and display unit typical of other terminals. This makes it possible for the terminal to perform processing operations when not in communication with the larger computer. A microcomputer is often used as an intelligent terminal.

GRAPHICS INPUT TERMINAL

Some input terminals are designed to translate input data recorded in graphic form into a form readable by the computer. A **graphics input terminal** allows a user to draw and revise an image (drawing) on the touch-sensitive screen using a light pen or some other input device. Once a designer is satisfied with the drawing, he or she can store it in the computer for further processing. Special devices, such as a digitizer or a graphics tablet, can convert the lines and curves in a drawing to digital data that a computer can store. Graphic input is used frequently by engineers and designers of automobiles, airplanes, and buildings.

GRAPHICS TERMINAL AND LIGHT PEN. A light pen is an input device connected to the computer by cable. It can sense light on the display screen and feed data into the computer. The image can be stored in the computer for later processing. *Courtesy IBM Corporation.*

ON-LINE PRINTING TERMINAL

For some applications it is necessary to have a hard copy of data that is keyed into a computer. For example, individuals entering input sales data from a remote terminal may want to retain a copy of customer-order data that is being communicated to a central computer. A **teleprinter** is an input device that provides a printed copy of data as it is keyed into a computer. It also can be used as an output device to record the results of information processing.

OFF-LINE INPUT DEVICES

Off-line input devices work independently of a computer. Therefore, unlike on-line data entry, *off-line data entry* requires two operations. First, input data is recorded in machine-readable form. Second, the recorded data is entered into a computer for processing. A number of different off-line devices are available to record input data in machine-readable form.

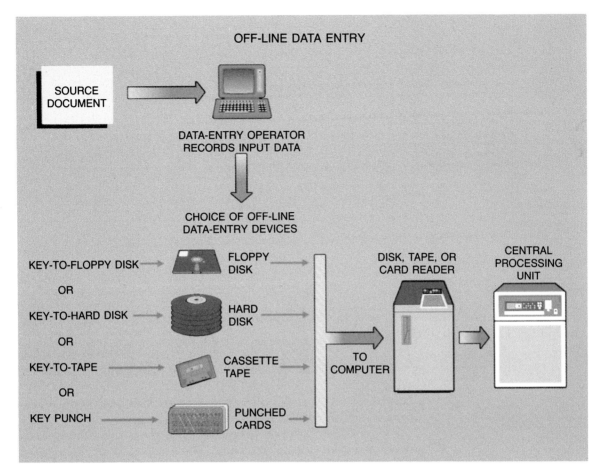

OFF-LINE DATA ENTRY

Within the figure:
OFF-LINE DATA ENTRY

SOURCE DOCUMENT

DATA-ENTRY OPERATOR RECORDS INPUT DATA

CHOICE OF OFF-LINE DATA-ENTRY DEVICES

KEY-TO-FLOPPY DISK → FLOPPY DISK

OR

KEY-TO-HARD DISK → HARD DISK

OR

KEY-TO-TAPE → CASSETTE TAPE

OR

KEY PUNCH → PUNCHED CARDS

TO COMPUTER

DISK, TAPE, OR CARD READER

CENTRAL PROCESSING UNIT

OFF-LINE DATA ENTRY.

PUNCHED-CARD DATA INPUT

Initially, all input data for computers had to be recorded on punched cards. As explained in Chapter 2, Dr. Herman Hollerith developed the punched-card concept of information processing for handling U.S. census data. Later, through the initiative of IBM, punched-card processing machines became widely used in business and government, before they were replaced by computers.

The 80-column punched card is the card most commonly used for the recording of input data. It gets its name from the fact that it is divided into 80 vertical columns. Each column can be used to represent an alphabetic or numeric character. This is possible because each of the 80 columns has 12 positions (rows) in which a rectangular hole can be punched.

The numbers 0 through 9 are represented by a single punch in a vertical column. For example, a 5 is represented by a punch in the 5-position of the column. The number of columns used to record data depends upon the size of the item. A number such

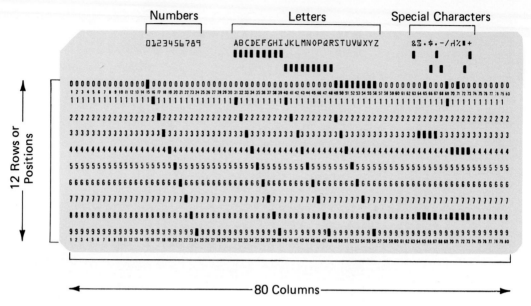

80-COLUMN CARD. There are 80 columns and 12 rows on an 80-column card. Columns go up and down; rows go across.

as 5,703 would take up four columns. (The comma is not recorded.) A letter can be recorded in a card column by punching a combination of two holes in the same column. Look at the figure to see how two punches record a letter.

Punched-card input is prepared on a machine called a keypunch or a card-punch machine. The keypunch (or data-entry) operator keys the number or letters recorded on a business document and the data is recorded in the form of punched holes. Usually, the accuracy of keypunched data is checked by a key verifying operation.

Once data is recorded on punched cards, it can be entered into a computer by a **card reader.** A card reader has photoelectric cells to sense punched holes and to transfer the data into the main storage unit of a computer for processing. Card readers vary in speed of operation, some handling as many as 2,000 cards per minute.

KEY-TO-TAPE AND KEY-TO-DISK INPUT DEVICES

In the 1960s newer types of data-entry methods were developed to overcome the disadvantages of punched-card input. The newer methods do not limit a user to a specified record length (for example, 80 characters). In addition, they provide a much more compact means of storing data. Punched cards are bulky to handle and cannot be erased or reused for data recording. The first improvement allowed operators to key input data directly onto a reel of magnetic tape. Then, in the 1970s, IBM developed an input device that enabled a data-entry operator to record input data on magnetic disk. **Key-to-disk input** is now the most popular method of off-line input.

Recording Data on Magnetic Media. Although there are many variations in key-to-disk input (and key-to-tape devices), most devices usually have a keyboard and display screen similar to that of the terminal display input device described earlier. But instead of having the input read directly into a computer as done with terminal input, the off-line key-to-disk and key-to-tape devices record the input data in the form of magnetized spots directly on disk or tape. Depending upon the particular machine, the magnetic spots are recorded most often on floppy disks (also called diskettes) or on hard disks. Less frequently, reels of magnetic tape contained in tape cassettes or tape cartridges are used for input (key-to-tape devices).

All machines permit the operator to enter the input data into a storage unit as it is keyed. The operator transfers the content of the storage unit for recording on disk or tape only after an entire record has been keyed. Thus, by rekeying she or he can make any corrections that may be necessary. In addition, the keyed data is often checked by a verifying operation. This is done by rekeying the input from the source document. The machine compares the data recorded in the two keying operations and points out any differences. The verifying operator must then determine which set of input data is correct.

Key-to-Disk Shared-Processor Systems. Large computer installations need many data-entry machines for input preparation. It may be economical in these situations to use more complex key-to-disk equipment that can make the data-entry task easier. In a **key-to-disk shared-processor system** a group of keyboard and display unit work stations (typically 2 to 64) is connected to a minicomputer with a large disk storage unit that can be used by all input stations. The input data keyed by each of the console stations is stored on the disk until the data-entry job is completed. Then the stored input is usually transferred to magnetic tape for entry into a larger computer for processing.

The processing capability of the shared processor, combined with the large disk-storage capacity, permits complex editing functions to be performed at each station. This ability can greatly simplify a data-input operation. For example, in a billing operation a data-entry operator can key in a customer's number and retrieve from storage the customer's name and billing address for use in invoice preparation. This information can be combined with sales data for that customer, and an invoice can be automatically prepared and printed by the computer. This reduces the amount of data to be keyed and also assures greater accuracy in input preparation.

Entry of Off-Line Input Data. Input data recorded on floppy or hard magnetic disks or tape cassettes by off-line data-entry devices will be transported to the computer where the data can be entered for processing using disk- or tape-reading devices connected to the computer.

Often, however, the data keyed off-line at various console stations is transferred to a reel of magnetic tape. The tape reel is then mounted on a **magnetic-tape drive** connected to the computer. This device, also known as a magnetic-tape input-output device, reads at high speed the input data recorded on the reel of tape and transfers it to the memory of the computer's processing unit. In the processing operation, new data may be written onto the tape. Thus, a magnetic-tape drive serves as both an input and an output device.

CHECK YOURSELF

Match each phrase with the word or phrase that best defines it.

1. On-line terminal that is very limited in its work ability.
2. Terminal that provides a hard copy of data keyed into a computer.
3. Input device that works independently of computers.
4. On-line data-entry device that can perform processing operations when not connected to the main computer.
5. Device that reads input data recorded on reels of magnetic tape.
6. Device that reads data recorded on punched cards.
7. General name for input device connected to a computer.
8. Another name for a video display terminal.
9. On-line terminal connected to a computer by communications lines.
10. Terminal used to translate images into input data.

a. Off-line data-input device
b. Teleprinter
c. Smart terminal
d. Intelligent terminal
e. Dumb terminal
f. On-line terminal
g. Card punch
h. Magnetic-tape drive
i. Remote terminal
j. Card reader
k. Video display unit or Cathode-ray tube
l. Graphics input terminal

Answers: (1) e; (2) b; (3) a; (4) d; (5) h; (6) j; (7) f; (8) k; (9) i; (10) l.

So far, you have learned about two different methods of data input. Under one method, on-line data input, a data-entry operator keys input data directly into a computer. In the second method, off-line data entry, a data-entry operator, using a device not connected directly to the computer, keys input data into machine-readable form. Then, in a separate operation, the machine-readable input is entered into a computer.

There is a third method of input preparation, usually called **source data automation.** In source data automation, manual keying of input data is eliminated. Instead, a machine reads data recorded on a source document and enters it directly into a computer for processing; alternatively, the machine may store the data on magnetic tape or disk for future automatic entry into the computer.

Source data automation is a very desirable method for data entry because it bypasses the manual keying of input that is both costly and time-consuming. One way of achieving source data automation is to have input data printed, typed, or marked so that it can be read by a scanning machine. Data entry by machine scanning is done in one of two ways—by optical reading or by magnetic-ink scanning.

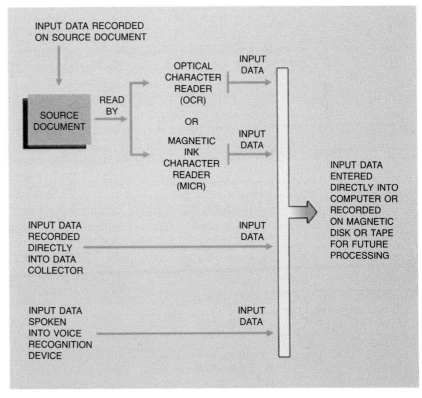

SOURCE DATA AUTOMATION.

OPTICAL SCANNING METHODS

Three different optical scanning techniques are used for data entry:

1. Optical reading of marks.
2. Optical reading of numbers, letters, and special characters.
3. Optical reading of bar codes.

Optical Reading of Marks. Optical scanning began with the development of scanning machines that read the pencil-marked answers students recorded on special multiple-choice test forms. Devices called *optical mark scanners* determined whether a student had marked a response in the correct column. Some machines can then score the tests from a given key of correct answers. More often, a scanner records the answer data on magnetic disk or tape for grading and analysis by a computer.

The same type of questionnaire document and the same scanning process is frequently used in business to record customer responses to market surveys.

Optical Reading of Numeric and Alphabetic Characters. The most widely used machine-scanning process is **optical character recognition** (OCR). In this type of scanning process, numbers, letters, and special symbols that are printed, typed, or handwritten on a source document are read and recorded as input data. The machines that do the scanning work are known as *optical character readers,* or sometimes *optical scanners.*

The OCR process is based on the use of a bright light source with a lens system to detect the pattern of a printed character. This pattern is matched against a master character pattern to identify the number or letter being scanned.

Optical character readers are used in a variety of different ways. Companies with large numbers of customers (such as utilities, retail stores, magazine publishers, and insurance companies) send to customers computer-printed bills that can be read by optical scanners. Customers are instructed to return the preprinted portion of the bill with their payment. When these documents, called **turnaround documents,** are returned by the customers, they are read by optical character readers that enter into the computer the data needed to credit the customers' accounts.

Optical character readers are often used in word processing work to convert a copy of a typed letter or a report to magnetic disk. The material can then later be retrieved and revised using a word processor. The U.S. Postal Service uses special optical scanners that read ZIP Codes on envelopes and direct sorting machines to sort the envelopes by their destination point.

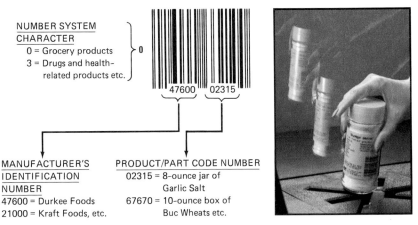

NUMBER SYSTEM
CHARACTER
  0 = Grocery products
  3 = Drugs and health-
      related products etc.

0

47600 02315

MANUFACTURER'S
IDENTIFICATION
NUMBER
47600 = Durkee Foods
21000 = Kraft Foods, etc.

PRODUCT/PART CODE NUMBER
02315 = 8-ounce jar of
        Garlic Salt
67670 = 10-ounce box of
        Buc Wheats etc.

UNIVERSAL PRODUCT CODE. An example of a UPC showing the manufacturer's identification number and product/part code number is shown at left. At right is the jar of Durkee Garlic Salt being passed over a scanner that reads the product code number and retrieves the price and description of the item from the computer. *Courtesy NCR Corporation.*

OPTICAL SCANNER. The salesman shown here is holding a scanning wand over the lampshade's bar code. The scanner reads the data, obtains the price and description of the item, and updates inventory and sales records. *Courtesy NCR Corporation.*

Optical Reading of Bar Codes. In addition to marks and alphanumeric characters, optical scanners can read bars or lines that are often seen printed on grocery items or other packaged goods. The most common bar code is the **universal product code** (UPC), which is used to identify products sold in retail stores. The UPC consists of a series of vertical bars of varying widths that represent a coded form of numbers. The information in the code identifies the manufacturer of the item, the particular product, and its cost.

Today, when you bring a load of groceries to a checkout counter in a modern supermarket, the bar code for each packaged item is read by an optical scanner. This is done by passing a hand-held scanning wand over the item or by moving the package across a fixed scanner. As each item is scanned, its bar code is read and the data sent to a central computer. The computer looks up the item price and description that are stored in memory, immediately transmits the price and item description back to the cash register at the checkout counter, and then updates its inventory and sales records. The cash register prints the item description and price on the sales slip given to the customer. Bar code systems are also widely used in factories to keep track of inventory and equipment.

The supermarket checkout system, of having input data entered into a computer at the location of the sale, is one example of a *point-of-sale* (POS) data entry system. Point-of-sale terminals are also widely used by sales clerks in large retail stores.

MAGNETIC-INK SCANNING METHODS

Magnetic-ink character recognition (MICR) was developed to help banks process the billions of checks that are written each year. MICR scanners read source documents on which data has been printed in a magnetic ink (iron oxide). A special typeface designed for data recording on documents to be processed by MICR machines was adopted by the American Bankers Association (ABA) as a national standard for use by banks throughout the United States.

Each bank issues to its customers sets of blank checks and deposit slips printed with the bank's identification numbers and the customer's account number. When the recipient of a check presents it to a bank for payment, a data-entry operator in the bank imprints the amount of the check in magnetic ink. Then an MICR machine scans the check, along with many other checks, to record the bank and customer identification numbers and the amount of the check. This input data is entered directly into a computer or stored on magnetic disk or tape for later input.

In the past, bank employees sorted the checks themselves so that the checks could be returned to customers along with statements of their accounts. This tremendous sorting job can

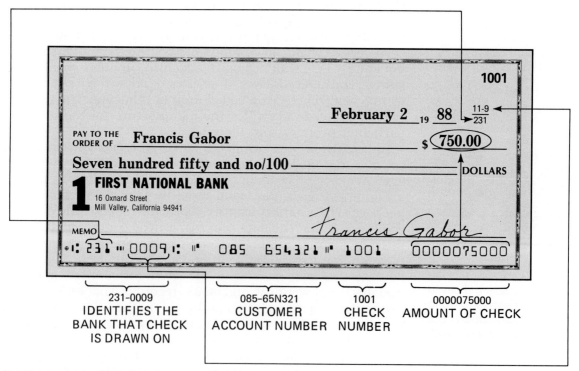

231-0009
IDENTIFIES THE
BANK THAT CHECK
IS DRAWN ON

085-65N321
CUSTOMER
ACCOUNT NUMBER

1001
CHECK
NUMBER

0000075000
AMOUNT OF CHECK

MAGNETIC-INK SCANNING. Banks use magnetic-ink scanning for recording of bank check data and for sorting of the checks. As shown on the check in the illustration, magnetic ink characters identify the bank on which the check is drawn, the customer account number, the check number and the check amount.

now be done by machines at the time that the data on the check is being scanned and recorded.

DATA-COLLECTION DEVICES FOR DATA ENTRY

In addition to optical and magnetic-ink scanning equipment, **data collection devices** can be used to record input data at the location where the transaction being reported takes place. These devices are commonly used in factories for the reporting of inventory stocks or the status of manufacturing jobs.

A variety of devices serve as data collectors. Hand-held terminals with simple keyboards can be carried through a manufacturing plant so that input data can be reported from many different locations. Bar code readers can be attached to the terminal to read in the bar code data printed on inventory or equipment in the plant. More complex systems of terminals are used to record input data about time worked or progress on manufacturing operations. In both cases, the input data is transmitted to a central computer for processing.

DATA ENTRY BY VOICE INPUT

For a long time, computer scientists have been trying to develop **speech-recognition devices** that can translate what is said by a person into machine-readable input data. The task is not an easy one. People say the same words in such dissimilar ways that no single pattern can be used for a given word. In addition, it is difficult to teach a machine to recognize the difference between similar-sounding phrases, such as "ice cream" and "I scream."

Limited speech-recognition equipment is now available, and it is employed mostly in situations where a person is engaged in some activity that otherwise occupies the hands, making the keying of input data impractical. This sort of situation occurs often in a manufacturing plant or research laboratory. For example, a factory inspector examining a manufactured product and a lab technician conducting an experiment often are not free to input data by hand.

Each type of speech-recognition device has a vocabulary of words specially designed for a particular application. The systems now available recognize only 100 to 200 words related to the task being recorded. Also, the recognition unit must be trained (or adjusted) to recognize the speech of a particular person. The person using the device wears a microphone headset and speaks the numbers or words into it. Wireless microphones are used where the user's mobility is important. Some speech-recognition devices are even available for use with personal computers. They can be programmed to reduce the number of keystrokes needed to use a typical word processing program, for instance. Instead of typing a command like SAVE, you simply say the word "save" and the computer saves your file.

SPEECH-RECOGNITION DEVICES. Speech-recognition devices translate what a person says into machine-readable input data. *Courtesy Texas Instruments.*

IBM and other companies are working on more advanced speech-recognition devices that will be able to recognize more than 10,000 words. When improved equipment is available at reasonable prices, voice-entry systems will become an attractive and efficient means of quickly feeding input information into a computer. In the future, automatic voice-recognition dictation equipment will take much of the drudgery and expense out of transcribing and typing spoken information.

CHECK YOURSELF

Supply the missing words.

1. The universal product code identifies by code numbers a ___?___ and its ___?___.

2. Banks use ___?___ character scanners for check processing.

3. What is spoken can be translated into input data by a ___?___ device.

REVIEW QUESTIONS

1. Define data entry.
2. Name three factors considered in the selection of a data-entry method and give a reason why each is important.
3. Describe three ways in which input data may be verified before being released for computer processing.
4. Define *batch processing* and give an example of its use.
5. Define *transaction processing* and give an example of its use.
6. Explain the meaning of the terms *on-line inquiry, interactive processing, computer-assisted instruction,* and *time sharing.*
7. State the main reason why transaction processing is not used for some computer processing.
8. Explain what an on-line terminal is and what the term *remote terminal* means.
9. Describe the features of three types of terminals that are used for on-line input.
10. Explain the difference between dumb, smart, and intelligent terminals.
11. Give an example of the use of a graphics terminal and of a teleprinter.
12. Explain the difference between off-line and on-line data entry.
13. Explain the meaning of *source data automation* and its primary advantage.
14. Describe three different optical scanning techniques used for data input and give an example of the use of each.
15. Explain how banks use magnetic-ink scanners for check processing.
16. Describe two situations in which speech-recognition devices may be useful for entry of input.

COMPARING IDEAS

The questions below are designed to help you think about what you have learned in this chapter. They are "thought" questions. There is no one correct answer.

1. If you are employed as an input clerk in an insurance office, you likely will be given a video display terminal with which to enter data about customers' insurance policies. What terminal features would be of greatest interest to you?
2. Optical scanning of the universal product code is now widely used as a data input method. Give an example of a product that you have actually seen identified by a UPC and explain how the use of this code number can simplify data input operations.

INFORMATION PROCESSING ACTIVITIES

Now you can try out the kinds of information processing activities business workers perform. Below is a summary of the work you will do. You will find the actual information and business forms you need in your *Information Processing Work Kit.*

1. As a data input clerk in a large bank you will code data on mark sense forms.
2. You will verify the accuracy of MICR coding on customer checks.
3. You will select the computer system (microcomputer, minicomputer, or mainframe) that should be used for some of the bank's data processing requirements.

HANDS-ON ACTIVITIES

1. Using one of yours or one of your parent's canceled checks, identify the following information printed in Magnetic Ink Characters:
   ■ The number of the bank on which the check is drawn
   ■ The account number
   ■ The check number
   ■ The amount of the check
2. In this chapter you learned how the universal product code, or bar code, which is used to identify a product, is read by an optical scanner and the information regarding the product get input into the computer in the first place?
   Stop and see the manager of a local store which uses an optical scanner to read the bar codes of products. Find out how the information about a new product or how the information that must be changed about an existing product, such as the price; gets input into the store's computer.

CHAPTER

5

COMPUTER PROCESSING AND DATA STORAGE

Performance Goals

☐ Describe four essential functions performed by a central processing unit.

☐ Explain the purpose of main memory and the difference between RAM and ROM memory.

☐ Describe how a computer control unit serves as a traffic director of computer devices and as a communications link with the computer operator.

☐ Give the functions of the arithmetic-logic unit and give two examples of computer logic operations.

☐ Identify at least three differences between microcomputer CPUs and those of mainframes.

☐ Explain the difference between direct-access storage and sequential-access storage and give an example of each type of device.

To convert input data into output information, a computer usually performs a variety of processing operations. Depending on the complexity of the information requirements, these operations may involve the classifying, calculating, summarizing, and sorting of data. During processing operations, input or file data must be retrieved from storage and worked on, and the results are then stored. Later, it is often necessary to retrieve these results from storage so that they may be further processed to produce the required output.

In this chapter we will examine the features of the computer hardware devices used to perform processing and data-storage functions.

COMPUTER PROCESSING UNITS

Every computer system needs a **central processing unit** (CPU). Regardless of a computer's size, the processing unit performs essentially the same four functions:

■ Stores the program of instructions and data being processed.

■ Interprets the instructions in the program according to the type and sequence of processing operations that are to be performed on input data.

■ Performs the varied arithmetic and logic operations that are necessary to convert the input data into output information.

■ Directs all other devices (input devices, auxiliary storage units, and output devices), telling each what to do and when to do it.

Because of the nature of these functions, the central processing unit often is called the heart of the computer, but it also serves as the machine's brain.

To perform its vital tasks, a CPU must have three mechanisms: a memory unit (main memory), a control unit, and an arithmetic-logic unit (ALU). In some microcomputers these three mechanisms are combined in a single printed-circuit unit. In most microcomputers, however, only the control unit and arithmetic-logic units are combined (in a unit called the **microprocessor**) and the main memory is housed separately. Large mainframe computers require many individual circuit boards to make up their powerful central processing units.

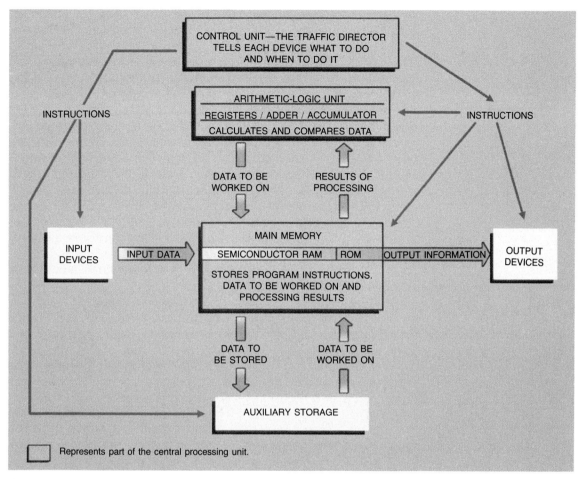

CENTRAL PROCESSING UNIT (CPU). The CPU is the computer mechanism that houses the arithmetic-logic mechanism, the main memory unit, and the control unit.

MAIN MEMORY

Main memory, primary storage, and *working storage* are interchangeable terms. They refer to a memory unit in the CPU that is used to store program instructions and data that must be readily accessible for a computer to perform its work at high speed. Programming instructions that are keyed into a computer or entered from magnetic disk or tape are stored in main memory. The computer retrieves the instructions along with the input data to be worked on, performs the operations called for, and returns the instructions so that they are available when needed again. The processing results are also stored in main memory until they are transferred to an output device.

You can think of main memory as a series of electronic storage locations, each identified by an individual number called a **memory address.** To indicate where a program instruction or an item of data is stored, the computer programmer uses an address, just as you use a street address to indicate where you live. The length of time needed to store (or write) data or to retrieve (or read) data from memory is called **access time.** The components used for a computer's main memory unit provide faster access time than those used for auxiliary storage.

Semiconductor Main Memory. Today semiconductors are used for almost all computer main memories. These storage units consist of tiny chips or wafers of silicon, often much smaller than a fingernail, on which hundreds of thousands of transistors and supporting circuitry may be microscopically etched. Each transistor acts as a gate that either allows electric current to flow or blocks it. The on-off positions of each transistor are used to represent the two bits (binary digits) in a binary code. (*Silicon* is a common metallic element, found as a compound in quartz, sand, and granite. A silicon wafer looks like a sliver of metal.)

Semiconductors have many advantages over other technologies used for main memory. They are more compact than other storage devices and provide faster access to data in storage at a lower cost. Each year improvements in manufacturing processes permit more storage capacity on a chip at a reduced cost per bit stored. In 1986 IBM introduced million-bit memory chips, each of which can store the contents of more than 50 pages of this book. By 1987, manufacturers in Japan and the

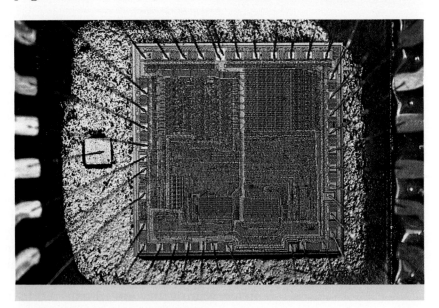

SEMICONDUCTOR MEMORY. Semiconductors consist of silicon chips on which transistors and support circuits are etched. *Courtesy Erich Hartmann, Magnum Photos.*

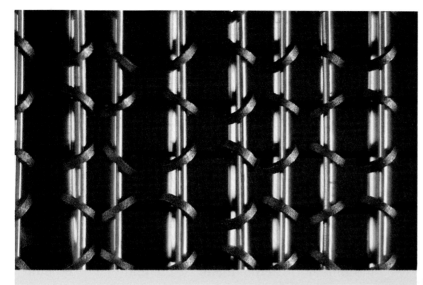

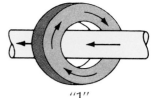

"1"
Magnetized in a
clockwise direction

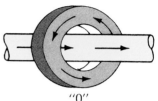

"0"
Magnetized in a
counterclockwise direction

CORE MEMORY. A close-up of a section of core memory (at left). Each doughnut-shaped core is about the size of a pin. A core is given the value of "0" or "1" according to the position in which it is magnetized (illustration at right). The two values represent binary digits or bits. *Courtesy IBM Corporation.*

United States were working on 256-million-bit memory chips that would be commercially available in the 1990s.

Semiconductor memory has one major disadvantage. Usually it is a **volatile memory,** which means that it works only in the presence of electric current. If a computer loses its source of power, all of the program instructions and data stored in main memory are lost, unless the information has been stored on an auxiliary memory unit.

Core Main Memory. In the 1960s and 1970s the most widely used main memories were made of magnetic cores. Magnetic core memory consisted of a large number of tiny doughnut-shaped rings made of iron. Wires were woven through each core. Current passing through these wires magnetized (or polarized) the core in either of two directions. One direction stood for the value of 0; the opposite direction had the value of 1. Thus, each core represented the two binary bits. Although magnetic core memory is now more expensive than semiconductor storage and provides slower access time, it is *nonvolatile* memory, which means it does not lose stored data when the computer has no power. The cores retain their magnetized states, and therefore retain the stored data, after electric current is turned off.

RAM AND ROM
MEMORY UNITS

The most common type of main memory is known as **random-access memory (RAM)** because the data contained in each storage address can be directly retrieved without regard for the sequence in which it was stored. A RAM device is sometimes called a *read-write memory,* which means that data can be stored (written) or retrieved (read) from each memory location. When data is stored in the memory, it replaces and erases data previously stored in the same location. On the other hand, when data is retrieved from storage, a copy of the data remains in storage. RAM semiconductor main memory is volatile, and does not retain stored data when the computer has no power.

In addition to RAM storage, semiconductor main memories usually include another type of memory, called **read-only memory (ROM).** The second type has data permanently or semipermanently recorded in it, which can only be read. No new data can be transferred into ROM during processing. ROM is used to store program instructions that the computer always needs in order to operate—for example, instructions that tell a computer how to get itself running when its on-off switch is turned on. When equipment is being made, each manufacturer stores such program instructions in the ROM unit of its computers, and the contents of these memory units cannot be changed by the users of the computers. As you may expect, unlike RAM memory, ROM is nonvolatile.

Variations of ROM permit a user to store, and in some cases to change, data stored in ROM. One example is a *programmable read-only memory* (PROM), which permits a user to initially store data but does not provide any means for changing the data once stored. Still other read-only memories permit a user to alter the data stored in ROM by a special process. Depending on the method of erasure, these memories are referred to as *erasable programmable read-only memory* (EPROM) or *electrically erasable, programmable read-only memory* (EEPROM).

CAPACITIES OF MAIN MEMORY UNITS

Memory capacities are usually classified by their size in terms of the number of bytes that can be stored in the unit. As explained in Chapter 3, for most computers a single letter or number is represented by an eight-bit code. The group of eight bits is called a *byte.* To store your social security number requires nine bytes (72 bits) of memory. Storing your name may require more memory. For example, the name Elvis Presley requires 13 bytes of storage, allowing for a space before the surname.

The number of bytes that can be stored in a computer's RAM main memory is usually expressed by using a number and the capital letter "K," as in 8K. In computer terminology, the letter "K" means 1024, even though the letter "K" stands for Kilo, which means 1000. An 8K memory can hold 8192 bytes and a 64K memory, 65,536 bytes. Microcomputers may have main memories as small as 4K, while some large mainframes can

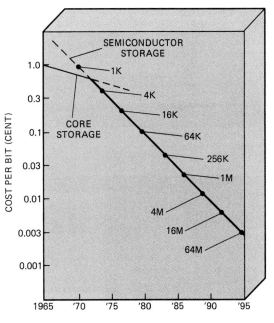

STORAGE CAPACITY AND COSTS. The trend has been for the number of bits that can be stored on a silicon chip to quadruple every 3 years. During the same period, the cost of a chip has tended to be cut in half. It is expected that this trend in semiconductor storage will continue. *Courtesy Donald H. Sanders, Computers Today, 1988.*

store as many as 128M characters in main memory. The capital letter "M" designates roughly one million bytes of RAM memory; it is referred to as a **megabyte** of memory.

In all sizes of computer systems, the potential capacities of RAM memory available to users has increased through the years as the manufacturing cost of making memory chips has decreased. In 1968 a 16-bit RAM chip cost $16; in 1980 a 4000-bit RAM chip cost $4; in 1986 a 256,000 RAM chip cost only $3.

Other variations in main memory units affect a computer's processing power. Some computers that store only a single character in each storage address are called *variable word-length* machines. A variable word-length gives the flexibility of using a varying number of storage locations depending upon particular input or output data requirements. For example, storage of a payroll social security number requires nine storage positions. A payroll rate will require only four storage positions. In other computers, each storage location of main memory holds more than a single character, and the capacity is described in terms of the fixed number of bits that can be stored in the location. For example, there are 16-bit-word memories, 32-bit-word devices, and others. Such memories are said to be *fixed word-length* storage units. They provide a more effective storage approach when processing requires computations with large numbers.

MEASUREMENT OF STORAGE UNIT OR CAPACITY

Measurement	Number of Bits or Bytes
Nibble	Four bits, half-byte
Byte	Eight bits
Kilobyte	1,024 bytes
Megabyte	One million bytes
Gigabyte	One billion bytes
Terabyte	One trillion bytes

CHECK YOURSELF

Match each phrase with the word or phrase that best defines it.

1. Most widely used technology for main memory.
2. Primary or working storage.
3. K in computer terminology.
4. Identification of storage location.
5. A read-write type of memory.
6. One million bytes of memory.
7. Heart of a computer.
8. It stores one character per location.
9. Time it takes to store or retrieve data.
10. It loses stored data when power is turned off.

a. Access time
b. Main memory
c. Variable word-length storage device.
d. Address
e. CPU
f. RAM
g. Volatile memory
h. Semiconductor memory
i. 1024
j. Core memory
k. ROM
l. Megabyte
m. 1000

Answers: (1) h; (2) b; (3) i; (4) d; (5) f; (6) l; (7) e; (8) c; (9) a; (10) g.

CONTROL UNIT

Without a control unit, a computer can do no work. The control unit manages the input devices, main memory, arithmetic-logic unit, auxiliary storage units, and output devices. In sequence, it interprets each instruction in a program, determines what has to be done to follow the instruction, and transmits to the appropriate device directions specifying the work to be done. For example, the control unit advises each input device what data to transfer, when to input it, and where to send that data. It arranges for data to move from memory to the arithmetic-logic unit, spells out the calculating and logic operations that are to be performed, and then arranges to send the processed results to storage or to an output device for printing or display.

In addition to acting as traffic director for the various computer devices, the control unit operates as a communications link with the equipment operator. Switches and push buttons that start, stop, and otherwise control the operation of a computer enable a machine user to communicate with the computer through the control unit. On a larger computer system, the control switches are usually mounted on a console equipped with a typewriter or a small printer and one or more video display terminals. The console can be used by the computer operator to enter small amounts of input data, such as a date, a con-

PROCESSOR CONTROLLER. The control unit of a mainframe computer manages the input devices, main memory, arithmetic-logic unit, auxiliary storage units, and output devices. *Courtesy IBM Corporation.*

trol figure, or a processing option. In turn, the control unit can send messages to the operator on the console printer or display terminal. These messages tell the operator about computer-detected errors that may interfere with executing the instructions in the computer program. Such errors may include the operator's failure to make available to the computer the appropriate input or output devices needed for that program, such as a particular tape or disk drive.

ARITHMETIC-LOGIC UNIT

As its name suggests, a computer's **arithmetic-logic unit** (ALU) has two functions: to perform calculations and to perform logic operations. Both types of operations are done at incredibly fast speeds, measured on some computers in **nanoseconds** (billionths of a second).

Arithmetic Operations. Computers are asked to do primarily addition, subtraction, multiplication, or division for business information processing. Occasionally, there may be the need for square root calculations. Research and scientific data processing, on the other hand, involves much more complex computational work. Nevertheless, the basic computer mechanisms used for both types of processing are similar.

An arithmetic-logic unit has **registers,** or special storage locations, to hold the data to be processed. A mechanism called an **adder** actually performs the required arithmetic operations, and the results of a calculation are placed in an **accumulator.** For example, to calculate someone's gross pay, the pay rate and total hours worked would be transferred from memory to registers. Then the adder would perform the required calculation (pay rate times hours worked). The result of the calculation (gross pay) would be recorded in the accumulator. As you have read in the last section, it is the control unit that gets these tasks done. It orders the pay rate and hours worked to be moved from memory to the registers, specifies the multiplication operation to be performed, and finally arranges for the gross pay to be printed on a paycheck.

Logic Operations. In computer processing, *logic operations* are based primarily on the computer's capacity to compare two values and to decide whether they are equal, or, if not, which value is greater and which is smaller. Depending upon the results of this comparison, the computer takes action as directed by its instruction program. The ability of the arithmetic-logic mechanism to make a comparison and to see the difference between two values is very important in information processing. For this reason, we will look at several examples of typical logic operations involved in processing information for business.

Almost every on-line inquiry information system in which an inquirer asks a computer to provide it with information contained in an electronic storage unit involves one or more logic operations. An example of this is the actions that occur when you want to withdraw money from your bank account, either through an automated teller machine or by presenting a check to a bank teller. In either case, you provide the bank's computer with your account number and the amount you want withdrawn. The computer first compares your account number with the account numbers stored in its customer account file. When the arithmetic-logic unit finds a match (an account number in the file equal to your account number), the computer has located your account file record. Next, the arithmetic-logic unit is asked to do another comparison—to match the requested withdrawal amount with your bank balance. If the computer determines that the bank balance is equal to or greater than the withdrawal request, you will be given the requested funds. If instead the comparison indicates that the bank balance is less than the withdrawal request, you will be advised that insufficient funds are available in your account.

Another common information processing operation that depends on the computer's ability to do comparisons is sorting. For example, given the need in payroll processing to sort employee records by social security number for tax reporting, the arithmetic-logic unit is told to compare one employee social security number with another. As a result of each comparison, it places the smaller of the two numbers before the larger number. By making repetitive comparisons, in a very short time the com-

SYMBOLS FOR LOGIC OPERATIONS

Symbol	Meaning
=	Is equal to
>	Is greater than
<	Is less than
<=	Is less than or equal to
>=	Is greater than or equal to
<>	Is not equal to

puter can arrange a file of social security records in ascending order.

CPU VARIATIONS IN SMALL AND LARGE COMPUTERS

Earlier, you read that based on its computing power a computer can be identified as a microcomputer, minicomputer, mainframe, or supercomputer. These differences are most obvious in the features of central processing units.

The entire CPU of a microcomputer can be mounted on a single circuit board. In contrast, a mainframe or supercomputer has many cabinets full of CPU integrated circuits. The CPU circuitry of a minicomputer usually will fit into a single cabinet.

Larger computers have more and larger registers than smaller machines have, and these speed up arithmetic and logic operations. Large main memories also speed up computer processing and make it possible for a machine to do more-complex operations. RAM main memories of mainframes and supercomputers are often many megabytes in size. By 1985 a CPU for one IBM mainframe (the IBM 3090, 400 processor) was equipped with up to 128 megabytes (128 million characters) of main memory. Microcomputers, on the other hand, are made with as little as 4K (slightly more than 4000 characters) of main memory, although for some business and personal uses memories as large as one megabyte (one million characters) are available. Minicomputers typically have larger main memories than microcomputers do.

A computer is called an 8-bit-, 16-bit-, or 32-bit-word machine depending upon its capacity to process a group of bits at one time. A 32-bit machine can transfer in one operation four times more data than an 8-bit machine can. On the whole, the greater the number of bits that can be handled at one time, the faster a computer can process data. By design, microcomputers typically have been 8-bit machines, minicomputers 16-bit machines, and mainframes 32-bit machines. The technology changes so quickly, however, that these differences among computers are not fixed. For example, in 1986 Intel introduced a new microprocessor chip (the Intel 80386), which can be used to make 32-bit microcomputers capable of processing about 4 million instructions per second.

CHECK YOURSELF

Supply the missing words:

1. The ___?___ unit serves as a traffic director of various computer devices.

AUXILIARY STORAGE

Main memory units are almost never large enough to store all the data involved in business or personal computing. Many banks, insurance companies, utilities, and other large corporations need to store electronically billions of characters describing the status of customer accounts. Even individuals who use home computers to keep track of personal finances find it necessary to have some type of auxiliary storage unit to supplement the main memory unit.

Semiconductors and magnetic cores are relatively expensive materials, so computer manufacturers have sought less expensive ways of storing data outside of main memory without significantly affecting machine processing time. Also, there is need for nonvolatile information storage so that data is not lost when power is turned off. Magnetic-disk and magnetic-tape auxiliary storage units fulfill these needs. They store in nonvolatile memory huge amounts of data that do not have to be retrieved frequently for processing. When data in auxiliary storage is needed for processing, it must be transferred to main memory.

Auxiliary storage units differ in their memory capacities. Small units may hold less than 100,000 characters of information, but others can store billions of characters.

CHOICE: SEQUENTIAL- OR DIRECT-ACCESS STORAGE

Auxiliary storage devices also vary in their access time, which is the amount of time needed to store or retrieve data. To a large degree, access time is determined by the method used to retrieve data. As explained earlier, main memory provides direct access to stored data, but this is not true of all auxiliary types of storage. Some provide only **sequential access** to stored data. In a sequential-access approach, file records are stored in sequence by a particular key found in all records. For example, employee numbers may serve as the key in a payroll file. Retrieval of one particular record stored in such a file requires

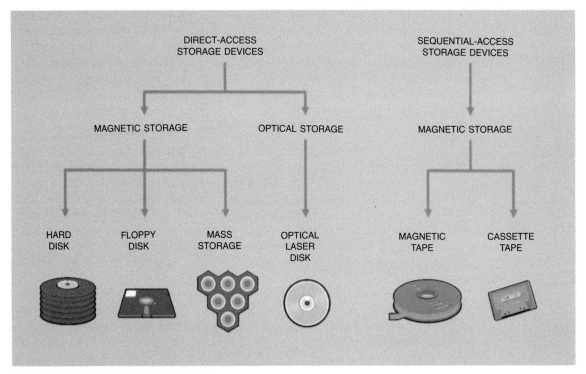

```
                    DIRECT-ACCESS                          SEQUENTIAL-ACCESS
                   STORAGE DEVICES                          STORAGE DEVICES


        MAGNETIC STORAGE            OPTICAL STORAGE          MAGNETIC STORAGE


   HARD      FLOPPY     MASS         OPTICAL          MAGNETIC      CASSETTE
   DISK       DISK    STORAGE         LASER             TAPE          TAPE
                                      DISK
```

TYPES OF AUXILIARY STORAGE DEVICES. Data that is used less frequently and that does not need to be retrieved immediately is kept in auxiliary storage.

searching sequentially through the entire file, record by record, from the beginning of the file until the desired information is found.

Faster access to stored data is provided by storage devices that permit **direct access** (or *random access*) to the data. Direct access means that it is possible to go directly to the location where the particular data required for processing is stored, without having to search through all of the records from the beginning of the file.

Direct-access storage units generally are more expensive than sequential-access devices. Nevertheless, in many information processing situations, the extra equipment cost is justified by the need for faster access time. Consider, for example, the supermarket checkout system described in the previous chapter. Each item you purchase is scanned at the cashier's counter so that a computer can retrieve a unit price from an auxiliary storage unit. By storing the price data for each item in a known location in a direct-access storage unit, the computer can retrieve it very quickly when needed. If the computer had to search the entire product file repetitively to retrieve a unit price for each item purchased, you would probably have to wait longer at the checkout station.

Sometimes faster access ability does not justify the extra cost of direct-access storage units. For this reason, computer users are offered a wide choice of auxiliary storage equipment. At present, magnetic-disk equipment is the most widely used type of direct-access auxiliary storage for both business and personal computing. Magnetic tape is the popular means of storing data for sequential access.

MAGNETIC-DISK STORAGE

Many different types of magnetic disks are used for data storage. All are thin, flat platters that look like phonograph records. The surfaces of the disk are coated with a material that can be magnetized. Data is stored on the disk in the form of magnetized spots recorded in concentric circles called *tracks.* The recording tracks on a magnetic disk are not connected to each other as they are on a phonograph record, where the track forms a continuous spiral from the outer to the inner edge of the record.

Devices called **disk drives** are used to write (or store) data on disks or to read (or retrieve) data already stored. The storing and retrieving of data is done by a **read-write head** in the disk unit.

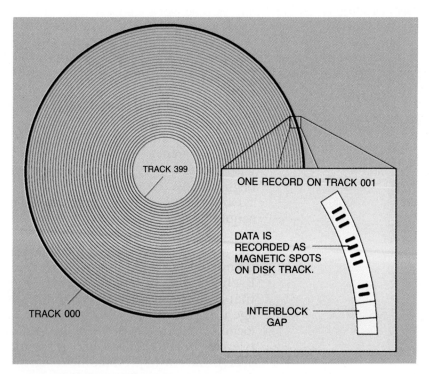

DATA RECORDING ON MAGNETIC DISK. Data is stored on the disk in the form of magnetized spots recorded in concentric tracks.

Data can be retrieved for processing by direct access to the track location where the data is stored. Direct access is achieved in different ways, depending on the particular disk drive being used. In some cases, disks are divided into segments known as sectors. Think of a pie cut into servings. The location of stored data can then be identified by its track and segment number. In addition to being able to access stored data directly, a read-write head can sequentially search stored data from the beginning of a file to its end.

Various types of disk drives are available for use on microcomputers and larger systems. Each is made to handle a particular type of disk, which may be a floppy disk or a hard disk.

Floppy Disks. The most common auxiliary storage unit for personal computers is one that handles **floppy disks,** also called *diskettes* or *flexible disks.* The disks get their name from their flexibility. Made of plastic, they can be bent slightly without damage. Because floppy disks are very easy to handle and to store, they can easily be distributed by mail.

Floppy disks, often called *floppies,* are available in three sizes. Originally, floppies of 8-inch diameter were used, but now 5¼-inch disks are more common. In both, the disk recording surface is protected by a cardboard envelope, except for a small

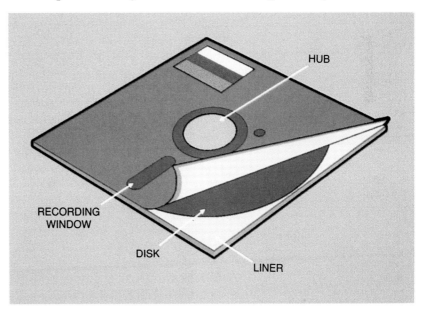

FLOPPY DISK. The floppy disk is the most common auxiliary storage unit for personal computers. The disk is enclosed in a protective jacket and the disk surface is cleaned by the jacket liner. The magnetic surface of the disk is exposed in the recording window which permits data to be read from or stored on the disk surface. The hole or hub in the center of the disk is used to mount the disk on the disk drive.

FLOPPY DISK. This floppy disk is 5¼ inches in diameter. In this illustration, the disk is being inserted into a disk drive. *Courtesy Apple Computer.*

opening to allow access for the read/write head. A smaller disk of 3½-inch diameter, called a *microfloppy,* was introduced in the early 1980s. Microfloppies are usually encased in a hard plastic case that can be inserted into the disk drive.

The storage capacity of floppy disks varies widely and is dependent on the type of disk and disk drive used. Data may be recorded on one or both sides of the disk and in some cases at double density, which permits storage of twice as many bytes in the same amount of space. A single-sided, single-density 5¼-inch floppy disk may hold only 160,000 bytes or characters. A double-sided, double-density disk may hold more than two million characters (two megabytes) of stored data.

Compared with hard disks, floppy disks are inexpensive, but their storage capacity is low and access time is high. For this reason, many users of microcomputers as well as larger computers use some type of hard-disk storage device rather than floppy disks.

Hard Disks. As the name indicates, **hard disks** are rigid, metal platters. Hard disks range in diameter size from 3½ to 14 inches. Typically, 3½-inch and 5¼ inch disks are used on personal computers. Because a hard disk does not bend, data can be packed much more closely together than on a floppy disk. This gives a hard disk higher storage capacity. Typical hard-disk units attached to microcomputers can store about 20 megabytes and larger units hold as many as 400 megabytes.

The capacity of some hard-disk devices attached to mainframes is measured in **gigabytes** (billions of characters).

In reading and writing operations a hard disk can make about 3600 revolutions per minute. A floppy disk makes 300 to 400 revolutions for similar operations. The faster rotating time gives more rapid access to stored data and, therefore, makes for speedier information processing.

Microcomputer and minicomputer users have popularized a hard disk called the **Winchester disk,** named for the technology used for manufacturing the disk. The Winchester disk is permanently sealed in a container to protect the disk surface from dust and dirt. This increases the reliability of data storage.

Disk Packs. For use with mainframe computer systems, several disks are usually assembled together to make a **disk pack.** Often, eleven disks are packaged together for mounting on a

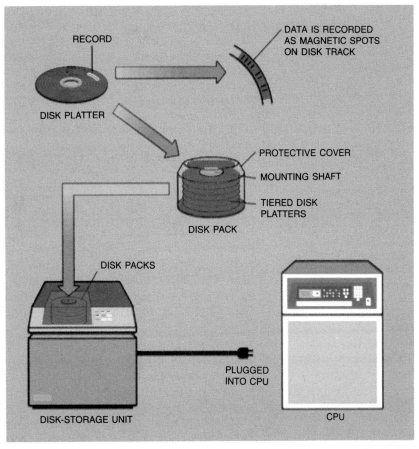

HARD-DISK STORAGE. Disk packs are mounted in the disk storage unit, which is connected to the computer.

DISK PACKS. Several disks are assembled into a disk pack, which can be put on or removed from a disk storage unit. This illustration shows a computer operator loading a disk pack into a disk drive. *Courtesy Sperry Corporation.*

disk drive spindle. Such a disk pack can store 200 megabytes of data. Disk packs are often removable and can be replaced by an operator in less than 1 minute.

Where even larger auxiliary storage capacities are required, the density of data recorded on disk is increased. In these cases, to ensure reliability of data reading and writing, the high-density disks are permanently housed in a disk-drive cabinet and cannot be removed by an operator. One such device, the IBM 3380 direct-access unit, can store more than 2.5 gigabytes. As multiple units may be connected to a single mainframe, a user has the potential of storing billions of characters.

MAGNETIC-TAPE STORAGE

Up until the late 1960s, magnetic tape was the most commonly used form of auxiliary storage. Magnetic-disk storage has become more popular since then because it permits direct access to stored data. As explained earlier, magnetic tape permits only sequential access to stored data.

Magnetic tape is actually made from a plastic material called Mylar, which is coated with a chemical that can be magnetized. The tape now commonly used is ½-inch wide and comes in lengths of 600, 1200, and 2400 feet. It is rolled on reels that

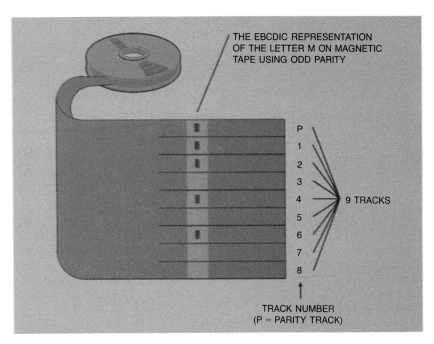

THE EBCDIC REPRESENTATION OF THE LETTER M ON MAGNETIC TAPE USING ODD PARITY

P
1
2
3
4   9 TRACKS
5
6
7
8

TRACK NUMBER
(P = PARITY TRACK)

DATA RECORDING ON MAGNETIC TAPE. Data is stored on the tape in the form of magnetized spots.

measure 10½ inches in diameter. A narrower and shorter strip of magnetic tape is packaged in cassette form for use on microcomputers. Magnetic tape for storing computer data is basically the same material used for videocassette recording.

Data is recorded on tape in the form of magnetized spots. Horizontally, a tape is typically divided into nine recording channels. Eight of these correspond to the eight-bit code positions used in the EBCDIC code to represent numbers, letters, and special symbols (see Chapter 3). The ninth channel is used to record a *parity bit* to detect errors in data recording. Thus, in a way similar to data representation on a punched card, a single vertical column on the tape contains a code representing a single character. In this case, the code is recorded by the presence or absence of magnetized bits.

A tape reel is mounted on a **tape drive** for writing data or for reading data. As on disk, writing data on tape automatically erases data previously stored in the same location. The number of bytes (characters) that can be stored per inch of magnetic tape, the **tape density,** varies by tape drive. Some store only 800 bytes per inch (800 bpi), others 1600 bpi, and a few as many as 6250 bpi.

Depending on the tape density and the particular tape drive used, from 15,000 to 1.25 million characters per second can be stored or retrieved from magnetic tape. As large as the higher

MAGNETIC-TAPE STORAGE. The photograph at left shows a computer operator mounting a reel of magnetic tape on a tape drive. At right, a tape librarian is retrieving a reel of magnetic tape from the tape library for delivery to the computer room. The tape library may contain thousands of magnetic tape reels. Each tape is labelled so that it can be easily retrieved when needed for computer processing. *Courtesy Control Data Corporation.*

figure may sound to you, the access time to data stored on magnetic tape is much slower than that to data stored on magnetic disk. Magnetic tape storage, however, is cheaper than disk storage. For these reasons, magnetic tape is now primarily used in two situations. It is used in many business installations to store copies of important data that is recorded on disk. Such **backup files** can be stored at another site (or archived) to provide security in case the disk file data is accidentally destroyed. Magnetic tape storage is also used in certain batch processing applications, such as payroll processing, where sequential retrieval and updating of file data can be an effective processing approach.

MASS STORAGE DEVICES

By combining the use of magnetic tape with a direct-access device, IBM and other manufacturers provide mass storage devices in which almost half a trillion characters of data (equivalent to the information on 27 million newspaper pages) may be stored.

To accommodate this amount of data, the IBM 3850 Mass Storage System is made up of thousands of small cylindrical cells assembled to look like the honeycomb of a beehive. Each cell contains a cartridge of magnetic tape on which data can be stored. To retrieve or store data, an access mechanism must first extract the cartridge from its cell and then read or write the data on tape.

Although mass storage devices offer larger storage capacities at cheaper prices than magnetic disks do, a disadvantage is their relatively slow access times to stored data.

MASS STORAGE. The IBM Mass Storage System contains honeycomb compartments where data cartridges are stored. A closeup of two data cartridges is shown here. *Courtesy IBM Corporation.*

NEW STORAGE TECHNOLOGIES

Since computers first became commercially available, a stream of technological developments has given us faster, more powerful, and much less expensive machines. The use of semiconductor memories for main memory and magnetic disks for auxiliary storage represent major steps in the improvement of computer performance. New designs and manufacturing techniques will speed up access time and increase the memory capacity of RAM chips and of magnetic disks, while decreasing component costs.

We should also expect new technologies inevitably to replace the semiconductor and magnetic-disk memories that now dominate the computer marketplace. Two new storage technologies deserve attention: magnetic-bubble memories and optical (laser) storage.

MAGNETIC-BUBBLE MEMORIES

Magnetic-bubble memories are another type of storage technology for main memory. Data is stored as tiny magnetic bubbles usually on a chip of magnetized material. The presence or absence of a bubble represents a bit of information. The computer reads the presence of a bubble in a given location as a 1. The absence of a bubble in the same location stands for a 0.

Because each bubble is only about one-twentieth the diameter of a human hair, many thousands of bubbles can be stored in a very small space. For reading and writing of data, the bubbles are moved electronically along tracks in the memory unit.

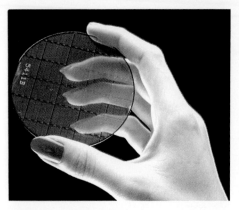

Courtesy Intel Corporation.

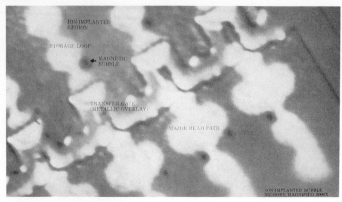

Courtesy AT&T Bell Laboratories.

MAGNETIC-BUBBLE MEMORIES. Data is stored in tiny magnetic bubbles. A bubble stands for "1" and a lack of a bubble stands for "0".

Compared to RAM semiconductor memories, magnetic-bubble storage units have several advantages. They can store more data per unit of space. Magnetic-bubble memory is also nonvolatile, retaining stored data when the power is turned off.

On the other hand, the bubble memories cost more than semiconductor storage. Bubble memories were introduced in 1977, but because of their relatively high cost, they are still not widely used. They are mostly installed in communication devices or portable computer systems.

OPTICAL (LASER) DISK STORAGE

There are similarities between an **optical disk** (sometimes called a *laser disk* or an *optical-laser disk*) and a magnetic disk. The principle of operation is the same for both. Bits of

LASER DISK. A laser beam is used to record and read data on a laser disk. A single optical laser disk can provide the same memory capacity as 15 magnetic tapes. *Jules Allen.*

information are stored in tracks on the disk, and the data can be read by a disk-reading device attached to a computer of any size. However, much more information can be stored in the same amount of space on an optical disk. For example, an optical disk the size of a 40-megabyte magnetic hard disk can hold 400 megabytes of data. Optical disks are also more durable and cannot be accidentally erased.

Data is recorded on an optical disk by a laser beam that burns tiny holes (pits) into a thin metal surface. The presence of a pit in a recording position represents a 1 bit, and the absence of a pit in the same location stands for a 0 bit. The pits are so small that they are not visible to the naked eye. Data recorded on the disk is also read by a laser beam.

At the present time, data recorded on most optical disks cannot be erased. New types of optical disks are being developed, however, which can be more easily written on and read from. One such optical-disk technology is called **WORM,** which stands for *write once, read many.* This technology allows the user to burn data onto a disk and read the data as often as necessary. WORM disks still cannot be erased. Thus, at present, optical storage is usually a read-only memory (ROM). Also, the time and cost of recording data are high, so only a few customers are using laser disks for business information processing. Some banks are recording copies of cancelled checks on optical disks, and the Internal Revenue Service is recording copies of income tax returns.

The publishing/information industry has identified a large market potential for so-called **CD-ROM optical disks,** which stands for compact disk, read-only memory. A CD-ROM optical disk is a 4.7-inch disk platter, the same size as the 45-rpm audio disk that has been widely used by the recording industry. The equivalent of 250,000 pages of text can be stored on one such disk. Magnetic storage of this amount of information would require 60 magnetic hard disks or 1500 floppy disks. Publishers believe that CD-ROM optical disks provide an important new way to distribute information. For example, the contents of an encyclopedia can be contained on one or two disks and displayed on a personal computer equipped with a CD-ROM disk drive. Educational and reference material recorded on optical disks may be retrieved and displayed on a home or business computer.

Erasable optical disks that can serve as a read-write memory are now in the experimental stage. If these become available at reasonable costs, optical laser technology may offer the most effective and reliable type of auxiliary storage and eliminate the need for tape backup files. Many experts believe that by the early 1990s, optical (laser) disks will replace magnetic disks as the preferred method for auxiliary storage.

CHECK YOURSELF

Match each phrase with the word or phrase that best describes it.

1. Hard magnetic disk sealed in a container.
2. Group of hard disks assembled together.
3. Device that reads or writes data on tape.
4. Way of safeguarding data stored on disk.

5. Possible future replacement for magnetic-disk storage.
6. Most common type of direct-access auxiliary storage.
7. A developing technology for main memory.
8. A small read-only, optical disk memory.
9. The smallest flexible disk.
10. Most popular type of sequential storage.

a. Disk pack
b. CD-ROM
c. Magnetic tape
d. Optical-disk memory
e. Magnetic-bubble memory
f. Winchester disk
g. Backup tape files
h. Microfloppy disk
i. Read-write head
j. Tape drive
k. Mass storage device
l. Magnetic disk

Answers: (1) f; (2) a; (3) j; (4) g; (5) d; (6) l; (7) e; (8) b; (9) h; (10) c.

REVIEW QUESTIONS

1. Describe four functions performed by every CPU.
2. Explain the purpose of main memory.
3. Define the following computer terms: *address, access time, volatile memory,* and *nonvolatile memory.*
4. Give three advantages and one disadvantage of using semiconductors for main memory.
5. Define and explain the difference between RAM and ROM main memory units.
6. How many characters of data are held in each of the following memories? 4K, 64K, and 256K bytes and 1 megabyte?
7. Explain the functions performed by a control unit.
8. Name three mechanisms in an arithmetic-logic unit and explain what each does.
9. Explain what is meant by the term *logic operations* and give two examples of typical information processing needs for these.
10. Name at least three differences between the central processing unit of a microcomputer and that of a mainframe.
11. Compare the retrieval of data by sequential access with direct-access retrieval. Which is faster and why?

12. What is the most common form of direct-access auxiliary storage? of sequential auxiliary storage?
13. Describe how data is stored on magnetic disk and the mechanisms used to read and write data on disk.
14. Compare three types of magnetic disks: a floppy disk, a microfloppy, and a hard disk.
15. What is a Winchester disk? a disk pack?
16. Describe how data is recorded on magnetic tape. Describe the device used to read and write data on tape.
17. What is the purpose of backup files? Describe one way of making them.
18. Describe a mass storage system.
19. What are the advantages and disadvantages of magnetic-bubble memories and how are they being used?
20. What are the advantages and disadvantages of optical-disk memories? How are they now being used, and what may be their future potential?

COMPARING IDEAS

The questions below are designed to help you think about what you have learned in this chapter. They are "thought" questions. There is no one correct answer.

1. If you purchase a microcomputer to use at home, what choices of auxiliary storage units will you have? Identify the factors that will influence your choice of storage units.
2. Explain why some businesses need mainframe computers. Give examples of particular companies in your area that may be using mainframes.

INFORMATION PROCESSING ACTIVITIES

Now you can perform many of the information processing activities business workers perform. Below is a summary of the tasks you will complete. You will find the actual data and business forms you need in your *Information Processing Work Kit.*

1. As an EDP research assistant for a major public library you will identify computer applications that require main memory only or also auxiliary memory capacity.
2. You will perform numeric sorting on test data to verify the effectiveness of newly acquired system hardware.
3. You will evaluate numerous databases and determine which the library should keep in random-access storage.

CHAPTER

6

COMPUTER OUTPUT

Information Processing Terminology

Input-output device
Output device
Hard copy
Typeset-quality print
Letter-quality print
Nonletter-quality print
Dot matrix
Character (serial) printer

Line printer
Page printer
Impact printer
Nonimpact printer
Daisy-wheel print unit
Monochrome
Soft copy
Scroll

Graphics output
Interactive graphics
Plotter
Microform (microimage)
Computer output
  microform (COM)
Voice-response device

Performance Goals

☐ List seven ways of reporting output information.

☐ Define the terms *letter-quality print* and *nonletter-quality print.*

☐ Explain the difference between character, line, and page printers.

☐ Compare the printing technology used in an impact printer with that of a nonimpact printer. Give three examples of each type of printer.

☐ Describe the features of a typical input-output device used to display statistical or text material. Give an example of how it is used in information processing.

☐ Explain two ways in which a computer can be used for graphics work, and give an example of each.

The information produced by computer processing may be reported in many forms. The desired objective is to produce output results in the particular form most useful for the people who require the information. This is true, for example, whether a mainframe is used to produce marketing information for a sales manager in a large corporation or a personal computer is used to help an individual keep track of family finances.

Today a variety of options are available for the reporting of output information produced by computer. Output information may be:

- Printed in statistical or text form
- Displayed in statistical or text form
- Printed or displayed graphically
- Recorded in microform
- Recorded as a voice response
- Recorded on punched cards
- Stored on disk or tape for future reporting

In this chapter, you will learn how each of these seven options can be accomplished. In some cases, devices used for the inputting of data are also used for the reporting of output data and therefore are called **input-output devices.** More often, reporting of information is accomplished with a device used exclusively for that purpose. In this case it is called an **output device.**

PRINTING OF STATISTICAL OR TEXT MATERIAL

Printing is one of the most popular ways of reporting information results produced by a computer. An output device called a *printer* can be attached to a microcomputer, a minicomputer, or a mainframe. The printer records processing results in a permanent form that human beings can read; it is often called **hard copy.** Printed output can consist of statistics arranged on a specially designed report form, or it can be text material reported as an answer to an inquiry posed to the computer, as a letter addressed to a customer, or as a legal document of many pages.

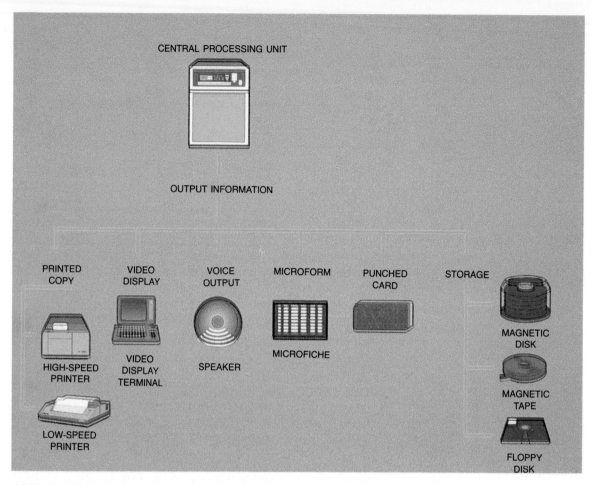

CENTRAL PROCESSING UNIT

OUTPUT INFORMATION

PRINTED COPY

VIDEO DISPLAY

VOICE OUTPUT

MICROFORM

PUNCHED CARD

STORAGE

HIGH-SPEED PRINTER

VIDEO DISPLAY TERMINAL

SPEAKER

MICROFICHE

MAGNETIC DISK

LOW-SPEED PRINTER

MAGNETIC TAPE

FLOPPY DISK

OPTIONS FOR REPORTING OF OUTPUT INFORMATION.

CRITERIA FOR SELECTION OF A PRINTER

A buyer of microcomputer equipment finds a number of different printers to choose from. An even greater variety is offered to users of larger computers. Before examining the types of printers now available, it is helpful to understand the particular features of most interest to users.

When selecting a printer, buyers usually consider four factors to be particularly important: quality of printing, speed of printing, capacity to meet special printing requirements, and equipment cost.

Quality of Printing. The print quality of a computer printer is usually judged by comparing its output to the output produced on a good typewriter on which numbers and letters are printed in a clear, solid form. When compared with such typed copy, computer print may be classed as of about equal quality, of an even better quality, or of a lower quality.

This is an example of typeset quality.

This is an example of letter quality.

This is an example of nonletter quality.

COMPUTER PRINT QUALITIES.

Typeset-quality print refers to a print that is better than letter-quality. It is produced by special electronic typesetting devices or laser printers. Typeset print quality is normally required for the printing of magazines, books, newsletters, advertisements, and special business reports.

Computer print which is about equal to clear, solid typed copy is said to be **letter-quality print.** This print can be produced by a so-called daisy-wheel printer, the features of which are described later. Letter-quality print is usually required for business correspondence, reports, payroll checks, customer invoices, tax returns, and other documents that are sent to outsiders.

The term **nonletter-quality print** refers to computer print that is of a poorer quality than typewriter print. There are, however, many levels of nonletter quality ranging from very poor copy to nearly letter-quality print.

A nonletter-quality computer printer typically records a number or letter as a series of dots. The dots are recorded in predetermined places in rows and columns that together form a **dot matrix.** The greater the number of dots used to form the letter or number, the better the print quality. In fact, some printers use so many dots that to the naked eye the characters printed appear as though they are solidly formed characters. Only when viewed by a magnifying lens can the individual dots be detected. Businesses usually do not use nonletter-quality printers to prepare business correspondence. However, nonletter print quality can be completely adequate for draft copies of letters or documents produced in the office or at home or for printed reports circulated internally within an organization.

Speed of Printing. Computer printers are often categorized by their printing speeds. There are low-speed, high-speed, and very high-speed computer printers. The slowest printers are **character printers,** or *serial printers* which print a single char-

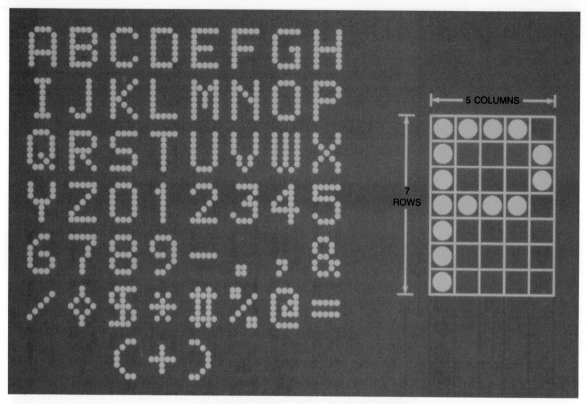

PRINT CHARACTERS FORMED BY A DOT MATRIX PRINTER. The characters shown at left were formed by a 5 × 7 dot matrix printer. The enlarged letter P at right shows more clearly the 5 columns and 7 rows in which dots are used to form characters. Depending on the printer, the matrix can include more or fewer columns and rows. The denser the dots, the better the print quality.

acter at a time. The printing speeds of character printers vary, ranging in speed from 15 characters per second to more than 300 characters per second. The slower machines print in one direction only, like a typewriter. The faster machines print in two directions, alternately printing from left to right, then from right to left (this is called *bidirectional printing*).

High-speed printers have the ability to print a whole line at a time rather than just one character at a time, and so are known as **line printers.** They can print at speeds from 300 lines per minute to as many as 3000 lines per minute. Even faster are the so-called very high-speed or **page printers.** Page printers, as you might expect, are designed to print a whole page of output at once. These machines can produce more than 3000 printed lines per minute, some printing more than 20,000 lines a minute.

Character printers are fast enough for most users of personal computers. Line printers, which print a whole line at a time (as opposed to individual characters), are nearly always used to print output from mainframe computers. Only companies such as banks, insurance companies, publishers, and utilities, with very large printing requirements need the printing speed capacities of page printers. These very fast machines can facilitate the task of preparing millions of customer statements each month.

Special Printing Capabilities. A user of any size of computer may have special printer requirements. Some need lightweight printers that can be carried easily. Salespeople, for example, often carry portable computers and printers to be able to prepare customer orders while with the customer. Other users need machines with special typefaces or symbols, such as those for printing scientific and technical formulas. Still others look for printers that can print extra-wide lines (132 characters) instead of the standard 80-character line width. The wider line is often needed for the printing of financial reports. The requirements for the handling of color and graphic presentations are more complex. These are discussed in a later section.

Equipment Cost. Few buyers of equipment are able to ignore the factor of equipment cost in their selection of a printer. As you may expect, better print quality and faster speeds come with more expensive machines.

In price, printers may range from less than $200 to hundreds of thousands of dollars. One user of personal computers may be satisfied with the capabilities of a $200 printer, while another finds that a $2000 printer is appropriate for her or his needs. Each prospective buyer of a computer printer therefore must consider the trade-offs in quality, speed, and cost necessary to meet the particular printing requirements to be satisfied.

TYPES OF PRINTERS

As in the case of storage units, different technologies are used to accomplish the printing of a character or number. An **impact printer** operates like a typewriter, producing printed results by the strike or impact of a metal character against an inked ribbon. The impact of the ribbon on paper results in the printing of characters on the paper. Impact printers can produce a number of copies at one time by using multiple copy forms. A disadvantage is that impact printers are noisy in operation.

Nonimpact printers are much quieter in operation because they produce printed results without any impact motion. Several different technologies are used to accomplish nonimpact printing. Laser printing is one method. Although nonimpact printers cannot produce multiple copies of documents at one time, many operate at such high speeds that they can produce

A VARIETY OF DESKTOP PRINTERS. *Courtesy IBM Corporation.*

many copies in the time it takes an impact printer to make one copy. Nonimpact printers thus eliminate the need to decollate (separate) multiple copy forms and to pull out carbon interleaves.

We will look at six different types of impact and nonimpact printers that are commonly used with small or large computer systems, or with both. Each is identified as to whether it is an impact or nonimpact printer. There are three of each kind.

The six printers are listed generally in order of their cost, though some of the printers are available in a wide range of model prices. The first machine listed, the thermal printer, is the least expensive and also the one with the poorest quality of type. The last machine, the laser printer, is the most expensive. It is also the fastest and has the best print quality.

Thermal Printer (nonimpact machine). The least expensive printer is the thermal printer. The thermal printer prints by "burning" character images into a specially made paper that is heat-sensitive. Characters and numbers are formed by the dot-matrix method. This type of printer is usually used only with smaller home computer systems and some types of portable computers and electronic typewriters. It produces a rather poor nonletter-quality print that tends to fade over time. Another disadvantage of using thermal printers is the high cost of the special paper these devices require.

Dot-Matrix Printer (impact machine). The dot-matrix printer is the most popular type of printer used with personal computers. Different combinations of pins making up a dot matrix represent particular letters or numbers (see illustration on page 134). Printing occurs when the pins press the ribbon against the paper. Although it produces nonletter-quality print, as described earlier, this type of printer is satisfactory for many tasks. The printing is usually done one character at a time. Relatively inexpensive printers are available in a range of operating speeds, varying from 15 characters per second to more than 300 characters per second.

Daisy-Wheel Printer (impact machine). A second type of printer popular with personal computer users is the daisy-wheel printer. This printer gets its name from its pinwheel-like print unit, called a **daisy wheel,** which resembles a daisy's flower structure. The characters are located at the end of thin petal-like fingers, connected to a circular carrier. Daisy-wheel print units are available in a number of different typefaces. They are also removable and interchangeable, which provides greater flexibility to suit user needs for varied printing. A daisy-wheel printer is usually slower and more expensive than a dot-matrix impact printer, but it has a better print quality. A daisy-wheel printer produces letter-quality print.

DAISY WHEEL PRINT MECHANISM. The daisy wheel is a pinwheel-like print unit. Each arm (spoke) of the wheel has a character at the end. When the printer is operating, the daisy wheel spins until the character to be printed is lined up with the hammer. Then, the character is struck against the hammer and ribbon, resulting in a printed character.

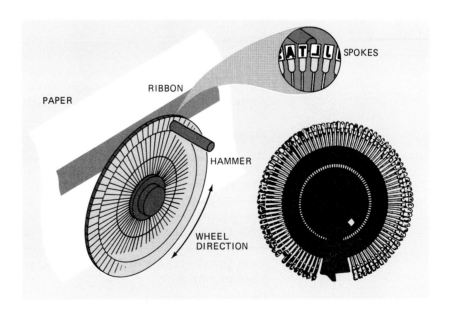

SPOKES

RIBBON

PAPER

HAMMER

WHEEL DIRECTION

LASER PRINTER. This laser printer is a letter-quality printer. *Courtesy Xerox Corporation.*

Ink-jet Printer (nonimpact machine). The ink-jet printer prints by means of tiny nozzles that spray liquid ink in the forms of print images directly onto the page. Actually, letters and numbers are formed from a number of tiny ink dots, but because many dots are used to make up each letter and number, solid characters are printed. Ink-jet printers produce high-quality print output. Different models of ink-jet printers operate at different speeds. Slower models are tailored for use on personal computers, and faster models for larger systems.

Band and Chain Printers (impact machines). For high-speed printing with minicomputers and mainframes, band printers or chain printers are commonly used. Both are impact-type printers, but they operate with different types of print mechanisms. The print unit of a band printer consists of a flexible rotating steel band that contains the characters used to form the print images. On a chain printer, the characters are mounted on a rotating chain. Both types of printers produce good print quality at high speeds, printing as many as 3000 lines per minute.

Laser Printer (nonimpact machine). The fastest and most expensive computer printers are laser printers. These machines accomplish printing by using laser technology. Tiny beams of laser light form the characters to be printed. A laser printer can print numbers and letters in varying sizes and type faces, and can even print the outline of a report form while data is being printed as output. Laser printing is of the highest print quality.

Originally, laser printers were designed for use with large computers to achieve high-speed letter-quality printing. Slower operating models are now made for use with personal computers. In 1986 Xerox introduced a desktop copier/laser printer. This machine acts as a computer printing device for a personal computer, but it also functions as an office copying machine. The Apple Macintosh computer can be used with the Apple Laserprinter to produce near-typeset-quality printouts for newsletters, advertisements, and company reports. This application is commonly called *desktop publishing.*

CHECK YOURSELF

Match each phrase with the word or phrase that best defines it.

1. Printer that forms character images by ink sprays.
2. One type of high-speed impact printer.
3. Numbers and letters that are printed in clear, solid form as if produced on a typewriter.
4. Output from a dot-matrix printer.
5. A machine that prints one character at a time.
6. A type of impact print unit that is used to produce letter-quality print.
7. A machine that prints one line at a time.
8. A printer that forms characters by laser beams.
9. A machine that prints a whole page at a time.
10. An output record in printed form.

a. Page printer
b. Daisy wheel
c. Laser printer
d. Letter-quality print
e. Character printer
f. Line printer
g. Ink-jet printer
h. Nonletter-quality print
i. Band printer
j. Soft copy
k. Input device
l. Hard copy
m. Thermal and laser printers

Answers: (1) g; (2) i; (3) d; (4) h; (5) e; (6) b; (7) f; (8) c; (9) a; (10) l.

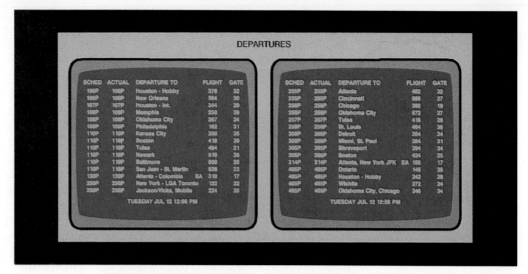

TERMINAL SCREEN SHOWING OUTPUT INFORMATION. Terminal screens at airports display arrival and departure flight information. The above shows two screens with information about afternoon flights from Los Angeles.

DISPLAY OF STATISTICAL OR TEXT OUTPUT

A video display terminal (VDT) is most often used to display statistical or text output that can be expressed in alphanumeric form—numbers and letters. The VDT also outputs graphics displays, which are discussed in the next section. As you read in Chapter 4, the same device can be used for the input of data. In this case, the VDT serves as an input-output device.

A VDT consists of a keyboard, which is used to input data, and a video display screen, also called a cathode-ray tube (CRT). The screen, or monitor, is the unit used to display output information. Most screens used to display statistical or text material are **monochrome,** which means that information is displayed in only one color. Screens are available that can display information in a number of different colors.

The typical display screen usually can show 24 lines of up to 80 characters on a line. This creates a maximum display of 1920 characters. Some microcomputer terminals have a smaller screen capacity, usually displaying 16 lines of 64 characters each. There are other variations in screen display capabilities. Some show letters only in upper-case format. Others can show both upper- and lower-case letters. The clarity (resolution) of the information displayed on screens also varies. On the whole, however, because VDTs are designed specifically to display computer output, they provide a better mechanism for the display of output information than do television sets. Only very simple home computers now use TV screens to display output results.

Computer output information displayed on a screen is called **soft copy.** Unlike the hard copy produced by a printer, the soft copy displayed on a VDT is not a permanent record. Nevertheless, the ability to display statistical and text information on a VDT serves an important function. It provides a computer user with faster and more convenient access to computer output information than can be achieved with printers.

Display of output information is particularly important in an inquiry type of information system. For example, when a customer calls a catalog mail-order company to find out the status of merchandise that he or she has ordered, the sales clerk who has received the call can key an inquiry into the computer and display the status of the customer's order on a screen. This step permits the clerk to give the customer an immediate answer. In other inquiry systems, users can call for display of reference information—for example, information about airline flight schedules. Others use display screens to browse (to **scroll**) quickly through a page or pages of reference material to find the particular information that is needed.

Display screen output complements print output. The screens provide quick access to particular items of information. Printers, on the other hand, provide a permanent and more complete record of processing results. For this reason, both printers and VDTs are usually found together as output devices on personal computers as well as on larger systems.

GRAPHICS DISPLAY AND PRINT OF OUTPUT

So far you have read about output devices that display or print alphanumeric information—that is, numbers or letters in the form of statistical reports or text material. **Graphics output** refers to charts, maps, drawings, newspapers, books, and even movies that are produced on a computer and then displayed as soft copy on a screen and/or printed as hard copy on paper.

USE OF COMPUTERS FOR GRAPHICS WORK

The explosive growth in computer graphics seems to support the old saying that one picture is worth a thousand words. Many users of personal computers as well as larger computers now have the computer hardware and the computer software (programs) to allow them to produce graphics output.

There are two ways in which a computer can be used for graphics work. First, it can be used to display and to print information in a pictorial form so that it may easily be understood. Second, it can be used to create designs for products or buildings and even works of art.

Presenting Output in Pictorial Form. Financial results, market research survey analyses, and almost all types of statistical information can be dull to read when presented in tabular form as columns of numbers or even as figures in a report. Most

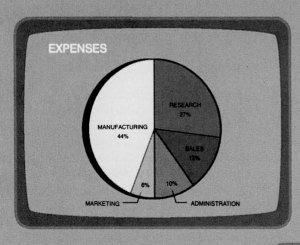

PIE CHART   Gets its name from its round shape which resembles pies that you eat. Pie charts are used to show the relationship of one part to a whole. The color (or shading) helps distinguish the parts of a pie chart.

BAR CHART   Represents the values of items by the length of bars, drawn vertically or horizontally. The longer the bar, the greater the value of the item represented by the bar.

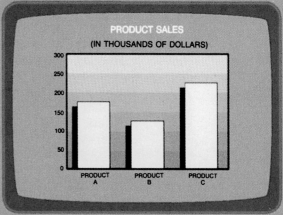

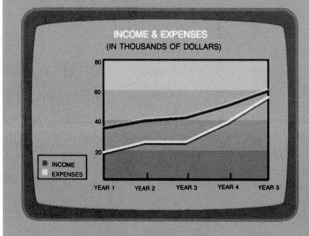

LINE GRAPH   Used to display trends of what is happening over a given time period. It is easy to see if a trend is going up or down when data is plotted on a line graph.

COMPUTER OUTPUT DISPLAYED IN PICTORIAL FORM ON A VDT SCREEN.

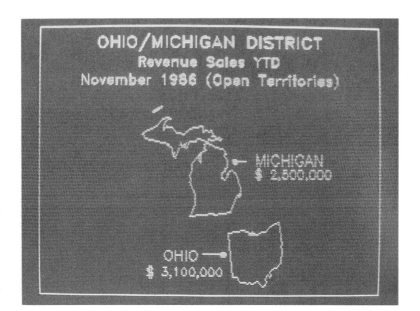

COMPUTER OUTPUT DISPLAYED IN MAP FORM. Businesses often use computer output to display facts in an easy-to-see format. The revenue from the Ohio/Michigan sales district is clearly displayed in the map shown. *Courtesy Decision Resources, Inc.*

of us have difficulty analyzing long columns of figures. To draw meaningful conclusions from a mass of numbers is not easy.

Decision makers in business particularly need statistical information produced by computers presented in a form that is easy to read. This can be done by displaying or printing the information in some type of chart, graph, diagram, or map form. Both black-and-white and color output is possible with many computers. The use to be made of the information determines which type of output is most appropriate. For instance, most business correspondence and reports are printed in black and white, while for slide presentations, many people prefer color output for greater clarity and impact. There are many different ways of presenting information in pictorial form as shown in the illustration on page 142.

You can see how much easier it is to make comparisons when figures such as product sales are presented on a multicolor chart rather than as printed columns of numbers. Charts also make it easier to detect business trends. For example, note how clearly the trend of business income and expenses is depicted by a line graph.

Computer Graphics for Product Design. The use of computer graphics for product design started more than two decades ago in the automotive and aircraft industries. Engineers involved in the design of new models of automobiles and airplanes recognized then that the computer could help them create a new automobile or airplane design.

The design process is much the same today. A designer draws a product design on a display terminal screen and can revise it for improvements a nearly endless number of times. When the design concept is satisfactory, whether it is for a new product or a new building, the computer can be asked to translate the screen model into complete design drawings and manufacturing or building specifications. This total process is now called CAD (computer-aided design) and CAM (computer-aided manufacture). CAD/CAM applications are more fully discussed in Chapter 8.

PRODUCT DESIGN. A designer draws and may later revise a product design on a display screen. Here, an engineer is working on fine-tuning a design for a car manufacturer. *Courtesy Evans & Sutherland.*

INTERACTIVE GRAPHICS. With interactive graphics, a user and a computer "communicate" to develop a design or drawing on a display screen. This artwork was produced by an engineer using a computer at Bell Laboratories. *Courtesy AT&T Bell Laboratories.*

The use of computers for product design work quickly spread to many other fields. Architects now design new industrial plants or office skyscrapers, hospitals, schools, and even homes with the aid of a computer. Fashion designers develop on computer screens their ideas for new dress or suit designs. Newspaper, magazine, and book editors use computer graphics to prepare page layouts that combine the text and illustration material. Movie producers in such hits as "E.T." have achieved special effects on film using computer graphics. A number of artists are achieving fame for drawings produced on a computer. All these applications involve **interactive graphics,** which means a communication between a user and a computer to develop a design or a drawing on a display screen. The user can store the image and later retrieve it from storage for modification. When necessary, the image can be recorded as hard copy on paper.

A user needs special software for interactive graphics and a graphics display terminal to develop a design.

GRAPHICS DISPLAY TERMINALS

A graphics display terminal differs from the regular video display terminal (alphanumeric terminal) described earlier in this chapter in several ways. The graphics terminal can display lines, curves, and drawings in addition to letters and numbers. It can also display information in a range of colors. Of course,

GRAPHICS DISPLAY. A graphics display terminal can produce images of relatively high quality. *Courtesy IBM Corporation.*

the more colors, the more expensive a graphics terminal. As many as 250 different colors can bring a terminal cost to well over $10,000. Most users are satisfied with four- to eight-color capacities.

Another difference between the two types of terminals is that the resolution (clarity and sharpness) of the image displayed on a graphics terminal is of much higher quality than that on the normal video display unit screen.

A graphics terminal used for creative design work usually has additional capabilities. A designer can use a number of devices to draw images on the screen, including a light pen, a mouse, and a graphics tablet. A *light pen* is a pen-shaped device with a light-sensitive cell at its tip that can be used to mark lines on the screen that the computer then stores in its memory. A *mouse* is a small, hand-held device that, when moved around on a flat surface, can control the movement and placement of the cursor. A *graphics tablet* is usually a pressure-sensitive tablet; when you write on it with a special pen, you can draw any image, which is automatically stored in the computer. No matter what type of graphics input device is used, the drawing can be redisplayed, made larger or smaller, or modified in any way

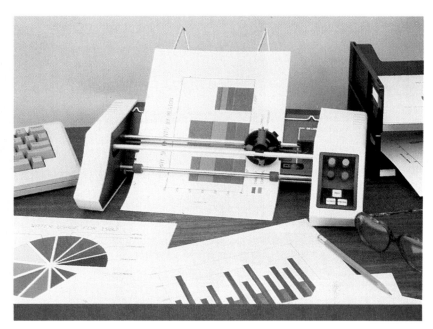

GRAPHIC PLOTTER. The graphic plotter shown here can be connected to a variety of computers to produce high-quality multicolored output in hard copy form. *Courtesy Hewlett-Packard Company.*

desired by the designer. If a user wants a hard copy of the design, a graphics printer is needed.

GRAPHICS PRINTERS

A variety of special printers designed specifically for graphics output are available. One type of graphics printer is called a **plotter.** Plotters are widely used to provide hard copy of graphics output in multicolored chart, graph, diagram, map, and other forms. Many of these machines create images by moving one or more pens over the surface of the paper on which the image is to be drawn. The pens can be equipped with ink supplies of different colors.

Operating on a different principle, a dot-matrix plotter forms graphic images as a series of dots, in this way resembling a dot-matrix printer. Laser printers and ink-jet printers also have the capacity to print graphics displays in multiple colors.

The cost of a graphics printer depends on the quality of the image produced and the speed at which the image can be made. Complex and expensive graphics printers are needed to handle the large volumes of high-quality printing work that is required to produce copy for advertisements, books, magazines, and films. Slower graphics printers with a range of print qualities are also available. There is even a wide choice of desktop models designed to meet the needs of personal computer users at relatively low costs.

MICROFICHE. Images of text and graphics can be stored on a small sheet of film called microfiche. The operator is holding a 4 × 6 microfiche (closeup shown at left) which contains a total of 270 pages of data. In the background is a microfiche reader which can be used to display in readable size any page of data recorded on the microfiche.

RECORDING OUTPUT IN MICROFORM

Banks, insurance companies, and other large businesses usually have huge numbers of business documents and reports that must be kept for accounting or general reference purposes. Storing this information in hard-copy form takes up large areas of expensive office space. In addition, retrieving a document or information when needed from such large files is slow.

For these reasons, many businesses are photographing key business documents, drawings, and lengthy reports printed by computer to reduce them to small film images called **microforms** or *microimages*. These images, too small to read without magnification, can be stored in several ways. The images may be recorded on rolls of film stored in cartridges called microfilm or on microfiche. A *microfiche* (pronounced "mī-krō-fish") is a 4- by 6-inch sheet of film on which as many as 200 or more pages of images can be stored.

Microfilm records can be produced by a special computer output device called **computer-output microfilm** (COM). A COM device records information at very high speeds on microfilm or microfiche. When the COM is attached directly to a computer for the recording of output in microform, it is said that the device is *on-line.* Often, the conversion is done *off-line;* the data to be filmed is first recorded on magnetic tape and, in a second operation, the tape information is recorded on film.

The information recorded on microfilm or microfiche by COM is indexed so it can be easily retrieved. The equipment used in the office for retrieving microimages is called a *reader* or a *viewer*. The reader enlarges and displays a microimage so that it can be read. Some readers are equipped with mechanisms to help locate the particular reference information needed by a user. Equipment is also available for making hard copies of microimages.

COM is practical when large volumes of information produced by the computer need to be printed and stored for occasional reference. Typically, payroll records, bank statements, customer invoices, and accounts receivable statements may be recorded in microform with considerable savings in space and reference retrieval time. Companies may also record pages of product and part catalogs in microform for internal and customer reference.

VOICE-RESPONSE OUTPUT

Computers have a limited capacity to provide output in the form of a human voice. A **voice-response output device** converts information stored in a computer into a spoken output message. The response is transmitted to the user who hears it on a telephone, on earphones, or on some other audio-receiving mechanism.

Most voice-response devices use a speech synthesizer to translate words stored in a computer's memory into a voice response. At present, the synthesizers have quite limited vocabularies and are slow in operation. In addition, the voice response that the machine makes sounds more mechanical than a human voice.

In spite of their limitations, voice-response devices have good uses. When you dial a telephone number that has been changed, you will likely receive a message from a computer voice-response device. The message may tell you: "The number you have dialed has been changed to 9-2-4 (pause) 7-1-1-8. Please make a record of this new number." If you have dialed a wrong number, the mechanical voice will advise you of your error. These applications of voice-response output save operator time for the telephone companies and also provide a faster (and more reliable) response to the caller.

Some banks also use voice-response output to reply to customer inquiries about their bank balances. A bank may have one or more voice-response output devices in its lobby, or you can call a special number from your home or work telephone. When a customer keys her or his account number into a special

VOICE RESPONSE. Data stored in a computer is output in the form of a synthe-sized human voice. *Doonesbury. Copyright © 1982 G. B. Trudeau. Reprinted with permission of Universal Press, Syndicate. All rights reserved.*

input device or into the telephone, the computer translates the amount of the customer's bank balance into a spoken response. The customer hears the response over the receiver. Super-markets are also beginning to use voice-response output at checkout stations to tell a customer the cost of each item purchased.

The use of voice-response output is expected to grow as ma-chine vocabularies increase and as the quality of the response is improved.

PUNCHED-CARD OUTPUT

What once was the only method of outputting information from a computer is now infrequently used—punched-card output. The output device used to record the results of computer pro-cessing in punched form is called a *card punch*. It can be com-bined with a punched-card reader that is used for input, or it can be a separate device.

Punching output on cards is such a slow operation that it is almost always done off-line. The output information to be punched is recorded first on magnetic tape, and in a separate operation the data is recorded as punched holes. Punched-card output is used primarily in the form of checks, which then can be easily reconciled when cashed. To attract a reader's atten-tion, magazine publishers sometimes forward to a customer subscription promotion material prepared in punched-card form. The card, when returned by a customer, can serve as an input document to enter subscription data. This is another example of a *turnaround document* that was described in Chap-ter 4.

STORAGE OF OUTPUT ON DISK OR TAPE

Magnetic-disk storage units and magnetic-tape drives are always made to serve as both input devices and output devices. A magnetic-disk unit can be considered an output device when results of computer processing are stored on the disk for future use.

Results of information processing can be recorded at very high speeds on magnetic tape. For this reason, output data is often recorded by computer on magnetic tape. The tape, in turn, is used to accomplish other output operations off-line from the computer. For example, a magnetic-tape drive can be attached to a printer or a COM unit and can produce required output without tying up computer processing time.

Output results produced and stored in a computer at one location can be transmitted thousands of miles away to one or more distant locations. At each remote location the computer output can be printed or displayed. In the next chapter, you will read about the methods used for the communication of data from one location to another.

CHECK YOURSELF

Match each phrase with the word or phrase that best defines it.

1. A device that outputs information as a spoken response.
2. A device that provides output in microform.
3. A screen that displays information only in one color.
4. A system to aid engineers in design work.
5. An output document later used for input data.
6. An output device connected directly to a computer.
7. A device that can display charts and drawings in color.
8. A 4- by 6-inch sheet of microfilm.
9. Output information displayed on a screen.
10. Communication between user and computer to develop a drawing.

a. COM
b. Soft copy
c. Interactive graphics
d. Microfiche
e. Hard copy
f. CAD
g. Graphics display terminal
h. Turnaround document
i. Voice-response output device
j. Monochrome screen
k. On-line device
l. Off-line device

Answers: (1) i; (2) a; (3) j; (4) f; (5) h; (6) k; (7) g; (8) d; (9) b; (10) c.

1. List seven options for the reporting of output information.
2. Name the four criteria usually considered in selection of a printer.
3. Explain the difference between letter-quality and nonletter-quality print and when each may be used.
4. How are computer printers classified by their printing speeds?
5. Explain how a character printer, line printer, and page printer work.
6. What special printer features may be important to some users?
7. Explain what trade-offs a potential buyer considers in selecting a printer.
8. Describe an impact printer and a nonimpact printer. Which of the two can prepare multiple copies of output at one time?
9. Name three types of impact printers and identify when each may be used.
10. Name three types of nonimpact printers and identify when each may be used.
11. How does a laser printer operate?
12. Describe the features of a typical VDT device that displays alphanumeric information.
13. Define the term *soft copy*. Under what situations is it a satisfactory form of output?
14. What does graphics output mean?
15. Describe two ways in which a computer can be used for graphics work and give an example of each.
16. What do CAD and CAM mean?
17. Explain three differences between a graphics display terminal and a regular (alphanumeric) display unit.
18. Describe how a graphics plotter may create an image.
19. What are the factors that determine the cost of a graphics printer?
20. Name two reasons why business documents are reduced to microform.
21. Explain how a COM device is used.
22. What is the difference between on-line and off-line output operations?
23. What is the function of a voice-response device? Explain two ways it is used in business.
24. Give one example of the use of punched-card output.
25. Explain how a magnetic tape drive may serve as an output device.

COMPARING IDEAS

The questions below are designed to help you think about what you have learned in this chapter. They are "thought" questions. There is no one correct answer.

1. A wide selection of printers is available to microcomputer users at home, in schools, or in business offices. Explain the specific differences

in the printers that are actually available for purchase at a local computer store or that you see advertised in papers or magazines.

2. If you are using a computer terminal to assist you in your work as an architect, what features of a terminal would be of greatest interest to you?

INFORMATION PROCESSING ACTIVITIES

Now you can perform many of the information processing activities business workers perform. Below is a summary of the tasks you will complete. You will find the actual data and business forms you need in your *Information Processing Work Kit*.

1. You will assist the members of the Information Systems staff at the corporate headquarters of The Copy Factory franchises. You will review questionnaires submitted by the outlet owners and recommend the appropriate output printer.
2. You will write the specifications that will be used in the purchase of a graphics output software package. You will design pie-chart and bar-graph output.
3. You will review a portion of an office operations manual and determine the appropriate output hardware to perform each task.

HANDS-ON ACTIVITIES

1. Use a magnifying glass and examine the print quality of a typed letter, a printout from a dot-matrix printer, a newspaper, a magazine, and this book. Describe the differences in quality as discussed in this chapter.
2. Assume that you and a good friend who lives in a distant city both belong to an on-line computer time share service. One day immediately after school you get on-line with your friend and begin to key a lengthy letter to tell your friend about your activities over the last month. Your parent comes home and becomes extremely upset when it is determined what you are doing. Write an explanation giving several reasons why your parent was so upset and a suggestion which you probably received.

CHAPTER

7

DATA COMMUNICATIONS AND COMPUTER NETWORKING

Information Processing Terminology

Data communications
Telecommunications
On-line inquiry system
Communications
  channel
Communications circuit
Telephone twisted-wire
  line
Coaxial cable
Fiber-optic (or optical
  fiber) cable
Microwave
  communications
Satellite communications

Bits per second (bps)
Bandwidth
Narrowband channel
Voiceband channel
Broadband channel
Simplex transmission
Half-duplex transmission
Full-duplex transmission
Modem
Acoustic coupler
Front-end processor
Networks
Computer networking

Star network
Ring network
Local area network
  (LAN)
Distributed data
  processing
Electronic mail
Teleconference
Electronic blackboard
Telecomputing
Videotex
Database
Electronic bulletin board

Performance Goals

☐ Name four types of needs for data communications and give an example of each.

☐ Define the term *communications channel* and describe five types of channels used for data communications.

- Define bandwidth and bps and describe how communications channels are classified by transmission speed.
- Name three alternative types of channel capacities for sending and receiving messages.
- Explain the function of a modem and describe how an acoustic coupler modem is used.
- Explain the difference between a *star* and a *ring network* design.
- Describe how private networks are used for distributed data processing, electronic mail, teleconferencing, and telecomputing.
- Name three large information suppliers for personal computer users and describe three categories of services they provide.

When computers were first used in business, the computer processor and all input and output equipment were generally located in one place, often in the same room. If a sales office in another city needed information from the computer, the output information usually would be printed and then mailed to the distant sales office. Until the early 1950s the only faster means of communicating data was via telegraph lines. Even then, data could be transmitted from one city to another only at a speed of about 600 characters per minute. This meant it took hours to transmit the content of a long report. As more and more individuals in business organizations came to depend on computer output, it became necessary to have faster ways to transfer data from one place to another.

The words **data communications** and **telecommunications** have the same meaning. Both refer to the electronic transmission of data from one location to another. Today some type of data communications capacity is very important to a variety of business organizations. Many users of personal computers also need data communications capacities. For this reason, before examining how data communications is accomplished, we should review more fully the typical needs for electronic communication of data.

USER NEEDS FOR DATA COMMUNICATIONS

Today data communications facilities are used to perform one or more of the following functions:

1. To transfer input data from one or more remote locations to a centrally located computer.
2. To distribute computer output results.
3. To handle on-line inquiries to a central reference point.
4. To exchange information from one computer to another.

COMMUNICATION OF INPUT DATA

Every day billions of characters of input data are being transmitted electronically from remote offices to computers for processing. Airlines receive requests for plane reservations by data communications from thousands of travel agents located throughout the world. Depending upon where you live, you too may be able to enter input data into an airline reservation system by using your telephone instrument as a data communications device. You press the telephone buttons to enter data about the day and month you want to fly, the place of departure, and the flight number.

Think of the data communications needs of an international bank that has individual bank offices in every large city in the world. Daily, each of the branch banks must communicate input data about thousands of banking transactions to a computer at the headquarters. High-speed methods of data communications are needed to ensure that records at headquarters each day accurately reflect the bank balances at each banking location.

COMMUNICATION OF COMPUTER OUTPUT RESULTS

Although a business may have hundreds, or even thousands, of computers in operation throughout its offices, some types of work may still be performed only at one location. The results of the computer processing done at the central location must be communicated to other locations of the business. For example, many large retail companies from which you can order merchandise by mail actually store their merchandise in many different warehouses located throughout the country. Nevertheless, the retailer usually requests that you and other customers send your orders directly to a central office.

The data about items ordered by a customer is entered as input in the central office, and a computer located there processes the customer's order to determine which of the warehouses has the particular material ordered by the customer, and which is located closest to the customer. The central computer then communicates to a receiving terminal located in the selected warehouse all of the data needed to prepare a shipping order. The shipping order is used by warehouse employees to select and to ship the material ordered by the customer. If electronic communication was not used between the central location and the warehouses, the handling of customer orders would take much longer.

COMMUNICATIONS IN ON-LINE INQUIRY SYSTEMS

In recent years there has been explosive growth in computerized **on-line inquiry systems.** These are systems in which a central reference file of computerized information is made available for access by data communications to users who may be spread throughout the country, or even the world. A user want-

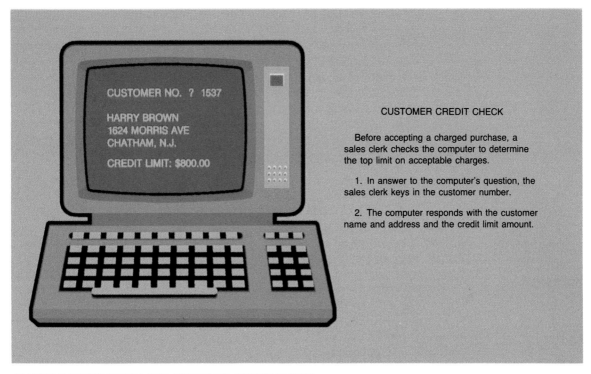

ON-LINE INQUIRY SYSTEM FOR CUSTOMER CREDIT CHECK.

ing to access the reference file sends her or his inquiry for information via data communications facilities. The answer to the inquiry is received from the computer via data communications. As an example, if communications facilities are available, a personal computer user in a very remote area may retrieve from a central computer file a variety of information ranging from summaries of news events, the latest stock prices, or schedules of sporting events.

A business organization may establish central computerized reference files that can be accessed by designated employees within the company. One typical application provides for maintenance of a customer reference file. In answer to a customer's request, a sales person within the company is able to access this file to learn about the status of a particular customer order.

EXCHANGE OF INFORMATION BETWEEN COMPUTERS

Large companies often want to transfer large amounts of data stored in a computer at one location to another computer at a distant location. Sometimes such a transfer is made in order to provide a backup copy of a file in a second location, for security. In other cases, duplicate copies of computerized file data are needed for processing in several locations. For example, it often is necessary in large companies to have an up-to-date file of product inventory information in several manufacturing locations. Whatever the reason, the transfer of file data from a computer in one location to a computer in another location can be done at high speed by modern data communications facilities.

Even the user of a personal computer may want to exchange data with another computer user. If both users have appropriate communications devices, the exchange of information can be very simple. Later in the chapter more will be said about the exchange of data among computer users and other new applications of data communications.

COMPONENTS OF A DATA COMMUNICATIONS SYSTEM

Whether a data communications system is designed to serve the user of a personal computer or a large business, it has three components: a *sending mechanism,* a *communications channel,* and a *receiving mechanism.* The same device often serves as both a sending and receiving mechanism, and its design depends in part upon the communications channel to be used. For this reason, your study of data communications systems starts with the subject of communications channels.

TYPES OF COMMUNICATIONS CHANNELS

Communications channels are pathways along which data can be transferred electronically from a sending location to a receiving point. The term **communications circuits** has the same meaning.

There are different types of communications channels. Some are actual lines that physically connect one location with another. These lines may be laid underground or underwater, or they may be stretched from one telephone pole to another. Other types of communications channels are not physical lines made of material that you can see or touch. Instead, these channels are simply the atmosphere or space through which the broadcast signals are transmitted.

The types of communications channels for data transmission include telephone twisted-wire lines, coaxial cables, fiber-optic cables, microwave systems, and satellite transmission.

Telephone Twisted-Wire Lines. The most commonly used communications channel for data transmission are telephone lines. These lines often are referred to as **telephone twisted-wire lines** because of the way they are made. A telephone twisted-wire line consists of two strands of copper wire (a pair of wires) twisted together and then strung from one location to another. One twisted pair can handle one telephone conversation or one transmission of data. Most often, bundles of hundreds of twisted-wire lines are combined in a single thick cable to provide greater transmission capacity.

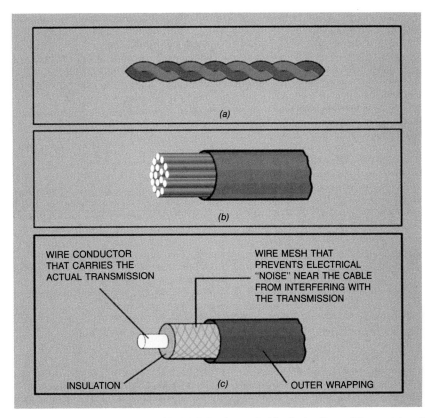

COMMUNICATIONS CHANNELS. (a) Telephone twisted-wire lines, (b) a cable of twisted-wire lines, and (c) coaxial cables are types of communications channels.

The use of telephone lines for data communications has a great advantage for both business and personal computer users. Existing telephone networks link together almost every location in this country and many cities throughout the world. If a telephone line is in place, a computer user only needs sending-receiving equipment to be able to send or receive data communications. Telephone lines, however, do not provide as fast a communication facility as newer types of channels do.

Coaxial Cables. Fast and high-quality data communications can be secured with coaxial cable channels. A **coaxial cable** consists of a conducting cylinder, with a single wire conductor running down its center, wrapped in insulation. Its characteristics permit faster transmission of data and less interference by static noise than is the case for telephone twisted-wire lines. Coaxial cables are usually run underground or under the ocean. They have provided an important means of voice and data communication between the United States and other countries of the world.

Chapter 7: Data Communications and Computer Networking   159

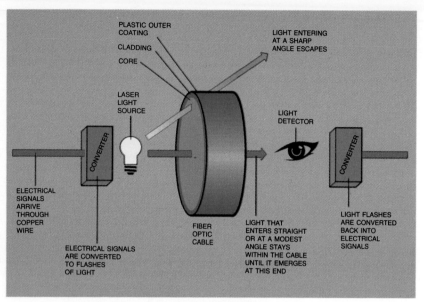

FIBER-OPTIC TRANSMISSION. A tiny, glass optical fiber is shown at left. At right is a diagram showing how a fiber-optic channel transmits information by means of laser light. *Courtesy Gould, Inc.*

Fiber-Optic Cables. A rapidly growing new technology, fiber optics, is replacing the older twisted-wire and coaxial cable technologies in voice and data communications facilities. A **fiber-optic** (or *optical fiber*) **channel** transmits voice or data communications by means of laser light beams flashing through tiny glass fibers no thicker than a human hair. Thousands of the glass fibers are incorporated in a fiber-optic cable which can carry over 100,000 voice conversations at one time. The cables are run underground or under the ocean between communications locations.

Fiber optic cables are much smaller and weigh less than either telephone twisted wire or coaxial cables. They provide much faster data transmission than the older technologies.

American Telephone and Telegraph (AT&T) planned completion of a trans-Atlantic fiber-optic network by 1988. In 1987, however, the AT&T director of engineering reported that sharks had destroyed four segments of cable strung along the ocean floor connecting the United States and Europe. Attracted apparently by the electrical current in the fiber-optic lines, the sharks had bitten through the cable. AT&T took steps to protect the cables from the gnawing sharks by placing the cables in armored jackets.

Microwave Communications Links. As stated earlier, data communications does not always require that some type of cable physically link a sending station to a receiving station. In

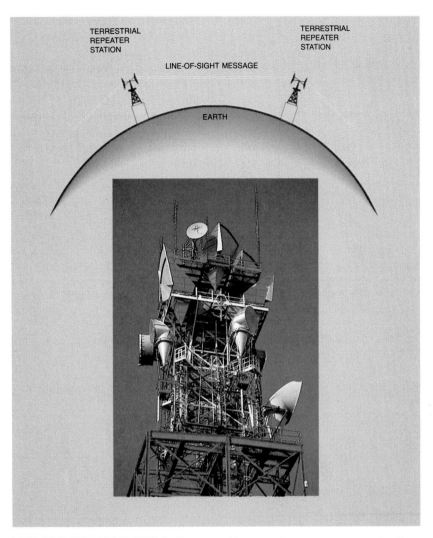

TERRESTRIAL REPEATER STATION

TERRESTRIAL REPEATER STATION

LINE-OF-SIGHT MESSAGE

EARTH

MICROWAVE TRANSMISSION. A diagram of how a microwave communications system works is shown above. At the bottom of the illustration is an actual microwave station. *Courtesy Mitchell Funk, The Image Bank.*

a **microwave communications system,** a sending station communicates data (or voice conversations) to a receiving station in another location by broadcasting signals.

Microwave sending and receiving stations are located on the ground. The signals broadcast by a sending station travel in a straight line. Any obstruction between the sending station and the receiving station will deflect the broadcast signals. Because the surface of the earth curves, microwave stations must be placed no more than 30 miles apart to avoid deflection of the signals. Data to be communicated from the East Coast to the

West Coast are broadcast from one microwave station to another. The receiving station then amplifies and retransmits the signals to the next station.

Microwave systems provide a faster means of transmitting data over long distances than do standard telephone lines or coaxial cables. Special coding and decoding equipment is sometimes used when sensitive or important information is transmitted, because anyone with microwave receiving equipment can pick up the signal, just as your radio picks up many different channels.

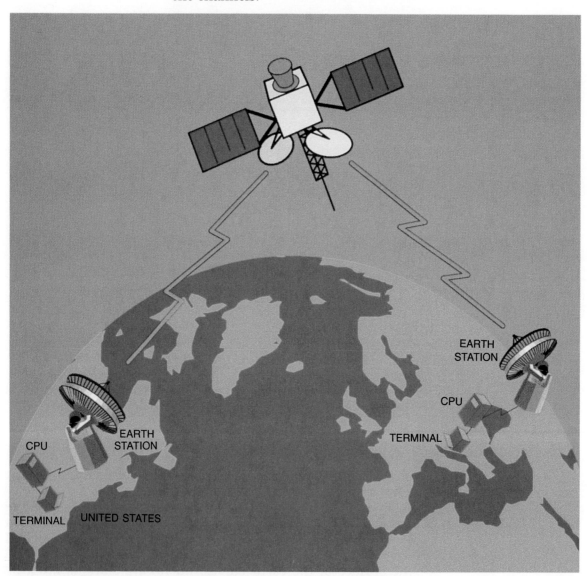

SATELLITE TRANSMISSION. Satellites make it possible to transmit data from one location to another many thousands of miles away.

Satellite Transmission. We are now accustomed to looking at television programs broadcast by satellite. Satellite transmission, for example, makes it possible for us to watch in our living rooms an Olympic sporting event that takes place in another country thousands of miles away. Business data can also be communicated by satellite. **Satellite transmission** is the broadcast of signals from an earth station to an orbiting satellite that amplifies and retransmits the signal to a receiving station on earth, thousands of miles away from the sending location.

The satellites used for video, voice, or data transmission are placed in orbit about 22,000 miles above the earth and travel at the speed at which the earth rotates. Therefore, they do not appear to change their position in the sky. The earth stations that send and receive communications are dishlike antennas.

Satellite data transmission has an advantage over microwave communications in that data can be transmitted over great distances without worry about obstruction. It is, however, a very expensive means of data communications and, therefore, is used primarily by large international companies that need to communicate volumes of information between distant locations at high speeds.

SPEEDS OF DATA TRANSMISSION

A communications channel is classified according to the speed at which data can be transmitted over the channel. Data transmission speeds are measured in terms of the number of bits that are transmitted each second—the **bits per second** (bps). Remember that typically 8 bits (or a byte) are used to represent a single letter or number. Therefore, a transmission rate of 9600 bps means that 1200 characters of information are being communicated each second.

Communications channels are classified by their data transmission speeds into three groups—low speeds, medium speeds, and high speeds. Communications technicians use the word **bandwidth** to describe each of these categories. The wider the bandwidth of a channel, the faster its data transmission speed.

- *Low-speed communications channels* (or **narrowband channels**) transmit between 40 and 300 bps. Telegraph lines are low-speed communications channels.
- *Medium-speed communications channels* (or **voiceband channels**) transmit between 300 and 9600 bps. The standard telephone lines provide medium-speed transmission.
- *High-speed communications channels* (or **broadband channels**) transmit more than 9600 bps. Some have transmission speeds of over 200,000 bps. Fiber-optic cables and microwave and satellite communications systems provide high-speed data communications.

DIRECTIONAL CAPACITY OF CHANNEL TRANSMISSION

Communications channels are classified still another way. This classification identifies a channel's capacity for message forwarding—that is, whether a message can be sent in one or both directions over the channel. There are three possibilities:

1. A **simplex channel** can transmit data in only one direction and cannot transmit a message in the opposite direction. For example, if a simplex line is used, a printing terminal can only receive messages and never send them. Simplex channels are not often used in modern data communications.

2. A **half-duplex channel** can be used to transmit data in both directions, but can operate in only one direction at a time. A terminal connected to a half-duplex channel can be used to send or to receive communications at different times.

3. A **full-duplex channel** can be used to send data in both directions over the channel at the same time. Although more expensive than the other two types of channels, full-duplex channels are needed to achieve high-speed data communications.

CHECK YOURSELF

Match each phrase with the word or phrase that best defines it.

1. Unit of measurement for data transmission speed.
2. A channel capable of transmitting more than 9600 bps.
3. A channel that can send data in both directions at the same time.
4. Communications transmitted via an orbiting body.
5. A channel that can send data in only one direction.
6. A low-speed communications channel.
7. A medium-speed communications channel.
8. Communications transmitted via a laser light beam.
9. Electronic transmission of data from one location to another.
10. Standard telephone line.

a. Voiceband channel
b. Fiber-optic channel communications
c. Half-duplex channel
d. Satellite communications
e. Bits per second (bps)
f. Simplex channel
g. Microwave communications system
h. Telecommunications
i. Broadband channel
j. Twisted-wire line
k. Full-duplex channel
l. Narrowband channel

Answers: (1) e; (2) i; (3) k; (4) d; (5) f; (6) l; (7) a; (8) b; (9) h; (10) j.

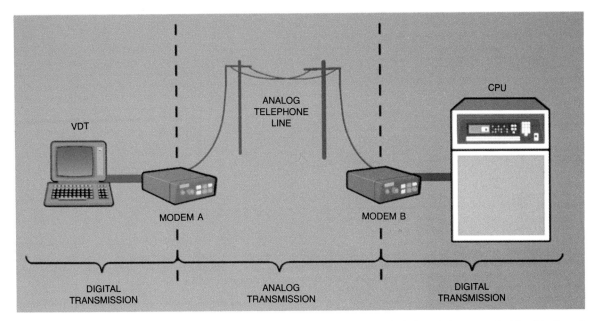

FUNCTION OF MODEM DEVICES. Data that is keyed at a terminal in digital signals is converted by Modem A to analog form so that it can be transmitted over the telephone line. When Modem B receives the transmitted data, it is reconverted back to digital form and passed to the computer CPU. When data is communicated from the computer CPU back to the terminal, these steps are reversed.

COMMUNICATIONS SENDING AND RECEIVING EQUIPMENT

A communications channel provides a link through which a sending location can forward a message to a receiving location. At each of the two locations, equipment is needed to send and to receive the message. A standard computer input-output device such as the video display terminal described in Chapter 4 can be used to send and to receive data communications. A printing terminal (Chapter 6) can be used to receive messages. At minimum, one additional device is needed to send or receive messages over voice communications lines. This device is called a modem.

Modem Devices. Telephone lines are designed to carry voice signals, which differ from computer signals. A voice signal is said to be an analog (or a wave-type) signal; and, as you read in Chapter 3, a computer signal is a digital signal represented by bits, which are on-off pulses.

Voice communications lines are designed to transmit messages in analog form. When using a telephone line for data transmission it is necessary, therefore, to convert computer signals into analog code at the sending station. When the message arrives at the receiving station, it has to be converted back into the computer code. These conversions are done by a device

MODEM. An internal modem is designed to be inserted into the microcomputer's CPU. *Will Faller.*

called a **modem.** The word modem comes from the two functions performed by the device: At the sending station, a modem *mo*dulates computer signals (converts them into analog signals), and at the receiving station, a modem *dem*odulates analog signals (converts them back to computer signals).

For data transmission via telephone lines, one modem is required at the sending station and a second modem at the receiving station. As a message is keyed at the sending station, the modem converts it to analog code and sends it over the communications channel. When the message is received, the second modem converts the message to digital code and sends it to the computer for processing. All this is done under communications program instructions.

Using regular home telephone equipment, a user of a personal computer can send messages to others or receive messages from others by adding a modem to her or his computer system and acquiring the appropriate software to perform data communications.

A modem may be built into a computer system or it may be purchased as a free-standing unit and then attached to a computer by cable. To perform its function, the modem must also be connected to a telephone line. This is done in one of two ways: first, the modem may be plugged directly into a telephone jack outlet; or, second, it may be attached to the telephone line by means of a special device called an acoustic coupler. An **acoustic coupler** is a special type of modem that has a cradle with

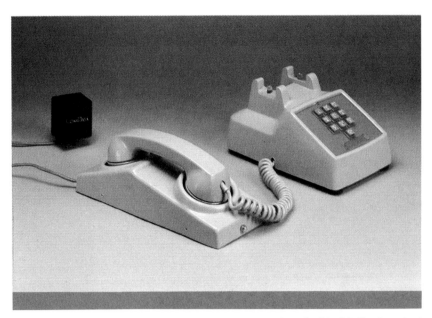

ACOUSTIC COUPLER. An acoustic coupler is a modem that holds the handset of a telephone. *Courtesy ComData Corporation.*

rubber caps designed to hold the handset of a typical home telephone. To send a message, the user dials the receiving party as would be done to place a telephone call. The telephone handset is placed in the cradle. This connects the terminal of the sender to the telephone line. Impulses from the terminal will be received into the handset and communicated over the telephone line.

An acoustic coupler modem is convenient for business people who travel from office to office. For example, a salesperson with a portable computer can stop at any pay telephone, dial the home office, place the handset in the acoustic coupler, and transmit customer order data to headquarters. It also provides a convenient means for a traveling sports reporter to transmit a story to his newspaper office. A reporter, while attending a sporting event in a distant location, can write up the story about the event on a portable computer terminal and then transmit it by the nearest telephone to a computer in the news office. The editor of the newspaper can then retrieve the story from the computer, edit it as necessary, and release it for insertion in the next edition of the newspaper.

Other Sending and Receiving Equipment. Computer users with high volumes of data communications need additional sending and receiving equipment to effectively handle their communications loads.

ACOUSTIC COUPLER.
Acoustic couplers can
be used with any tele-
phone anywhere. *Cour-
tesy Bohle/Epson Corpora-
tion.*

There are several reasons why additional communications equipment may be needed. One reason is to make effective use of high-speed communications channels. Broadband communications lines that transmit at high speeds are expensive. Special devices are made to help a business transmit as much data as possible in the shortest period of time, thereby keeping the costs of communications down. These special devices, called *multiplexers* and *concentrators,* act as an interface between modems and computers to schedule effective use of high-speed communications channels.

A second reason for using special communications equipment is to ensure that the processing units of large computers involved in data communications are used effectively. A large computer system may have hundreds of terminals accessing it at one time. Often, in this situation, a minicomputer is used to relieve the larger computer of the functions necessary to handle communications of data to and from the terminals. In this case, the smaller computer is called a **front-end processor.**

STAR NETWORK. Many terminals or computers are connected to and can communicate directly with a central computer to form a star network.

COMPUTER NETWORKING

To permit fast exchange of information, computers, terminals, and other electronic office equipment may be organized in communications systems, called **networks.** The term **computer networking** has come to mean the sharing of information among computer devices and their users by means of communications systems.

NETWORK DESIGNS

There are two basic designs of computer networks. These are referred to as *star* and *ring networks.*

A **star network** consists of a central computer to which many terminals and remote computers in different locations are connected by communications lines. The line connections thus form a starlike pattern. In this type of network, each terminal and remote computer can communicate directly with the central computer but not with each other. A message directed from one remote computer to another must go through the central computer before being routed to the appropriate network component.

A star network is often used in time-sharing systems in which a number of different users share a large central computer facility. In this case, such users usually have no need to communicate with each other.

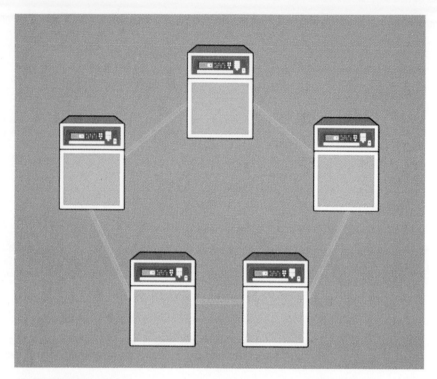

RING NETWORK. Terminals and computers in a ring network communicate directly with each other.

A **ring network** is a network without a central computer. Instead, the network consists of a series of computers and terminals connected on a communications line so that each component on the line is able to communicate directly with any other component. Each component in the ring is assigned an address. A sending component must use the appropriate address to direct a message to a receiving unit.

A ring network is generally used to handle the exchange of information among computer users and facilities within a single organization or group of organizations.

PRIVATE NETWORKS   In recent years many large businesses, government agencies, hospitals, and universities have established private data communications facilities to permit the exchange of information among computer devices and people within the organization.

One type of private network is a **local area network** (LAN) system. A local area network links by communications lines (usually telephone lines) computers, terminals, and other elec-

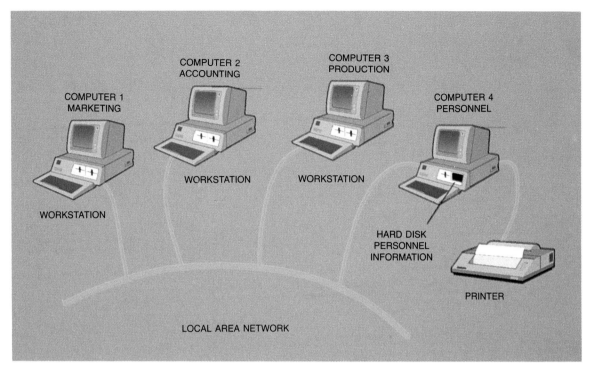

LOCAL AREA NETWORK (LAN). A local area network links various types of hardware located within a small geographic area.

tronic equipment located within a relatively small geographic area. For example, a local network system may be used by a business organization to link computers and other electronic equipment located in a single office building or factory. It is also used by some universities to link computer users on a college campus. Such a system permits users to transfer data from one computer to another, to input data into a computer for processing, or to have processing results reported on a high-quality printer and then copied. Also, terminal users connected to the network can address and forward electronically messages to other terminal users on the network. Later, you will learn more about the use of networks for the exchange of electronic mail.

Advanced local networks in some business organizations include word processing machines, microfilm equipment, optical scanners, and typesetters as well as computers, high-quality printers, and copying machines. The purpose is to permit the transfer of copy from a word processing unit to a high-quality printer or to a computer storage unit, or from a computer storage unit to a copying machine, microfilm unit, or typesetter. Such a network provides a means of achieving greater office automation.

Chapter 7: Data Communications and Computer Networking   171

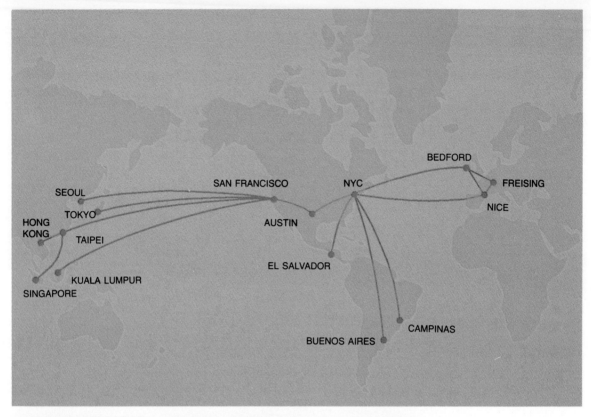

CORPORATE INTERNATIONAL NETWORK. Large international corporations such as Texas Instruments, Inc. have installed complex networks to link together terminals and computers located in offices and plants around the world. ©
Courtesy Texas Instruments.

The same functions performed in a local communications network can be performed over wider geographic areas. In addition to telephone lines, which are typically used in local networks, a complex system of coaxial and fiber-optic cables and microwave or satellite transmission may be used to form a nationwide or worldwide communications network. Such a system is usually designed to handle voice communications as well as data transmission.

Large international companies often have sophisticated data communications systems to permit the exchange of data among computers and terminals spread around the world. For example, Texas Instruments, a large manufacturer of computers and microprocessor chips, has a network that interconnects over 7000 terminals and hundreds of computers located in Dallas, Texas, and in other manufacturing and sales distribution sites located in Europe, South America, and the Far East.

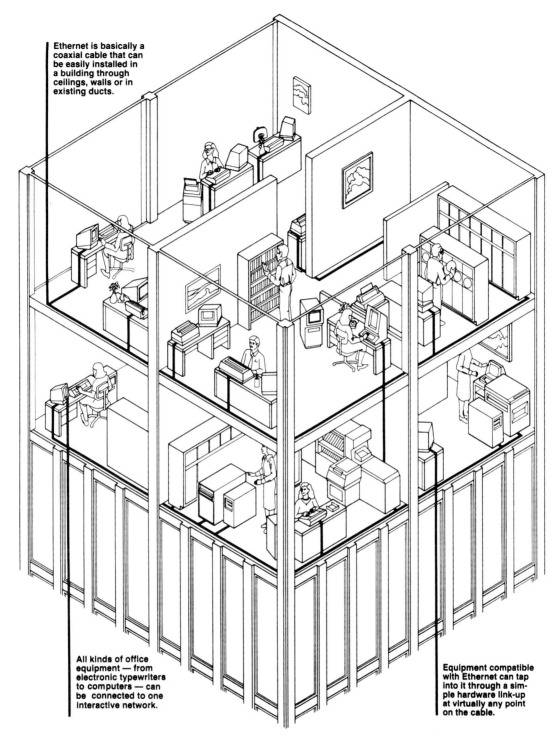

Ethernet is basically a coaxial cable that can be easily installed in a building through ceilings, walls or in existing ducts.

All kinds of office equipment — from electronic typewriters to computers — can be connected to one interactive network.

Equipment compatible with Ethernet can tap into it through a simple hardware link-up at virtually any point on the cable.

LOCAL AREA NETWORK. The diagram shows a popular local network system developed by Xerox Corporation called ETHERNET. It permits more than 1,000 workstations within an office building to be linked together by cable so that information can be exchanged and hardware shared among the workstations. *Courtesy Xerox Corporation.*

Match each phrase with the word or phrase that best defines it.

1. Device that relieves a large computer of communications functions.
2. Private network serving a single office building.
3. Sharing of information between computers and their users over communications lines.
4. Voice transmission signal.
5. Data (or digital) transmission signal.
6. Modem that holds telephone handset.
7. Network design in which components can communicate with each other.
8. Device that converts analog to digital (or data) signals.

a. Star network design
b. Computer networking
c. Modem
d. Bit on-off pulse
e. LAN system
f. Acoustic coupler
g. Ring network design
h. Analog wave
i. Front-end processor

Answers: (1) i; (2) e; (3) b; (4) h; (5) d; (6) f; (7) g; (8) c.

DISTRIBUTED DATA PROCESSING

One reason why a business may establish a private communications network is to provide the means of accomplishing distributed data processing. **Distributed data processing** (DDP) means dividing (or distributing) computer processing work among two or more computers that are located in physically separated sites but are connected by communications lines.

When computers were first used in business, processing was centralized. There was good reason for this: The early machines were large, expensive, and difficult to program, operate, and maintain. It was more effective to have a single group of experts at one location responsible for the operations.

This is no longer true. Computers are now distributed throughout business organizations, and where necessary, communications networks provide the means of transferring data back and forth between the computers for processing. For example, the Bank of America has more than a thousand branch offices in California and other countries of the world. Each branch office has some computer processing capabilities to handle input transactions. The bank also has two large central computing facilities, one in Los Angeles and the other in San Francisco. The central computers receive input transactions from branch computers, process the transactions, and communicate output information back to the branch offices. The central computers also serve as backups to each other.

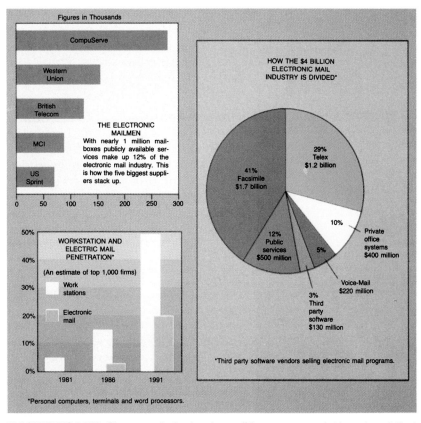

Figures in Thousands

CompuServe

Western Union

British Telecom

MCI

US Sprint

THE ELECTRONIC MAILMEN
With nearly 1 million mailboxes publicly available services make up 12% of the electronic mail industry. This is how the five biggest suppliers stack up.

0 50 100 150 200 250 300

WORKSTATION AND ELECTRIC MAIL PENETRATION*

(An estimate of top 1,000 firms)

Work stations

Electronic mail

50%
40%
30%
20%
10%
0%

1981   1986   1991

*Personal computers, terminals and word processors.

HOW THE $4 BILLION ELECTRONIC MAIL INDUSTRY IS DIVIDED*

41% Facsimile $1.7 billion

29% Telex $1.2 billion

10% Private office systems $400 million

5% Voice-Mail $220 million

3% Third party software $130 million

12% Public services $500 million

*Third party software vendors selling electronic mail programs.

ELECTRONIC MAIL. The use of electronic mail has grown quickly; a trend that will continue. The other two graphs show major suppliers of E-Mail and how the industry is divided. *Courtesy Crain's New York Business.*

ELECTRONIC MAIL

The use of local area or worldwide private networks to exchange messages among users was mentioned earlier. **Electronic mail** is the name given to a mail system that uses computers and communications lines to transmit messages from one user to other users. Messages may be in the form of letters, memos, reports, or graphic displays.

Each participant in an electronic mail system is assigned an electronic (or computer) mailbox with a specific address. To send a letter to a particular participant, the sender keys the message on his or her terminal, edits it, keys in the computer mailbox address of the individual or individuals to whom the message is to be sent, and directs the terminal to send off the letter.

The message is transmitted electronically at fast speed to the personal computers of the persons to whom it is directed, where it is placed in the computers' auxiliary storage unit. When the user of a computer that has received a message begins to use the computer, a message appears on the display screen saying that mail has been received. She or he can then display the full text of the letter, and if necessary arrange to have it printed.

Electronic mail certainly provides a faster and more efficient way of delivering messages. Think also of all the paper that can be saved by this type of mail service.

TELECONFERENCING AND TELECOMPUTING

Communications networks are now widely used for new forms of conferences that involve discussions among people who are in various geographic locations. Business and educational institutions have found that teleconferencing and telecomputing can reduce the time and costs spent by staff members in traveling to meetings that are held away from the office.

A **teleconference** is a conference of people in different physical locations who, through communications networks, exchange ideas as though they were meeting in person. One type of teleconference is a telephone hookup (a conference call), which connects all the conference participants so that they may exchange ideas. Comments made by any one individual are heard by all participants.

A more sophisticated type of teleconference provides for a video hookup from one location to another so that people actually can see one another during the conference discussion. In some cases, the video picture is limited to a one-way transmission, and only what is happening at the central point is transmitted by video to remote sites.

An **electronic blackboard** may be used for presentations in teleconferences. As a conference leader writes on a blackboard

TELECONFERENCING. Without having to travel to a central point, people in different locations can exchange ideas through teleconferencing. Under computer control, video images can be displayed in multiple locations. *Courtesy AT&T Bell Laboratories.*

that is usually located in a central site, the image is transmitted to dozens of remote conference locations where it is displayed on television screens. This type of equipment is often used by automotive companies when engineers physically separated from one another want to discuss alternative designs for automotive equipment.

A new form of teleconference is telecomputing. **Telecomputing,** also called *computer conferencing,* is an interactive discussion between participants in different locations who communicate with each other through personal computer terminals. In one form of telecomputing, all participants are on-line at the same time, sharing their ideas and posing questions to others by keyboarding them on their terminals. As an alternative, a particular telecomputing conference may extend over several days or a week; during some of the time some of the participants may not be active. Instead, a participant may choose to comment on or ask questions about certain subjects on the conference agenda.

McGraw-Hill, a large publisher, has been a leading sponsor of computer conferences for business, scientific, and educational people. In 1986, for example, it held a worldwide telecomputing conference to discuss the problems raised by the nuclear reactor accident at Chernobyl in Russia shortly after the accident happened. It linked by communications lines the personal computers of several hundred conference participants located throughout the world, including thirteen of the world's top nuclear power experts. The conference participants posed questions, by computer, to the experts or submitted their own views on the conference subjects. Copies of the questions and comments were made available to all conference participants through their computer terminals.

PERSONAL COMPUTER NETWORKS

Commercial communications networks have been established to serve varied needs of personal computer users. Many of the services are similar to those provided by the so-called videotex information systems that are now available in many parts of the world. **Videotex** is a two-way information service sent over a subscriber's telephone line or two-way cable television channel. A subscriber to a videotex information service can request information by depressing keys on a small hand-held terminal. The requested information is displayed on a home TV screen.

Information suppliers offer to personal computer users a broader range of information services than presently available to subscribers of videotex systems. Also, the equipment used to request and to receive information via a personal computer is not the same as that used in videotex. A personal computer user requests information by dialing a supplier of the information and keying and transmitting the information request via his or her computer terminal. If the individual requesting the information is a subscriber in good standing (has paid the starting, monthly, or annual charge for the service), the requested information is transmitted back to the personal computer over telephone lines.

There are hundreds of electronic information services available to personal computer users. Among the largest of these suppliers are:

- The Source, owned by the Source Telecomputing Corporation.
- CompuServe, owned by H&R Block, the income-tax service organization.
- Dow Jones News/Retrieval Service, owned by the Dow Jones Company, publisher of the Wall Street Journal and other financial services.

The commercial information suppliers offer a wide variety of services to personal computer users. Most of these can be classified in one of four groups: information reference services; electronic mail and bulletin board communications; networking; and banking, shopping and other transaction processing.

Information Reference Services. Through an information supplier, a computer user anywhere in the country where telephone connections are available can access computerized reference files. These files can be used to retrieve information about current and historical events, the latest stock and bond prices and other financial data, real estate listings, medical and legal information, local theater listings, schedules and results of sporting events, weather forecasts for locations around the world, and a host of other subjects.

The reference information just described is stored in **databases,** the name given to collections of computerized data organized to permit easy access and retrieval. All together, there are thousands of reference databases now available for access by a computer user who must be willing, of course, to pay a fee for the information.

Electronic Mail and Bulletin Board Communications.
You have already learned that mail can be transmitted from individual to individual over private networks within a single organization. The commercial information suppliers also provide electronic mail service to their subscribers. For example, a subscriber to CompuServe living in New England can address a letter to another personal computer subscriber in California. The message is transmitted over the CompuServe communications network. The procedures for sending and transmitting such a message are the same as those described earlier in the section dealing with electronic mail.

CompuServe, The Source, and even individual personal computer users have set up **electronic bulletin boards** for the posting of messages to be read by other personal computer users. An electronic bulletin board serves the same purpose as a bulletin board you may have in school, where a student can post a message—perhaps one asking for a ride to a particular place on a particular day. The difference is that the information on your bulletin board is written on paper. To post a message on an electronic bulletin board, one inputs the message on a computer terminal. The message is then transmitted to the supplier's computer and placed in a storage unit allocated to bulletin board messages. A subscriber can use her or his terminal to scan and retrieve the contents of electronic bulletin board messages.

Networking by Personal Computer. Such business information services as CompuServe and The Source also encourage networking among the personal computer users who subscribe to their services. A subscriber to CompuServe may join one or more of over 40 different *special interest groups* (SIGs), 16 of which are for business or professional people. These include a medical SIG and another one for individuals interested in public relations and marketing. On-line conferences are held by the different SIGs. Members of the medical SIG, for example, often discuss by computer terminal their experiences with various medical treatments.

Networking by computer permits a personal computer user to "meet" people who can give the user assistance or advice on a business or personal matter. Some users have even successfully used computer networks to hunt for new job opportunities.

Banking, Shopping, and Other Transaction Processing. A fourth category of service offered by information suppliers allows subscribers to execute banking, shopping, or other transactions through a commercial network. Banking by computer means that using your terminal you can access the records of your bank to determine the balance in your account and authorize the bank to pay particular bills for you. This can save you the time needed to write out and mail a check to pay a bill or to go in person to pay what you owe in cash.

It is possible now to buy a book, a bond or stock, a TV set, or almost any item you may need while remaining at home. Shopping by computer means that using your terminal you may scan a product catalog, identify the item you need, and authorize the supplier to send the item to you. CompuServe offers its subscribers a shopping catalog listing more than 250,000 brand name products that may be purchased by computer users at a discount.

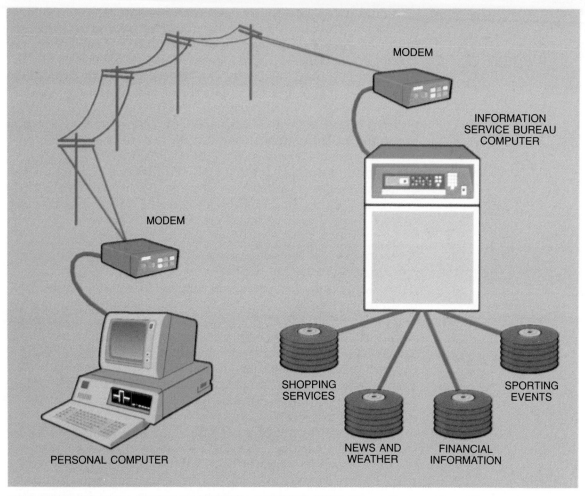

INFORMATION SERVICES OFFERED TO PERSONAL COMPUTER USERS. Information suppliers offer a wide variety of services to personal computer users. These are obtained by accessing databases in the information service bureau computer by using telecommunications.

The planning and making of travel arrangements illustrate another type of transaction processing that can be done by personal computer. Through The Source or CompuServe networks, subscribers can examine hotel guides and advertisements of special travel packages, look up airline schedules and fares, book a room at a hotel, buy an airline ticket, or arrange for a car rental.

Each year the number of information services offered to computer users expands, and the possibilities for future growth of the industry appear almost endless. This is another indication that you are living in the midst of an Information Revolution.

CHECK YOURSELF

Match each phrase with the word or phrase that best defines it.

1. Mail service that uses computers and communications lines for the exchange of messages.
2. Conference of people in different locations by means of a communications network.
3. Electronic device that can transmit a blackboard image to remote locations.
4. Posting of electronic messages to be read by computer users.
5. Dividing computer processing among two or more computers.
6. A two-way information service by telephone or cable TV line.
7. A collection of computerized data organized to permit easy access and retrieval.
8. Conference conducted by computer terminal exchanges of messages.

a. Teleconference
b. Electronic mail
c. Electronic blackboard
d. Distributed data processing (DDP)
e. Telecomputing
f. Database
g. Computer processor
h. Videotex
i. Electronic bulletin board

Answers: (1) b; (2) a; (3) c; (4) i; (5) d; (6) h; (7) f; (8) e.

REVIEW QUESTIONS

1. Give examples of four different types of business needs for data communications facilities.
2. Define the term *on-line inquiry system* and give an example of such a system.
3. What is a communications channel?
4. Describe five types of communications channels and an advantage of each.
5. Explain how data transmission speeds are measured.
6. What are the differences between a simplex channel, a half-duplex channel, and a full-duplex channel?
7. Describe the function of a modem and explain how it gets its name.
8. Explain how an acoustic coupler is used.
9. Give two reasons why computer users with high volumes of data communications may need special sending and receiving equipment.
10. Define the word *network* and explain the difference between a star network and a ring network.
11. Describe how a local area network may be used.

12. Define the term *distributed data processing* and give an example of its use in business.
13. Explain how an electronic mail system works.
14. What is an electronic blackboard and how can it be used in business? In a school?
15. Explain why and how telecomputing is used for conferences.
16. Name three suppliers of information services to personal computer users and the types of services that are offered.
17. Define the term *database* and give an example of a database.
18. What is an electronic bulletin board?
19. Explain how a personal computer may be used for shopping.

COMPARING IDEAS

The questions below are designed to help you think about what you have learned in this chapter. They are "thought" questions. There is no one correct answer.

1. Name five types of communications channels that can be used for the electronic transmission of data, and give an example of a business situation under which each may be the practical choice.
2. Given the assignment of investigating the practicality of operating an electronic mail system among four retail stores (or four schools) in your state, what factors and costs would you have to identify?

INFORMATION PROCESSING ACTIVITIES

Now you can perform many of the information processing activities business workers perform. Below is a summary of the tasks you will complete. You will find the actual data and business forms you need in your *Information Processing Work Kit.*

1. As a data entry clerk for an international oil company, you will help prepare hardware specifications for telecommunications equipment.
2. You will examine current computer hardware to determine what type of data network exists.

SOFTWARE PROJECT

2

USING WORD PROCESSING: 2

As you learned in Part 2, computer systems include specialized methods of data input, storage, processing, and output. As you progress in your information processing career, you will learn to identify and operate a wide variety of computer devices. All of these devices have one purpose—to produce useful business information.

In this software project, you will update a business catalog under the direction of your supervisor. This activity will be very similar to the tasks you might complete in your first information processing job. Sales information is always rapidly changing and represents an area where computers are often used. You should look for the use of word processing techniques in the businesses that you visit.

The Video-II-Go video tape rental store is very pleased with the results of its word processed (personalized) letters to prospective members. The membership list is growing every day. Pat Brown now wants to begin a new service by mailing a Customer Service List to members each month. This list will contain "New Releases" and "Top Five Videos."

Each time a new video tape is purchased, it is given a rental number and added to the master list of video tapes. Now that Video-II-Go has a computer system with word processing software, producing a list of new releases will be much easier. It is also important to keep the list as current as possible since the other video stores are competing for Pat's customers.

INFORMATION PROCESSING PROBLEM

This business needs to update a list of new releases (in catalog format) as quickly and easily as possible.

INFORMATION PROCESSING SOLUTION

This task can be performed using a microcomputer and the existing word processing software application package.

The following listing of video tapes was typed by Pat Brown last month, duplicated and given out to customers who entered the store. As you can see, this data represents a substantial amount of input data. In particular, the "Top Five Videos" section must be revised to reflect the popularity of each tape during the previous month. Note that entries have been made on the previous month's listing to help you prepare the listing for the coming month. Tapes are dropped from the "New Releases" list after they have been listed for two months.

```
    VIEO-II-GO                                    CUSTOMER SERVICE LIST

                                New Releases

              Title                        Tape No.          Daily Rate

         All Quiet For Now                  T602               2.00
         Before You Say Goodbye             T512               2.00
  Drop   Fitness For All                    T506               1.50
         Kiddie Corner                      T601                .99
         Superdome II                       T603               2.00
         Tax Preparation Video Guide        T604               1.50
  Drop   The Connection                     T503               2.00
  Drop   Wait for Summer                    T501               2.00
         Zest                               T509               2.00

                            Top Five Videos


         Reserve these titles early.

                    1.   Wildfire II             T405
                    2.   Space Chase             T408
                    3.   Suspicion of Guilt      T412
                    4.   Make it Happen          T511
                    5.   Wait for Summer         T501
```

The following video tapes were purchased during the month. They should be added to the "New Releases" section in alphabetical order.

```
    VIDEO-II-GO                                      NEW PURCHASES

                    Title            Tape No.    Copies    Price/Day

              Smiling                  T701        1         2.00
              Banbury Clock            T702        1         2.00
              Awesome Dawn             T703        2         2.00
              Aerobics for Fun         T704        2         1.50
    COMPLETED BY ____T. C.____              DATE ___April 9___
```

KEYBOARDING ACTIVITIES

1. Enter the sample Customer Service List data using available microcomputer hardware and a word processing software package. You should not enter the video tape titles that have been deleted.
2. Update the listing by adding the data for the new purchases (in alphabetical order) from the New Purchases list.
3. The tape rental data for the end of this month is as follows:

Title	Number of Rentals
Suspicion of Guilt	43
Wildfire II	38
Wait for Summer	33
Space Chase	31
Make it Happen	28

Update the "Top Five Videos" section of the listing to indicate the new favorites.
4. The price for renting tape No. T604 has been reduced. The daily rate should be changed to $.99.
5. Print a copy of the finalized customer service list and submit it to your supervisor for approval or revision.

ENRICHMENT ACTIVITIES

1. If your software allows the merging of text into an existing file, add the finalized customer service list to one of the letters produced in Software Project 1. Modify the letter to indicate that a sample video tape listing is enclosed. Produce a sample new customer letter with new releases and submit it to your supervisor.
2. Create a *master list* of all video tape data now on the computer by moving data until the listing is in ascending numerical order by tape number. Do not reenter any data; use the copy or move function. Include the tape number, title, and rental price on your master list.

PART 3

3

COMPUTER INFORMATION SYSTEMS

CHAPTER

8

INFORMATION SYSTEMS FOR BUSINESS AND PERSONAL COMPUTER USERS

Information Processing Technology

Information system
Procedure
Inventory
Accounts receivable
Accounts payable
General ledger
Income statement
Balance sheet
Integrated system
Management
 information system
 (MIS)

Decision support system
 (DSS)
"What if?" decision
 making
Business modeling
Administrative support
 system
Electronic calendar
Desktop publishing
Computer-aided design
 (CAD)

Computer-aided
 manufacturing (CAM)
Robotics
Debit card
Computer-assisted
 instruction (CAI)
Simulation
Special interest group
 (SIG)

Performance Goals

☐ Define the terms *information system, procedure,* and *integrated system.*

☐ Give the reasons why accounting systems were the first business systems to be computerized, and identify six such systems.

☐ Explain the purpose of a management information system, a decision support system, "what if?" decision making, and business modeling.

☐ Define the term *administrative support system,* and give four examples of such systems.

☐ Describe the use of computer-aided design (CAD) and computer-aided manufacturing (CAM) systems.

☐ Describe four different kinds of specialized information systems.

☐ Name four types of uses for home personal computers, and give two examples of each.

The computer is so widely used now that hardly a day passes without it affecting your life. If you go to a library to borrow a book or video cassette, shop at a supermarket, make a purchase in a department store, fly on an airplane, deposit money in a bank, pick up a hamburger at a fast-food restaurant, or take a college entrance exam, you will probably make a transaction that a computer has to process. In this chapter you will learn about many of the typical uses of business and personal computers.

THE NEED FOR INFORMATION SYSTEMS

As you read earlier, the purpose of information processing in business is to produce information that can be used to: (1) operate a business, (2) satisfy outside needs for information about the business, and (3) make plans about future business activities. Whether a business is large or small, its owners or managers must develop a system for meeting these information needs in a step-by-step manner. Your telephone company, for example, must have a systematic means of identifying the long distance calls you make and recording for each call both the destination point and the number of minutes you talked. Even the owner of a very small business must have a system for keeping track of his or her business transactions, such as the quantity of items that are sold and the selling price and cost of each item.

An **information system** is a collection of the specific human and machine efforts required to produce information about a particular business activity. A billing information system, for example, consists of the many manual and machine operations that must be performed to bill customers. Often the word *application* is used interchangeably with the term *information system*. For example, a billing information system may be called a *billing application.*

Within each system, the operations to be performed are usually grouped into one or more procedures. A **procedure** defines the step-by-step manual and machine operations that must be performed to accomplish a particular task within a system.

A large information system, such as payroll, contains a number of different procedures, each one defining the series of operations required for a specific task within the system. One procedure in a payroll system, for example, defines the steps required for recording time worked by each employee during the pay period. Another payroll procedure defines all the operations that payroll clerks and the computer must perform to prepare payroll checks. The steps in these payroll procedures are followed each pay period. This systematic way of handling payroll information ensures that employee checks are prepared accurately and on time.

BUSINESS INFORMATION SYSTEMS

Every business has a number of different information systems. Each is designed to produce information about a particular activity in the business. You will find similar information systems in many different businesses. Business accounting systems, for example, are found in almost every type of business organization, small or large.

BUSINESS ACCOUNTING SYSTEMS

The first business system operated on a computer was a payroll system. This system was installed in 1954 by the General Electric Company. Shortly after that, a large utility company in New York City started to use a computer for customer billing. Since then, in most companies, computerization has started with payroll, billing, and other accounting systems. There are good reasons for this. Payroll, billing, and most of the other accounting systems involve a large number of repetitive operations. With the help of computers, these operations can be accomplished much faster and more accurately, and usually at a lower cost.

Before computers were available, these repetitive operations had to be done by hand. Imagine the difficulty of keeping track of, summarizing, and storing all the information on sales, expenses, and all the other factors involved in running a business. Business managers were quick to realize that by computerizing many of these operations, the work could be accomplished much faster, more accurately, and less expensively than by any other means.

Because accounting systems were the first applications to be computerized, they are often considered routine. Nevertheless, they are still important computer activities in every company. There are six key business accounting systems, which handle the following functions:

- Customer order entry and billing
- Inventory management
- Payroll
- General ledger accounting
- Accounts receivable
- Purchasing and accounts payable

The objectives of each of these systems and a sample of the system outputs are shown in the illustration on pages 191–193.

CUSTOMER ORDER ENTRY AND BILLING

Primary Purposes of System:
To record an incoming customer order, authorize shipment of merchandise ordered by a customer (or to provide the services that are requested), and produce a bill (customer invoice) to send a customer who does not pay in advance.

All businesses try to enter customer orders promptly and ship the ordered merchandise as soon as possible. Once this is done, the customer can be billed. Billing is done with a customer invoice. As shown in the example, an invoice typically lists the number and price of each item and the total amount to be paid by the customer.

CUSTOMER INVOICE

GOOD TIMEſ PAPER COMPANY
610 West 23d Street
New York, NY 10011

Sold To
CONSUMER NOTES
950 JEFFERSON DRIVE
WASHINGTON, DC 20560

Account No. 84239

Invoice Date 11/15/-

Terms of Sale 30 DAYS

Late Payments 1.5 PERCENT INTEREST

Item Number	Item Description	Transaction Code	Quantity	Unit Price	Total Price
401	WRITING PAPER	1	12	12.00	144.00
225	DESK CALENDARS	1	10	7.50	75.00
334	DESK SETS	1	24	50.00	1,200.00
				TOTAL	1,419.00
			SHIPPING CHARGES		15.00
Please pay this amount.					1,434.00

Transaction Codes

1. Charges
2. Payments
3. Credit Memos
4. Miscellaneous Debits
5. Miscellaneous Credits
6. Returned Check

INVENTORY MANAGEMENT SYSTEM

Primary Purposes of System:
To keep accurate track of the number of each product or (supply item) on hand and to help management determine whether the amounts on hand are adequate to fulfill the expected sales.

The number kept on hand of each product is that product's inventory. Since any inventory or combination of inventories represents a financial investment, the owner or manager wants to keep inventories as low as possible. The objective is to have just enough items to fill customers' orders but not so many as to create excess or unsaleable supplies. A computer print-out such as that shown to the right helps management achieve these objectives.

INVENTORY MANAGEMENT REPORT

INVENTORY MANAGEMENT REPORT

GOOD TIMES PAPER COMPANY   03 31 19--

PRODUCT CODE NO.	PRODUCT DESCRIPTION	BALANCE ON HAND	REORDER POINT	NET INV. POSITION	OPEN ORDERS	NET AVAIL. INV.
1201	BIRTHDAY CARDS	8,713	5,000	3,713		3,713
1202	NOTE PADS	2,401	5,000	-2,599		-2,599
1203	PLACE CARDS	1,205	1,000	205		205
1204	NOTEPAPER	20,405	10,000	10,405		10,405
1205	CONGRATULATORY CARDS	5,880	6,000	-120	5,000	4,880
1206	SYMPATHY CARDS	3,110	2,000	1,110		1,110
1207	THANK-YOU NOTES	105,210	100,000	5,210		5,210
1208	ANNOUNCEMENT CARDS	15,712	15,000	712		712
1209	ANNIVERSARY CARDS	12,400	20,000	-7,600	15,000	7,400
1210	GIFT CARDS	300	1,000	-700	500	-200
1211	AIRMAIL PAPER	14,251	10,000	4,251	10,000	14,251

EXAMPLES OF BUSINESS ACCOUNTING SYSTEMS.

PAYROLL SYSTEM

Primary Purpose of System:
To pay employees for their services.

Every business has additional payroll obligations. Employees must be given accurate statements detailing regular and overtime earnings and all deductions made from gross pay (see example.) Reports on employee deductions for taxes must be prepared for federal, state, and local agencies including a quarterly report on social security taxes. Because the payroll is usually the largest operating expense of a business, a payroll system also is designed to produce many analyses of payroll costs, such as the breakdown of payroll expense by product line.

PAYROLL CHECK AND REGISTER EARNINGS STATEMENT

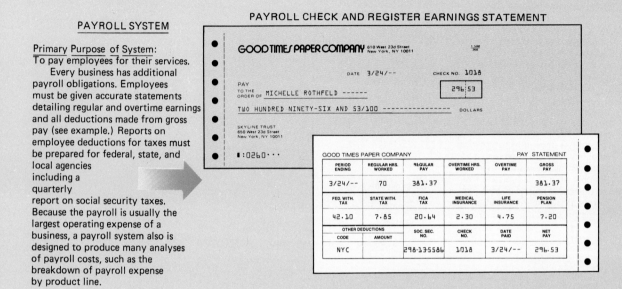

GOOD TIMES PAPER COMPANY 610 West 23d Street New York, NY 10011

DATE 3/24/--   CHECK NO. 1018

PAY TO THE ORDER OF MICHELLE ROTHFELD ------   296│53

TWO HUNDRED NINETY-SIX AND 53/100 ---------------- DOLLARS

SKYLINE TRUST
650 West 23d Street
New York, NY 10011

⑆:0260···

GOOD TIMES PAPER COMPANY   PAY STATEMENT

PERIOD ENDING	REGULAR HRS. WORKED	REGULAR PAY	OVERTIME HRS. WORKED	OVERTIME PAY	GROSS PAY
3/24/--	70	381.37			381.37

FED. WITH. TAX	STATE WITH. TAX	FICA TAX	MEDICAL INSURANCE	LIFE INSURANCE	PENSION PLAN
42.10	7.85	20.64	2.30	4.75	7.20

OTHER DEDUCTIONS		SOC. SEC. NO.	CHECK NO.	DATE PAID	NET PAY
CODE	AMOUNT				
NYC		298-13-5586	1018	3/24/--	296.53

GENERAL LEDGER ACCOUNTING SYSTEM

Primary Purposes of System:
To keep track of how much money a business makes and how much the business is worth.

The financial transactions of a business are summarized by a general ledger system. One output from the system is called an income statement. As illustrated, this statements lists the major sources of income, the major items of expense, and the net income (or loss) earned by the company for the month and cumulatively year-to-date. A balance sheet report summarizes what business owns (its assets) and what a business owes to others (its liabilities). The balance sheet gives a picture of the net worth of the business, the difference between the assets and liabilities.

INCOME STATEMENT

Month Ended December 31, 19XX

Revenue		
Fees		18,300 00
Expenses		
Salaries Expense	10,100 00	
Utilities Expense	300 00	
Supplies Expense	1,250 00	
Rent Expense	5,000 00	
Depreciation Expense—Equipment	500 00	
Total Expenses		17,150 00
Net Income for the Month		1,150 00

EXAMPLES OF BUSINESS ACCOUNTING SYSTEMS (*cont'd*).

ACCOUNTS RECEIVABLE SYSTEM

Primary Purposes of System:
To keep an accurate record of the amount owed by each customer and to aid management to follow-up customers for overdue payments.

In business, the term used for the money customers owe for products or services is called accounts receivable. An accounts receivable system keeps track of the amounts owed and paid by customers. Because about 90% of all transactions in the U.S. is done on credit, a good accounts receivable system is important to most businesses. Such a system usually produces as output a monthly report listing all overdue amounts broken down by the length of the overdue period as shown here.

AGED ACCOUNTS RECEIVABLE REPORT

December 31, 19XX

ACCOUNT WITH	BALANCE		CURRENT		PAST DUE—DAYS 1–30		31–60		OVER 60	
Anton, Janet	180	00	180	00						
Ardath, Robert	210	00			150	00	60	00		
Aston, Thomas	104	00							104	00
Baltus, Ida	80	00	80	00						
Barton, Leslie	62	00	42	00	20	00				
Bender, Harold	225	00	85	00	100	00	40	00		
Benson, Mary	48	00					32	00	16	00
(All Other Accounts)	10,748	00	9,075	00	1,050	00	360	00	263	00
Totals	11,657	00	9,462	00	1,320	00	492	00	383	00

ACCOUNTS PAYABLE SYSTEM

Primary Purposes of System:
To keep track of the amounts the business owes to others and to produce checks to pay these amounts.

To operate businesses' purchase of supplies, equipment, and other materials and services. Although some small purchases may be made in cash, most companies charge their purchases. When a business does not pay for purchases in cash, it must record the amount that is charged as an accounts payable in an accounts payable system.

The illustrated report helps management to determine the bills which must be paid by a given date to maintain a good credit rating for the company.

CURRENT ACCOUNTS PAYABLE REPORT

January 31, 19XX

NAME OF CREDITOR		DUE DATE	BALANCE	
Active Paper Goods		2-15-XX	310	00
Best Products Corporation		2-20-XX	275	00
Chase Company		2-7-XX	1,450	00
Miller Distributing Company		2-10-XX	1,130	00
Total			3,165	00

EXAMPLES OF BUSINESS ACCOUNTING SYSTEMS (*cont'd*).

INTEGRATED SYSTEMS

Often data produced in one system is used in another system. For example, data about merchandise sold to customers is typically used in the customer order entry and billing system of a business and in its inventory management system. Computers provide the means of sharing data among systems. Computer systems that share the same data are said to be **integrated systems.** In Chapter 11 you will read more about computer software that is used to integrate accounting and other systems.

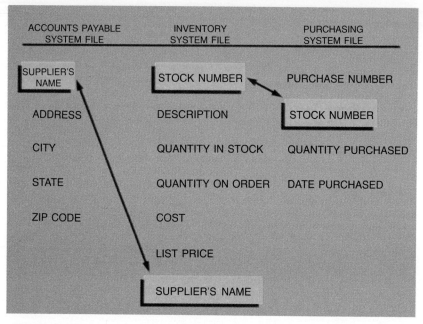

ACCOUNTS PAYABLE SYSTEM FILE	INVENTORY SYSTEM FILE	PURCHASING SYSTEM FILE
SUPPLIER'S NAME	STOCK NUMBER	PURCHASE NUMBER
ADDRESS	DESCRIPTION	STOCK NUMBER
CITY	QUANTITY IN STOCK	QUANTITY PURCHASED
STATE	QUANTITY ON ORDER	DATE PURCHASED
ZIP CODE	COST	
	LIST PRICE	
	SUPPLIER'S NAME	

INTEGRATED SYSTEM FILES. Integrated systems are computer systems that share the same data.

CHECK YOURSELF

Match each phrase with the word or term that best defines it.

1. Systems that share data.
2. First business system to be computerized.
3. Report of income and expenses.
4. Amount of product kept on hand.
5. Operations that accomplish a specific task in a system.
6. Human and machine efforts required to produce information about a specific business activity.
7. System to keep track of how much a business makes and what it is worth.
8. Report of what a company owns and what it owes to others.
9. Document to bill customers who do not pay in advance.
10. Amounts owed to a business by its customers.

   a. Payroll
   b. Balance sheet
   c. Inventory
   d. Customer invoice
   e. General ledger
   f. Information system
   g. Income statement
   h. Procedure
   i. Accounts receivable
   j. Payroll check
   k. Integrated systems
   l. Aged trial balance

Answers: (1) k; (2) a; (3) g; (4) c; (5) h; (6) f; (7) e; (8) b; (9) d; (10) i.

After key accounting systems are computerized, a business usually develops management information systems and decision support systems.

Management Information Systems. The first type of a computer system designed for management is called a **management information system** (MIS). The purpose of a management information system is to help management direct, assess, and plan business operations.

Initially, many computer experts attempted to design one MIS system for an entire business. The objective of the system was to provide information about all aspects of the business to all levels of management. The experts soon recognized that because different managers required different types of information, a single MIS system for a business would not be able to meet the needs of all the different users. For this reason, many companies now have a number of different management information systems to satisfy the needs of the various managers.

The owner or president of a large discount store, for example, wants information that shows how the entire business is running—what the total product sales are, whether the total expenses are under control, and whether other goals of the business are being met. In contrast, managers who work for the top executive need detailed information about what is happening in the departments for which they are responsible. For example, the manager of the store's television department needs detailed

Courtesy Honeywell, Inc. *Courtesy Sperry Corporation.*

MANAGEMENT INFORMATION SYSTEM (MIS). A management information system is a computer system designed to assist management with the direction, assessment, and planning of business operations. The output from a management information system may take the form of hard copy reports as shown in the illustration at the left or be displayed on a terminal screen as shown at the right.

information about the sales of different TV models and how these compare with sales objectives. On the other hand, the manager of the kitchen appliance department is interested in data about sales of refrigerators, microwaves, and other cooking appliances.

In a typical MIS system, information may be reported at daily, weekly, or monthly intervals. The information is usually provided to managers as a standardized printed report, though it may be displayed on a computer output terminal in tabular or graphic form.

Decision Support Systems. In the 1970s, a second type of computer system was developed to aid business management. The newer systems, called **decision support systems** (DSS), are interactive computer systems.

Using a decision support system, a manager is able to get the information needed to assess and plan a business activity when he or she needs the information. The manager retrieves the information directly from a DSS database. The information is displayed in tabular or graphic form on a computer terminal, but hard copies of the displayed material can be printed.

Decision support systems permit a manager to test the impact that alternative actions might have on the business. For example, the management of a large chain of motels tested on a computer the likely results of lowering room rates. They found that reducing the daily rates by 15 percent would cause more people to stay at the motels. The net result would be more revenues, a higher occupancy rate, and higher profits. Testing the

CURRENT QUOTES ENHANCED //CQE

HON SY IBM DEC HWP

STOCK	BID CLOSE	ASKED OPEN	HIGH	LOW	LAST	VOL (100'S)
HON	57 1/8	57 1/4	57 3/8	56 7/8	57 1/4	1283
SY	51 1/4	51	51 1/2	50 5/8	50 5/8	2360
IBM	128 5/8	128 1/4	128 5/8	128 1/8	128 1/4	6134
DEC	103 3/8	103	103 1/2	102 7/8	103	2073
HWP	34	33 7/8	34 3/8	33 3/4	33 7/8	3663

NEWS AVAILABLE FOR HWP 2:10PM

DECISION SUPPORT SYSTEM (DSS). A decision support system is a type of computer software system designed to aid management in its decision-making. The stock price figures displayed on the terminal screen shown here aids an investment manager in making decisions about the buying and selling of stocks. *Courtesy Dow Jones and Company.*

impact of alternative actions, such as changes in room rates, is called **"what if?" decision making** in business. The assessing and planning of future business policies can be greatly aided by decision support systems that permit a manager to do such analyses.

Another technique, called **business modeling,** allows a manager to predict the future of the business under different conditions. For example, managers can predict change in sales if the population of particular western states increases, as forecasted, while the population of certain midwestern states decreases or remains the same. Using historical data for the company, the manager can project the future effect on company sales of such changes in population or changes in many other factors, such as the cost of raw materials, foreign competition, or new tax laws.

Databases are needed to implement decision support systems. Often, businesses rely on databases provided by information suppliers for general economic, financial, and business information. You read about such information providers in Chapter 7. A variety of software packages are also available to assist businesses in implementing decision support systems. You will learn about these in Chapter 11.

ADMINISTRATIVE SUPPORT SYSTEMS

Computer systems that automate office functions more fully are called **administrative support systems.** Such systems are typically designed to handle typing, editing, printing, collating, mail delivery, and record storage and retrieval functions. Computerization of these activities can reduce office paperwork and increase office productivity.

Word Processing and Electronic Mail. In an earlier chapter, you read about the development of word processing equipment and software that more fully automates typing operations. This equipment provides a means of revising or adding to typed material at a later time. Word processing provides a more flexible and efficient means of creating, storing, retrieving, revising, and printing correspondence, contracts, proposals, reports, and other documents. When mailing lists are maintained in word processing systems, personalized letters can easily be prepared for selected names on the lists.

When computer terminals (or individual personal computers) are available at individual work stations, each individual can do word processing when necessary. In addition, the terminal can be used for other applications, such as the electronic mail service you read about in Chapter 7. This permits the electronic exchange of messages between individuals both inside and outside an organization. It reduces the need for paper correspon-

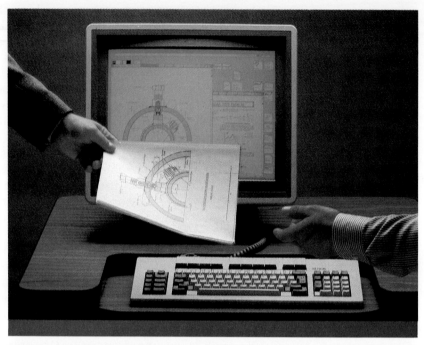

DESKTOP PUBLISHING SYSTEM. New desktop publishing hardware and software allow a user to combine text and graphics to produce professional-looking documents. *Courtesy Xerox Corporation.*

DESKTOP PUBLISHING OUTPUT. More and more business newsletters are being produced using desktop publishing software and laser-jet printers.

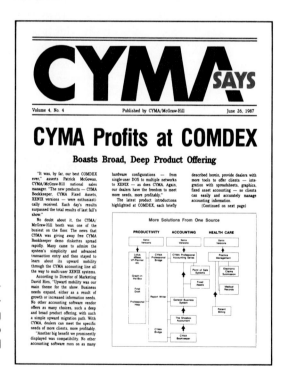

dence and mail delivery service. Often, an **electronic calendar** service is associated with word processing and electronic mail systems. The purpose of electronic calendars is to keep track, by computer, of the daily appointments for individual managers and of the meetings and conferences that are scheduled to be held in the office.

Desktop Publishing. In the mid-1980s, a new type of administrative support system, called desktop publishing, was introduced. **Desktop** (or electronic) **publishing** is the process of creating on a personal computer a document that looks like a professionally designed and printed document.

It is possible for an individual with a desktop publishing system to produce a high-quality advertising promotion piece, a newsletter, a manual, or even a 400-page book. Different sizes and styles of typefaces are available to the system user. Specialized software for a microcomputer and laser printer instructs the computer to size and insert photos, graphics, and line drawings into the text copy. Desktop publishing systems are popular because they reduce the time and expense in text composition, design, and paste-up operations.

PRODUCT DESIGN AND MANUFACTURING CONTROL SYSTEMS

The application of computer technology to factory work and manufacturing followed the use of computers in offices, and productivity in the factory has improved dramatically through the use of computers. Factories use computers in two major ways: to aid in the design of products and to manage and control the manufacturing process.

Computer-Aided Design. In the mid-1960s, engineers at General Motors worked with computer programming specialists at IBM to develop a system that would simplify the process of preparing engineering drawings of all the parts that go into each automobile model. The result was the first **computer-aided design** (CAD) system. A CAD system allows an engineer to design products, machines, and buildings on a computer video screen rather than on paper. The designer can refine the drawing as many times as necessary.

More advanced CAD systems allow a designer to enlarge or reduce any part of the object. The video screen provides a three-dimensional image of the object, which can be rotated to check side views or views from the top or bottom. Some CAD systems allow the designer to animate the part, or simulate the motions the real product or part will need to do. The designer can see whether the part will work as expected before the machine is built, saving both money and time.

COMPUTER-AIDED DESIGN (CAD). A designer can design and refine products, machines, and buildings on a computer screen rather than on paper. In this illustration a product designer at Daimler-Benz is using a CAD/CAM system for designing an automobile. *Courtesy IBM Corporation.*

General Motors estimated that the use of CAD systems cut in half the time required to design an automobile. The use of CAD systems spread quickly to the aviation and other industries. Now, many architects who design buildings and room interiors generate their drawings by computer instead of drawing pencil sketches. With a computer, the architect has to draw only one seat in a school auditorium. The computer draws in all the other seats and provides a perspective of how they look from all angles. Fashion designers also use CAD systems to develop drawings of coats, dresses, and even shoes.

Computer-Aided Manufacturing. In the 1980s considerable progress has been made in using computers to manage and control manufacturing processes. **Computer-aided manufacturing** (CAM) systems help factory managers in two ways. First, computer systems can be designed to schedule all factory activities required to produce a product when needed. IBM, for example, uses computers to schedule all the labor steps and material requirements necessary to finish construction of a mainframe computer by the date it is to be shipped to a customer.

Computers can also be used to direct and control the operation of a factory machine so that it produces a part exactly according to the specifications provided by a CAD system. Other CAM systems are designed to direct machines to assemble a

ROBOTS. Robots, which are controlled by computers, can be made to perform manufacturing tasks, such as testing computer hardware (at left) or welding motorbike parts (at right).

group of parts, weld the parts together to form an automobile body, and then spray-paint the body.

Designers of high school and college class rings use a CAD/CAM system first to design the ring, then to manufacture the molds used to cast the rings. The computerized design of the ring can be rotated, shown from any direction, enlarged or shrunk, and modified in any way necessary to develop a final design. Another program is used to take the design from the CAD system and control a computerized milling machine to automatically produce the mold needed to make the ring. The drawing can be stored in computer memory and later retrieved as often as necessary to be altered. Whenever desired, copies of the drawing can be printed.

An exciting form of CAM is **robotics,** the use of robots controlled by computer to perform the same work humans do. Robots are now used to perform many jobs that are too monotonous or too dangerous for humans: for example, lifting heavy loads of material, welding aircraft or automobile bodies, or removing red-hot materials from furnaces or polluted materials

Chapter 8: Information Systems for Business and Personal Computer Users   201

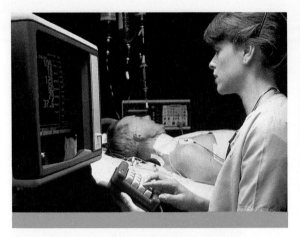

ELECTRONIC PATIENT MONITORING SYSTEM. Doctors in hospitals use computers to monitor a patient's progress and check on the effect of medical tests and drugs (at left). At right, monitoring systems are checked periodically at the nurse's station. *Courtesy Hewlett-Packard Company.*

from nuclear plants. Robots usually have arms and hands that are controlled by computer systems. Also, a computer-controlled camera placed inside a robot gives it the ability to recognize different objects. Sensors within its hands give the robot the ability to gauge the temperature, weight, or strength of the materials it is handling. The technology of robotics is rapidly being improved, and the applications are expanding. You will read more about new developments in this field in Chapter 14.

Computer-Integrated Manufacturing. A **computer-integrated manufacturing** (CIM) system connects and integrates all the manufacturing tasks in a typical factory so that the process can be automated and controlled from a central computer system. Apple Computer Company uses hundreds of Macintoshes networked together to monitor and control the manufacture of Macintosh computers. Oil refineries use CIM to monitor and control the entire process of turning crude oil into various petroleum products, all from a control center.

SPECIALIZED INDUSTRY INFORMATION SYSTEMS

In addition to the widely used systems already described, hundreds of specialized systems have been designed for particular types of businesses. These often involve specially designed equipment in addition to computers. Examples of these have been cited in earlier chapters; for example, the use of specialized input scanners in supermarkets to read product code numbers. In this chapter you will read about specialized information systems developed for four diverse industries—medicine, banking, law enforcement, and education.

The medical profession has begun to use computers more and more to aid in the care of patients. Both hospitals and individual physicians use computer systems to keep track of the medical histories of their patients and to bill them for the services provided. Hospitals also need other administrative systems to maintain up-to-date inventory records of various supplies, including the inventory available in their blood banks, the amount and type of drugs in storage, and the type of equipment available.

More specialized computer systems have been developed to help doctors and nurses diagnose patient illnesses and monitor their conditions. A physician may call on a computer to evaluate possible causes of symptoms reported by a patient, such as dizziness or chest pains, and to interpret the results of blood pressure, x-ray, and other types of tests. Through special sensors attached to a critically ill patient and a computer, a nurse is able to monitor the patient's temperature, blood pressure, heartbeat rate, and other conditions. Once patients are hooked up to the system, the computer will issue a warning signal at the nurses' station if it senses a change in any patient's condition.

Computers are used in many types of specialized medical equipment, such as magnetic resonance images (MRI), computer axial tomography (CAT) scanners, and portable heart monitors. Both MRI and CAT scanners take thousands of electronic pictures of the body or the head or the leg; then a computer processes this data and creates a three-dimensional image of the body. This allows the doctor to diagnose the patient's condition more accurately and to plan surgery and treatment better. Portable heart monitors have built-in computers that detect, record, and report abnormal heart conditions; the doctor can use this information to treat the patient more effectively.

Computers will never replace doctors or nurses, but they free medical workers from some of the more time-consuming routine work, leaving more time for treating difficult cases and tending to other patients' needs. In the process, health care should become more reliable and less costly.

Banks are large users of computers. Many examples of computerized banking have already been cited. The recording of deposits and withdrawals, calculation of interest earned on savings accounts, and updating of customer loan records for repayments are only a few of the tasks done by computers in a bank.

One of the first specialized industry computer systems was developed for the banking industry. It was developed to record and sort the billions of bank checks that must be processed

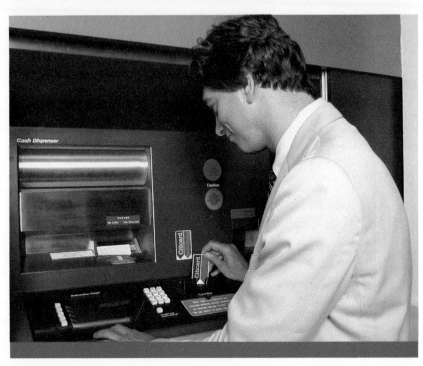

AUTOMATIC TELLER MACHINE (ATM). A customer can now take care of many bank transactions 24 hours a day without the aid of a teller. *Courtesy CitiBank.*

daily. The task is done by the magnetic ink character input equipment that you read about in Chapter 4.

A recent advance in computerized banking systems provides 24-hour banking service to customers. Specially designed automatic tellers connected to a bank's computer are placed outside the bank building, in shopping centers, or in supermarkets. At any time of day, seven days a week, a customer may insert his or her plastic bank card in the machine, key in an identification code and the amount of cash to be withdrawn, and push a button to withdraw the money from the machine.

Banks are promoting a new computerized service: the use of bank **debit cards** for payments of purchases. A customer may use a bank debit card to pay for purchases at designated supermarket checkout counters or in stores. As soon as a supermarket or store cashier uses a debit card to ring up a purchase, the amount of the sale is deducted from the customer's bank account and added to the account of the supermarket or store. If the customer had used a credit card instead of the debit card, he or she would normally receive by mail a bill for the purchase, which would then have to be paid in cash or by check. Think of the work saved by debit card use.

LAW ENFORCEMENT DATA NETWORK. Police use computer terminals in their cars to check with the main computer for stolen car reports or other violations of the law.

LAW ENFORCEMENT

The U.S. government, an early user of computers, first processed population data with them at the Bureau of Census. Since then, the federal government has become the largest user of computers in the country. Checking of tax returns, preparation of Social Security checks, keeping track of military supply inventories, and forecasting of weather are only a few of the uses of computers in government.

Computers are also being used to aid law enforcement efforts throughout the country. The FBI's National Crime Information Center (NCIC), located in Washington, D.C., maintains a computer system that can be used by police units in all states. The heart of the NCIC system is an up-to-date database containing nationwide information on stolen property, criminals, and missing persons. Through a communications network, police stations in each state equipped with computer terminals are linked to NCIC. Local law enforcement officers may access this database.

Suppose, for example, a police officer in a patrol car in New Jersey stops a speeding car from Texas for a traffic violation. The officer immediately notifies police headquarters by radio communication of the car's license plate number and the driver's name and license identification. Using the computer terminal, a police officer at headquarters immediately sends an inquiry to the NCIC database to determine whether the automobile is on the list of stolen vehicles and whether the

COMPUTER-ASSISTED INSTRUCTION (CAI). With computer-assisted instruction, the student interacts with the computer, which has been programmed to present a particular course of study. *Courtesy Apple Computers.*

driver is wanted by the police. The inquiry is answered within seconds, and the information is then transmitted to the patrol car so the officer on the scene can take the proper action.

EDUCATION

Initially, educational institutions used computers for administrative tasks, such as the scheduling of classes, scoring of tests, and maintenance of student grade records. Now attention is focused on the use of computers to aid the teaching and learning process.

The term **computer-assisted instruction** (CAI) means the use of computers to help a student learn. CAI does not mean teaching students about computers, though that may be one of the instructional programs. CAI is a system of individualized instruction that uses a computer to assist the instructor. Using a computer terminal, a student interacts with the computer, which has been programmed to present a particular course of study—for example, math, spelling, or geography. Under a CAI program, each student works individually with a computer at his or her desired pace. The computer assigns material to learn and then quizzes the student about this material, giving feedback and direction when the student has not fully mastered the material.

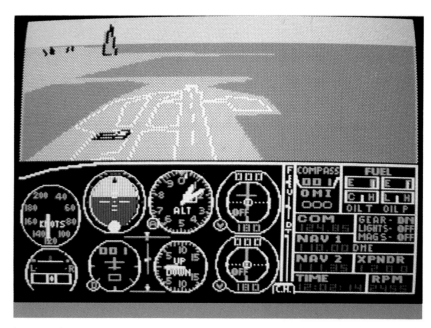

SIMULATION. By using a real-life computerized model, simulated programs can help train employees to react under certain conditions. A flight simulation pattern, as shown here, can teach a pilot how to land a plane. *Direct Positive Imagery.*

CAI instructional programs originally concentrated on drill and practice exercises, such as math problems. Now, CAI is used for a variety of courses in educational institutions ranging from preschools to universities. Industry also uses CAI programs to train employees. CAI programs can train employees how to sell more effectively, how to run a factory, or how to use a particular piece of computer hardware or software. Utilities use CAI to train operators of nuclear power plants how to handle emergencies. At home, a personal computer user may learn to read a foreign language through a CAI instructional program.

Another educational technique that uses computers is called simulation. In computer terminology, **simulation** means representing the behavior of a system in a real-life situation by a computerized model. Computer simulation programs were developed first to aid in the instruction of airplane pilots. Through displays on a computer screen of what a pilot actually flying an aircraft would see, a student pilot can be taught how to fly and land the plane under certain conditions.

Computer simulation techniques are now used for driver training, ship pilot training, train engineer education, and many other occupational training programs. Obviously, in all these activities it is safer, and usually cheaper, to learn how to react to particular dangerous situations at a computer terminal than to learn in life itself. Simulation techniques also help teachers explain basic concepts in science and math. How gravity works, for example, can be illustrated on a computer screen.

Earlier, you read about business modeling that permits managers to test the potential impact of alternative actions. A business model is a form of simulation.

CHECK YOURSELF

Match each phrase with the words or term that best defines it.

1. Testing the impact of alternative business actions.
2. The process of creating quality printing with a personal computer.
3. Drawing images on a computer screen.
4. The system that helps management direct, assess, and plan.
5. A computer record of appointments and meetings.
6. An interactive type of management information system.
7. The use of computers to help a student learn.
8. The system that helps factory managers schedule and make products.
9. Using machines that are operated by computers to perform work.
10. Bank cards that can be used to pay for purchases.

a. Electronic calendar
b. Decision support system
c. Desktop publishing
d. CAD
e. MIS
f. "What if?" decision making
g. CAM
h. Debit cards
i. Robotics
j. NCIC
k. CAI

Answers: (1) f; (2) c; (3) d; (4) e; (5) a; (6) b; (7) k; (8) g; (9) i; (10) h.

SYSTEMS FOR HOME PERSONAL COMPUTERS

Many of the typical business systems described in this chapter are now operated on personal computers. By 1986 about three-quarters of American businesses employing more than 100 employees were using personal computers. Some of the largest companies, such as General Motors and General Electric, were using as many as 20,000 personal computers. Many of these, of course, are linked by communications networks to each other and/or to mainframe computers.

Millions of personal computers are also installed in homes. Some of these are used by doctors, lawyers, landlords, stockbrokers, insurance agents, accountants, writers, and other individuals who are self-employed and maintain offices in their homes. Others are used by parents for work and education or by

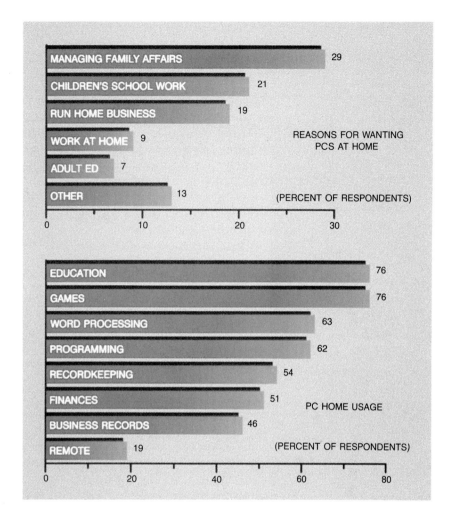

MANAGING FAMILY AFFAIRS 29
CHILDREN'S SCHOOL WORK 21
RUN HOME BUSINESS 19
WORK AT HOME 9
ADULT ED 7
OTHER 13

REASONS FOR WANTING
PCS AT HOME

(PERCENT OF RESPONDENTS)

0   10   20   30

EDUCATION 76
GAMES 76
WORD PROCESSING 63
PROGRAMMING 62
RECORDKEEPING 54
FINANCES 51
BUSINESS RECORDS 46
REMOTE 19

PC HOME USAGE

(PERCENT OF RESPONDENTS)

0   20   40   60   80

USE OF PERSONAL COM-PUTERS AT HOME. Shown is the results of a 1987 survey conducted to find out why people wanted PCs at home and how PCs were being used at home. While in-home PCs are still mostly used for education and entertainment, an increasing number are being bought for office and home work-related tasks. *Survey by C&SN/SRI Research.*

students to write reports, learn a language, or play games. A wide choice of systems exists to meet the needs of these people, including systems to handle billing, inventory, accounts receivable, accounts payable, payroll, general ledger, word processing, and graphics design.

Nowadays many farmers also have computer systems. For example, the owners of Underwood Ranches, a large grower of vegetables in California, use a personal computer to keep track of the harvest yields of various crops. Midwest dairy farmers maintain records on their computers of each cow's milk production.

COMPUTER GAMES

According to a survey taken in 1986, home personal computers are often used for entertainment, specifically the playing of electronic games. Playing computer games on a personal computer is a form of interactive computing. The player interacts with images shown on a computer screen through the computer keyboard or some other input device.

EDUCATION AT HOME

Many computer-assisted instruction programs of the same type as those used in schools are available for purchase by home personal computer users. They are designed for different ages, ranging from preschoolers (ages three to five) to adults. The majority of computer home education programs concentrate on drill and practice exercises for math, spelling, grammar, and punctuation. Programs that deal with social studies, geography, astronomy, and languages are just a few examples of the programs also available.

WORD PROCESSING AND ADMINISTRATIVE SYSTEMS

The 1986 survey of home computer users showed that word processing on home computers was rapidly becoming as popular as game playing. Often, even at home, letters, notes, and memos can be written more easily on a computer using word processing software than on a typewriter. Freelance writers prepare manuscript copy for articles and books at home, and students can prepare reports and essays on personal computers at home or at school.

As you will read in Chapter 11, many software packages for word processing and other administrative tasks are available to home computer users. If a member of the family is active in volunteer work, membership lists for the organization can be kept current on the computer and used to prepare mailings announcing meetings and special events. Addresses of friends of the family, schedules of family members' appointments, and even favorite recipes can be stored in the computer, retrieved, and printed when needed.

Some people also keep records of family finances on home computers. While most of us can use a hand calculator to balance a checking account, keeping accurate track of the value of holdings of stocks and bonds, and of various insurance policies and the items covered by each, is more difficult and often warrants use of a computer.

USER NETWORKING AND DATABASE ACCESS

The use of home computers for computer networking and database access is growing rapidly. As explained in Chapter 7, by adding a modem to a personal computer, a user gains the capacity to communicate with other computer users and to access central databases of reference information.

The commercial communications networks that are established to serve personal computer users promote the formation of **special interest groups** (SIGS) among their members. Special interest groups are composed of members interested in discussing among themselves topics of mutual interest. Usually, the topics center around hobbies, such as stamp or coin collecting, automobile racing, jazz music, or even computers themselves. There are thousands of such groups, and each usually has an *electronic bulletin board* on which an individual member may post a message for others to read. Mostly, however, members exchange ideas and advice by data communications with one another, keying (and receiving) their messages on computer terminals or personal computers. One commercial communications network (The Source) boasts that such computer networking has resulted in a number of marriages among SIG members.

Chapter 7 identifies the types of reference information that a personal computer user is able to retrieve from central databases maintained by commercial information suppliers. By 1986 it was estimated that about 3000 different databases were available for access by personal computer users. As you can imagine, these cover almost every subject and interest you can think of, ranging from scientific reports and studies, to electronic encyclopedias, to electronic catalogs. On-line banking and shopping services are still another use of home computers.

COMPUTER-CONTROLLED HOUSEHOLD DEVICES

Individual microprocessors are now commonly used in individual household appliances and in automobiles. The "on" and "off" functioning of a refrigerator or a microwave oven, for example, is controlled by a microprocessor. In the case of the refrigerator, sensors connected to the microprocessor tell it when the air in the refrigerator or freezer has gotten too warm. The microprocessor then directs the cooling unit to operate. Modern automobiles contain many computers (microprocessors) that control everything from the amount of fuel injected into the engine to regulation of the car's speed with the cruise control device. Even the AM/FM stereo cassette player in the car may have a microprocessor controlling its operations.

In the same manner, home computers can be used to turn lights on and off at specified times and to control thermostats and air-conditioning systems so that desired temperatures are maintained. Fire alarm and burglar alarm systems protecting a home are often computer-controlled, and a computer can even determine when the grass and garden need to be watered and control the operation of an outdoor sprinkler system.

CHECK YOURSELF

Supply the missing words.

1. School reports can be prepared on home personal computers equipped to do __?__ __?__ .
2. To access a commercial database, a home personal computer must have a __?__ device.
3. The most popular use of home personal computers is for playing __?__ __?__ .
4. Computer-aided design systems, first developed by General Motors and IBM, appeared in the __?__ .
5. Computer groups formed to exchange ideas over communications networks are called __?__ __?__ groups.

Answers: (1) word processing; (2) modem; (3) electronic games; (4) 1960s; (5) special interest.

REVIEW QUESTIONS

1. Define the terms *information system, application,* and *procedure.*
2. Explain why business accounting systems were the first to be computerized. List six such systems.
3. Explain the purpose of a customer order entry and billing system.
4. Define *integrated system.* Give an example of data sharing between systems.
5. Give two objectives of an inventory management system.
6. Define *accounts receivable* and name two purposes of an accounts receivable system.
7. Define *accounts payable* and name two purposes of an accounts payable system.
8. Describe four functions performed in a payroll system.
9. What is the purpose of a general ledger system? an income statement? a balance sheet?
10. What is the purpose of a management information system?
11. How does a manager use a decision support system?
12. Give three examples of administrative support systems.
13. Explain the purpose of desktop publishing.
14. Define *CAD* and give an example of its use.
15. What is a CAM system and how may it help a factory manager?
16. Explain why robots are used in a factory.
17. List some ways in which computers are used in medicine.

18. What is the purpose of an automatic teller? a bank debit card?
19. Describe how computers may be used in law enforcement.
20. Explain the use of computer-assisted instruction and simulation.
21. Name five types of self-employed people who may use a home personal computer.
22. What is a SIG? Why do people use home personal computers for networking?
23. Give three other popular uses of home personal computers.

COMPARING IDEAS

The questions below are designed to help you think about what you have learned in this chapter. They are "thought" questions. There is no one correct answer.

1. Identify the specific types of information systems (applications) that you would expect to find in the office of a large discount store in your area.
2. Describe the uses that could be made of a desktop publishing system in your school.

INFORMATION PROCESSING ACTIVITIES

Now you can try out the kinds of information processing activities business workers perform. Below is a summary of the work you will do. You will find the actual information and business forms you need in your *Information Processing Work Kit.*

1. As a programming trainee at a store that sells motorbikes and motorcycles, you will determine back-order delivery dates, given system specifications.
2. You will classify common software products given four applications categories.

HANDS-ON ACTIVITIES

Design a decision support system (DSS) based on "what if" decision making on whether or not you should buy tickets for an upcoming concert. Do this by drawing a decision tree with Yes or No branches.

CHAPTER

9

DEVELOPING INFORMATION SYSTEMS

Information Processing Terminology

Systems analyst
System development
Systems analysis
System feasibility report
System design
Data dictionary
Input control
File

Database
Record
Data field
File maintenance
Database administrator
System flowchart
Service bureau
System specifications

System checkpoints
System implementation
Operational
System test
Debug
System conversion
Parallel systems
System audit

Performance Goals

☐ Describe the work of a systems analyst. Name the four phases of work involved in system development.

☐ Define the term *systems analysis.* Describe four tasks involved in systems analysis.

☐ Describe the contents of a system feasibility report.

☐ Define the term *system design.* Describe six tasks involved in system design.

☐ Define and give an example of a *file,* a *database,* a *record,* and a *data field.*

☐ Give an example of file maintenance by transaction processing; by batch processing.

☐ Explain the function of a system flowchart and the value of good system programming specifications.

In the last chapter you read about many different types of information systems used to operate and manage businesses. How do these systems come into being? Who is responsible for planning, developing, and implementing a business information system? These questions and others are answered in this chapter.

Trained individuals called **systems analysts** are usually responsible for developing new or improved information systems and supporting procedures. Larger businesses usually have systems analysts on staff to work on various information system projects. Smaller businesses may hire only a computer systems consulting company on an as-needed basis to develop the necessary procedures and systems. In all situations, a systems analyst must be able to work well with others because much of the work involves evaluating the needs and coordinating the efforts of other people. He or she must find out from management what it expects from the company's information system. A systems analyst also talks with other employees to get their ideas about how work may be performed more effectively. The systems analyst is also responsible for consulting with equipment suppliers and programming technicians on the selection of computer hardware and other office equipment.

The process of creating a new system or revising an already existing system is called **system development.** System development typically involves a four-step process:

1. Systems analysis
2. System design
3. System implementation
4. System evaluation and maintenance

Effective coordination of system development work is essential because the operation of an information system depends on many individuals working together as a team. For example, data-entry clerks are needed to carry out input operations, and computer operators are needed to run the equipment. Of course, computer programmers are needed to prepare the written instructions for processing the information. Many employees work together to operate the information systems developed by systems analysts.

Chapter 9: Developing Information Systems   215

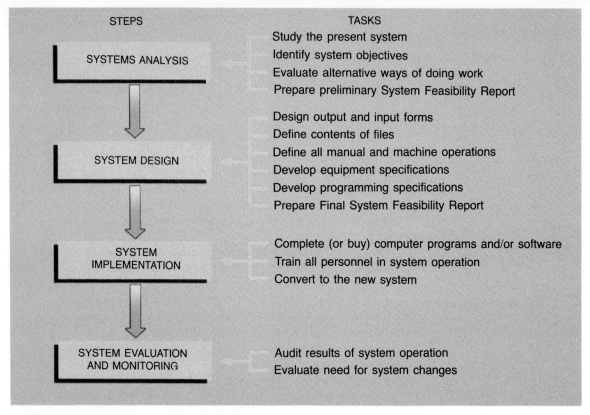

STEPS	TASKS
SYSTEMS ANALYSIS	Study the present system Identify system objectives Evaluate alternative ways of doing work Prepare preliminary System Feasibility Report
SYSTEM DESIGN	Design output and input forms Define contents of files Define all manual and machine operations Develop equipment specifications Develop programming specifications Prepare Final System Feasibility Report
SYSTEM IMPLEMENTATION	Complete (or buy) computer programs and/or software Train all personnel in system operation Convert to the new system
SYSTEM EVALUATION AND MONITORING	Audit results of system operation Evaluate need for system changes

SYSTEM DEVELOPMENT IS A FOUR-STEP PROCESS. Each step in the process requires a systems analyst to perform a number of work tasks.

STEP 1: SYSTEMS ANALYSIS

The first phase of system development work is known as **systems analysis.** The purpose of systems analysis is to identify exactly what a new or revised computer system is supposed to accomplish and what benefits the company should obtain from the system. Systems analysis is also called *problem analysis* because it involves problem solving—figuring out the particular requirements for a given system.

Usually, systems analysis work is divided into four tasks:

1. Study the present information system.
2. Identify the system objectives.
3. Evaluate alternative ways of meeting the objectives.
4. Prepare recommendations to management for implementing the system.

Suppose you are working as a systems analyst in the headquarters office of a supermarket chain. Management has received complaints from customers about the service at the checkout counters in a particular store. You are asked to do an analysis of

SYSTEMS ANALYSIS. One of the tasks of a systems analyst is to collect information about all aspects of an existing system including the work flow and procedures. The analyst must also find out from users how well the present system is working. *Courtesy Honeywell, Inc.*

the checkout system. You would begin by making a study of the store's present information system.

STUDYING THE PRESENT SYSTEM

The systems analyst's first task is to study the operation, procedures, and components of the existing information system. In the supermarket example, the systems analyst would study all aspects of the store's operation, including the checkout system, inventory control procedures, and type of equipment currently used. The analyst would review any complaints about the store received from employees or customers. If customers are complaining that the checkout lines are too long, the analyst will need to offer a solution in his or her recommendations to management.

Studying the present system involves gathering lots of information from many different people. All the people who are affected by or who use the system must be involved in the analysis process. The manager of the supermarket should be asked to evaluate how well the present system meets his or her needs. The checkout clerks should be asked to describe the checkout procedure and indicate what kinds of problems the current system might be causing for them or the customers. To fully analyze the current system, the analyst should even study the type of training the clerks receive and the type of equipment they must use. Customers should also be interviewed to find out whether they have any complaints or suggestions for improving the current system.

**IDENTIFYING
SYSTEM OBJECTIVES**

The next step in systems analysis is to evaluate the facts that have been gathered in the study of the present system. The purpose is to develop a set of objectives that state exactly what the system is supposed to accomplish now and in the future. The objectives should include a definition of the output information required from the system, the policies to be followed in the processing operations, the amounts and type of input data, the present and future volumes of work that have to be handled, and the amount of time allowed for these operations. Many other system objectives may also be established, such as the need to minimize job training time or the need to reduce customer waiting time by a certain percent.

Think of the objectives that could be established for the supermarket system:

■ Provide receipts for customers that list the description and price of each item purchased.
■ Provide daily information about the sales and inventory balance of each stock item in the store, and provide for automatic reordering of items when the inventory is low.
■ Establish a system capacity that will permit the handling of 25 percent more customers each year for the next five years.
■ Speed up the checkout process so that on average it should take no longer than three minutes to pass through the store's checkout station.
■ Simplify the checkout system so that a trainee can perform the job reliably after having four hours of instruction.

**EVALUATING
ALTERNATIVE
SYSTEMS**

A set of system objectives, such as those listed above for a supermarket, provides a basis for comparing the present system with alternative systems.

A systems analyst starts the evaluation process by defining the degree to which an existing system actually meets each of the objectives. If the system fails to meet one or more of the objectives, the analyst asks what changes will be necessary to make the current system meet the required objectives. The systems analyst evaluating the procedures in a supermarket may note that the present system would work better if there were twice as many checkout stations. On the other hand, although increasing the number of checkout clerks would speed up the checkout process, it still might not satisfy all the system objectives. This would be true if the checkout clerks use an old type of cash register that requires them to manually enter the price of each item purchased by a customer. This type of machine is unable to print item descriptions of purchases on a customer receipt or to provide sales or inventory records of items sold. Thus, if one of the system objectives is to give the customer itemized descriptions of purchases, simply adding checkout lanes with old cash registers would not be a satisfactory way of meeting all the system objectives.

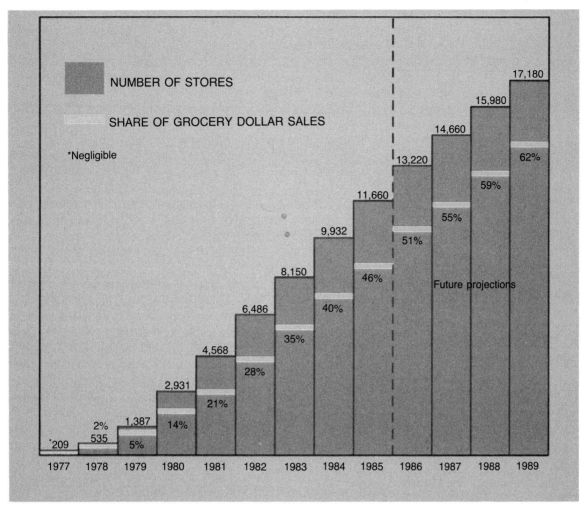

THE GROWING USE OF SCANNING-INPUT TERMINALS IN SUPERMARKETS. In 1977 only 209 supermarkets in the U.S. used scanning terminals at checkout stations. By 1985 more than 11,000 supermarkets had installed scanning terminals. These markets accounted for almost half of the grocery sales in the U.S. *Source of data: A.C. Nielson.*

If an existing system and the equipment used in it cannot be modified to meet the system objectives, the systems analyst must seek alternatives. For example, in order to meet the system objective stated above, it is likely that the systems analyst in the supermarket would determine that a computerized scanning terminal is needed at each checkout station. As you read in Chapter 4, a scanning input terminal reads the Universal Product Code (UPC) on a packaged item, which allows a computer to retrieve the current price for that item from its memory. The cash register prints the item description and the price on the receipt. At the same time, the sale is recorded for inventory and sales reporting purposes. The use of scanning terminals in a supermarket speeds up the checkout process, makes the process more reliable, and reduces the time required to train checkout clerks.

A systems analyst must also identify disadvantages of adopting new systems, particularly the costs involved in changing to the new system. In the supermarket study, for example, the costs of purchasing or leasing the scanning terminals and computer equipment and the expense of preparing the computer programs needed to operate the system must be estimated.

PREPARING A PRELIMINARY SYSTEM FEASIBILITY REPORT

The systems analysis phase is concluded by the preparation of a preliminary **system feasibility report.** This report summarizes the findings of the systems analysis phase. Its purpose is to compare the suitability (feasibility) of the present system with that of alternative systems.

Typically, the report starts with a statement of the system objectives. This is followed by an evaluation of how well the present system is meeting the current requirements and how adequate it will be for future needs. If the present system has shortcomings, the systems analyst points out the specific operating problems. For example, the analyst might point out that the current checkout procedure used in the supermarket takes too long, is error-prone, does not provide the required output, and is difficult to learn.

Each alternative to the present system is described, and the advantages of each are fully discussed in the report. The major benefits resulting from a new system may include the following: faster processing of data or availability of new data, more reliable performance of the work, and a possible reduction of operating costs.

The systems analyst also identifies any disadvantages that might result from a change in systems and includes estimates of the costs of changing the system and operating the new or revised system. Disadvantages might include the high cost of purchasing new equipment and the added expense of training all employees how to use the new system. However, it is usually not possible at this stage of system development work to estimate accurately the total costs of changing to and operating the new system. The figures in the preliminary system feasibility report will be updated if the system development work continues.

On the basis of the findings and recommendations of the systems analyst, management will decide whether to proceed with the development of a new or revised system. If management decides that the project is worth pursuing, the next phase of work to be done by the systems analyst is system design.

STEP 2: SYSTEM DESIGN

The second phase of system development work is known as **system design.** The purpose of system design is to identify exactly *how* a system will accomplish the objectives identified in the systems analysis work.

Six tasks are normally involved in system design work. To complete a system design, a systems analyst must:

1. Design the output and input formats.
2. Define file contents and updating methods.
3. Describe all manual and machine processing operations.
4. Prepare equipment specifications.
5. Develop system specifications for programming.
6. Prepare a final system feasibility report for management.

DESIGNING OUTPUT AND INPUT FORMATS

You are accustomed to thinking about information processing as a sequence of input, processing, and output operations. In system design work, however, a systems analyst works backwards, starting with the design of formats for output information. This is because the most important part of system development work is to provide users of the system with the information they need at the time they need it and in the most usable format for their needs.

Output Formats. The systems analyst must find out from users the reporting forms that meet their particular needs. This includes defining the items of information the user wants, the time at which the information is made available, the media to be used for reporting the information, the format for printing

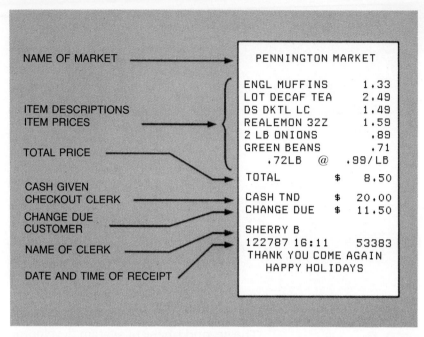

NAME OF MARKET	PENNINGTON MARKET

ITEM DESCRIPTIONS
ITEM PRICES

TOTAL PRICE

CASH GIVEN
CHECKOUT CLERK

CHANGE DUE
CUSTOMER

NAME OF CLERK

DATE AND TIME OF RECEIPT

```
PENNINGTON MARKET

ENGL MUFFINS      1.33
LOT DECAF TEA     2.49
DS DKTL LC        1.49
REALEMON 32Z      1.59
2 LB ONIONS        .89
GREEN BEANS        .71
   .72LB   @    .99/LB

TOTAL        $    8.50

CASH TND     $   20.00
CHANGE DUE   $   11.50

SHERRY B
122787 16:11      53383
THANK YOU COME AGAIN
    HAPPY HOLIDAYS
```

DESIGN OF SYSTEM OUTPUT FORMATS. A systems analyst designs formats for the reporting of output information in the form most useful to users. This example shows the format a systems analyst designed for printing out customer receipts at Pennington Supermarket's check-out stations.

the information in report form or displaying it on a screen, and even the colors, if any, to be used in graphic presentations.

To design the output formats for the supermarket system is relatively straightforward. The information to be printed on the customer's receipt and its sequence should be determined. In addition, the format for the display of sales and inventory information that the manager wants to be able to access on a terminal screen needs to be decided.

Input Formats. Once the requirements for output information have been completed, the systems analyst determines the type of input data needed to produce the required output. Often, a **data dictionary** is prepared listing each item of data required to operate the system.

The analyst identifies where each item of input data can be obtained (captured) and the quantity of input data required. He or she must also determine whether the data has to be coded and how the coding is to be accomplished. Next, the analyst decides how the data should be entered into the system. In Chapter 4, you read about a variety of devices available for data

DESIGN OF SYSTEM INPUT FORMS. Once systems analysts know what output information is required by users, they can design formats for entering data needed to produce the output. Here, a user is entering data needed for preparing a business financial plan. *Courtesy Xerox Corporation.*

entry. The systems analyst will try to select a cost-effective data-entry method that also ensures a high level of accuracy in the input operation. If display units are required for data entry, the screen formats needed to guide data-entry operators in the input operation must be designed. Because reliability of input data is so important to information processing, systems analysts also establish **input controls** to assure correct entry of all the data.

DEFINING FILE CONTENTS AND UPDATING METHODS

To operate, a business system normally needs one or more **files** containing data about the particular aspect of business for which the system is designed. A file is a collection of related information kept in storage. For example, a payroll file contains data about the pay rates of each employee in a business, and a customer file contains data about each customer, such as name, address, and credit rating. Where possible, a systems analyst tries to design a file that may be shared by two or more systems. This step eliminates duplication of efforts when different users need the same file data. In systems terminology, a file that is shared is called a **database.** As you read earlier, a database is organized to permit easy access to and retrieval of the stored data. For example, information in a database containing customer data could be used in a word processing application to generate a personalized thank-you letter to a customer and in

ORGANIZATION OF A DATABASE OR FILE. A database or file stored in magnetic tape or disk is divided into records. Each record, in turn, is subdivided into data fields. The illustration shows a product database (simplified) designed for the supermarket system that has been described. It contains a record for each item sold in the supermarket. Each product record contains identifying data about the product, unit price, inventory balance, and accumulative product sales.

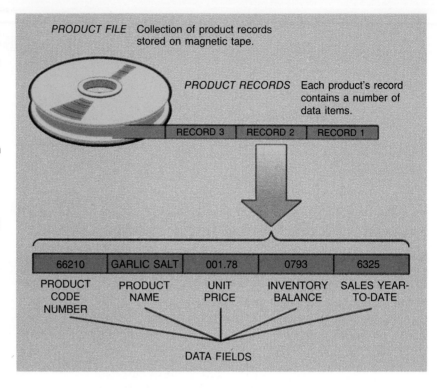

PRODUCT FILE   Collection of product records stored on magnetic tape.

PRODUCT RECORDS   Each product's record contains a number of data items.

RECORD 3   RECORD 2   RECORD 1

66210	GARLIC SALT	001.78	0793	6325
PRODUCT CODE NUMBER	PRODUCT NAME	UNIT PRICE	INVENTORY BALANCE	SALES YEAR-TO-DATE

DATA FIELDS

a billing system to generate a bill for items purchased by the customer during the month.

File Contents.   Data in a file, or database, is subdivided into records. Whether a file is stored on a magnetic or optical disk, or a reel of magnetic tape, it is organized into individual records. A **record** contains a collection of data about one particular person, object, event, or transaction. For example, a payroll file is made up of a group of records, one for each employee in the company. An inventory file contains a record for each item stored in inventory. Many people maintain at home a file containing a record of the name, address, and telephone number of each of their friends and associates.

Each record in a file or database is subdivided into several areas called **data fields,** or simply *fields*. A data field consists of one or more characters that make up an item of data. For example, in the payroll file, employee name and pay rate are two important data fields. Data recorded in a field may be alphabetic only, numeric only, or alphanumeric (both alphabetic and numeric).

File and Database Maintenance. The process of updating records in a file or database so that they contain the latest information is called **file maintenance.** In the file maintenance operation, whether it is done by a computer or manually by a file clerk, new records are inserted in the file, data in existing records is changed, and inactive records are removed.

It is important that the task of file or database maintenance be handled accurately and reliably. For this reason a **database administrator** may be assigned the full-time responsibility for seeing that the information in a file or database is kept current and accurate. He or she is greatly aided by computer programs (database management systems) that are specifically designed to organize and maintain information in databases.

As you read in Chapter 4, either a file can be updated as transactions occur (transaction processing) or input transactions can be held for later updating of a file or database (batch processing). The systems analyst must determine which of the two methods best meets the needs of the users of the system. Depending upon the type of input required to update the data fields in a file, a combination of transaction and batch processing is sometimes used for file maintenance.

The systems analyst for the supermarket may decide to establish one common database for the system. This would be a product file containing one record for each item stocked in the store. The information in this database would be used for customer checkout, sales analyses, and inventory management reporting. Through the scanning terminals, checkout clerks would have access to file data on item price and description.

In the supermarket system, transaction processing occurs when the scanner reads a product code on an item purchased by a customer. The description of the item and its price are immediately retrieved from the database, displayed at the checkout terminal, and printed on the customer's receipt. At the same time, the quantity purchased is added to the sales data in the database and subtracted from the inventory balance.

The systems analyst may decide, however, that the input for the supermarket inventory receipts need not be handled on a transaction processing basis (recorded when received). Instead, inventory receipts would be entered on a batch processing basis just once a day. In many businesses, a crew of data-entry clerks and computer operators comes in at night to update all the computer files. In the supermarket example, all receipts for goods delivered during the day, such as milk, bread, meats, or bakery goods, would be entered into the computer at night. The quantity of each item received would then be added to the inventory balance for that item.

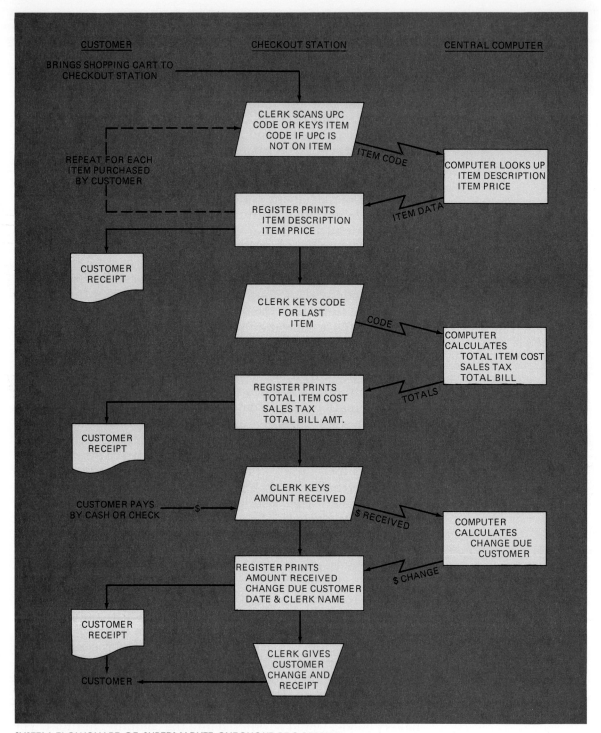

SYSTEM FLOWCHART OF SUPERMARKET CHECKOUT PROCEDURE.

Once the output, input, and file maintenance requirements for a system are established, the systems analyst must define and prepare descriptions of all the processing operations that are required to convert the input data into the required output information. The processing steps from input to output are usually documented in flowchart (graphic) form.

A **system flowchart** depicts the series of manual and machine steps that make up the particular system being designed. Using a standard set of flowchart symbols, a systems analyst traces, step by step, the operations that have to be performed in the system from beginning to end.

Special symbols are used in the drawing of system flowcharts. The more commonly used symbols are shown in the illustration on page 248. A systems analyst writes a very brief explanation of the operation inside each symbol outline. The simplified system flowchart shown on page 226 illustrates the operations performed at a supermarket checkout station, as discussed earlier. Usually, many flowcharts must be prepared to show all the steps in all the procedures of a typical business information system. Computer programs are available to simplify and speed up the preparation of complex flowcharts.

The fourth task in system design is to specify the requirements for the computers, communications, and all the other equipment needed to operate the information system. The computer equipment already installed in a business may possibly be able to handle the new system requirements without change. In other cases, although sufficient computer processing time is available, additional main memory capacity, additional auxiliary storage units, and/or different types of input-output terminals may be needed. In order to speed up the checkout process at the supermarket, the analyst probably would decide that new scanning devices and electronic cash register terminals should be installed at each checkout station.

If sufficient computer processing capacity is not available on the present equipment, management may decide to acquire additional equipment or to upgrade the existing central processor so that it can handle the processing requirements of the new system. This may mean getting a more powerful processing unit for an existing microcomputer, exchanging a microcomputer for a minicomputer, or moving from a minicomputer to a mainframe computer.

A systems analyst may decide that none of the equipment alternatives just described can satisfactorily meet the processing requirements for a new system. With management, he or she will need to investigate a number of alternatives, one of which

SERVICE BUREAU. A service bureau provides information processing services for a fee to subscribers.

might be the use of a computer service bureau. A **service bureau** is a company that will provide information processing services for a fee. The fee, of course, is based on the workload to be handled. A small company may gain valuable experience by using a service bureau as an introduction to computer processing before buying a system for use on-site. It also may prove to be the most economical way of handling their requirements on a permanent basis.

Once decisions are reached about the type of computer hardware and supporting equipment to be acquired, a systems analyst prepares a list of equipment specifications to obtain equipment cost estimates from hardware manufacturers. These specifications are reviewed by management and other personnel before being sent out to the various suppliers who will bid for the right to supply the equipment.

The analyst must also consider whether it is better to write the required programs or to buy the software as well as the needed hardware. Computer equipment is almost always purchased from outside vendors, but many businesses find it cheaper or more efficient to develop software programs themselves. The analyst must look at the costs of developing programs and of acquiring them from a software company. Many factors affect this decision, including costs, staff capabilities, and the technical specifications of the program.

DEVELOPING SYSTEM SPECIFICATIONS FOR PROGRAMMERS

A fifth task of system design is the development of detailed **system specifications** for the computer programmers who write the instructions telling the computer how to perform its processing work. These specifications define the organization of the individual programs that make up the system. They also clarify the logic to be followed in the processing steps. Well-written and complete system specifications decrease the chance for error in interpreting not only the data to be processed but also what each processing operation should accomplish. They can also reduce the time needed to prepare computer programs.

When developing the system specifications for a computer information system, the systems analyst establishes various **system checkpoints** (checking and control operations) needed to ensure accurate processing of data. The programmers who write the programs for each subsystem must design tests for data accuracy at each checkpoint.

PREPARING A FINAL SYSTEM FEASIBILITY REPORT

Only after completing these five tasks of system design work can a systems analyst evaluate the benefits and costs of converting to and operating the system (determine its feasibility). He or she then prepares a final system feasibility report for management. This report contains the recommendations of the analyst, with the following background information:

- An explanation of the benefits offered by the system, along with an identification of any negative effects of the system. Usually, this includes a statement of the impact of the system on staffing and on the organization structure.
- A financial statement of the costs of converting to and operating the system and a cost/benefit analysis.
- A description of the system outputs, data inputs, file maintenance activities, and processing steps.
- Equipment specifications.
- System specifications for computer programming.
- A listing of all the steps that are necessary to implement the new system and a proposed timetable showing how long it would take to complete the implementation operations.

The report of the systems analyst allows management to decide whether to proceed or to discontinue efforts to implement the new system.

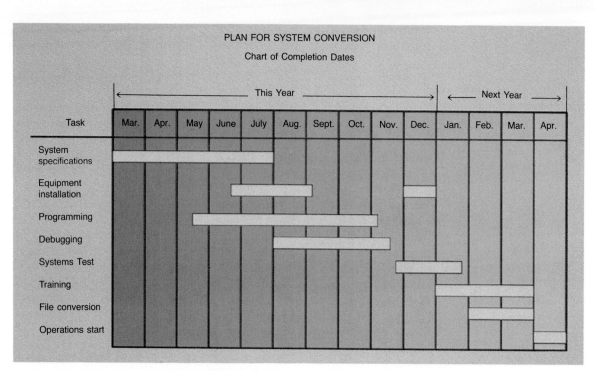

PLAN FOR SYSTEM CONVERSION

Chart of Completion Dates

SYSTEM IMPLEMENTATION SCHEDULE. When a large system is to be implemented, a systems analyst usually prepares a schedule of the major steps that have to be completed to convert to the new system. As shown in the illustration, the schedule may be in graphic form. The beginning of each bar indicates the starting date for the work task and the end of the bar marks the date by which the task is to be completed. For example, the writing of system specifications is scheduled to start on March 1 and be completed by August 1.

CHECK YOURSELF

Match each phrase with the word or term that best defines it.

1. The means of assuring correct data entry.
2. A file shared by different users.
3. A list of data items required to operate a system.
4. The person responsible for keeping a database current and accurate.
5. A company that provides information processing services for a fee.
6. A description of a system in pictorial form.
7. The operation of updating file information.
8. Items of data in a record.

a. Data dictionary
b. Database
c. Input control
d. System design
e. System flowchart
f. Service bureau
g. Systems analyst
h. Data fields
i. Database administrator
j. File maintenance

Answers: (1) c; (2) b; (3) a; (4) i; (5) f; (6) e; (7) j; (8) h.

STEP 3: SYSTEM IMPLEMENTATION

Management's approval to proceed with the installation of a new system triggers a number of actions. **System implementation** refers to the steps that are necessary to install a new system and put it into operation.

IMPLEMENTATION TASKS

SYSTEM IMPLEMENTATION. Preparing job training manuals explaining how a new system works is an important task in system implementation. Training sessions are also usually required. *Courtesy IBM Corporation.*

After arrangements to acquire new computer systems, devices, or components are made, the task of translating system specifications into programs is started. The systems analyst also develops a job training manual for the employees who will be involved in operating or using the new system. Such a manual includes descriptions of the specific operations data-entry operators must perform to prepare input for the system. The manual also explains how output information is to be printed or shown and how users can generate needed reports.

Training classes are held to introduce employees to the features and operation of the new system, particularly if new equipment is involved. Often, employees who will operate the new equipment are sent to technical training classes conducted by the equipment manufacturers.

How a changeover to a new system is planned and executed has a major impact on the system's performance and acceptance. For this reason, systems analysts spend a good deal of time ensuring the effective installation of a new system. The more sophisticated the equipment selected for a system, the longer it can take to make it **operational** (in proper working condition). Completion of computer programs may take months or even several years, depending on their complexity.

The next chapter describes the tasks involved in writing computer programs. But one responsibility a programmer has, beyond creating programs, is to test the programs he or she has written. Once all the programs for a system have been completed and individually tested, they must be tested as a whole. To do this, a systems analyst supervises a **system test** to determine that, when the programs are linked together in a network, they work satisfactorily. Actual items of input data taken from the business activity are used in the system test. The systems analyst must make sure that the system produces the correct output information. If errors occur, the system must be **debugged** to find the source of the problem. The problem can be caused by errors in the program itself, faulty hardware, inaccurate data input, or inaccurate database information. Debugging the programs (or *troubleshooting* the system) can be an expensive and time-consuming process.

SYSTEM CONVERSION

The process of changing an old system to a new system is called **system conversion.** For example, changing from an old type of

SYSTEM AUDIT. At regular intervals, after a new system has been installed, a business may have a systems analyst perform a system audit. One of the purposes of an audit is to determine whether output information is being produced accurately and on schedule. *Courtesy Prime Computer, Inc.*

type of cash register to new computerized scanning devices at supermarket checkout stations would involve a system conversion.

A new system may be phased in slowly, one piece at a time. When one part is working satisfactorily, the next part of the system is installed. In other cases, a company may continue to use the old system along with the new one for some time. When the new and the old system are operated at the same time, they are said to be **parallel systems.** For instance, when a word processing system is installed, many secretaries continue to use a typewriter for many tasks until they feel comfortable with and are fully trained on the new system. The accuracy and effectiveness of the new system can be proved by comparing its results with the results of the old system. Only when the systems analyst and management are satisfied that the new system is operating well should the use of the old system be discontinued.

STEP 4: SYSTEM EVALUATION AND MAINTENANCE

Once a new system has been operational for some months, its performance should be evaluated to determine whether the system is actually achieving the results that were expected. The evaluation process, sometimes called a **system audit,** should examine the degree to which each of the predicted benefits of the system is being realized. Whether the output information is produced accurately, on time, and in the right format is part of the evaluation. Also, it is important to determine whether the operating costs of the system are within the expected ranges and, if not, the reasons for this.

A system audit serves several purposes. It points out any deficiencies in the system that must be corrected. It also teaches a systems analyst how a system design for other systems may be improved.

In a typical business, as long as a system continues to operate, there will be a need for system maintenance work. Some changes may be needed to correct or improve minor operations. Most often, however, system maintenance is needed to accommodate changes in business requirements that originate from expansion of the business or demands for information from the outside.

If a system has been designed properly, minor changes can be easily accommodated. In any case, it is important that good computer program documentation exist. The individual who prepared the original programs may have been promoted to another job or may no longer be with the company. Only if good program documentation exists can programmers make changes in programs they themselves may not have written.

SYSTEM LIFE CYCLE. Once a system is installed, it must be evaluated at regular intervals to determine whether it still offers the best way of accomplishing business objectives. Every system has a life cycle, meaning that at some time in the future there will be a better way of accomplishing the work.

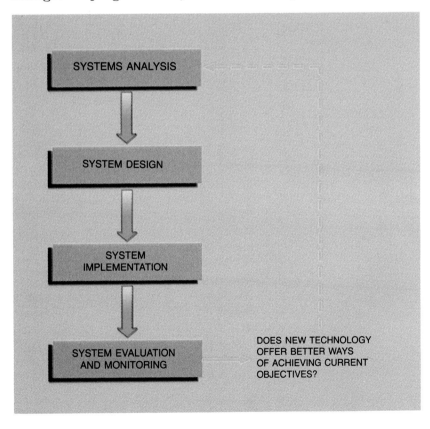

SYSTEMS ANALYSIS

SYSTEM DESIGN

SYSTEM IMPLEMENTATION

SYSTEM EVALUATION AND MONITORING

DOES NEW TECHNOLOGY OFFER BETTER WAYS OF ACHIEVING CURRENT OBJECTIVES?

ShopRite in Kingston checks out Posi-Talker

The Posi-Talker is positively the last word in supermarket checkout techniques, according to Dorothy Strauber, director of consumer affairs for Foodarama Inc., the owner of the ShopRite in Kingston, Franklin Township.

A few weeks ago, the newly renovated ShopRite installed the talking scanning device, which not only silently records the price of the item on a store inventory tape but also verbalizes that price to the consumer.

The Posi-Talker also enables the consumer to receive a detailed register receipt that describes the individual items purchased. For example, instead of just saying "grocery" item for 49 cents, the Posi-Talker tape will describe "ShopRite green beans, 16 ounce" for 49 cents.

"The reaction of the public has been 99.9 percent fabulous. People are amazed, but pleasantly amazed," Dorothy Strauber said.

Kingston ShopRite store manager Debbie Durant confirmed Ms. Strauber's reading of Posi-Talker's popularity. "We have gotten a lot of 'oooohs and aaaaahs,'" Ms. Durant said. "People are surprised that it talks, but they seem to like it."

NEW TECHNOLOGY FOR SUPERMARKETS. This news item discusses a new type of equipment for supermarket check-out stations. Such new developments stimulate businesses to evaluate whether the new equipment offers a better way of performing work. *Courtesy Princeton Packet (N.J.), Jan. 1987.*

This is one reason why buying commercial software for a particular application is preferable to developing software internally. The manufacturer keeps the program updated and documented and supplies technical support to users.

Some time in the future, the business requirements for a system designed this year may change drastically. Or, it is possible that in ten years a new generation of computers, or improved input and storage devices, will offer much more efficient ways of achieving the system objectives. Whatever the reason, it is likely that some time in the future a systems analyst will decide that a system installed this year needs major modification. This will lead the analyst back to the first step in system development (systems analysis), which you read about earlier in this chapter. So you see that system development is a never-ending cycle. Businesses will always need to find better ways of performing work.

Match each phrase with the word or term that best defines it.

1. An evaluation of how well a system is performing.
2. The process of changing from an old to a new system.
3. A system in proper working condition.
4. A test to make sure that when computer programs are linked together, they work satisfactorily.
5. Testing by operating a new system and an old system at the same time.

a. An operational system
b. A system having program bugs
c. Program test
d. System test
e. System audit
f. System conversion
g. Parallel systems

Answers: (1) e; (2) f; (3) a; (4) d; (5) g.

REVIEW QUESTIONS

1. What is the chief responsibility of a systems analyst?
2. Name four steps involved in system development work.
3. Explain the purpose of systems analysis.
4. Describe four tasks performed in systems analysis.
5. Identify the contents of a preliminary system feasibility report.
6. What is the purpose of system design work?
7. List the six tasks involved in system design.
8. Explain why a systems analyst starts with output in system design.
9. What is a data dictionary?
10. Explain the purpose of input controls.
11. Define the following terms: *file, database, record, data fields, file maintenance,* and *database administrator.*
12. Describe a system flowchart.
13. Identify the ways in which the machine processing requirements for a new system may be met.
14. What are system checkpoints?
15. List the contents of a final system feasibility report.
16. Explain why system implementation work is important.
17. Describe the tasks involved in system implementation.
18. Give two ways of accomplishing system conversion.
19. Explain two benefits of a system audit.
20. Why is system development considered a never-ending cycle?

COMPARING IDEAS

The questions below are designed to help you think about what you have learned in this chapter. They are "thought" questions. There is no one correct answer.

1. List the skills, education, work experience, and personality traits that a systems analyst requires to handle a complex systems development project competently.
2. Which of the four steps in system development do you think is most difficult? Give the reasons for your choice.

INFORMATION PROCESSING ACTIVITIES

Now you can perform many of the information processing activities business workers perform. Below is a summary of the tasks you will complete. You will find the actual data and business forms you need in your *Information Processing Work Kit*.

1. You will make hardware purchase recommendations based on a set of system specifications.
2. You will apply your knowledge of standard flowcharting symbols in preparing an oral systems presentation.
3. You will complete a system flowchart.

USING SPREADSHEET SOFTWARE

As you learned in Part 3, a business can have many different information systems. Often, when businesses start using computers they develop separate systems to handle each decision-making problem. If designed properly, it should be possible to integrate two or more computer applications so that they can share the same data. This eliminates a great deal of data entry and reduces errors. We will apply this technique in Software Project 6.

In this software project you will help produce the data needed to create payroll checks under the direction of your supervisor. Financial information must always be double checked for accuracy. Imagine how you would feel if you did not receive an accurate payroll check!

The Video-II-Go store is gaining in popularity. In order to meet the increased customer demand, Pat Brown has hired two additional part-time students to help out during the weekends. This change has made payroll preparation a bit more difficult since part-time checks are usually made out for different amounts each week. Pat hopes that the store's new microcomputer can help.

Each time part-time employees come to work for Video-II-Go they are given a timesheet to record their hours. Pat Brown tells the new employees what the hourly rate is, and explains the exceptions to that rate. At Video-II-Go part-time employees receive an extra $.75 per hour for working on the weekends or holidays. In addition, after six months they receive a $1 per hour increase on the original hourly rate. From this total (or gross) amount, deductions must be made for social security tax before a check is issued. As the number of part-time employees increases, the number of calculations increase.

INFORMATION PROCESSING PROBLEM

This business needs to rapidly and accurately calculate the amount due each part-time employee every two weeks. This includes computing total pay, total deductions, and check amount for each employee as well as the overall total of each item for all part-time employees. The full-time employees are issued weekly payroll checks through an outside payroll service.

INFORMATION PROCESSING SOLUTION

The manual calculations involved in preparing the part-time payroll data can be greatly reduced by utilizing the existing microcomputer hardware and acquiring an electronic spreadsheet software package. This package will not be used to produce the actual checks. It will, however, perform all of the necessary calculations.

Electronic spreadsheet software allows you to create common accounting reports using the calculation and capabilities of a computer. The major elements of spreadsheet software include:

COLUMNS The vertical spaces that start from the top and extend to the bottom of the worksheet are lettered and referred to as **columns.**

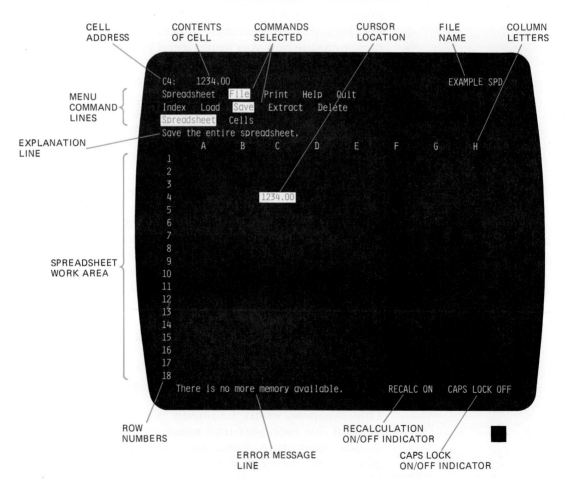

ROWS	The horizontal spaces that start at the left and extend to the right across the worksheet are labeled numerically and are referred to as **rows.**
CELLS	The point where a column letter and a row number meet is referred to as a **cell.** This is similar to reading a road map. Thus, the first cell on a spreadsheet can be identified as Cell A1.

The example above shows the organization of the McGraw-Hill Spreadsheet program. Your supervisor will demonstrate the use of an electronic spreadsheet software package to you before you begin the keyboarding activities.

KEYBOARDING ACTIVITIES

1. Unless your supervisor has provided you with a prepared spreadsheet, you will need to label the columns and rows in order to record the information from the Accounting Worksheet. The social security label should start in cell A1.

VIDEO-II-GO   ACCOUNTING WORKSHEET

SS Number	Hours	Pay	FICA −6%	Fed. −12%	State −3%	Check Amt.
416-44-1211	20	80.00	4.80	9.60	2.40	63.20
511-21-4441	18	72.00	4.32	8.64	2.16	56.88
518-56-4567	23	92.00	5.52	11.04	2.76	72.68
434-23-4534	20	80.00	4.80	9.60	2.40	63.20

Completed by _____ P. B. _____   Date __ May 15 __

2. You will also need to enter the appropriate formulas for the cells that will be computed. The contents of a cell can be a label (words), value (number), or formula (mathematical instructions). The instructions look like formulas for solving common problems. The check amount for the first employee, for example, would be calculated by taking the contents of the Pay cell minus the sum of the FICA, Fed., and State tax cells. Remember, what makes a spreadsheet so useful is that the computer will recalculate the value of a cell automatically after you change the contents of any cell in the worksheet.

Here is a listing of the cells that will be entered and those that will be computed.

Entered	Computed	Formulas
SS Number	Pay	Hours × 4.00
Hours	FICA	Pay × 6%
	Fed.	Pay × 12%
	State	Pay × 3%
	Check Amt.	Pay − (FICA + Fed. + State)

When the labels and formulas are completed, enter the SS Number and Hours from the Accounting Worksheet so it resembles the handwritten entries.

Compare the computed totals with the totals on the Accounting Worksheet. They were double checked. Your spreadsheet should have the same data items and totals.

3. Add the following new employees to the file from the Time Sheet list.

VIDEO-II-GO   TIME SHEET for   Rachel Thomas

Rate 4.00   Social Security No.   372-59-6312
==

Date	Hours	Pay	Approval
May 3	5	20.00	P.B.
5	7	28.00	P.B.
6	4	16.00	P.B.
10	8	32.00	P.B.
TOTALS	24	96.00	P.B.

VIDEO-II-GO   TIME SHEET for   Michael Soo

Rate 4.00   Social Security No.   431-23-4530
==

Date	Hours	Pay	Approval
May 1	4	16.00	M.T.
4	8	32.00	M.T.
10	3	12.00	P.B.
13	5	20.00	M.T.
TOTALS	20	80.00	P.B.

The worksheet still does not account for extra pay for working on weekends and holidays, or for wages for part-time employees that have been with Video-II-Go for over six months. First, add a column between Hours and Pay for special hours (Spec. Hours), then make the following changes:

SS Number	Hours	Spec. Hours
416-44-1211	16	4
511-21-4441	11	7
518-56-4567	18	5
434-23-4534	14	6
372-59-6312	16	8
431-23-4530	10	10

Pay should now be calculated as: (Hours $\times$ 4.00) + (Spec. Hours $\times$ 4.75) except for employee 518-56-4567 who has been with Video-II-Go for seven months. The formula for this person should be: (Hours $\times$ 5.00) + (Spec. Hours $\times$ 5.75).

4. Print a copy of the current month's worksheet and submit it to your supervisor for approval or revision.

ENRICHMENT ACTIVITIES

1. Add a year-to-date total pay column which could carry forward the amount paid from one month to the next. This is important since there is a limit on the amount of salary that is taxed for FICA (social security). Assume that the pay total was exactly the same last month. Show the year-to-date pay (YTD/PAY) on a revised spreadsheet. You may delete the deduction columns on your revised spreadsheet.
2. Prepare a worksheet that would show the effect of giving each employee a $1.15 per hour raise. This kind of report would help the owner make important salary decisions.

PART 4

COMPUTER PROGRAM-MING AND SOFTWARE

CHAPTER 10

CONCEPTS OF PROGRAMMING

Information Processing Terminology

Computer software
System specifications
Program flowchart
ANSI
Machine language
Assembler language
Symbolic form
Higher-level languages
Query languages
Compiler

COBOL
BASIC
Logo
Pascal
Ada
C
Diagnostics
Desk debugging
Documentation
Database management

Operating system
Applications package
Turnkey package
Support software
Utility program
Sort/merge utility
Cross-reference utility
File-handling utility

Performance Goals

☐ Compare and contrast business, technical, and general-purpose programming languages.

☐ Describe how a program flowchart for a typical accounting application works.

☐ Explain the importance of properly documenting a program.

☐ Describe the essential accounting functions on the computer, using software packages.

☐ Identify at least two types of utility packages for improving programming or processing efficiency.

PROGRAMMING A COMPUTER. A computer programmer writes the code that instructs the computer on which processing activities need to be accomplished. *Will Faller.*

You read earlier that a computer converts data to information by following specific instructions. The instructions and other procedures the computer uses to process data are known as **computer software**. In this chapter you will learn more about the steps involved in programming, or writing instructions for, a computer.

You will become familiar with a broad range of programming languages, and will learn how to modify an existing program. You will read about recent developments in computer software that enable businesses to process data efficiently. You will also learn how international software standards are making computer software increasingly portable and how special programs can help managers and professionals manage their time better.

PROGRAMMING A COMPUTER

Engineering groups and research labs hire as programmers applicants with strong backgrounds in mathematics or science. Businesses, on the other hand, generally look for training in business math, information processing, accounting, or record-keeping. What is important in programming a computer is to pay careful attention to the needs of the end user of the resulting information. The program must successfully convert the raw data the programmer starts out with into usable information. The number of programming instructions will range from a few to many thousands, depending on the system requirements and user needs.

THE STARTING POINT: SYSTEM SPECIFICATIONS

You are programming a computer when you write instructions for a specific application. A programmer needs to have a clear understanding of both the data to be input and the information required by users.

In writing a program for processing a payroll for hourly workers, the analyst will start out with data on time cards that are either handwritten or punched at a time clock. The analyst begins by visualizing the process. The input data needs to be considered first. The time-card data can be converted to machine-readable form or keyed directly into the computer at a video display terminal. What are the data fields? The analyst must consider the types of data fields present, the number of characters needed for each field, and many other factors. Do the fields contain enough characters for employee names, for employee departments, for employee ID numbers?

Developing the programming instructions calls for great care. Because computers do *exactly* what they are told, an omitted or incorrect step means the computer will not be able to process the data properly. You can imagine how important the computer instructions for airplanes are. Modern passenger jets are almost completely automated, with computers doing everything but taking off and landing the planes. If the program instructions were incorrect or important data was entered wrong, the results could be catastrophic.

A programming project generally begins with a set of **system specifications** defining the work to be done. After the systems analyst determines the steps to be performed, the work of the programmer begins.

CREATING THE PROGRAM

The systems analyst reviews the specifications with management and then gives them to the programmers who will write the program. There are four major steps in writing a program.

1. Planning and flowcharting
2. Coding
3. Testing and debugging
4. Documentation

Planning and Flowcharting. A good way to keep track of what is happening to the input data as a result of each step is to draw a flowchart. Starting with the specifications and plan the analyst provides, a **program flowchart** is generated that graphically shows each action the computer is to take. The flowchart enables the programmer to identify appropriate decisions each

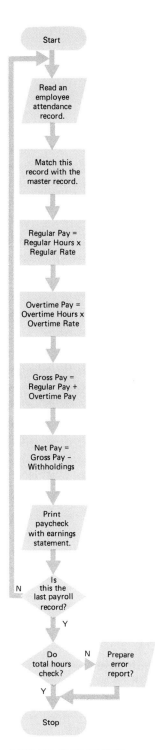

PAYROLL FLOWCHART.

time there is a choice to be made and then to follow the data through the process to be sure the steps will produce the desired results. An example of a decision that might need to be made is whether or not to pay an employee for overtime. Using a special program, the computer would check the number of hours worked by each employee. If an employee worked more than 40 hours, it would calculate the necessary extra pay. If the employee worked 40 hours or less, the computer would skip the part of the program that calculates overtime pay and continue with the next step.

Each flowchart is a series of rectangles, diamonds, circles, and other shapes. These shapes are used as symbols for particular operations in the data processing cycle. The geometric shapes shown here are the standard symbols established for flowcharting by the American National Standards Institute (**ANSI**). They are important symbols because they indicate the specific steps the computer is asked to perform.

- A rectangle specifies an operation, such as adding the hours worked each day to compute the total number of hours worked during that week.
- A diamond shape indicates a decision. For example, in a payroll program, for each hourly worker it is necessary to make a separate decision. A typical decision in a payroll program is based on whether the employee worked overtime— more than 40 hours.
- The parallelogram represents input or output steps. Examples are reading (entering) input data or writing (printing) output data.
- Arrows show the sequence in which the steps are to be carried out. For example, the computer is instructed to read in an employee's time record and compute regular and overtime pay.

Using the weekly payroll example, assume that the analyst is asked to review the employee data and then to list the employees who worked overtime (more than 40 hours per week). The programmer would need to use two decision diamonds in the program flowchart (see page 249).

- The first diamond asks the computer to decide for each employee whether the total hours worked exceeded 40.
- The second diamond asks the computer to decide each time an employee record is examined whether it is the last record.

When there are no more records, the computer has finished its work and must be told to stop processing. Until it is told to do this, it will continue to process the next employee record.

The flowcharts a programmer creates for a typical business application are more involved than this example. Flowcharting all the steps in a payroll or other application often calls for many

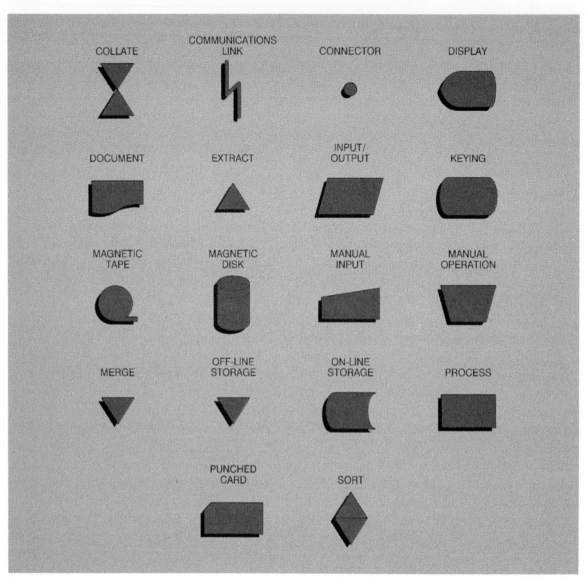

COLLATE

COMMUNICATIONS
LINK

CONNECTOR

DISPLAY

DOCUMENT

EXTRACT

INPUT/
OUTPUT

KEYING

MAGNETIC
TAPE

MAGNETIC
DISK

MANUAL
INPUT

MANUAL
OPERATION

MERGE

OFF-LINE
STORAGE

ON-LINE
STORAGE

PROCESS

PUNCHED
CARD

SORT

FLOWCHART SYMBOLS.

pages of flowcharting symbols. Each such flowchart, called a *program flowchart,* provides the programmer with a means of checking the data flow. It makes possible an early check on the completeness and logical order of a program. It also provides a framework for performing the next part of the programming task: coding, or writing, the program.

Selecting a Programming Language. Today we can discuss as many as four generations of languages for computers. These four generations include machine-oriented, symbolic, English-

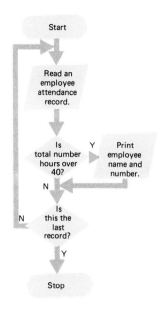

FLOWCHART FOR REPORT-
ING OVERTIME WORK.

like, and query languages. Specialists sometimes classify languages in different ways, but the distinctions that follow are common.

1. *Machine-oriented languages.* In the early days of computers, the programmer who wrote instructions for the computer had to write programs in a numeric form understood by the computer. These programs, written in 0's and 1's, were called either *binary* or **machine language.**

2. *Symbolic-form languages.* The next step in the development of programming languages as we know them was the symbolic form, commonly called **assembler language.** The expression **symbolic form** refers to the use of a letter, a numeral, or some other image to represent an idea to be communicated. Symbolic form permitted programmers to write instructions as a combination of alphabetic and numeric codes that could be quickly read and processed by a computer.

3. *Higher-level languages.* A tremendous breakthrough in the simplification of programming came with the development of the so-called **higher-level languages.** Each of these languages was designed to
   - Provide a means of writing computer instructions similar to English.
   - Enable computer users to move programs from one computer processor to another more easily.

4. *Query languages.* A recent step to make communication with computers easier was the development of a group of programming languages known as **query languages.** These languages allow the user to instruct the computer

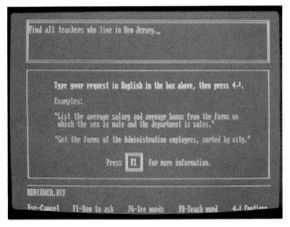
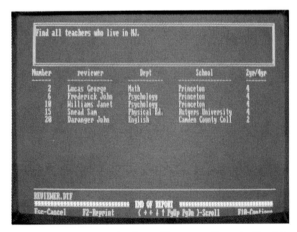

QUERY LANGUAGES. Query languages allow the user to instruct the computer by asking questions in English that are interpreted by the software program. *Will Faller.*

by answering questions or issuing commands provided for by the language. IBM developed SQL (Structured Query Language) to provide a standard syntax for retrieving information from database management systems. A standard syntax is an established arrangement of symbols or words that has a common meaning around the world.

Coding the Program. The word **programming** is sometimes used interchangeably with the word *coding*. Both words are used to indicate the programmer's use of a programming language to translate each instruction into a form the computer can understand. Since a computer processes data only if it is told exactly what to do, coding from a flowchart can involve hundreds or even thousands of individual written instructions. The programs designed to fly the Space Shuttle include hundreds of thousands of lines of code and instructions. Each instruction tells the computer which operation is to be performed and on what data. The program in the payroll example given earlier must include several sets of instructions. These include reading the overtime hours recorded on magnetic tape and multiplying the overtime hours by the overtime rate to obtain overtime pay. The overtime pay must then be added to the base salary to arrive at the employee's final weekly pay.

Unfortunately, a computer can carry out the instructions in a program only in numeric form. This means that either the programmer or the computer must convert the instructions to numeric form. As you read earlier, programmers using the first computer models had to understand and write programs in machine language. Each computer manufacturer developed a numeric code suitable for its computer model. The programmer

CODING THE PROGRAM. After flowcharting a procedure, the programmer has to write the code that will tell the computer exactly what must be done. Here, a programmer is reviewing a payroll program written in COBOL. *Will Faller.*

```
SAMPLE PROGRAM-ASSEMBLER OUTPUT & DIAGNOSTICS                              PAGE    2

  LOC  OBJECT CODE   ADDR1 ADDR2 STMT  SOURCE STATEMENT              F08APR--  5/17/--

  001000                       35  SAMPLE START   X '1000'                    SAMP0020

                               36  *                                          SAMP0030

                               37  FIRST  ENTREE                              SAMP0040

  001000 90EC D00C 0000C  38+FIRST  STM    14,12,12(13)-SAVE CALLER'S REGS IN SAVEAREA

  001004 05C0             39+       BALR   12,0-SET UP ADDRESSABILITY (BASE REG 12)

  001006                  40+       USING  *,12-TELL ASSEMBLER REG 12 IS BASE REG
```

ASSEMBLER LANGUAGE. An assembler language is a symbolic form of coding that translates programs into machine language.

had to develop instructions in detail, then translate the instructions into numeric form. A great deal of time was thus spent on each computer program.

As computers became more widely used to process business information, the variations in numeric codes from manufacturer to manufacturer created difficulties that resulted in a great many errors. Programmers who had learned how to code instructions for one machine had to learn a whole new coding system to write computer programs for another machine. Also, large businesses that used computers made by different manufacturers could not run the same programs on the different machines.

Computer manufacturers and large-scale computer users, such as businesses and government agencies, began sending representatives to meetings to develop standard language specifications that would work for all computer models. The goal was to enable programmers to write instructions in a form as close to ordinary English as possible. Grace Hopper, at the time Captain of the U.S. Navy, was responsible for developing the first assembler program in the early 1950s. Later she headed a team of Navy programmers who developed a program to test COBOL compilers to see whether they met certain standards. (A **compiler** is a special computer program designed to translate a program from a high-level, English-like programming language into a machine-readable binary format such as a machine language.) Partly because of her work, COBOL became one of the few languages that is standardized internationally.

COBOL can be said to have international standardization because programmers worldwide use the same syntax. Because of such standardization, programmers can move from one employer or country to another and use the COBOL syntax they are familiar with. Such standardization also means that a COBOL program can be used with the computers of various manufacturers. One of the oldest higher-level languages, COBOL has continually had new features added to its syntax by computer manufacturers. Because of the ongoing efforts of Grace Hopper and others who have participated in committees on international standardization, COBOL can still be used around the world.

There are numerous higher-level languages, some intended for a broad range of applications and others for very specific applications. Besides COBOL, some of the most popular of these languages are BASIC, Logo, Pascal, C, and Ada. The more widely used programming languages are listed below. Following the list is a brief description of six of the nine languages.

Language	Year Developed	Use of Language
FORTRAN	1957	Scientific and technical work
COBOL	1960	Business systems
BASIC	1965	General-purpose work
PL/1	1965	Business and scientific work
RPG	1966	Business reporting
Logo	1968	Fundamental problem solving
Pascal	1971	General-purpose work
C	1972	General-purpose work
Ada	1982	Large programs

1. One of the most effective higher-level languages developed for business so far is **COBOL** (COmmon Business-Oriented Language). COBOL, which has been expanded by its developers since its specifications were first released in 1960, has been standardized as American National Standard COBOL. Computer manufacturers provide users with compilers, which convert or translate each statement written by the programmer into machine language. A COBOL compiler translates each COBOL programming instruction into several machine-language instructions.
2. **BASIC** (Beginner's All-purpose Symbolic Instruction Code) has grown in popularity as a language for information processing because it:
   - Is easy to learn.
   - Can be used for educational, business, and technical work.

COBOL Coding Form

Date **Dec. 8, 19--**

Student/Programmer **Fred Converse**

Program **PAY**

Page No.	Line No.	C	A Margin	B Margin			Identification
009010	520		IF H (D) GREATER 40	GO TO 550-CALC-OVERTIME.			
009020	530		MOVE H (D) TO R.				
009030	540			GO TO 570-CALCULATE-PAY.			
009040							
009050	550		550-CALC-OVERTIME.				
009060	550		COMPUTE O = H (D) - 40.				
009070	560		MOVE 40 TO R.				
009080							
009090	570		570-CALCULATE-PAY.				
009100	580		COMPUTE P1 = R * P.	NOTE CALCULATES REGULAR PAY.			
009110	600		COMPUTE P2 = O * P * 1.5.	NOTE CALCULATES OVERTIME PAY.			
009120	620		COMPUTE G = P1 + P2.	NOTE CALCULATES GROSS PAY.			
009130	640		COMPUTE W = G * .2.	NOTE CALCULATES WITHHOLDING.			
009140	660		COMPUTE N = G - W.	NOTE CALCULATES NET PAY.			
009150							
009160	670		670-ADD-TO-RUNNING-TOTALS.				
009170	680		ADD R TO T1.				
009180	690		ADD O TO T2.				
009190	700		ADD P1 TO T3.				
009200	710		ADD P2 TO T4.				
009210	720		ADD G TO T5.				
009220	730		ADD W TO T6.				
009230	740		ADD N TO T7.				
009240							

CODING FORMS. A page of a COBOL coding form for a payroll program is shown here. A coding form is completed before the program is entered into the computer.

```
10 REM THIS PROGRAM ILLUSTRATES THE
20 REM USE OF THE OR STATEMENT
30 LET A=10
40 LET B=20
50 LET C=30
60 IF A=B/2 or C=A+B THEN 80
70 STOP
80 IF B=C-A OR B=A*2 THEN 100
90 STOP
100 IF A=10 or B=20 OR C=30 THEN 120
110 STOP
120 END
```

SAMPLE OF A BASIC PROGRAM.

Chapter 10: Concepts of Programming   253

```
TO SQUARE
FORWARD 50
RIGHT 90
FORWARD 50
RIGHT 90
FORWARD 50
RIGHT 90
FORWARD 50
RIGHT 90
END
```

SAMPLE OF A LOGO PROGRAM. This logo program is used to teach the computer how to draw a square.

- Is available on many microcomputers and minicomputers.
- Is interactive and therefore easy to test and debug.

Students often learn BASIC as their first programming language. One drawback is that BASIC may not be suitable for the large-scale information processing applications found in many businesses.

3. The **Logo** programming language was developed at MIT by Seymour Papert. It is designed to teach problem solving and programming to children. Logo differs from the other languages in the following ways:

- Logo provides commands that offer graphics, data processing, and file creation.
- Logo uses a triangular object called a "turtle" to produce screen graphics through specific commands. It permits children to draw and manipulate images on the screen.

4. The **Pascal** programming language (named for the seventeenth century philosopher and mathematician Blaise Pascal) is a more recent general-purpose language. It has most of the advantages of BASIC. In addition, it:

- Is appropriate for both large and small applications.
- Is structured (in sections) in such a way that large programs can be distributed for team programming.
- Makes it easier for a programmer to understand and alter work done by another programmer.

Pascal has recently become available on a wide range of large and small computer systems.

```
PROCEDURE COMPUTEPAY;
    BEGIN
        IF HOURS [COUNT] > 40.0
            THEN
                BEGIN
                    REGULARHOURS [COUNT] := 40.0;
                    OVERTIME [COUNT] := HOURS [COUNT] - 40.0
                END
            ELSE REGULARHOURS [COUNT] := HOURS [COUNT];
        REGULARPAY [COUNT] := RATE [COUNT] * REGULARHOURS
        [COUNT];
        OVERPAY [COUNT] := 1.5 * RATE [COUNT] * OVERTIME [COUNT];
        GROSSPAY [COUNT] := REGULARPAY [COUNT] + OVERPAY [COUNT];
```

PASCAL. This program is written in Pascal. Since ANSI has not yet standardized Pascal or BASIC, the details of these languages vary from manufacturer to manufacturer. The printout produced when this program is executed is shown below and on the next page.

```
EXECUTE PAY
LINK:      Loading
[LNKXCT PAY execution]
INPUT          : TTY:
OUTPUT         : TTY:
MASTER         : MASTER.DAT
PROGRAM REPORTS PAY INFORMATION FOR THE FOLLOWING PEOPLE.
NAME           NUMBER
------------------------------------------------------------------
MYRON FURTH    1234
JUDY SOKOL     4321
LARRY CHAN     2468
HELEN KELLY    1357
INPUT EMPLOYEE NUMBER 1234
HOURS WORKED 40
ARE THERE ANY MORE? (Y OR N) Y
INPUT EMPLOYEE NUMBER 4321
```

SAMPLE OF A PASCAL PROGRAM.

```
HOURS WORKED 42

ARE THERE ANY MORE? (Y OR N) Y

INPUT EMPLOYEE NUMBER 2468

HOURS WORKED 38

ARE THERE ANY MORE? (Y OR N) Y

INPUT EMPLOYEE NUMBER 1357

HOURS WORKED 40

ARE THERE ANY MORE? (Y or N) N

HOURS FOR ALL EMPLOYEES HAVE BEEN ENTERED.

                            PAY REPORT
```

NAME	HOURS		PAY		GROSS PAY	WITH- HELD	NET PAY
	REG	OVR	REG	OVR			
MYRON FURTH	40.0	0.0	220.00	0.00	220.00	44.00	176.00
JUDY SOKOL	40.0	2.0	180.00	13.50	193.50	38.70	154.80
LARRY CHAN	38.0	0.0	171.00	0.00	171.00	34.20	136.80
HELEN KELLY	40.0	0.0	190.00	0.00	190.00	38.00	152.00
TOTAL	158.0	2.0	761.00	13.50	774.50	154.90	619.60

```
INPUT CONTROL VALUE FOR TOTAL HOURS

WORKED THIS WEEK BY ALL EMPLOYEES

160

NO ERROR HOURS CHECK
```

5. The **C** programming language was created by Dennis Ritchie of Bell Laboratories. It was developed as a programming language for writing systems software and evolved into a general-purpose language. The C language's important features are that it:
   - Is concise, with only 30 or so required commands.
   - Has flexible commands that allow it to be used with new and developing systems.
   - Is portable, meaning that it can be used on a variety of computers, from small to large.

6. **Ada** was developed by the Honeywell corporation under the direction of the U.S. Department of Defense. The purpose of introducing this general-purpose language was to reduce the department's rapidly escalating software costs by using one language instead of different languages that

```
struct address *sls_store(i,top) /* store in sorted order */
struct address *i;       /* new element to store */
struct address *top;     /* start of list */
{
  static struct address *last=0; /* start with null link */
  struct address *old,*start;

  start=top;

  if(!last) {  /* first element in list */
    i->next=NULL:
    LAST=i;
    return i;
  }

  old=NULL;
  while(top) {
    if(strcmp(top->name,i->name)<0) {
      old=top;
      top=top->next;
    }
    else {
      if(old) {  /* goes in middle */
        old->next=i;
        i->next=top;
        return start;
      }
      i->next=top; /* new first element */
      return    i;
    }
  }
  last->next=i; /* put on end */
  i->next=NULL;
  last=i;
  return start;
}
```

SAMPLE OF A C PROGRAM.

were used depending on the work that had to be done. The U.S. Bureau of Standards increased the use of Ada in major system development projects because of the ease of

```
BEGIN
  WHILE Remaining_Set_1_Members /=NULL AND
        Remaining_Set_2_Members /=NULL LOOP
    DECLARE
      Next_Set_1_Member:
        Integer RENAMES
        Remaining_Set_1_Members.Member_Part;
      Next_Set_2_Member:
        Integer RENAMES
          Remaining_Set_2_Members.Member_Part;
    BEGIN
      IF Next_Set_1_Member<Next_Set_2_Member THEN
        Insert_At_End
          (Next_Set_1_Member,Last_Result_Cell);
        Remaining_Set_1_Members:=
          Remaining_Set_1_Members.Next_Cell_Part;
      ELSIF Next_Set_2_Member<Next_Set_1_Member THEN
        Insert_At_End
          (Next_Set_2_Member,Last_Result_Cell);
        Remaining_Set_2_Members:=
          Remaining_Set_2_Members.Next_Cell_Part;
      ELSE  -- Same value belongs to both sets.
        Insert_At_End
          (Next_Set_1_Member,Last_Result_Cell);
        Remaining_Set_1_Members:=
          Remaining_Set_1_Members.Next_Cell_Part;
        Remaining_Set_2_Members:=
          Remaining_Set_2_Members.Next_Cell_Part;
      END IF;
    END;
  END LOOP;
```

SAMPLE OF AN ADA PROGRAM.

reusing programming code. Ada, a trademark of the Department of Defense, has a couple of major features. It:

- Promotes the development of portable, modifiable programs.
- Can be used for a wide range of major development projects, including operating systems, simulations, and communications.

COBOL continues to be the most widely used language for business. RPG (Report Program Generator) is used for programming simple business procedures. FORTRAN (FORmula TRANslation) is used for information processing that involves numerous mathematical formulas. There are hundreds of other programming languages, ranging from the general to the specific. The trend in an organization's selection of programming languages is toward those that combine learning ease for the user and flexibility of application. The selection of languages will also become more and more standardized as many less useful or less powerful languages disappear, and the more powerful and more flexible languages, such as COBOL and C, remain and become the standards.

Testing and Debugging the Program. When a program has been written and recorded on an input medium, it must be tested on the computer. The skilled programmer checks his or her work throughout the work assignment to make sure the work will be completed accurately and on time. This means the program will run as planned, performing accurately the operations specified. It also means the computer output will be in the proper form.

Each time part of a programming assignment is completed, the programmer needs to double-check the code for accuracy and completeness. Such a manual self-check is called **desk debugging.** A programmer who carefully checks his or her own work saves computer processing time because the computer finds fewer errors. This is true for both errors in the logic of the program (the plan itself) and errors in the syntax used in coding the instructions.

Because a computer program is usually very complex, desk debugging often cannot catch every error. A coded program must always be read into the computer, translated into machine language with a compiler, and run-tested. The computer itself issues error messages, often called **diagnostics,** which flag mistakes in coding. When the programmer corrects coding errors in the program, he or she checks the output to see whether the results, format, and output medium are as expected.

```
0040:    STATEMENT DELETED DUE TO ERRONEOUS SYNTAX.   CLXSE
0050:    PROCEDURE-NAME IS UNRESOLVABLE.    3000-GET-A-RECORD
0001:    /F/ FILE NEVER CLOSED.
0002:    /F/ FILE NEVER CLOSED.
```

DIAGNOSTICS. Diagnostics are computer-generated error messages that flag system problems or mistakes in coding. The COBOL diagnostics shown above, tell the programmer to look at lines 40 and 50 of the code for possible errors. The messages for these lines refer to errors in syntax. While two files were opened in the program, neither was closed after processing. This caused the appearance of the two messages noted as 0001 and 0002.

Once all the obvious coding errors have been corrected, a program is tested using a set of test data for which the correct output and responses are known. This is sometimes called a *simulation.* The program uses the test data to generate output data. Errors in the logic of the instructions (such as dividing, instead of multiplying, two numbers) are usually found using this technique.

It may require weeks of effort to find and correct all the errors made in planning and coding a lengthy or complex program. But, only after the testing operation has resulted in a complete and accurate program should a computer program be used to process actual business or scientific data. You obviously would not want to fly an airplane if the programs operating the flight controls had not been thoroughly tested.

Documenting the Program. Illustrations, comments, and explanations, called **documentation,** must be prepared for each working program. Documentation typically includes flowcharts and written explanations (narratives) of the purpose of the program and each routine in it, sample input and output, and a test run. Also, within the program itself, the programmer writes many comments that describe what is taking place in that section of the program or what kind of input is being processed. Documentation is prepared to meet two needs:

1. To provide the information that a computer operator needs to run the program or that might be needed later if the program had to be updated (for example, to compute overtime pay after 35 hours instead of after 40 hours). The person who is asked to update a program needs detailed

program flowcharts and explanations of each section of coding. Without clear and complete documentation for such a project, a programmer might be forced to "reinvent the wheel" by rewriting sections of the program or the entire program. This duplication of effort would waste valuable time and energy.

2. To provide the general information the user needs to input data accurately and to generate necessary output information easily. For example, the documentation would detail the information the payroll department would need to input and keep up to date, such as current tax tables. The user for whom the processing work is done needs information such as the requirements of the data-entry operations and descriptions of each printout prepared by the computer.

CHECK YOURSELF

Supply the missing words.

1. The business programmer should have one or more courses in ___?___ ___?___, information processing, accounting, or recordkeeping.

2. Developing appropriate instructions for computer information processing is called ___?___.

3. In the early days of computers, programming instructions were written in ___?___ language.

4. The person who defines the system specifications is called a ___?___ ___?___.

5. To show the steps in a computer program graphically, the programmer prepares a ___?___.

6. The flowcharting symbol used to show that a decision must be made has the shape of a ___?___.

7. The flowcharting symbol generally used to show a process is a ___?___.

8. An example of a symbolic programming language is ___?___.

9. One of the oldest programming languages important in business information processing is ___?___.

10. A language translator used with a higher-level programming language is called a ___?___.

11. The programmer's self-check is called __?__ __?__.
12. Computer-generated error messages are often called __?__.
13. The illustrations and explanations that should accompany the computer printout of a working program are called __?__.
14. A recent development in communication between computers and computer users is __?__ language.
15. A relatively new programming language that is portable, powerful, and concise is known as __?__.
16. A language created under government supervision, primarily for major development projects, is __?__.

Answers: (1) business math; (2) programming; (3) machine; (4) systems analyst; (5) flowchart; (6) diamond; (7) rectangle; (8) assembler; (9) COBOL; (10) compiler; (11) desk debugging; (12) diagnostics; (13) documentation; (14) query; (15) C; (16) Ada.

SOFTWARE DEVELOPMENTS

According to the National Bureau of Standards, software has evolved more slowly than hardware. The chief development is a change from user-developed software to manufacturer-developed software. In other words, instead of each company developing custom software for its internal applications, software manufacturing companies develop generic applications software and sell these programs to many different users. The change from user-developed to manufacturer-developed software applies to the three broad classifications of software: operating systems, applications software, and support systems. It also applies to a classification of software known as *utility programs.*

Every business wants to keep its costs down and its prices competitive, so there is a great interest in making the development and use of computer hardware and computer software more efficient. The hardware developers have produced computers that are less expensive, more reliable, and faster than earlier models. In spite of inflation, most computer systems cost considerably less than their more primitive predecessors. The software developers have also found better ways to use computer systems to produce the desired results at less cost to the user. There have been major developments in four classifications of computer software:

1. Operating software
2. Applications software
3. Support software
4. Utility software

COMPUTERS IN THE OFFICE. A travel agency would find it impossible to operate today without a computer.

OPERATING SOFTWARE

An **operating system** is a set of manufacturer-developed programs that performs the following functions:

- First, an operating system reduces programmers' workload because it contains coded instructions for certain repetitive operations that are required for every computer job, such as the instructions for transferring input data into the computer memory or for printing out a document.
- Second, an operating system makes the computer operator's job easier by performing such tasks as keeping track of the running time of each job.
- Third, an operating system makes it possible to maximize the use of the computer hardware. For example, an operating system schedules the sequence of multiple jobs to perform the work in the shortest possible time.

Today's operating systems can acknowledge processing requests from remote terminals, allocate the necessary resources, and run the jobs on the central processing unit. (A remote terminal is located in a different room, or even a different building, from the computer.) The terminal operator stores data, processes data, and retrieves data by working at the terminal keyboard. Telephone lines transmit the keyed data and instructions to the computer's central processing unit.

Operating system software is being made increasingly user-friendly, with interfaces to both applications software and support software. Computer manufacturers and computer users continue to work to develop more effective ways of communicat-

APPLICATIONS PACKAGES. Financial applications packages are available for almost every business or administrative function.

ing with the computer and to reduce the need for human intervention. This is necessary because, while unit computer processing and storage costs have been decreasing rapidly, the systems and programming costs for designing and installing computer systems have risen steadily due to increasing system complexity and higher labor costs.

APPLICATIONS SOFTWARE

Lower-cost computer hardware designed for smaller businesses and for individual departments in larger organizations has created a strong demand for business and scientific software. Today, there is a tremendous range of off-the-shelf software for virtually every business or administrative function. Programs for doing accounting, business graphics, financial analysis, and word processing are all available from many different manufacturers. Users purchase or lease such applications packages directly from software developers or through computer stores.

Applications packages, sometimes called *canned programs*, can be much less expensive for the user than the customized software packages that once had to be developed on a user-by-user basis because of a lack of software standards. Applications packages can be obtained for all computer models. Whether or

TURNKEY PACKAGE. The Cascade CAD system shown above is an example of hardware and software dedicated to a specific task. *Source: Cascade Graphics Systems.*

not a potential application is available for a particular computer model depends on how widespread the need for that application is and whether the users of that application have typically purchased their computers from the same manufacturer. Software developers are unlikely to produce software for a computer system unless they expect a large number of users and potential customers.

When hardware and software are combined to perform a specific business task, the combination is referred to as a **turnkey package.** This arrangement is common when small businesses make their first computer purchases. Of course, the drawback of a commercial applications package is that it may not exactly satisfy a user's particular requirements. If an applications package must be extensively revised, purchasing or leasing may be more expensive in the long run than paying to develop a custom-made program.

SUPPORT SOFTWARE

The third key area for software development, **support software,** is the software that falls between the applications software and the operating system. Examples of support software include database management systems and communications software.

Database management software is another type of program package that can be purchased from computer manufacturers or software service companies. This set of standard machine instructions makes it easier for a programmer to write a program that handles the storage, updating, and retrieval of data in a file, such as a computer file used for billing. Information in

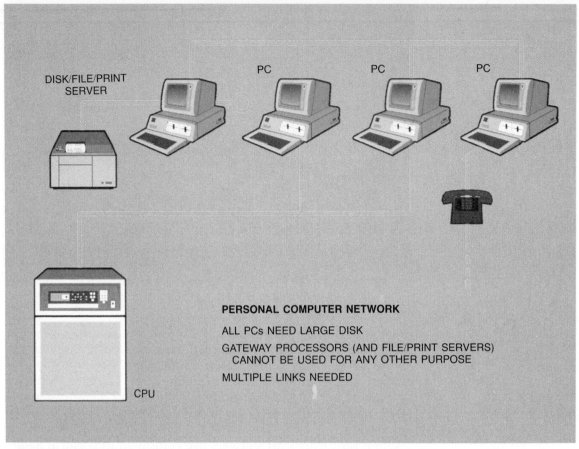

DISK/FILE/PRINT SERVER

PC   PC   PC

PERSONAL COMPUTER NETWORK

ALL PCs NEED LARGE DISK

GATEWAY PROCESSORS (AND FILE/PRINT SERVERS) CANNOT BE USED FOR ANY OTHER PURPOSE

MULTIPLE LINKS NEEDED

CPU

PERSONAL COMPUTER NETWORK. Networking PCs allows for services to be available on every desk and for expensive resources to be shared. *Reprinted from April 1984 issue of Data Communications. Copyright © 1984 by McGraw-Hill, Inc. All rights reserved.*

the database, for example, a set of customer names and addresses, can be used by other applications and programs to generate output. A word processing application can access the names and addresses in the database to generate a personalized business letter, and a billing program can use the same information to produce a customer invoice.

Communications software helps more and more users work with centralized databases, such as corporate databases and commercially available databases. It also helps users communicate with one another, using either manufacturer- or user-developed models for message transmission. Communications software is designed to act as a traffic manager in handling incoming and outgoing information.

UTILITY SOFTWARE

In ordinary English, something that has "utility" is considered useful. A **utility program** is a collection of instructions designed to perform common programming functions. Such functions might include sorting, copying, editing, deleting, and printing. These programming aids, also called *software utilities,* have been greatly improved and expanded in recent years. Examples include sort/merge, cross-reference, and file-handling packages. These preprogrammed tools can save hours of programming time. A sort/merge utility program, for example, can be inserted into another program, eliminating the need to write hundreds of instructions to tell the computer how to sort data.

Sort/Merge Utility Program. A **sort/merge utility** program arranges file records sequentially, then combines the entries in two files. For a sort/merge application, the programmer names both the input file and the output file, specifying the files to be sorted. The sort/merge program then performs the sorting of the files. For example, if an insurance company wants to sort clients by birth dates, the programmer indicates the beginning and ending fields, and the program will sort the list of clients in descending or ascending order by birth date. Many companies use mailing list programs with sort utilities. If a company, like your local telephone company, can presort its mail by zip code, the post office charges less for postage. So, using a sort program, the company can sort thousands of customer addresses by zip code. When the mailing labels are printed, they are grouped by common zip codes. Imagine how time-consuming it would be to sort thousands of telephone bills by hand.

A merge operation combines two files into one file. For example, a mutual fund company might merge two sets of client files by birth date to send mailings that take into account typical financial planning needs for a particular age group. Or a sales representative might want to send a personalized letter to his or her customers. A merge utility can merge the name and address data in one file into the text data in another file to generate a personalized letter.

File-Handling Utility Program. A **file-handling utility** program converts files from one format into another and manages the process of reading a file from one medium (such as a disk) and writing it on another (such as a printer). With a utility program providing management of output, you can select the number of lines per page, single-spacing or double-spacing, and indention.

Cross-Reference Utility Program. A **cross-reference utility** program can examine hundreds of lines of program code and locate a trouble spot. In general, such a program is developed to save programming time. A cross-reference utility program also eliminates the need to write instructions for common types of operations that must be performed in many programs. For example, in letter-writing campaigns, a brokerage firm may need to refer to an electronic file for information about investments that are likely to be of interest to clients. A cross-reference program saves a lot of handwork in identifying the appropriate brochures to enclose with each letter.

CHECK YOURSELF

Supply the missing words.

1. An ___?___ ___?___ is a set of manufacturer-developed programs that make the programmer's job easier and the computer hardware more useful.
2. A ___?___ utility program can save a great deal of time by having the computer reuse instructions that would otherwise need to be re-created for different programs.
3. Software houses and computer manufacturers can supply ___?___ ___?___, which eliminate the need to hire a programmer.
4. ___?___ ___?___ aid programmers by eliminating the need to program common types of applications.
5. A ___?___ utility program arranges file records sequentially and then combines the entries from two files.
6. A ___?___ utility program converts files from one format to another, then arranges for a file to be sent from one medium to another.

Answers: (1) operating system; (2) cross-reference; (3) applications programs; (4) Utility programs; (5) sort/merge; (6) file-handling.

REVIEW QUESTIONS

1. Name one business, one technical, and one general-purpose programming language.
2. For the payroll flowchart shown in this chapter, describe the input, then describe the output.
3. List in ordinary English the several processes that take place in moving from the input phase to the output phase.
4. Name one similarity and one difference between the input and the output.
5. Mention two reasons why an employer would expect programmers to do a good job of documenting their programs.
6. How many types of software are there?

7. How are operating systems software becoming more user-friendly?
8. What is a utility program? Describe one example of such a program.

COMPARING IDEAS

The questions below are designed to help you think about what you have learned in this chapter. They are "thought" questions. There is no one correct answer.

1. If you were a programmer, would you prefer to write a program in assembler language or in a higher-level language? Why?
2. Are employers in your area likely to hire systems analysts? What types of employers? In which industries?
3. Would you prefer to create a compiler for a computer manufacturer or an applications program for a computer user? Why?

INFORMATION PROCESSING ACTIVITIES

Now you can try out the kinds of data processing activities business workers perform. Below is a summary of the work you will do. You will find the actual information and business forms you need in your *Information Processing Work Kit.*

1. You will work as a programmer trainee in a large computer service bureau. You will develop a flowchart for a check approval procedure.
2. You will sort and classify customer requests matching the requirement with the appropriate computer language.

HANDS-ON ACTIVITIES

Prepare a simple flowchart to describe how to add any series of exactly five numbers and compute the average. Then, if computers are available, use any available programming language to write a short program to perform this task.

CHAPTER

11

SOFTWARE APPLICATIONS PACKAGES

Information Processing Terminology

Packaged software
Customized software
Horizontal software
Vertical software
Word processing
  software
Telecommunications
  software

Baud rate
Menu-driven
Single-purpose software
Integrated software
Database management
  system

Free-form package
File manager
Electronic spreadsheet
"What if" questions
Decision support
  software

Performance Goals

☐ Distinguish between customized and off-the-shelf software.

☐ Distinguish between horizontal and vertical market software, and give at least one example of each.

☐ List five benefits of software packages.

☐ Describe at least five types of software applications packages that help automate the preparation of typical business reports.

☐ Distinguish between single-purpose and integrated software packages.

☐ Define the term *decision support system* and provide at least two examples.

☐ Name six examples of business and industrial databases.

☐ Describe an electronic spreadsheet and give at least one example of appropriate use.

WORKING WITH A PERSONAL COMPUTER. Managers can accomplish a great deal of work using portable computers on business trips. *Richard Hackett.*

In this chapter you will learn about a broad range of software. You will become familiar with software designed to create documents, monitor performance, and send and receive data. You will also learn whether it makes sense to buy software created for a large number of users with similar needs or to pay a higher price to have software professionally developed to meet the needs of one organization.

You will also learn about several electronic tools that aid managers and professionals, and sometimes consumers as well, in making reasoned decisions about important questions. These tools include specialized software, databases, and spreadsheets.

PACKAGED SOFTWARE

Computer programs written for a large number of users with similar needs are called **packaged software** or *off-the-shelf software*. As more and more organizations have installed computers and automated their offices and production operations, packaged software has become increasingly useful to developers of programs and users alike. Manufacturers now find it profitable to sell packaged software because of the large number of potential sales. Examples of packaged software for microcomputers include Lotus 1-2-3, dBase III, MacWrite, and Excel. Users find it practical to purchase such software because off-the-shelf software is less expensive than customized software.

VERTICAL SOFTWARE. Vertical software is used in related operations in specialized areas, such as insurance. Shown here are a general commands screen (at left) and a formula test for a single limit liability premium (at right).

You can think of **customized software** as made-to-order software—that is, software designed and developed to meet the specific requirements of the end user.

General-purpose software packages that can be used by any type of business are known as **horizontal software.** They perform one or more functions for business in general. Examples of such software are word processing and financial management packages, such as Microsoft Word and Lotus 1-2-3. Software written for a specific business or profession, such as an insurance agency or a law practice, is known as **vertical software.** Vertical software is also known as special-purpose software—software related to operations in specialized areas, such as insurance, stock brokerage, banking, or hospital administration. Another example of vertical software is a client accounting package for a medical practice. Such a package keeps track of time spent with or working for a client, out-of-pocket expenses, and third-party reporting, such as a doctor's charges or lab fees that will be paid by an insurance company.

Both horizontal and vertical software packages created by commercial software developers provide at least five benefits to users.

1. *Immediate availability.* Less time is required to develop the program than with customized software.

2. *Known cost.* The cost of a software package is the price quoted.
3. *Lower cost.* The price of packaged software is often considerably less than the cost of customized software because many users are, in effect, dividing up the development cost.
4. *Better documentation.* Usually, software packages come with more complete and accurate descriptions and explanations than customized software.
5. *Reliability.* Software packages developed by reputable firms have generally been thoroughly tested under typical user conditions. Such firms also tend to provide updates for programs that are sensitive to changes needed by many users.

Applications needed by both large and small organizations include word processing, telecommunications, accounting and business management, database management systems, electronic spreadsheets, and graphic applications.

WORD PROCESSING APPLICATIONS

Although industrial productivity has increased visibly over the past 15 years or so, productivity experts report that office productivity has increased at a much slower rate. Computerization has played a great role in the increased productivity of the factory, just as it has in that of the finance and accounting departments that help a company track its performance.

Until the late 1970s, computers were used primarily for processing data and converting it to information valuable to those who would receive it. Offices that processed a large number of lists, letters, and catalogs often used special typewriter-like devices that provided some automation. But, it was not until companies like IBM and Wang developed electronic devices called word processors that words were electronically stored, edited, and retrieved in a way similar to the way numbers were being processed.

Word processing software, like other types of software, is designed to perform a number of functions the user needs or wants. Like software in general, word processing software is designed to perform one or more steps that would otherwise be repetitive and time-consuming. Word processing software is available for individuals who only need some basic functions and for businesses that produce documents with complex tables, charts, and footnotes. A discussion of both the basic and the supplemental functions of word processing software follows.

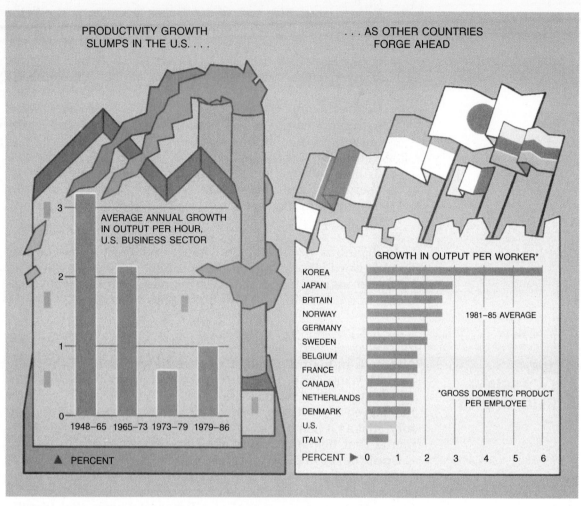

PRODUCTIVITY GROWTH SLUMPS IN THE U.S. . . .

. . . AS OTHER COUNTRIES FORGE AHEAD

AVERAGE ANNUAL GROWTH IN OUTPUT PER HOUR, U.S. BUSINESS SECTOR

3

2

1

0

1948–65 1965–73 1973–79 1979–86

▲ PERCENT

GROWTH IN OUTPUT PER WORKER*

KOREA
JAPAN
BRITAIN
NORWAY
GERMANY
SWEDEN
BELGIUM
FRANCE
CANADA
NETHERLANDS
DENMARK
U.S.
ITALY

1981–85 AVERAGE

*GROSS DOMESTIC PRODUCT PER EMPLOYEE

PERCENT ▶ 0 1 2 3 4 5 6

GROWTH IN INDUSTRIAL PRODUCTIVITY IN THE UNITED STATES AND INTERNATIONALLY. *Reprinted from April 20, 1987 issue of Business Week by special permission. Copyright © 1987 by McGraw-Hill, Inc.*

BASIC FUNCTIONS

Basic functions common to most word processing programs include text editing, electronic storage and retrieval, and automatic pagination and printing. Text editing functions include the ability to correct spellings, change words within a sentence, move sentences and paragraphs around, and/or change the size or style of typeface. Electronic text storage allows users to store their documents on a diskette or hard disk and later retrieve them for editing or printing. Automatic pagination and printing includes automatically setting the horizontal and vertical margins and line spacing. As you type text into the computer, the word processor automatically returns the carriage at the end of the line. This is called *automatic wrap-around*. Normally, the user can reset the tabs, margins, and line spacing to whatever setting he or she requires. Most word processors also

SIMPLE WORD PROCESSING SOFTWARE. Most word processing programs include text editing, electronic storage and retrieval, and automatic pagination and printing. *Source: McGraw-Hill Word Processing. Will Faller.*

have standard page lengths built in, so the text automatically skips to the top of the next page when it hits the bottom margin. All word processors allow the user to control the printing function, including the quality of printing, the type of printer, and the amount of output to be printed at one time.

SUPPLEMENTAL FUNCTIONS

Different users need different special functions to meet their needs. For instance, a student writing a Ph.D. thesis in engineering needs a powerful word processing package that can write formulas, integrate graphs and charts, and use many different symbols and characters. The owner of an electronics store, on the other hand, needs a very simple word processing program that can be used to write letters to customers or to write advertising copy. The electronics store owner does not need, and would not want, the more complex, more expensive program used by the Ph.D. student.

Developers of word processing software are adding new features and new functions to these programs all the time. Dozens of different commercial software packages are available, each of which has different special applications. For instance, there are desktop publishing programs that allow you to write text in multiple columns, easily add pictures and graphics, and print out the results on a high-quality laser printer. A desktop publishing type of word processor would be very useful to someone writing a newsletter or creating copy for a newspaper. On the

```
        C:SP12.DOC  PAGE 1 LINE 14 COL 64           INSERT ON
                   < < <    M A I N   M E N U    > > >
    --Cursor Movement--   : -Delete-  :  -Miscellaneous-  : -Other Menus-
  ^S char left ^D char right :^G char  :^I Tab  ^B Reform : (from Main only)
  ^A word left ^F word right :DEL chr lf:^V INSERT ON/OFF  :^J Help  ^K Block
  ^E line up ^X line down   :^T word rt:^L Find/Replce again:^Q Quick ^P Print
     --Scrolling--         :^Y  line :RETURN End paragraph:^O Onscreen
  ^Z line down ^W line up   :        :  :^N Insert a RETURN :
  ^C screen up ^R screen down:        :  :^U Stop a command  :
  L----!----!----!----!----!----!----!----!----!----!----!---------R
  Applying  the formulas of figure 6-14 we find the following  (all
  division remainders are ignored):

              2,137 (200 + 6)
    ^B146^ + --------------- = 146 + 214 = 360 ~B
                  2,048

  The  results  of our calculation indicate that the tracks of  the
  2314  disk  will  accommodate ^S20 physical  records^S  consisting  of
  eight logical records of 25 bytes each.  Each logical record will
  contain a six-byte key or record identifying the control field.        "
                                                                         "
                                                                         "
  1HELP   2INDENT 3SET LM 4SET RM 5UNDLIN 6BLDFCE 7BEGBLK 8ENDBLK 9BEGFIL 10ENDFIL
```

ADVANCED WORD PROCESSING SOFTWARE. Sophisticated word processing programs include additional functions such as spell checking, drawing programs, special character capabilities, and footnoting. *Source: WordStar.*

other hand, a college student writing a paper for biology class would find a more basic word processing package both easier to learn and more useful.

Supplemental functions include such things as spell checkers, drawing programs, special character capabilities, and footnoting. Before choosing a word processing program (or any program, for that matter), the user must decide which features will produce the kinds of documents he or she needs, and can then choose the word processing program that best meets those needs.

TELECOMMUNICATIONS PACKAGES

As you read in Chapter 7, telecommunications is the transfer of information over telephone lines or through some similar technology. Data can be transferred from computer to computer using a device called a modem and a basic communications software package. With this equipment, a computer user can send and receive text and data to and from computers in another room or in another country. Information providers, such as MarketScope, can send information on the stock market over telephone lines to subscribers' personal computers. Users can send information to one another to report on business developments. For example, perhaps a bank's management wants each branch to report weekly on the number of loans made to small businesses for a special marketing campaign. Each bank sends

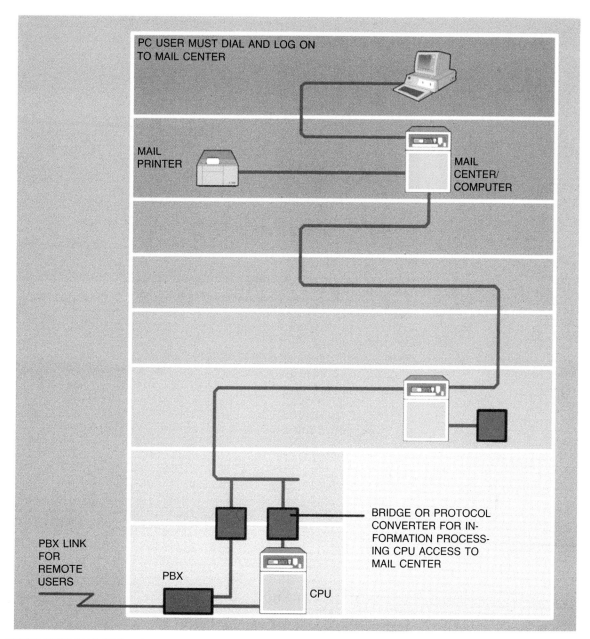

ELECTRONIC MAIL LINK. PC users can send mail to each other in one location or to users around the world. PBX is a Private Branch Exchange used for communications. *Reprinted from April 1984 issue of Data Communications. Copyright © 1984 by McGraw-Hill, Inc. All rights reserved.*

the information electronically to the main office. That office receives and analyzes the information, and then sends a summary to all the branches electronically.

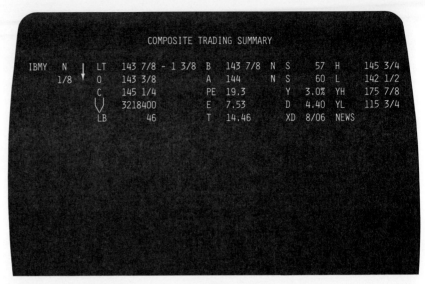

COMPOSITE TRADING SUMMARY

IBMY	N		LT	143 7/8 - 1 3/8	B	143 7/8	N S	57	H	145 3/4
	1/8		O	143 3/8	A	144	N S	60	L	142 1/2
			C	145 1/4	PE	19.3	Y	3.0%	YH	175 7/8
				3218400	E	7.53	D	4.40 YL	115 3/4
			LB	46	T	14.46	XD	8/06 NEWS

ELECTRONIC DATABASES. More and more people are depending on electronic information to keep up to date in their fields. Above is a computer
screen showing IBM stock trading figures provided on-line by MarketScope
(Standard & Poor's).

Telecommunications packages are available in at least two
major versions:

1. Basic functions
2. Electronic mail

BASIC FUNCTIONS

In the 1960s and 1970s, organizations added terminals connected to the central processing unit by telephone lines, which
enabled users at many locations to use the central computers.
In the 1980s, as personal computers became popular in business and government, users required packaged software for
their own local processing needs, such as departmental budgets
or traffic scheduling. However, users still needed company data,
and the company still wanted reports from all its locations. To a
large extent telecommunications software alleviates this problem.

Basic functions of telecommunications software include
sending and receiving data, storing information, and phone
dialing. Most telecommunications packages allow for different
settings, including speed of transmission, data size, and type of
communications device. The speed of transmission refers to the
rate of speed at which bits of information are to be sent or received. This is referred to as the **baud rate** (pronounced "bōd").
The baud rate can range from 300 to over 20,000, depending on
the type of modem, the type of communications link (i.e., telephone lines or high-speed fiber optic cable), and the type of

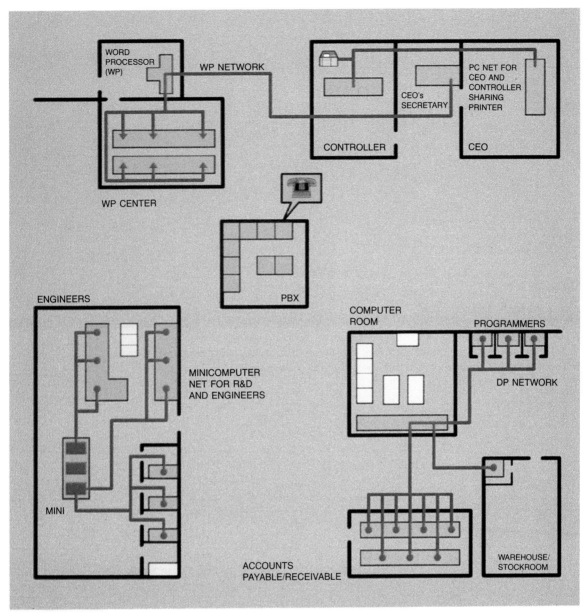

TELECOMMUNICATION PACKAGES. Telecommunications software provides the means for communicating computer to computer over telephone lines. People working in the executive word processing, engineering, accounting, and computing offices can all exchange information using telecommunications. *Reprinted from April 1984 issue of Data Communications. Copyright © 1984 by McGraw-Hill, Inc. All rights reserved.*

computer. The higher the baud rate, the faster a file can be transferred. If you are using long distance telephone lines, the faster you can complete a data transfer, the lower the telephone charge will be.

The data size tells the computer how many pulses (bits) make

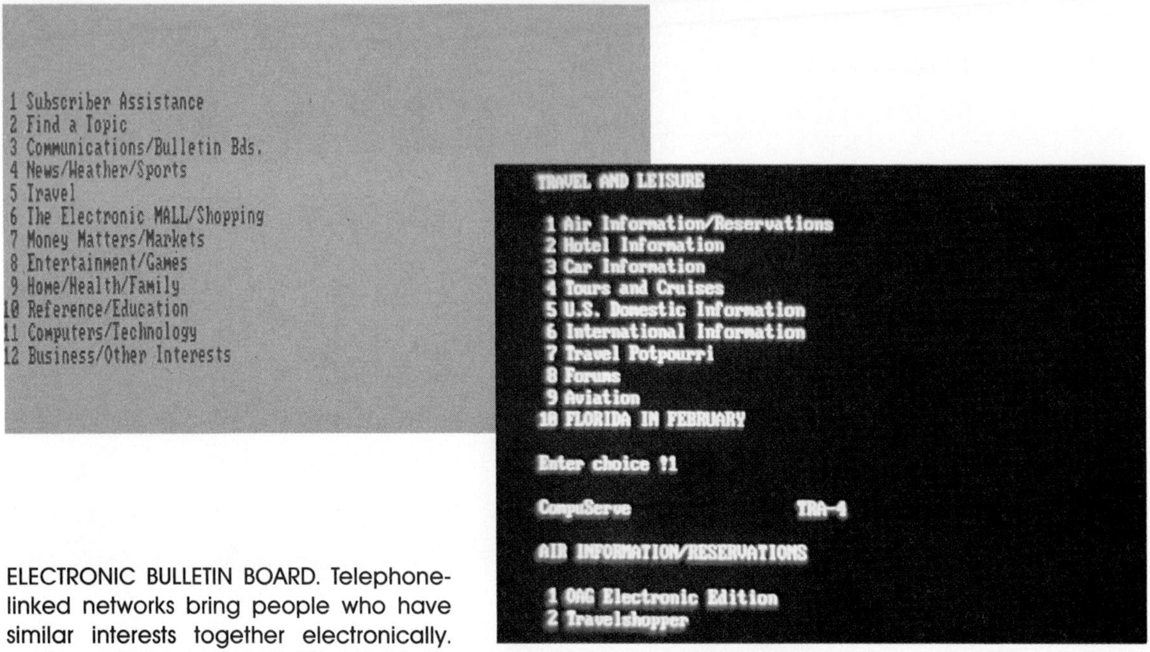

```
1 Subscriber Assistance
2 Find a Topic
3 Communications/Bulletin Bds.
4 News/Weather/Sports
5 Travel
6 The Electronic MALL/Shopping
7 Money Matters/Markets
8 Entertainment/Games
9 Home/Health/Family
10 Reference/Education
11 Computers/Technology
12 Business/Other Interests
```

```
TRAVEL AND LEISURE

1 Air Information/Reservations
2 Hotel Information
3 Car Information
4 Tours and Cruises
5 U.S. Domestic Information
6 International Information
7 Travel Potpourri
8 Forums
9 Aviation
10 FLORIDA IN FEBRUARY

Enter choice !1

CompuServe                    TRA-1

AIR INFORMATION/RESERVATIONS

1 OAG Electronic Edition
2 Travelshopper
```

ELECTRONIC BULLETIN BOARD. Telephone-linked networks bring people who have similar interests together electronically. For example, when subscribers enter CompuServe they can choose a special interest group from the screen shown at left. If the user chose 5, Travel, the screen on the right would appear offering more specific subjects to choose from. *Courtesy CompuServe.*

up each character. As you may remember, some computers use 8 bits to define a character, and other computers use 7 bits. A telecommunications program must be set correctly to receive words of the correct size. The type of communications device used to transfer data is also important. Different signals are required if a touch-tone phone is used, as opposed to a rotary dial phone.

ELECTRONIC MAIL

Recent developments that broaden the scope of electronically sending and receiving mail are the electronic bulletin board and computer conferencing. Such systems are comprised of telephone-linked networks that bring people who have similar interests together electronically. For example, a major information provider has conducted teleconferencing sessions for subscribers to one of its computer magazines. One user sends a message that he would like information on a particular type of hardware or software. Another user responds that she is familiar with two or three suppliers of that hardware. On a larger scale, politicians across the country could exchange their ideas on the latest tax proposals, without leaving their offices.

```
Mail #64695
From: jbaiter@MIX
Date: Tue, 18 Aug 87 10:42:04 EDT
To: lgettelman@MIX
Cc: rodell@MIX,
    jjohnson@MIX,
    kfjelsted@MIX,
    sbouchard@MIX,
    jbaiter@MIX
Message-Id: <memo.64695@MIX>
Subject: NEWSLETTER

IBM RE-ENTERs EDUCATIONAL MARKET

IBM has announced a new computer model for the home and
school market.  The new machine called the Personal System/2
Model 25, comes with a standard keyboard, 512K, a 3 1/2 inch
disk drive capable of storing 720K of data and, a quick and
fairly powerful 8086 microprocessor with the ability to run
must software designed for larger PC's.  Priced between
.More...
```

ELECTRONIC MAIL. More and more people are communicating by electronic mail. Here, a memo about including an announcement on IBM hardware in a newsletter is being sent electronically to co-workers. *Source: MIX. Will Faller.*

CHECK YOURSELF

Supply the missing words.

1. ___?___ ___?___ is another name for off-the-shelf software that is created for a large number of users with similar needs.

2. Another name for software created to meet the needs of a specific user is ___?___ ___?___.

3. A key difference between horizontal and ___?___ software is the type of user served.

4. Development time is a critical issue when deciding between ___?___ software and customized software.

5. ___?___ ___?___ software performs one or more steps that are generally repeated in preparing documents.

6. Functions that enable a user to move copy, adjust spacing, and change the type are called ___?___ functions.

7. With ___?___, businesses can send and receive text and data at terminals or personal computers.

8. An electronic bulletin board system is a ___?___ ___?___ that enables users with similar interests to communicate electronically.

Answers: (1) Packaged software; (2) customized software; (3) vertical; (4) packaged; (5) Word processing; (6) text-editing; (7) telecommunications; (8) telephone-linked network.

ACCOUNTING AND BUSINESS MANAGEMENT APPLICATIONS

Several types of accounting and accounting-related software packages have become popular because a number of software developers have created programs that meet typical needs at attractive prices. Programs included in this area are:

1. Accounts receivable software packages
2. Accounts payable software packages
3. Payroll software packages
4. General ledger software packages
5. Integrated accounting software packages

Single-purpose software packages perform one type of function, such as accounts receivable or accounts payable. In contrast, **integrated software** packages provide several different functions and allow for reference from one data file to another. For instance, some integrated microcomputer software packages offer word processing, database, spreadsheet, and communications capabilities in one product. With integrated software, related programs, such as payroll and general ledger, can refer to the same data stored in a common database.

Typically, buyers of accounting and business management software packages usually obtain recommendations for software from their accountants and information processing personnel or from outside consultants, who may also install the software, train the employees who are to use the software, and develop procedure manuals for ongoing reference. This help in software planning and implementation is commonly chosen by users ranging from small businesses purchasing their first personal computers and software packages to Fortune 500 companies seeking to expand their capability as their businesses grow in size. Because some major corporations have combined their accounting and financial management systems, many firms now refer to finance and accounting software as F&A software.

The following software packages are used by both small and large businesses. The differences in capability have more to do with the number and size of the data fields and the overall flexibility of the programs to accommodate company expansion than with the basic accounting functions themselves.

ACCOUNTING SOFTWARE PACKAGES. Accounting operations are ideally suited to computer processing as is evident by the wide variety of accounting software programs available today. *Julius Allen.*

ACCOUNTS
RECEIVABLE
SOFTWARE
PACKAGES

These programs include instructions for maintenance of customer account files, production of monthly invoices, balancing of accounts, processing of payments, issuance of overdue statements, triggering of debt collection procedures, and management reports. An accounts receivable software package helps to maximize profits and minimize losses from bad debts.

ACCOUNTS
PAYABLE
SOFTWARE
PACKAGES

A typical accounting software package usually includes a scheduled payments file, a paid-but-not-cleared check file, and a historical file. Accounts payable packages provide capabilities for checking supplier invoices, planning payments, scheduling and sending payments, reconciling payments, and allocating payments to different units of the corporation.

PAYROLL
SOFTWARE
PACKAGES

As you read in the last chapter, payroll data includes employee identification, time worked, pay rates, deductions, earnings, and cumulative earnings. Payroll packages perform data entry functions and process payroll output, which includes paychecks, earnings statements, and payroll reports. Some payroll packages also include employee services, benefits administration, and government reporting.

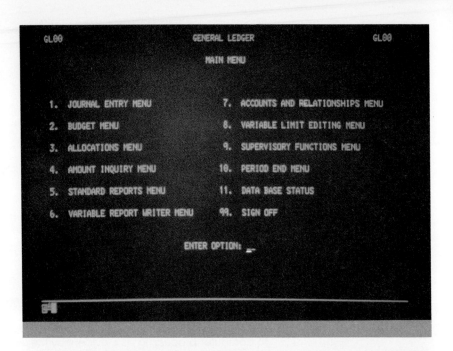

GENERAL LEDGER SOFTWARE. A general ledger accounting system is an easy operation to perform using the proper software. *Courtesy Computer Associates, Inc.*

GENERAL LEDGER SOFTWARE PACKAGES

General ledger packages include a master account file, account posting distribution files, and historical ledger data files. These packages provide management with information on the firm's financial position. The example of a general ledger for ABC Business Machines, Inc., includes headings for petty cash, cash in the bank, accounts receivable, inventory, furniture and fixtures, and accumulated depreciation.

INTEGRATED ACCOUNTING SOFTWARE PACKAGES

Integrated packages combine the various accounting functions into one integrated package. Such packages typically include accounting, tax accounting, a control system, auditing, and tele-communications. They also include links to sales, inventory, banking, personnel, and payroll. Integrated accounting packages, which have been the most popular, are also the most expensive because of the larger number of functions performed.

DATABASE MANAGEMENT SYSTEMS (DBMS) APPLICATIONS

A collection of data fields organized to fit the information needs of multiple users is known as a *database.* It is a collection of information organized in a meaningful way. A database can take many forms—it can be clothes listed in a catalog, an inventory of camping gear, a price list, or educational loan sources. As you read earlier in this book, a *file* is an organized collection of records treated as a unit. For example, the employees at a branch office might represent a file. But all the files containing

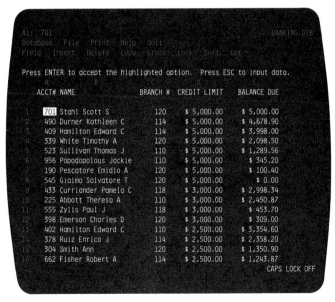

DATABASE SOFTWARE. Electronic filing systems such as the bank's list of customers and their lines of credit is a good example of how fields and records are organized in a database. *Source: McGraw-Hill Database.*

information on the employees at both the main office and all the branch offices together make up the company's employee database.

A **database management system** (DBMS) organizes the electronic files that make up the database. It permits users to define a file, the records in a file, and the fields within the records. In an employee skills database, for example, there might be a file for each type of employee, such as a programmer, records of the present assignment and previous work done by each programmer, and particular programming languages each programmer can use efficiently. There are three main types of database systems:

1. Free-form packages
2. File managers
3. Database management systems

FREE-FORM PACKAGES

Free-form packages, which are comparatively low-priced, permit a number of patterns of data entry. To use such a system of organizing data, you place a key word at both the beginning and end of each entry. The key word acts as a signal to the computer as to where a particular record begins and ends.

FILE MANAGERS

Unlike a free-form package, a **file manager** has a specific format, or template, for determining field length and content. (The length of a data field is the number of characters in the field.)

DATABASE MANAGEMENT SYSTEMS

Like a file manager, a *database management system* allows for data storage with preformatted fields. Unlike a file manager, which is usually set up for one purpose, a full database management system has a number of applications, such as mailing lists, accounting, and payroll.

Because they are both less expensive to buy and simpler to learn, individuals tend to choose free-form programs for personal use. For business, employees who need to use database management systems often choose full systems because they provide for a number of applications. Which database program a business purchases depends on the amount and type of data to be entered and stored, the type of applications to be used to access the information, and the type of output required. A large department store chain needs a different type of database to store sales or product data than a small variety store with only a few types of product needs.

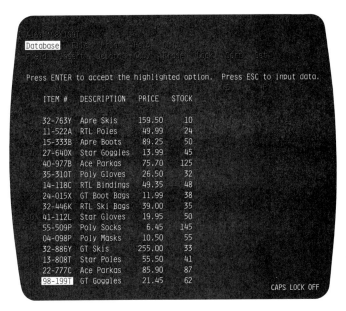

A16: '98-199T

```
Database  File  Print  Help  Quit
Field  Insert  Delete  Copy  Erase  Look  Sort  Get

   Press ENTER to accept the highlighted option.  Press ESC to input data.

   ITEM #   DESCRIPTION  PRICE   STOCK

   32-763Y  Apre Skis    159.50    10
   11-522A  RTL Poles     49.99    24
   15-333B  Apre Boots    89.25    50
   27-640X  Star Goggles  13.99    45
   40-977B  Ace Parkas    75.70   125
   35-310T  Poly Gloves   26.50    32
   14-118C  RTL Bindings  49.35    48
   24-015X  GT Boot Bags  11.99    38
   32-446K  RTL Ski Bags  39.00    35
   41-112L  Star Gloves   19.95    50
   55-509P  Poly Socks     6.45   145
   04-098P  Poly Masks    10.50    55
   32-886Y  GT Skis      255.00    33
   13-808T  Star Poles    55.50    41
   22-777C  Ace Parkas    85.90    87
   98-199T  GT Goggles    21.45    62
                                      CAPS LOCK OFF
```

INVENTORY FILE. An electronic database is an ideal software package for inventory management. A ski shop can list all the items they sell and easily update their inventory daily. *Source: McGraw-Hill Database.*

CHECK YOURSELF

Supply the missing words.

1. Packaged software that attempts to maximize profits and minimize losses from bad debts is an __?__ __?__ package.

2. Packaged software that can check supplier invoices and schedule and send payments is an __?__ __?__ package.

3. Payroll software performs both data entry and __?__ processing.

4. A type of software that enables managers to look at the company's financial position is known as a __?__ __?__ package.

5. An accounting package that usually combines a control system and auditing with accounting, tax accounting, and telecommunications is an __?__ package.

6. A collection of information such as midterm exam scores for an entire high school math class is, in the language of information processing, a type of __?__.

7. Two other types of database management systems are file managers and __?__ __?__.

8. A major difference between a free-form package and a file manager is ___?___.

9. Both database management systems and ___?___ ___?___ allow for data storage with preformatted fields.

10. Unlike a file manager, a full database management system provides for a number of ___?___.

Answers: (1) accounts receivable; (2) accounts payable; (3) output; (4) general ledger; (5) integrated; (6) database; (7) free-form packages; (8) format; (9) file managers; (10) applications.

ELECTRONIC DATABASES FOR DECISION SUPPORT

Just as users can access data supplied by their employers or professional organizations, they can access data organized and managed by companies that provide information that, in effect, rent the data. By the late 1980s, databases provided information serving virtually every type of business and consumer need.

DECISION SUPPORT. Users can subscribe to databases organized and managed by outside companies that provide needed information. Financial analysts need up-to-the-minute information on stock and bond prices. *John McGrail, 1986.*

MEDICAL DATABASE. On-line information is available from numerous sources, covering a wide variety of subjects. Here, an example from Medline, a database provided by Nexis, keeps doctors up-to-date on changes in their field.

This information ranged from stock or bond quotes to wall coverings, and from scholarships to vacation homes. Users can subscribe to databases covering just one subject, such as medicine, or to databases covering thousands of subjects ranging from sports to politics to electronics.

There are now literally thousands of commercially available databases, and demand for data by both consumers and businesses is expected to continue to increase rapidly, at least through the early 1990s. Government agencies, commercial publishers, professional associations, and database distributors sell access to their databases. Typically, end users can choose from regular business hours, evening/weekend hours, and 24-hour-a-day service. Users pay an annual subscription fee in addition to charges for the actual time they use the database. The charge per minute can range from a few cents during the evening to a multiple of that for daytime use. A third type of charge is the expense to the user for transmission of the information over telephone lines while linked to the database.

Examples of commercially available databases valuable in business and industry are the following:

1. *Legal databases.* Laws, court cases, and legal interpretations are collected, indexed, and stored by firms specializing in legal databases. The Mead Corporation's Lexis is an example of such a database.

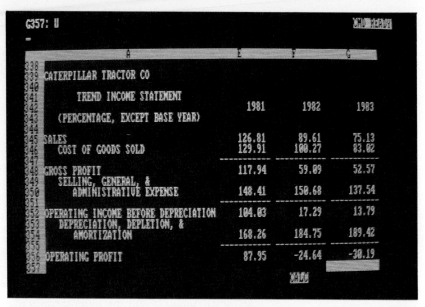

A FINANCIAL DATABASE. A sample screen from CompuStat illustrates information obtained from a financial database. Shown here are the 1981 to 1983 operating profits for Caterpillar Tractor Co. *Courtesy Standard & Poor's CompuStat Services.*

2. *Economic databases.* National data on population growth, production, imports, exports, and other statistics of interest to business planners and financial analysts is collected on various country markets, such as the United States, Canada, the United Kingdom, France, West Germany, and Japan. Major providers of economic data include McGraw-Hill's Data Resources, Inc., and International Data Corporation.

3. *Financial databases.* Data is collected on the stocks, bonds, and other securities of corporations, government agencies, and investment companies. The Dow Jones Industrial Average (DJIA) is an example of one such database. Standard & Poor's CompuStat is another example of a financial database.

4. *Credit databases.* Information on the creditworthiness of both businesses and consumers is a major database business today. A number of organizations collect information on the earnings and spending of credit seekers and sell this information to organizations to which these businesses and individuals have applied for credit. The purchasers of the information include a broad range of financial institutions that issue credit cards and companies that provide goods and services on credit. Dun & Bradstreet is the chief supplier of credit information on busi-

A CREDIT DATABASE. A sample of a credit profile of an individual including information such as present address, employment history, and credit history. *Courtesy Equifax, Inc.*

nesses. Many organizations offer credit information on individual consumers. These organizations typically specialize in such sectors as retail, banking, and insurance.

5. *Industrial databases.* Data is collected on the financial performance of firms in major industries, such as insurance, banking, securities, and health care, and on trends that are likely to affect future performance. A.M. Best is an example of a database provider for the insurance industry.

6. *Specialty databases.* Data on the firms in a particular industry is collected by both private firms and industry associations. For example, a tremendous amount of information is available on both the insurance and the construction industries because of their size and their impact on the overall economy. McGraw-Hill's Dodge Division is the leading source of U.S. national and regional construction data.

Most of the databases mentioned above are available through a personal computer and in print form. More and more of the databases will also become available on CD-ROMs. Such firms as Dow Jones, Dun & Bradstreet, and McGraw-Hill are among the largest providers of databases. These and other firms that collect and organize information for users in business, industry, and the professions are known as *information* or *content providers.*

Examples of North American firms that provide paid access to data collected and organized by others include Dialog, BRS, and

DATABASE AVAILABLE ON CD-ROM. The entire *Encyclopedia of Science and Technology* easily fits on one compact disk. *Courtesy McGraw-Hill's Professional and Reference Division.*

QL. Such firms are sometimes described as database distributors or electronic distributors.

Telephone linkage to such databases is provided by AT&T, the regional Bell operating companies that were formerly part of AT&T, other telecommunications firms, and private networks developed for specific transmission services. One example of a private network is PHINet, Prentice-Hall's electronic tax database. Telecommunications firms can be described as access providers.

CHECK YOURSELF

Supply the missing words.

1. Data collected on stocks, bonds, and other securities can be found in ___?___ databases.

2. There are ___?___ of commercially available databases for business, professional, and consumer use.

ELECTRONIC SPREADSHEET SOFTWARE

A writer of fact or fiction employs word processing software to record, revise, store, and print out words. Many novelists and magazine writers are enthusiastic users of word processing software. In much the same way, numbers-oriented people such as budget managers and financial analysts use electronic spreadsheets.

Electronic spreadsheets appear as a series of rows and columns in a grid pattern. They allow users to record, for example, sales and expenses for each product line and then show future sales under different circumstances. If you've sold about 100 magazine subscriptions during the spring campaign each year, you are probably going to assume sales of 100 for this year's spring campaign. This assumption or other typical business

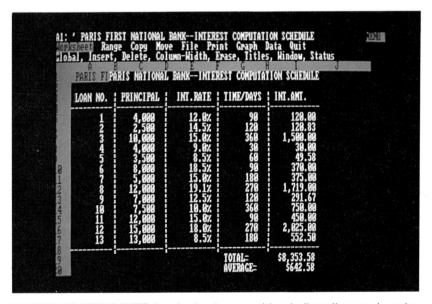

ELECTRONIC SPREADSHEET. An electronic spreadsheet allows the user to enter data into a matrix displayed on the screen. The software does calculations such as addition, subtraction, division, and multiplication. *Courtesy Lotus Development Corporation, 1987. Used with permission. Will Faller.*

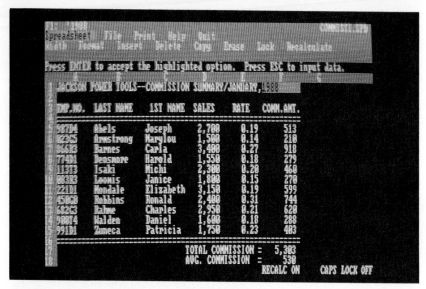

SPREADSHEET SOFTWARE. An electronic spreadsheet is used to quickly calculate the commissions earned by sales representatives of Jackson Power Tools, Inc. *Source: McGraw-Hill Spreadsheet. Will Faller.*

assumptions can be written as instructions to an electronic spreadsheet that will adjust the entries already in the spreadsheet. This enables the computer to calculate the numeric changes automatically.

Electronic spreadsheet applications are usually described in three ways:

1. Basic functions
2. "What if" scenarios
3. Overall forecasting

BASIC FUNCTIONS

As with other types of business software, there are spreadsheets for beginners and spreadsheets for experienced users. Since the key function of a spreadsheet is to help the user evaluate sales, expenses, or other data from past years and project their values in future years, all spreadsheets involve the recording and computing steps of the information processing cycle. For any spreadsheet application you will record the numbers for the first year, past or present, and specify the relationship between that year and future years. For example, this year you save $25 a month for a car. You expect to be able to save 20 percent more next year. You can express these relationships electronically year by year and determine when you will have enough saved for your car. The owner of a small business can use a spreadsheet to keep track of sales, expenses, and profits for the current year or develop a budget forecast for next year based on this year's data. Spreadsheets are powerful and flexible tools businesses can use to manage their finances and to plan future projects and marketing campaigns.

"WHAT IF" SCENARIOS

Before investing money, a business may wish to explore a number of possibilities hypothetically. Let's say, for example, that a gasoline distributor would like to project gasoline sales in each region of the country. Since usage is likely to vary with weather conditions, employment conditions, and gasoline prices, the distributor may want to try out several possible conditions for each region. For instance, what happens to sales and net profits for next year if the weather is extremely cold, normal, or warmer than normal? Each paired condition and projected result is called a *scenario.*

People who make projections generally look at conditions they would like to have, conditions they would not like to have, and conditions in between. The gasoline distributor may decide to increase gasoline distribution to the Sunbelt area if good weather conditions are expected and a high level of employment (more people driving regularly to work) seems likely. In the Sunbelt, given these conditions, local residents and tourists will use their cars more often, travel farther, and use more gasoline. The reverse is likely to be true for the Northeast if much snow is predicted in urban areas, layoffs are increasing, or gasoline prices are rising.

Questions that electronic spreadsheet users develop to help identify conditions and project results are called **"what if" questions,** think about these "what if" questions, then develop your own.

- If hourly accounting fees are raised by 10 percent and salaries by 5 percent, what is profit likely to be?
- If sales of party favors for New Year's Eve double, does a third production shift need to be added?

Software packages that help managers ask and answer "what if" questions are sometimes called **decision support software** systems because they help managers make decisions.

FORECASTING

Spreadsheet programs allow managers to forecast future sales, profits, or other business factors quickly and easily. Before computers became widely used, forecasting and financial projections had to be done by hand. This was tedious and inflexible. If one number in the forecast changed, or if the manager decided, after the fact, that he or she needed to do a "what if" analysis, all the numbers used in the projection had to be recalculated by hand. With electronic spreadsheets, managers can look at dozens of scenarios, ask lots of "what if" questions, and modify or update data whenever necessary, without having to do any manual calculations. The computer automatically does the necessary adding, subtracting, dividing, or multiplying.

GRAPHICS APPLICATIONS

Earlier you may have learned about various types of charts and graphs which are used to create visual images of relationships between several levels of information. For example, an investment company may use a bar graph to show how well a particular type of investment has done over a period of five years or more. A corporation may use a pie chart to show the percentage of revenue and profit contributed by each major product line. The Federal Reserve Board may use a line graph to show the rate of inflation over a period of several years.

A graphics program asks questions that enable the user to enter information that can be compared year by year or on some other basis. You provide the information by answering the questions. Then your computer draws a graph or chart of some type on the display screen with the information transformed into a visual image. When you are satisfied with the results, you can have the printer print it. Some programs, such as Lotus 1-2-3, can load information directly from the spreadsheet and automatically draw line graphs, bar graphs, or pie charts to show the information graphically. Computer graphics are useful to business managers, architects, engineers, and many

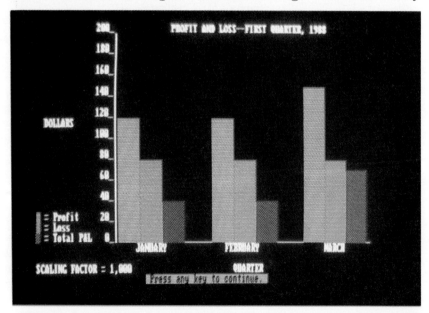

GRAPHICS APPLICATIONS. A graphics program allows the user to examine data and trends in a visual representation. Here, the profit and loss for 1988 is shown in a computer generated bar graph. *Source: McGraw-Hill Graphing. Will Faller.*

other professionals. Business managers use graphics to summarize large quantities of numerical data in a format that's easy to read and understand. Scientists and engineers use graphics applications to generate graphs, charts, and drawings. A mechanical engineer can use a CAD package to design a new bicycle or a new car. The scientist might use a graphics package to generate a line chart summarizing data collected in an experiment.

CHECK YOURSELF

Supply the missing words.

1. A type of software package called an ___?___ ___?___ enables users to record numeric data and then project future data.
2. Electronic spreadsheets appear as a series of rows and ___?___ in a grid pattern.
3. Spreadsheets include both the ___?___ and the computing steps of the information processing cycle.
4. A description of a condition, combined with a projected result, is often called a ___?___ .
5. A type of question electronic spreadsheet users develop to help identify conditions and project results is called a ___?___ question.
6. ___?___ software helps managers ask and answer "what if" questions.

Answers (1) electronic spreadsheet; (2) columns; (3) recording; (4) scenario; (5) "what if"; (6) Decision support.

REVIEW QUESTIONS

1. What is a single-purpose software package?
2. What is integrated software? Give an example of such software.
3. What is the difference between horizontal and vertical software?
4. What are five benefits of both horizontal and vertical general-purpose software packages over customized software?
5. What are three basic functions of word processing software? What are three supplemental functions?
6. Name five basic types of accounting and business management software packages.
7. Describe three types of databases.
8. Describe how spreadsheets are used in business.

9. Give an example of how a "what-if question" could be used in the planning process of a record store.
10. Describe two ways in which a graphics application can be used in business.

COMPARING IDEAS

The questions below are designed to help you think about what you have learned in this chapter. They are "thought" questions. There is no one correct answer.

1. Think about the decision to plan and create a computer payroll program for your bank. Now think about whether it would be better to create such a program solely for your bank or to select a program written for banks in general. Give two advantages of each approach. Which approach would you use? Why? Can you think of any other information that would be useful to have in making this decision?

2. If application software packages become more popular, what do you think will happen to job opportunities for systems analysts and programmers? Explain your answer.

INFORMATION PROCESSING ACTIVITIES

Now you can perform many of the information processing activities business workers perform. Below is a summary of the tasks you will complete. You will find the actual data and business forms you need in your *Information Processing Work Kit.*

1. You will complete a word processing proofreading task required when using an applications software package.
2. You will perform the steps required to verify data on an electronic spreadsheet.

HANDS-ON ACTIVITIES

Locate five software programs in use at your school. For each program, classify it as packaged or customized, horizontal or vertical, and single purpose or integrated. Also, list the type of application such as accounting, word processing, graphics, and so forth.

SOFTWARE PROJECT 4

USING DATABASE SOFTWARE

As you learned in Part 4, businesses must decide if the software required to meet their information needs should be created or purchased. Most small businesses buy application packages that can be used with a limited amount of computer knowledge. You have already utilized two popular application packages, word processing and spreadsheet, in completing the previous software projects. In this project you will sort video tape rental information to help Pat Brown make some important business decisions.

The number of titles in the Video-II-Go catalog is growing rapidly. Pat Brown is pleased with the growth of the business, but has several questions on future tape purchases. It would be very helpful to be able to sort rental information in a variety of ways. At the present time this is not possible using handwritten reports. The owner hopes that the store's microcomputer can help.

Each time a tape is rented, a mark is made on an index card for the tape. The index card includes all the information about the tape (title, purchase price, rental price, etc.). The owner uses these notes to prepare a worksheet that describes how often each tape is rented. In the past, this has been a fairly easy task. However, as the number of video tapes increases, the amount of time required for this task will increase.

INFORMATION PROCESSING PROBLEM

Like any business, Video-II-Go needs to spend its money wisely. The owner needs to rapidly add copies of tapes that are rented frequently to the store's inventory, and reduce the rental price on less popular titles. The owner needs a rapid and accurate way to access the information that is recorded on the video tape index cards.

INFORMATION PROCESSING SOLUTION

The amount of manual sorting involved in preparing the rental worksheet can be greatly reduced by utilizing the existing microcomputer hardware and acquiring a database program. The database can eventually be used to replace the index cards. For now, the owner would like to start by preparing a variety of reports based on the rental worksheet data.

Database software allows you to input data records (like the information on index cards) into a computer's memory. All of the records make up a database. Each record contains the same categories of information called fields. Fields can contain alphanumeric or numeric information. The categories (fields) of information contained on each index card include Tape No., Title, No. of Rentals, Fee, and No. Out of Stock.

Your supervisor will demonstrate a database program to you before you begin the keyboarding activities.

The following worksheet was prepared by Pat Brown from the information on the index cards for last month.

VIDEO-II-GO				RENTAL WORKSHEET
Tape No.	Title	No. of Rentals	Fee	No. Out of Stock
602	All Quiet For Now	28	2.00	0
512	Before You Say Goodbye	24	2.00	4
506	Fitness at 50	14	1.50	0
601	Kiddie Corner	9	.99	0
511	Make it Happen	18	2.00	1
412	Suspicion of Guilt	43	2.00	12
408	Space Chase	31	2.00	2
603	Superdome II	23	2.00	4
604	Tax Preparation Video Guide	5	1.50	0
503	The Connection	40	2.00	10
501	Wait for Summer	19	2.00	7
405	Wildfire II	38	2.00	2
509	Zest	21	2.00	1

COMPLETED BY _____ *P. B.* _____   DATE _____ *April 30* _____

KEYBOARDING ACTIVITIES

1. Unless your supervisor has provided you with a prepared database, you will need to label the fields in the database to record the information from the Rental Worksheet. You would start with the Tape No. category and end with No. Out of Stock. The categories (fields) of information contained on each index card include:

   The No. Out of Stock field contains the number of times in the month that a customer wanted to rent the tape and it was not available.

Field	Type	Size (Maximum characters)
Tape No.	Numeric	4
Title	Alphanumeric	30
No. of Rentals	Numeric	4
Fee (Rental)	Numeric	4
No. Out of Stock	Numeric	2

2. Once the database fields have been created, enter the data for the records shown on the Rental Worksheet.

3. Display or print a sample report after sorting the title field in alphabetical order. Compare the database report with the Rental Worksheet. They should contain the same information.

4. Display or print a sample report after sorting the No. of Rentals field in ascending numerical order. Be sure to have your supervisor review your output.

5. Display or print a sample report after sorting the No. Out of Stock field in ascending numerical order. Have your supervisor review your output.

6. Display or print a sample report after sorting the Tape No. field in descending numerical order. Have your supervisor review your output before going on to the next step.

7. Make a duplicate copy of the database file for the current month so that you will be able to modify the report for next month. You will not want to erase the data for the current month in case you want to refer to it in the future.

ENRICHMENT ACTIVITIES

1. If your database software allows you to pull specific records from the database:

   ■ Sort the Title field in ascending order.
   ■ Pull all the records for tapes that were rented more than 25 times.
   ■ Print a copy of the records of the 7 tapes that were rented more than 25 times.

2. Review the catalog you produced in Software Project 2. A similar listing can be produced using database software. Use database software to prepare two versions of the catalog. Print a list in alphabetic order by title, and a numeric listing by daily rate.

Software Project 4: Using Database Software   301

PART 5

OPPORTUNITIES IN INFORMATION PROCESSING

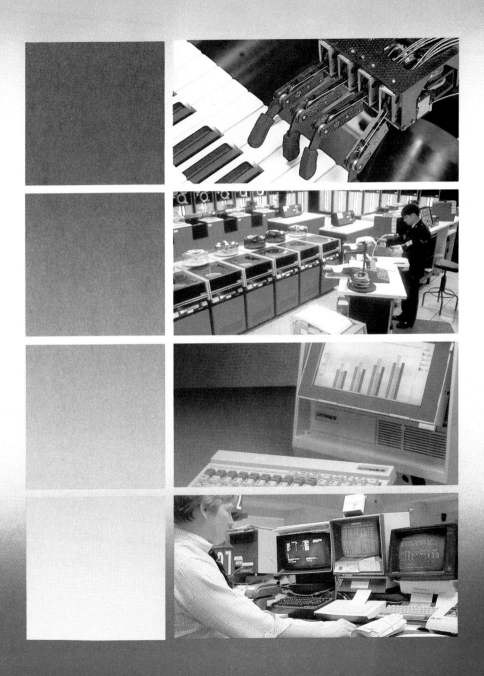

CHAPTER

12

INFORMATION PROCESSING IN THE PRIVATE AND PUBLIC SECTORS

Information Processing Terminology

Telecommunications
Robotics
Centralized computing

Management information systems
Information systems technology

Decision support systems
Decentralized computing

Performance Goals

☐ Compare a service economy and a manufacturing economy.

☐ Discuss at least two trends in information processing.

☐ Distinguish between a centralized and a decentralized computing unit.

☐ Describe one computer application for each of four types of service businesses.

☐ List at least two issues relating to a company's plan to convert from centralized computing to decentralized computing.

Earlier in this textbook, you read about the origins of the mainframe computer. Early forecasts of the demand for mainframe computers predicted very little usage because of the enormous amount of space and expense required for such equipment. Although usage greatly exceeded those early forecasts, computer purchasers were limited to large organizations, such as banks, insurance companies, and government agencies.

Over the years, most other medium- and large-sized organizations became interested in computers as newer models came to require less space and became less expensive. During this period, minicomputers and small business computers became increasingly popular. This equipment began to appear in business offices in the late 1970s, as their development focused on greater capabilities and storage capacity. Since the late 1970s, microcomputers have increasingly won a place in the accounting, finance, planning, and marketing departments of both service and manufacturing firms.

TREND TOWARD A SERVICE ECONOMY

In 1900, more people were working on farms than in factories or in offices. The economy of the United States, based primarily on agriculture, was what is known as an *agrarian economy*. By 1930, however, the United States had changed to an industrial, or *manufacturing, economy*. This means there were more people employed in factories than on farms. By this time, office workers also outnumbered farm workers, but office jobs were still fewer in number than factory jobs. From the early 1930s on, the need for office workers in the United States grew tremendously. By 1960, the number of people employed in offices exceeded the number of people employed in factories. This is the environment you will encounter as you seek your first information processing job.

The U.S. Census Bureau predicts that office employment will continue to grow. By the early 1990s, at least 50 percent of U.S. workers will have some kind of office job. This means that more than 57 million people will be doing office work. Since information processing represents a larger and larger share of office jobs, office workers need to have a strong background in this area.

THE COMPUTER AS A PRODUCTIVITY TOOL

A *manufactured good* is something tangible, like a pair of shoes, a car, or a television set. A *service* is something that is produced and consumed at the same time. For example, a haircut is a service; so is a college education. These are obviously services because no goods change hands, only money. Education and haircuts are invisible commodities that nevertheless have value to their "owners." A fast-food restaurant is also considered a service business, yet you receive tangible hamburgers and milkshakes in exchange for your money. A *service economy* is one that is based primarily on the sale of services rather than on the sale of goods.

WESTWARD HO! In 1803 the Louisiana Purchase opens the frontier to settlers and prospectors. The fertile plains and the mineral-rich mountains provide ample resources. *Courtesy Culver Pictures, Inc.*

AGRARIAN SOCIETY. On Southern plantations, agriculture remained the basis of the economy while factories spring up in the North. *Courtesy Culver Pictures, Inc.*

THE RAILROAD. The first transcontinental line, completed in 1869, symbolizes a new age of industrial progress. *Courtesy Culver Pictures, Inc.*

THE AUTOMOBILE. Henry Ford introduces mass production for a mass market in 1908, as communications, electricity, and other advances sweep the nation. *Courtesy Culver Pictures, Inc.*

FINANCIAL CENTER. Wall Street grows with the economy. After World War I, the U.S. becomes a creditor to the world. *Courtesy UPI/Bettmann Newsphotos.*

POSTWAR BOOM. Its industrial plants undamaged, the U.S. emerges as a superpower after World War II. New technologies and pent-up consumer demand spur growth. *Courtesy UPI/Bettmann Newsphotos.*

FOREIGN RIVALS. The U.S. begins to lose its lead in the 1970's. As foreign competition builds in the 1980's imports grow and steel mills are shuttered. *Courtesy UPI/Bettmann Newsphotos.*

HIGH TECH. Technology is now the big hope. A manufacturing economy built on super-chips, fiber optics, and superconducters could give the U.S. a new competitive edge. *Andrew Popper.*

TOWARD A SERVICE ECONOMY.

When economists speak of *productivity,* they are referring to the relationships between the steps required to produce a good or a service and the actual results. For example, if fewer workers are needed to produce an automobile in a set amount of time in Japan than are needed for an equivalent model in the United States, Japanese automotive workers are considered more productive. North American businesses are enormously interested in increasing productivity because they want their goods to sell overseas. Similarly, they want their goods to be lower priced for the same quality than goods imported from other countries.

Because computers can have a tremendous impact on both office and industrial productivity, they are becoming more and more visible in the workplace. Experts predict that by the early 1990s more than 20 percent of the work force (close to 12 million people) will have jobs with information processing titles. Moreover, since many other jobs will increasingly depend on computers, it would be very unrealistic to expect to succeed in the work force without at least a basic understanding of computers and information processing. In fact, corporate recruiters now report a need for computer literacy no matter what the position. Experts claim that many organizations have equipped at least 60 percent of their managers with personal computers.

CHANGES IN THE POPULATION BASE

Whether you live in an urban, suburban, or rural area, you have probably noticed that there are more service workers and fewer factory workers. The fact is that fewer and fewer manufacturing, or factory, jobs are available in this country. As wages rise, manufacturers move production and assembly plants to other countries where workers' wages are lower or productivity is higher. At the same time, more U.S. workers are acquiring a higher education and a higher standard of living, resulting in greater spending for services most individuals and families used to perform for themselves. Some of these include child care, house cleaning, gardening, laundry, and food preparation.

Two major changes in the population are the significant increase in two-career couples and the aging of the population. Since the early 1960s, many women who traditionally would have married and had children shortly after school have instead either married later or postponed having children. The net economic effect of these two-career couples is twofold: They have less time for taking care of themselves and their homes, and they have more *disposable income,* or money to spend after taking care of their basic needs for home, food, and clothing.

Such men and women rely more on full-service laundries, fast-food outlets and other restaurants, house or apartment cleaning services, and other help they can pay for, rather than doing the work themselves.

Another way these trends show up is in the increasing demand for personal computers, modems, and access to electronic databases. More and more individuals who take office work home need the same types of computing tools and information there that they have at the office.

OPPORTUNITIES IN SERVICE BUSINESSES

By 1990 there was a major decline in the number of teenagers, a moderate increase in the number of elderly, and a very large increase in the number of North Americans between the ages of 25 and 44.

As the population ages, workers move into higher income brackets, have greater buying power, and save a higher percentage of their earnings. Such developments should mean greater demands for both retailing and financial services, including banking, securities, and insurance. Workers will save money in traditional bank accounts, invest in securities and mutual funds, and insure their financial well-being through life insurance, health insurance, and annuity programs. You will read more about the particulars of such financial services in other courses. In this course, you will learn about both the outlook for careers in these industries and the types of positions available.

OPPORTUNITIES IN SERVICE BUSINESSES. People in the financial sector depend heavily on computers in daily operations. *Courtesy John Coletti, Uniphoto Picture Agency*

Similarly, as the population grows older, there will be a greater need for health care services and for financial services, such as those provided by banks, securities firms, and insurance companies. There will also be increased demand for retailing services, for food preparation and specialty items, and for hospitality services, such as hotels, restaurants, and transportation. Below is a summary of the expected impact on information professionals.

- *Retailing information.* Retailing organizations, such as department stores, specialty shops, and restaurants, will need more managers, accountants, and information professionals as they continue to expand from local and regional organizations to national and international organizations. Typical information requirements and objectives will include the monitoring of sales receipts by region, by store or outlet, by season, or by department or salesperson. For example, a specialty store may want to compare the sales productivity of the cheese section, the meat section, and the salad section. A clothing store catering to young professionals may want to measure productivity by comparing sales of men's business clothing and women's business clothing, men's sportswear and women's sportswear, and men's accessories (such as scarves, belts, and hats) and women's accessories. A fast-food chain may need to keep track of sales by store, by region, or by type of meal (breakfast, lunch, or dinner). Using this information, the managers can decide which stores need to advertise more, where new stores should be located, or what new types of food should be offered on the menu.

- *Hospitality information.* Travel agents and travel services will need more computers and information professionals to organize and monitor fares, discounts, schedules, and restrictions. Information professionals will need to monitor sales figures seasonally and regionally; they will also need to provide agents with comparative information on full fares and discounted fares of airlines, hotel chains, and car rental services. Faster information access will help agents respond to customers more quickly, by telephone or in person.

- *Financial services information.* Financial services organizations, such as banks, securities firms, and insurance companies, will need more planning and marketing specialists as they continue to offer a greater range of services. They will also need more service representatives to sell the services and handle customer needs and more information professionals to collect and organize data and interpret it for management. Information professionals help sales and marketing professionals compare financial products for customers in terms of expected return, total cost (sales charges plus annual management fees, if any), and tax information.

■ *Health care information.* Health care organizations, such as hospitals, medical labs, health maintenance organizations, nursing homes, and professional corporations of doctors and dentists, will need information professionals to track appointments, manage patient records, and process billing and insurance forms and payments. Information professionals will also be asked to produce reports that help these organizations determine which days and hours they should be open for appointments, how much time there should be allowed between steps of physical checkups for lab work and evaluation, and how much fees should increase each year to allow for desired profit and cover expense increases.

As the price-performance ratio of computers continues to improve and it becomes less and less expensive for employers to equip their employees with computers, more and more office workers are expected to have desktop or portable computers.

The chart below shows that there are likely to be fewer information processing positions in such businesses as aerospace, automobile, and industrial equipment manufacturing than in the service industries. However, there will be many opportunities available for well-trained, dedicated information specialists in a variety of different businesses and industries. Examples of a few of the opportunities available follow.

PERCENT OF TOTAL NUMBER OF DATA PROCESSING WORKERS	INDUSTRY FIELD OF EMPLOYMENT
22.5%	Service industry, excluding computer services
18.7	Manufacturing plants, excluding computer manufacturers
13.7	Banking, finance, insurance, and real estate services
12.3	Computer service companies
10.4	Retailing and wholesaling establishments
9.9	Government agencies
6.3	Computer manufacturers
4.4	Transportation and communication companies
1.8	All other
100.0%	

Biotechnology. Breakthroughs in biology and other sciences have made possible some amazing new products, processes, and business opportunities. Research in the field of biotechnology should lead to new types of drugs and pharmaceuticals, better agricultural techniques, and many new medical techniques and procedures. Information professionals will be needed both by the biotechnology industry doing the research and by all the other organizations that will apply and use the new technology. All these businesses will need information experts to operate the computers and electronic equipment used to keep track of accounting, financial, and managerial information, as any other business does. But these high-technology companies will also need information specialists who can use computers to design new machines or products, to analyze the results of scientific experiments, or to develop new applications software for customers. Many other people will be needed to build, maintain, and repair computer and information processing equipment.

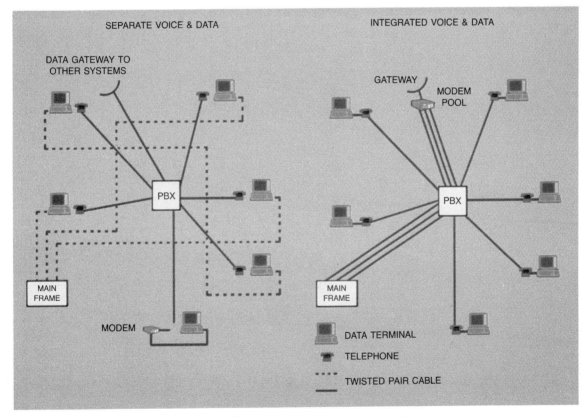

TELECOMMUNICATION SYSTEMS. Opportunities for information workers in telecommunications are expected to grow rapidly in the next few decades. *Courtesy Crain's New York Business.*

Telecommunications. Telecommunications, as you may remember, is a key part of many information processing systems. Opportunities for information workers in the telecommunications industry are expected to grow rapidly in the next few decades. AT&T was, until the early 1980s, the largest telecommunications company in the world. After deregulation and the breaking up of AT&T, many new telecommunications companies were created, such as MCI, U.S. Sprint, U.S. West, and NYNEX.

Many new companies, both in the United States and around the world, have entered the business of manufacturing a wide variety of telecommunications equipment, such as digital switching devices, computers, telephone systems, and fiber optics. Besides the general information specialists needed to operate each of the businesses in this industry efficiently, other people will be needed to design new equipment, develop new software programs, and organize the computer systems needed to tie all this equipment together and keep track of all the information and data being generated. All types of information professionals will be needed in this industry, ranging from junior programmers to systems analysts to hardware designers and engineers.

ROBOTICS. Specialists will be needed to design new automated equipment and the software to control it. Here, a robot is shown testing a piano keyboard.
Courtesy Malcolm S. Kirk, Peter Arnold, Inc.

Robotics. With new inventions and new breakthroughs in computer technology, more and more automated equipment and robots will become available to all kinds of businesses. Large and small companies are developing and building new types of automated equipment and robots. Other businesses are buying the equipment and using it to manufacture a wide variety of products, from computer chips to automobiles. Information processing professionals will be needed to develop information systems designed to provide management with the data and information necessary to run a successful business. Specialists will be needed to design the new automated equipment, to develop the software controlling the robots, or to design computer-integrated manufacturing systems to tie the operation together into a network. Systems analysts will be needed to evaluate the information needs of users, the system costs, and the computer hardware and software alternatives available to the company. Programmers will be needed to write the instructions the computer requires to process the information correctly.

Computer Hardware and Software. Both the computer hardware and software industries offer exciting opportunities for information professionals. Existing companies, like IBM, Apple, Tandy, and DEC, will continue to need people to design new computers and software. For new companies, like the Thinking Machine Company, to succeed, a ready supply of dedicated information workers must be available to develop new software and new technologies for designing computers. Software developers like Microsoft, Lotus, and IBM will also need systems analysts and programmers to develop new applications software and to design systems that enable computers to become more intelligent and efficient.

Manufacturing industries will continue to have many opportunities for information professionals in large and small companies. Increased competition and constantly changing technology make the available opportunities that much more challenging and exciting.

CHECK YOURSELF

Supply the missing words.

1. By 1930, the United States had changed from an agrarian economy to an industrial or __?__ economy.
2. Health care is an example of a __?__ industry.

OPPORTUNITIES IN A CENTRALIZED COMPUTING ENVIRONMENT

In order for computer equipment to be used efficiently and economically, it is frequently located in one place in a large business, such as a bank, a securities firm, or an insurance company. This is called a **centralized computing** environment. When such equipment is centralized, it can be shared by everyone in the company who has information processing needs. Responsibility for overseeing the computer activities of the entire firm is assigned to a director (or even a vice president) of *management information systems* (MIS) or *information systems technology* (IST). These are both names for the computer services function. Still another name sometimes used for this function is *decision support systems* (DSS).

The computer services function is increasingly part of a large management unit known as finance and administration. Within the computing function, there are typically two major units: (1) systems and programming, which may be further divided into units that develop computer applications for particular divisions of the company, such as finance and accounting, sales and marketing, and human resources; and (2) computer center operations. These units would probably be found in either a service or a manufacturing company. A manufacturing company might also have a manufacturing unit.

For a large staff there may be more than one supervisor. When a systems and programming unit is divided into several specialized functional units, there is probably a supervisor for each such unit.

Careers in information processing management are discussed in Chapter 13. For now you need to know the basic responsibilities of management. These include setting priorities, establishing schedules, and following up to see that projects are completed properly and on time. Management generally sets performance standards and evaluates employees against these standards. The evaluation form used by Diversified Financial

Confidential Office Employee Performance Appraisal Record

062 136 9745	Laura Chen	80	Information Systems	Denver	01 15 —
Soc. Security No.	Employee Name	Div.	Department	Wk. Loc.	Date of Hire

Position Title: **Programmer** How Long Under Your Supervision? **6 months** Postpone this Appraisal Until (Date): **not applicable**

Performance Comments

What aspects of the employee's duties are handled in an outstanding manner? *This employee's very pleasant "will do" manner helps her to work effectively with other employees, but she does not speak up at meetings.*

What aspects of the employee's duties are not handled as well as should be expected? *This employee must learn to participate more in department planning.*

Performance Rating

Considering all performance factors, please check the statement that most nearly fits this employee's overall performance on the current job in the last twelve months:

☐ A. Superior performance. Consistently exceeds job standards.
☐ B. High standard of performance. Consistently meets, and occasionally exceeds, job standards.
☒ C. Performance normally expected of qualified employee.
☐ D. Performance not up to desired standards; should show improvement.
☐ E. Poor performance. Cannot be retained on job without immediate improvement.

Development Plans

State your plans and objectives for improving the employee's performance (consider increased responsibility, coaching, on-the-job training, etc.)
We are asking her to report briefly on work-related problems.

If formal training programs will help the employee, please code (using the course list in the instructions) those programs that the employee needs:

1 **03*** 2 _____ 3 _____ 4 _____ *03: Program debugging*

Promotion Readiness (Please check the most appropriate statement)

☐ A. Has demonstrated capacity for continued growth; can move now or within six months to a higher level of responsibility.
☐ B. Has demonstrated capacity for continued growth, but needs six to twelve more months at present level before significant move can be made.
☐ C. Has demonstrated capacity for growth, but probably will not be ready for movement to levels of higher responsibility within the next twelve month period.
☒ D. Appears, at this time, to be limited to present position or to a comparable level of responsibility.

Please explain any factors limiting transfer or promotion possibilities: *See above. This employee will be reevaluated in six months.*

Employee Potential

Indicate next position, if any, you believe employee could perform: *See above.*

Appraisal Discussion (REQUIRED)

What comments were made by the employee when performance and future were discussed? *The employee describes herself as inexperienced in public speaking but knows this is important in climbing the business ladder.*

If this appraisal will not be discussed with the employee; explain why: *not applicable*

Appraised By: *Martin Hoffman* Date **7/16/—**
Appraisal Approved By: *Shirley Amato* Date **7/17/—**

EMPLOYEE PERFORMANCE APPRAISAL. Together the manager and the employee address achievements and performance gaps, agree on necessary steps to achieve end goals, and plan for training to make the employee more effective in his or her work.

Services Corporation is shown on page 315. Notice that the evaluator (the supervisor) is asked to comment on the employee's current performance and career goals. The evaluator must also make suggestions about specific steps the employee should take to improve on-the-job performance. The form shown is for formal evaluation. A good supervisor or manager keeps employees informed throughout the year on how well they are doing their jobs.

Although large companies traditionally had their information processing departments set up in a centralized fashion, more and more of these companies have converted their information units to decentralized computer environments.

OPPORTUNITIES IN A DECENTRALIZED COMPUTING ENVIRONMENT

In a centralized environment, the corporate staff performs a wide range of information processing activities for the various parts of a business as well as for the corporation's internal and external (government and stockholder) reporting needs. In a **decentralized** (or distributed) **computing** environment, by contrast, most of the information processing needs of the business units are performed within those units. The corporate computing unit concentrates on the corporation's reporting needs. In some corporations the corporate computing unit also has a group of computing consultants who work with the business units to identify needs, develop specific plans, and meet those needs using present staff, new employees, or external staff hired by the day (per diem) for computer application projects. Such projects are managed by either the business unit or the corporate computing unit, depending on the corporation's policies and procedures.

Before you seek a permanent job in a computing environment, it is a good idea to find out how the firm is organized. You may want to ask friends, family, or instructors whether they have any relevant information. You may also want to ask the company for an annual report or other descriptive literature. For many firms you can obtain information from your local library.

OPPORTUNITIES IN A GOVERNMENT COMPUTING ENVIRONMENT

Just as the use of computers in business has increased, more and more computers are being used at all levels of government. The country's growth in population, together with a more complex set of government-sponsored programs and tax laws, has increased the need for information processing. This is true for both federal and local agencies, where a steady stream of changes in financial aid programs and income tax provisions is likely to occupy many information processing professionals for a long time.

Whether at the federal or the local level, the opportunities for

GOVERNMENT COMPUTING ENVIRONMENT. Computers have become an integral part of government operations. The Air Force is just one example of government's dependence on computer systems. *Courtesy U.S. Air Force.*

information professionals available in government are very similar to those available in the private sector. The main difference is that government usually doesn't sell services or manufactured goods, but is responsible for managing programs and projects that have been mandated by law. Managing people, money, and information are all important functions of government organizations. Information professionals are needed to develop computer systems to manage money collected by taxes and paid out for medical care or to build roads. Governments around the world collect, store, and distribute incredible amounts of information about their countries, from research programs on the mortality rate of whooping cranes in Florida to the tax returns of small businesses in New Zealand. All this information must be entered as input, processed, and stored by various types of information systems.

In government, as in business, many clerical positions and middle-management positions are being eliminated as a result of computerization, while positions are being created for employees who plan, develop, and maintain computer programs, electronic databases, and electronic transmission systems for information and funds. For example, it will become more common for individuals to file their tax returns by electronically keyboarding their income and deductions and then sending these electronic entries to appropriate government agencies.

Computers run by trained government employees will need to review these electronic returns just as traditional hand-written returns are reviewed.

CHECK YOURSELF

Supply the missing words.

1. Most organizations have a number of units that require computers and ___?___ processing.

2. Examples of likely company needs for information include business planning, client services, order processing, marketing services, and ___?___ ___?___ ___?___.

3. An example of an information processing need for a marketing services unit is the measuring ___?___ of particular mail campaigns.

4. Tax information is (likely, not likely) ___?___ to be a need of a financial services organization.

5. A ___?___ ___?___ is a summary of specifics a customer has agreed to in making a purchase.

6. Responsibilities of the finance and administration unit are likely to include ___?___, tax, and corporate reports.

7. When a computing unit is shared by a number of units with information processing needs, that unit is said to be ___?___.

8. Abbreviations of typical names for a centralized computing unit are MIS, ___?___, and DSS.

9. An information processing manager can be expected to be responsible for setting priorities, establishing ___?___, and following up to see that projects are completed properly and on time.

10. The primary difference between a centralized computing unit and a ___?___ unit is the location of the processing function for that business unit.

Answers: (1) information; (2) finance and administration; (3) productivity; (4) likely; (5) sales confirmation; (6) payroll; (7) centralized; (8) IST; (9) schedules; (10) decentralized.

REVIEW QUESTIONS

1. Describe a service economy, and list two major trends that contribute to the change from a manufacturing economy to a service economy.

2. List four industries that are expected to have rapid growth in information processing employment through at least the early 1990s.
3. Describe one type of information likely to be needed by each industry you mentioned in your answer to Question 2.
4. List four areas of opportunity for information processing specialists in manufacturing.
5. Explain why opportunities are expanding in two of the areas you listed in Question 4.
6. Describe the key difference between a centralized computing unit and a decentralized computing unit.
7. List one trend in the staffing of large organizations, whether government or business.

COMPARING IDEAS

The questions below are designed to help you think about what you have learned in this chapter. They are "thought" questions. There is no one correct answer.

1. As the assistant to the regional manager of a large data communications company, you will simulate the use of an electronic spreadsheet in computing business data.
2. Why do you think many organizations place the computing or information processing unit under finance and administration?

INFORMATION PROCESSING ACTIVITIES

Now you can perform many of the information processing activities business workers perform. Below is a summary of the tasks you will complete. You will find the actual data and business forms you need in your *Information Processing Work Kit.*

1. As the assistant to the regional manager of a large data communications company, you will simulate the use of an electronic spreadsheet in computing business data.
2. You will produce several "what if" business predictions using simulated electronic spreadsheet data.

CHAPTER

13

CAREER OPPORTUNITIES

Information Processing Terminology

Software engineer
Systems analyst
Systems programmer
Computer programmer

Equipment analyst
Data-entry operator
On-line terminal
  operator

Computer operator
Computer graphics
  specialist

Performance Goals

☐ Describe the three basic career clusters found in the information industry and end-user organizations.

☐ Explain the typical opportunities for specialized training in a career cluster.

☐ Describe the educational background, training, and work experience required for a computer career.

JOB CLASSIFICATION SYSTEMS

Many employers have what they call job classification systems. These systems, often developed jointly by management and outside consultants, organize jobs into groups and then compare their relative worth. Such determinations are usually made on the basis of the scope and difficulty of the job responsibilities and the know-how and skills needed to do the job properly.

Job classification systems attempt to look at the education, training, and work experience an individual needs to be successful in each job. They also look at the pay rates offered by employers in the area and determine how these pay rates compare with those for other jobs the employer believes are comparable in level of difficulty.

A SAMPLE
JOB-RATING
SYSTEM
(PEERS)

The U.S. government assigns codes to industry clusters, such as construction and communications. The government, more specifically the U.S. Department of Labor, also assigns codes to jobs, including jobs in information processing. These codes are called DOT numbers because they are listed in a book called the *Dictionary of Occupational Titles* (DOT). This book describes each of the jobs it lists and its relationship to other jobs in that career cluster. You can read more about the demand for workers in particular industries in government publications such as the *U.S. Industrial Outlook* and the *U.S. Employment Outlook*. Your instructor or school library may have copies of government or other reference books on the outlook for particular industries and jobs.

There are additional aspects of job rating that these books do not fully cover. To describe the several characteristics that are particularly important in rating jobs in information processing, the authors of this book have developed a special job rating system. This system, called the PEERS job rating system, provides PEERS ratings for each job description in this chapter.

A PEERS rating describes a job in five ways. Each way is called a job characteristic. The five characteristics of each job the PEERS system rates are listed below. Notice that the first letters of the five job characteristics spell out the word PEERS.

Physical activity and environment
Experience
Education
Responsibility and job complexity
Skills

Meaning of the PEERS Ratings

CHARACTERISTIC	RATING OF 1	RATING OF 2	RATING OF 3
Physical activity and environment	Very little effort and comfortable surroundings	Some standing and lifting and/or some noise	Quite a lot of standing and lifting and/or noisy surroundings
Experience	Entry level	One or more years	Two or more years
Education	High school	Vocational/technical training or some college	Four-year college degree
Responsibiity and job complexity	Closely supervised; simple tasks	Lightly supervised; more complex tasks (with guidelines given)	Little supervision; many decisions to make in performing job operations
Skills	Few, if any	Some specialized	Many highly specialized

Each PEERS characteristic can be rated on a scale from 1 to 3, with 3 points assigned to the most demanding jobs. The table that follows shows the meaning of the ratings for each characteristic, depending on the quantity and quality of that characteristic in a particular job.

To see how the PEERS rating system works, look at the rating for a programming trainee. The first rating of 1 means the job calls for little physical effort and the work is done in comfortable surroundings. A rating of 1 for experience means no experience is required. The education rating of 2 means the job calls for a fairly high level of education. The 3 rating for responsibility means there is often little supervision. An employee working in a programming environment is expected to be a self-starter and to be highly motivated to do an excellent job. A PEERS rating of 3 for skills shows that programming trainees need highly specialized skills to do well in their jobs.

Programming Trainee

P	E	E	R	S
1	1	2	3	3

Physical Activity and Environment. A PEERS rating of 3 means the job is repetitive, requires substantial travel, and has an environment that is perhaps uncomfortable. For example, data-entry and on-line terminal operators often work in a large room and must stay at their work station except for very specific work breaks. By contrast, a job in which a worker sits in a quiet area and programs or keyboards all day would receive a rating of 1. This might describe the typical programming environment or the environment for an on-line terminal operator assigned as a secretary in a legal or planning department.

Experience. Experience refers to exposure to similar responsibilities and requirements in a previous job. Entry-level jobs, such as computer operations trainee or programming trainee, have a PEERS rating of 1 because they require little, if any, previous experience. A job as a computer operator or computer programmer, which requires some experience, has a PEERS rating of 2. A job such as systems analyst, which requires substantial experience as a programmer and a good deal of exposure to typical business problems, has a PEERS rating of 3. A job with a PEERS rating of 3 should be assigned only to an individual with two or more years of experience in performing the job functions.

Education. The PEERS rating for education provides a scale of the amount of education needed for each information processing job. Jobs that require a high school diploma have a PEERS rating of 1. Most entry-level jobs that are computer-related require a high school diploma or some college. A rating of 2 means that vocational/technical training or a two-year college degree is needed. Jobs that nearly always call for a four-year college degree have a rating of 3.

Responsibility and Job Complexity. A complex job is one in which an employee must perform many different tasks. A person in an entry-level job does not do as many things as a person in a more advanced job. A beginning data-entry operator or on-line terminal operator may work at first with only one type of input data. This person's job is pretty basic. Also, such a trainee is closely supervised until he or she is familiar with all the job operations. Such a job has a rating of 1 for Responsibility and Job Complexity. An experienced on-line terminal operator, by contrast, may enter several kinds of data in a day. This operator's job is more complex. Also, since the operator is experienced, there is less supervision.

People who have been promoted are less closely supervised as they perform their job functions. Their jobs also become much more complex. A very complex job or a job in which a person has many decisions to make in performing the job has a Responsibility and Job Complexity rating of 3. (The PEERS ratings given in this chapter for Responsibility and Job Complexity in entry-level jobs are for workers with very little experience.)

Skills. Skills are special abilities that one learns. The PEERS ratings for Skills give you an idea of how many skills you must have for a particular job. Jobs with a PEERS rating of 1 require few, if any, specialized skills. A rating of 2 indicates that some specialized skills are necessary. For a job with a rating of 3, you must have many highly specialized skills that must be kept up to date. Taking vocational/technical school courses and getting on-the-job training are the best ways to develop and maintain specialized job skills.

CHECK YOURSELF

Supply the missing words.

1. The U.S. government gives code numbers to jobs and these codes are listed in a book called the __?__ __?__ __?__ __?__ .

2. Two books that describe the outlook for particular types of employment are the U.S. Industrial Outlook and the __?__ __?__ __?__ .

3. A job that requires a worker to perform many different tasks is said to be __?__ .

4. The authors of this book have created a system to describe and compare information processing jobs; this system is identified by the letters __?__ .

Answers: (1) Dictionary of Occupational Titles; (2) U.S. Employment Outlook; (3) complex; (4) PEERS.

The development and management of information processing systems require the efforts of many people. Included in the chain are a broad range of professionals and technicians, from hardware and software systems designers to computer operators, sales specialists, computer technicians, and many others. In addition, human effort is needed for the planning, development, and maintenance of the applications programs, large and small, that organizations use for ongoing processing. In this section you will learn about careers in computer hardware and software development, computer sales and sales support, and information management and processing.

There are many career opportunities in the information processing field. Because the educational requirements, need for specialized work experience, and suitable personality characteristics vary considerably from one cluster to another, you may find it helpful to picture a career ladder. Think of each step (rung) of the ladder as another job. The higher steps represent more advanced jobs. The jobs become more demanding as you climb the ladder. The lowest step on a career ladder is often a trainee job.

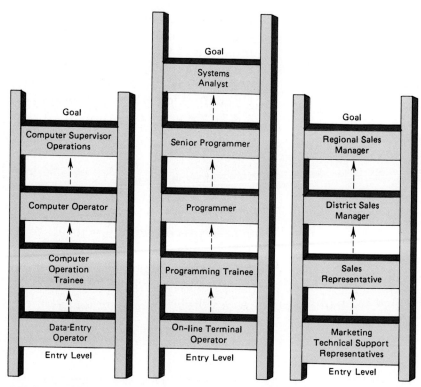

CAREER LADDERS. These ladders show three different types of information processing careers. Which one interests you the most?

CAREER OPPORTUNITIES

COMPUTER HARDWARE AND SOFTWARE CAREERS

The demand for systems analysts and computer programmers is expected to outpace the number of qualified applicants for the next several years. Demand for computer hardware designers is also good. It is especially good for engineers and designers with training in computer-aided design (CAD) and computer-aided manufacturing (CAM). The reason demand in these fields is so high is that all organizations, but particularly manufacturing companies, are trying to increase the productivity of their work force. Computerizing any routine steps that can be done by computer will reduce the number of steps that must be performed by human beings and thus save the company money. The several job clusters and specialized positions that follow have very specific requirements. The job titles themselves are descriptive of both the function and the technology.

COMPUTER HARDWARE JOB OPPORTUNITIES

The demand for engineers and designers trained in CAD/CAM techniques is very strong, but the greatest overall increase in computer employment is expected to be for computer service technicians. This is because of the need for assistance in constructing computer systems and for ongoing service and repairs once the equipment is in use.

Computer Hardware Designer. Computer engineers and designers do the research and development work that makes computer systems possible. Electronic engineers may redesign old equipment or develop new products that reflect major changes in technology. Typically, hardware designers have a graduate degree in electronic engineering.

Computer Hardware Designer				
P	E	E	R	S
2	2	3	2	3

COMPUTER HARDWARE DESIGNER. Computer engineers and designers are needed to do the research and development work that makes computer systems possible. The 3.5-inch micro-Winchester drive system shown here stores 10 megabytes of data. *Courtesy Hewlett-Packard Company.*

<table>
<tr><td colspan="6">**Computer Research Scientist**</td></tr>
<tr><td>P</td><td>E</td><td>E</td><td>R</td><td>S</td></tr>
<tr><td>2</td><td>1</td><td>3</td><td>2</td><td>3</td></tr>
</table>

Computer Research Scientist				
P	**E**	**E**	**R**	**S**
2	1	3	2	3

Computer Service Technician				
P	**E**	**E**	**R**	**S**
3	2	2	1	2

Computer Research Scientist. Large computer manufacturing companies sometimes hire computer professionals who are familiar with research techniques to develop alternative methods, techniques, and production materials. Computer research scientists responsible for original research usually have graduate degrees in electronic engineering, applied mathematics, or computer science. Research technicians working for these scientists usually need a four-year college degree.

Computer Service Technician. Hardware technicians assist designers and engineers in creating new hardware by testing and inspecting parts and finished machines. Technicians are sometimes also asked to design some of the smaller components of a new machine. Computer technicians known as field engineers install new computer systems, provide routine maintenance for customers, and make needed repairs.

Because computers require regular maintenance as well as emergency repairs, demand for technicians continues to grow. Technicians typically need a two-year technical program at the high school or junior college level. There should be especially good advancement opportunities for technicians who can iden-

COMPUTER SERVICE TECHNICIAN. Hardware technicians assist designers and engineers in creating new hardware such as this new portable computer by testing and inspecting parts and the finished product. *Courtesy Datavue Corporation, Norcross, Georgia.*

tify hardware problems before machines break down and cause processing delays.

COMPUTER SOFTWARE JOB OPPORTUNITIES

Recent developments in computer technology have made possible the hardware wiring of a large number of applications and operating programs. These instruction sets are wired directly on the silicon chips you read about earlier in this book. Although this progress in electronics affects the need for the programmers who used to write those instructions, the increasing demand for both systems and applications software for businesses and individuals will generate more jobs in analysis and programming than will be eliminated. Such new positions as *quality assurance assistants,* people who specialize in testing software, will definitely impact on the number of jobs available in information processing.

Software Engineer			
P	E	E	R	S
1	1	3	2	3

Software Engineer. This is a relatively new job category. A **software engineer's** responsibilities are similar to those in many other engineering professions. Mechanical engineers, for instance, might be given a project to design a machine to make potato chips more efficiently. The mechanical engineer would define all the objectives of the new machine, including size of chips, speed of operation, safety, and cost. The software engineer does the same thing, except that he or she is responsible for designing new software programs. A typical project for a software engineer could be to design a new software program to produce graphs and charts. A software engineer needs a four-year degree and might also need a master's degree.

Systems Analyst			
P	E	E	R	S
2	3	3	3	3

Systems Analyst. A **systems analyst's** job is to analyze a company's information needs or problems, including input, output, and processing requirements, from a productivity viewpoint. End-users, such as business managers or sales managers, ask a systems analyst to design a system that will provide the information they need to manage their businesses or departments. For example, a business manager or sales manager may request a monthly or weekly sales report showing sales by region, by product, or by salesperson.

The analyst presents the system design to the managers of the businesses or departments that will use the system. When the system plan is approved and the design work is under way, the analyst coordinates the training needed to make the system operate. It is the analyst's responsibility to instruct programmers in developing the software needed to run the entire computer system and to specify the commercial software and hardware needed to meet the needs of the users.

A systems analyst must be a good planner and must communicate well. Many analysts who start out as programmers are

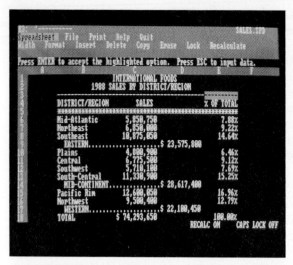
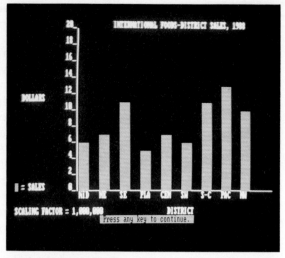

SALES INFORMATION. Managers depend on information, like the report shown on-screen here, to make business decisions. The systems analyst includes such output formats in the system plan. *Source: McGraw-Hill Spreadsheet. Will Faller.*

promoted because of their knowledge, planning skills, and people skills. Nearly all have a four-year college or graduate degree in computer science or mathematics. Many analysts also have training in insurance, banking, brokerage, or other fields relating to specific applications in large or growing industries. The U.S. Department of Labor forecasts a need for 400,000 analysts by the early 1990s.

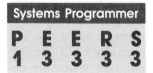

Systems Programmer. A **systems programmer** develops instructions that tell the computer how to operate itself and the peripheral equipment connected to it. This professional maintains the computer's operating system programs, making sure the computer programmers are properly using the operating system. Systems programmers are also involved in the design of data communications networks linking several business units or departments in a large organization.

Most systems programmers are college graduates with degrees in programming and systems analysis. Many employers give preference to those graduates with some business courses in their background. Because these professionals recommend computer operating systems and software packages to management and because many of these packages are designed to increase the efficiency of the firm's accounting and financial operations, there is especially good demand for systems programmers with a strong accounting background. Systems programmers are employed by large organizations, such as insurance companies, banks, government agencies, manufacturing companies, and management consulting firms.

Senior Computer Programmer. **Computer programmers,** also called applications programmers, write instructions that tell the computer what tasks to perform. They also adapt packaged software to a firm's particular needs. Large organizations often assign several programmers to the same project. Working together under the supervision of one or more senior programmers may be less experienced programmers, called junior programmers, and programming trainees.

System flowcharts developed by a systems analyst are used by a senior programmer, who develops program flowcharts and computer programs for the applications outlined in the system flowcharts. Using these charts and programs for reference, the senior programmer supervises the less experienced programmers in writing computer programs. The junior programmers convert each flowcharting instruction into a programming language as they write the programs step by step.

To manage a programming project successfully, a senior programmer must be skilled in writing instructions for a computer (coding). Many programmers can write computer instructions

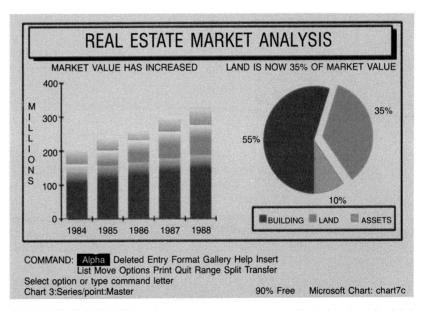

COMPUTER PROGRAMMER. Computer programmers write instructions that tell the computer what tasks to perform and adapt packaged software to their firm's particular needs. *Courtesy Microsoft Corporation.*

in several programming languages. Other programmers specialize in just one programming language.

Junior Computer Programmer. A senior programmer asks a junior programmer to do small tasks or write parts of a program. A junior programmer may be given just one program flowchart from a system or subsystem to work on at a time. (Computing hourly earnings is an example of one part of a payroll system.) Converting the program flowchart into a programming language, the junior programmer writes the detailed programming instructions. Each set of instructions is then tested through the input, processing, and output operations before the program is used for information processing.

Junior Computer Programmer				
P	E	E	R	S
1	2	2	3	3

Programming Trainee. The U.S. Department of Labor forecasts demand for half a million programming jobs by the early 1990s. Based on trends in the 1980s, it is likely that employers will favor trainee applicants with a college degree. Employers are also expressing interest in the ability of job candidates to communicate with people as well as with the computer.

Programming Trainee				
P	E	E	R	S
1	1	2	3	3

As a programming trainee, you would perform a number of beginning tasks under the supervision of an experienced programmer. These tasks might include making changes in a computer program and revising the written descriptions (the documentation) that should accompany computer software. In addition, you might be asked to convert each flowcharting instruction into a programming language. Opportunities for training and promotion are expected to come fastest to those candidates with specialization in a particular field such as insurance, banking, and brokerage because of the demand for programs to manage information in such organizations.

Equipment Analyst. When computer systems are developed, equipment decisions often have to be made. If a computer is to be purchased, what type, size, and make will it be? What special peripheral equipment will be needed?

Equipment Analyst				
P	E	E	R	S
2	3	3	3	3

Equipment analysts must know the job to be performed and what equipment, new or used, is available to perform it. They must be sure the equipment they buy will do the job efficiently and economically. Since information processing equipment can be bought from many manufacturers, an equipment analyst has to consider each sales presentation carefully before making a purchase recommendation to management.

Most equipment analysts have work experience in both computer programming and systems analysis. They usually have a college degree, and they are able to prepare well-written reports to support equipment recommendations.

EQUIPMENT ANALYST. As in other industries, buying computer equipment for a financial institution requires a knowledge of the end-user's needs and what equipment is available to meet those needs. *John McGrail, 1986.*

COMPUTER SALES AND SALES SUPPORT CAREERS

There is tremendous demand for computer professionals skilled in computer technology, human relationships, oral and written communications, and basic management. These professionals are employed to sell computer systems, peripheral equipment, operating systems, and applications software packages. Professionals are also needed to provide advanced technology support for the marketing of computer products.

Sales Representative				
P	**E**	**E**	**R**	**S**
2	**2**	**3**	**2**	**2**

Sales Representative. Computer sales representatives generally have a particular geographic territory in which to identify firms likely to need their company's products. These professionals contact potential customers to discuss their processing needs, budgets, and time frames. They match customer needs with company products and develop proposals that show how the products meet these needs.

Computer sales representatives need to understand computer terminology, to be capable of analyzing business needs, and to be proficient at business math and communication. They need to be self-confident and persuasive and to manage and organize their time well to achieve the levels of sales production expected of them. Most hardware and software employers look for a four-year college degree, including computer courses. Major hardware and software manufacturers also prefer job candidates with a master's degree in business administration, accounting, marketing, or computer science.

SALES REPRESENTATIVE. Computer sales representatives match customer needs with company products.

Marketing Technical Representative

P	E	E	R	S
2	2	3	1	2

Marketing Technical Support Representative. These professionals, sometimes called systems engineers by the large computer hardware manufacturers, are also part of the sales organization. They provide technical support to sales representatives in marketing computer products. Often they are asked to develop technical presentations and to provide customer training. To be hired by a major employer for an entry-level technical support position, individuals usually need a four-year degree in computer science. There may also be opportunities with smaller

TECHNICAL SUPPORT. An IBM instructor explains the operation of an IBM product to customers in classrooms across the country from an IBM television studio in Washington, D.C. *Courtesy IBM Corporation.*

employers for those who have had intensive training in a two-year technical program. The best advancement opportunities for these professionals often involve transferring to either a sales or a systems analysis position.

INFORMATION MANAGEMENT AND PROCESSING CAREERS

A number of jobs in information processing involve the management of information as it is prepared for processing, while it is being processed, and as it is prepared for reporting. Basically, these are the functions of input preparation, computer operations, and output preparation.

Skill in keyboarding is required for both jobs in data entry, or input preparation, and jobs in computer operations, or management of information processing. Individuals assigned to the data-entry function are typically called data-entry operators or on-line terminal operators. Those who are primarily responsible for computer operations include computer operators and computer operations trainees. Those who are important in computer output include both computer graphics specialists and technical writers. Prospects for jobs in computer graphics are excellent. Another area of specialization that seems to be growing is in database management. Positions such as *database administrator* and *database management assistant* are sure to gain popularity in the near future.

Data-Entry Operator

P	E	E	R	S
1	1	1	1	2

Data-Entry Operator. A **data-entry operator** uses input devices to enter data for use as input. This task consists of keyboarding data recorded on source documents. As the operator keyboards the data, it is recorded on magnetic disks or tapes.

Machine operation includes selecting various codes and format indicators to allow for machine interpretation of the various data fields. Data-entry operators must work carefully and accurately if the data is to be usable for processing. Typically, these operators need a high school diploma. They will need to take additional courses in business and computer technology if they want to advance to other positions, such as computer operator or computer programming trainee.

On-Line Terminal Operator

P	E	E	R	S
1	1	1	1	2

On-Line Terminal Operator. One type of data-entry worker is an **on-line terminal operator,** who enters data directly into a computer. The data is stored in an area called a buffer. The operator can check the visual display or the printed output, depending on the equipment used, then make corrections as needed. The corrected data can be entered right away, or it can be stored in a buffer. When the stored data is needed, it can be moved to the central processing unit. The major advantage of such on-line data input is that the computer checks and verifies the data as it is entered. Reductions in the cost of equipment ensure that on-line applications will continue to increase in the years ahead. Like other data-entry operators, on-line operators must be very accurate in their work. The educational requirements are the same.

Computer Operator

P	E	E	R	S
3	2	2	2	2

Computer Operator. As you know, a computer system is made up of a central processor and the input and output devices needed to perform the required information tasks of the organization. All these pieces of equipment are under the control of the computer console. A specially trained **computer operator** enters processing instructions at the console. This operator may also load magnetic disks or other input-output media. In a large department, these tasks will be performed by junior computer operators. The computer operator must keep an up-to-date log (record) of all computer information processing activities. This professional must also make sure all related computer equipment is kept in working order.

The computer operator works with programmers and systems analysts on problems of work flow. This operator also works with computer technicians to ensure regular maintenance and repairs to prevent and resolve machine failures. The computer operator must have a thorough knowledge of one or more computer systems. This individual usually needs at least a two-year college degree and also at least six months' work experience in information processing.

Computer Operations Trainee				
P	E	E	R	S
3	3	1	1	2

Computer Operations Trainee. A large data center may hire one or more high school graduates with no training or work experience. These employees are called computer operations trainees. Through on-the-job training, these trainees learn to operate computers and peripheral equipment and to load and unload input-output media. Sometimes these beginners are given the chance to be in a training program sponsored by the computer manufacturer whose system is used.

Computer Graphics Specialist				
P	E	E	R	S
1	1	3	2	3

Computer Graphics Specialist. A **computer graphics specialist** designs visual displays and presentations for computer output. Examples of such graphics presentations include economic forecasts for particular countries and industries or drawings of building or equipment plans. Other examples are bar graphs, pie charts, and line graphs showing industrial production, population trends, or employment patterns. The U.S. Department of Labor forecasts a demand for 600,000 computer graphics specialists by the early 1990s. It is likely that another 300,000 people will be employed to apply graphics technology. An example of this might be the use of computer graphics to create presentation slides or overhead transparencies.

COMPUTER GRAPHICS SPECIALIST. Computer graphics specialists design visual displays and presentations for computer output, such as the financial trends shown. *Courtesy Telerate Systems, Inc.*

Computer graphics specialists need to be well grounded in computer-aided design (CAD) and computer-aided manufacturing (CAM). They will also be specialists in particular fields, such as architecture, industrial engineering, commercial art, or statistics. They will need to be skilled at determining useful graphics and at converting their ideas into finished products. Typically, they will have a graduate degree in one or more technical fields, such as engineering or architecture. Those who apply the technology may have somewhat less formal and technical education, depending on whether they work for a computer graphics manufacturer or an end-user of this technology.

Technical Writer. These professionals work closely with the research and design staffs to describe the operations and relationships of computer systems, operating systems, computer software, information processing, and data transmission. Computer hardware manufacturers, software developers, consulting firms, and magazine publishers are increasingly looking for technical writers. The most skilled technical writers have salaries equivalent to those of engineers.

Writers describing office automation systems and other technology must understand how the systems work. They need training and/or work experience in computer programming and a four-year college degree. A technical, scientific, or business

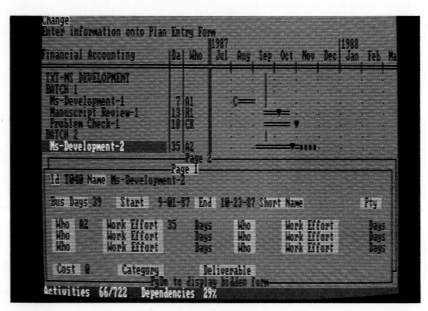

TECHNICAL WRITER. A technical writer helps make a program user-friendly. The screen above is from Project Workbench, a project management program. It is difficult to use the software efficiently without the documentation. *Will Faller.*

degree is useful because the systems are usually designed for business, research, or management information. The individual needs to be capable of understanding the technology, interviewing the systems developers, and managing what is often a demanding work schedule. Of course, written communication skills must be excellent.

SPECIALIZED TRAINING IN INFORMATION PROCESSING

Most computing jobs are in large metropolitan areas, such as Atlanta, Boston, Dallas–Fort Worth, Los Angeles, New York, Chicago, San Francisco, and Washington, DC. In general, the East Coast and California, with less than half the population of the United States, generated more than 70 percent of the country's total economic growth during the middle and late 1980s.

The large metropolitan areas named above are most likely to have excellent computer courses in their high schools and colleges, providing a good supply of job applicants to local employers. Some of the major employers in these areas are likely to offer special training programs for entry-level employees who are college graduates. These programs are usually geared to hardware design, systems analysis and development work, applications programming, or sales and marketing training.

Other organizations that provide career planning information, job descriptions, employment trends, salary information, and training programs are spread throughout the country. Information can generally be gathered from those organizations in person, by mail, or by telephone. See the table below for sources of additional information.

AMERICAN FEDERATION OF INFORMATION PROCESSING SOCIETIES
Suite 800
1815 North Lynn Street
Arlington, VA 22209

ASSOCIATED INFORMATION
MANAGERS
Suite 400
316 Pennsylvania Avenue, NW
Washington, DC 20003

ASSOCIATION FOR SYSTEMS
MANAGEMENT
24587 Bagley Road
Cleveland, OH 44138

COMPUTER AND BUSINESS EQUIPMENT MANUFACTURERS ASSOCIATION
Suite 500
311 First Street, NW
Washington, DC 20001

DATA PROCESSING MANAGEMENT
ASSOCIATION
505 Busse Highway
Park Ridge, IL 60068

EDP AUDITORS ASSOCIATION
373 South Schmall Road
Carol Stream, IL 60187

INDEPENDENT COMPUTER
CONSULTANTS ASSOCIATION
P.O. Box 27413
St. Louis, MO 63141

OFFICE TECHNOLOGY MANAGEMENT
ASSOCIATION, INC.
Suite 101
9401 West Beloit Road
Milwaukee, WI 53227

NATIONAL ASSOCIATION FOR WOMEN
IN COMPUTING
Suite 44
55 Sutter Street
San Francisco, CA 94104

SOURCE EDP PERSONNEL SERVICES,
INC.
Suite 227
2 Northfield Plaza
Northfield, IL 60093

CHECK YOURSELF

Supply the missing words.

1. The development and management of information processing systems require both professionals and ___?___.

2. The lowest step on a career ladder often represents a ___?___ position.

3. Demand for systems analysts, computer programmers, and computer hardware developers is great because of strong interest in ___?___.

4. There are ___?___ types of career opportunities for computer service technicians.

5. Certain types of programming jobs are being reduced in number because of new developments in ___?___.

6. Programming trainees are now evaluated for their ability to communicate with ___?___ as well as with computers.

7. Opportunities in programming will be more plentiful for applicants with both a ___?___ ___?___ and a specialized industry background.

8. There is tremendous need for computer programmers who are skilled in ___?___ and marketing.

9. Two types of jobs requiring keyboarding skill include data-entry operator and ___?___ ___?___ operator.

10. A computer ___?___ trainee learns to operate computers and peripheral equipment and to load and unload input-output media.

11. Two types of opportunities exist in computer graphics technology—one in design and one in ___?___.

Answers: (1) technicians; (2) trainee; (3) productivity; (4) two; (5) electronics; (6) people; (7) college degree; (8) sales; (9) on-line terminal; (10) operations; (11) applications.

REVIEW QUESTIONS

1. In the PEERS job rating system, what does PEERS stand for?
2. List three types of job opportunities in computer hardware.
3. List five types of job opportunities in computer sofware.
4. List two types of job opportunities in computer sales and sales support.
5. Name two data-entry positions.
6. Give two examples of information processing jobs that require a high level of education.
7. Give two examples of information processing jobs that need especially strong people skills.

COMPARING IDEAS

The questions below are to help you think about what you have learned in this chapter. They are "thought" questions. There is no one correct answer.

1. Take a field trip to a corporate data center. Describe the career ladder of greatest interest to you in terms of the company you visit.
2. Find out the salaries in your area for the jobs described in this chapter. Explain how these pay rates relate to a job rating system that takes into account the scope and difficulty of the job.

INFORMATION PROCESSING ACTIVITIES

Now you can perform many of the information processing activities business workers perform. Below is a summary of the tasks you will complete. You will find the actual data and business forms you need in your *Information Processing Work Kit*.

1. You will visit a local employment agency that specializes in information processing careers and will be given an interest test.
2. You will take an acheivement test in clerical speed and accuracy.
3. You will be given a test to measure your programming aptitude.
4. You will fill out a career planning questionnaire.
5. Using the questionnaire in Activity 4 you will complete a career evaluation planning sheet.
6. You will use the planning sheet to determine which jobs suit you best.
7. You will prepare a career ladder based on jobs that you are considering.

SOFTWARE PROJECT

5

USING GRAPHICS SOFTWARE

As you learned in Part 5, all businesses use computers in different ways to meet their information needs. Generally speaking, the larger the business, the more complex the computer applications. Some large businesses employ hundreds of workers in their information processing departments. When it comes to decision making, however, it is very often up to a single individual who must analyze business data to make a decision. This usually involves the use of one or more of the software application packages you have used in the Video-II-Go projects. In this project you will help convert sales data into a graphic format (such as bar charts and point graphs).

One of the most important activities in any business is sales. Since most owners cannot handle all sales personally, they must rely on their employees to process daily business transactions.

Since sales activity is so important, Pat Brown is constantly trying to think of ways to motivate all Video-II-Go employees to have customers rent more tapes. The latest idea is a $100 bonus to the employee who signs up the most new video club members each month. In order to motivate employees Pat would like to post the results daily on a wall chart. The store's computer system should be a big help in providing the needed information.

INFORMATION PROCESSING PROBLEM

Motivating employees can be accomplished in a variety of ways. The sales contest will require daily updates of membership sales. Pat would also like to see the data displayed in some graphic output format. This format should focus attention on the desire to be "first" rather than on the actual number of sales. What is needed is a rapid method of converting numeric sales data into a visual format that will help motivate the employees.

INFORMATION PROCESSING SOLUTION

The data for the sales contest is easily collected. A Sales Summary Worksheet will be posted at the cash register. Each time a membership is sold, the salesperson will update his or her daily totals. The totals on the daily worksheet will be used to produce the sales contest report. Producing the numeric data in the form of a wall chart as the owner wishes will require a great deal of manual design work. This effort can be greatly reduced by utilizing the existing microcomputer hardware and acquiring a graphics software package.

Graphics software allows you to create graphs and charts based on numeric data. The data can be keyboarded or can be converted from existing files. Graphics software can be simple or complex. In most cases, it is used to convert business data into a more useful or convincing format. The most common output formats are bar charts, point or line graphs, and pie charts. Most graphic output can be labeled in a horizontal (left and right) as well as a vertical (up and down) way. The software

---

VIDEO-II-GO   SALES SUMMARY WORKSHEET

Membership sales for the month of _____ *June* _____

Today's date _____ *June 1* _____

Salesperson	Sales this month	Sales this Date	Total
Anne	0	5	5
Marty	0	8	8
Mike	0	3	3
Rachel	0	4	4
Pete	0	1	1
TOTALS	0	21	21

VERIFIED BY _____ *P. B.* _____   DATE _____ *June 2* _____

```
VIDEO-II-GO                                    SALES SUMMARY WORKSHEET

Membership sales for the month of _____June_____

              Today's date _____June 30_____

   Salesperson         Sales this month     Sales this Date      Total

  _Anne_____         ____18____           ___8____          __26__

  _Marty_____         ____35____           ___9____          __44__

  _Mike_____         ____15____           ___2____          __17__

  _Rachel_____         ____10____           ___5____          __15__

  _Pete_____         ____25____           ___7____          __32__

  _____         _____           _____          _____

  _____         _____           _____          _____

  _____         _____           _____          _____

  TOTALS                ___103____           __31____          _134__

  VERIFIED BY __P. B._____        DATE __July 1_____
```

also makes it easy to display a report title that could additionally include the date.

Your supervisor will demonstrate the use of a graphics software package to you before you begin the keyboarding activities.

KEYBOARDING ACTIVITIES

1. Unless your supervisor has provided you with a prepared graphics format, you will need to select the output format (bar chart, point or line graph, or pie chart) and label each figure. Video-II-Go would like to use a bar chart format to compare the membership sales activity of its five employees. It is suggested that the total number of memberships sold be displayed on the vertical axis (the y-axis) and the name of the salesperson be displayed on the horizontal axis (the x-axis).

2. Once the labels have been created, enter the first day's sales from the total column on the first Sales Summary Worksheet. Enter the report title, "Daily Video Club Sales— June 1."
3. Using the output capability of the graphics software, display or print a graphic report. Have your supervisor review your output before going on to the next step.
4. Using the existing output format, enter the month's sales from the total column on the second Sales Summary Worksheet. Enter the report title, "June Video Club Sales."
5. Using the output capability of the graphics software, display or print a graphic report. Have your supervisor review your output.

ENRICHMENT ACTIVITIES

Using the data below, prepare a new graph that will show each employee's sales total for July as it compares to his or her previous month's total.

JULY	
Name	Total
Anne	15
Marty	24
Mike	23
Rachel	36
Pete	21

PART
6

THE FUTURE

CHAPTER

14

TRENDS IN INFORMATION TECHNOLOGY

Information Processing Terminology

Technology
Information processing
  technology
Serial processor
Parallel processor
Connection Machine
Superconductive
  circuitry

Josephson junction
Nanosecond
Picosecond
Optical computer
Transphasor
Femtosecond
Artificial intelligence (AI)

Expert system
Database
Electronic funds transfer
  (EFT) system
Cashless society
Password
Hacker

Performance Goals

☐ Define the terms *technology* and *information processing technology.*

☐ Explain the difference between serial and parallel processing and the advantage of parallel processing.

☐ Describe what is meant by computers made with superconductive circuitry and optical computers. Explain why each type of computer has the potential for faster processing than semiconductor computers.

☐ Explain the purpose of artificial intelligence (AI) research. Describe two areas of AI research work.

☐ Describe the capabilities of intelligent robots. Give examples of the kinds of work they can perform.

☐ Describe how the personal computer of the 1990s may differ from today's personal computer.

In many countries around the world, growth in agriculture and in industrial production together with improvement in the standard of living has been made possible by advances in technology. Simply defined, **technology** is the application of scientific knowledge to improve ways of doing things. More specifically, **information processing technology** is the application of science to improve methods of information processing.

Fifty years ago, information processing technology was concerned primarily with the development of better typewriters, adding machines, punched-card machines, and other types of mechanical office equipment. Today, research focuses on such subjects as electronics, optics, and superconductivity to find ways of improving computers and communications systems.

It is difficult even for expert computer scientists to predict with certainty the important technological breakthroughs that will occur in the future. Remember that less than fifty years ago Thomas J. Watson, Sr., founder of IBM, predicted that there would never be enough customers to justify the manufacture of computers by IBM. In view of the fact that there now are millions of computers in operation throughout the world, Watson's prediction seems ridiculous. He was wrong simply because he could not envision the varied ways in which computers could be used.

By the year 2001, computers certainly will be used in many ways not thought of today. The purpose of this chapter is to explore some of the advances in information technology likely to occur in the next 10 to 20 years. Then, we will look at how these advances may change the ways you will live and work.

ADVANCES IN INFORMATION PROCESSING TECHNOLOGY

Since computers began to be used in business information processing in the early 1950s, enormous improvements have been made in computer hardware and software, and associated communications technologies. Improvements in input, processing, storage, output, and communications equipment, discussed in

THE 4-MILLION-BIT CHIP. Each chip measures only 6.4 millimeters by 13.3 millimeters but can store about 400 pages of typed data. The chip's memory cells are so small that 48,000 of them will fit in an area the size of the period at the end of this sentence. *Courtesy IBM Corporation.*

earlier chapters, have led to faster, cheaper, and more reliable information processing.

As described in Chapter 2, developments in electronics technology, particularly in semiconductors, led to significant improvements in computers. The availability of large-scale integrated (LSI) circuits, and then very-large-scale integrated (VLSI) circuits, made possible the miniaturization of computer components and the development of the microcomputer. In turn, the availability of inexpensive microcomputers, together with larger memory units and improved techniques for communicating data, led in the 1980s to a spectacular increase in the use of computers in business and personal affairs.

Still, future advances in technology should bring significant improvements in at least four areas:

- Much faster computers will reduce processing time.
- Smarter computers will perform tasks not possible with today's computers.
- Intelligent robots will be available to perform complex tasks in industrial plants, offices, and homes.
- Personal computers will become more versatile in their capabilities.

FASTER COMPUTER PROCESSING

In spite of the progress that has already been made in producing high-speed computers, thousands of computer scientists are working in laboratories all over the world to improve pro-

THE 4-MILLION-BIT CHIP
AND GREAT MEMORIES
OF THE FUTURE

1-Million-Bit Chip

In August 1985, IBM began the world's first successful mass-production of a million-bit memory chip. Today our most advanced million-bit chip is faster than any in the industry, and million-bit chips are already in IBM mainframe, intermediate-size and new models of the RT PC computers.

4-Million-Bit Chip

On February 25, 1987, IBM announced a four-million-bit memory chip. It has four times the storage capacity of any memory chip used in computers today, and is being developed on the same manufacturing line used for volume production of IBM's million-bit chips. The four-million-bit chip can store about 400 pages of double-spaced typewritten text. And it can "read" them in one-quarter of a second. Its memory cells are so small that 48,000 of them fit in an area the size of the period at the end of this sentence.

And although the four-million-bit chip is big news, it's just the beginning of the story. There's a lot more going on in IBM research and development.

16-Million-Bit Chip

IBM is developing a memory chip that would quadruple the memory capacity of the four-million-bit chip. Selected portions of a 16-million-bit chip have already been fabricated and are being tested.

64-Million-Bit Chip

Working toward even denser chips, IBM designers and researchers are devising a memory chip that would store 64 million bits of information.

256-Million-Bit Chip

Looking even further ahead, IBM researchers are already investigating how to create a memory chip that would incorporate circuit lines only several hundred atoms wide.

COMPUTER MEMORIES OF THE FUTURE. This announcement of future computer memory capacities appeared in many newspapers and magazines in March 1987. *Courtesy IBM Corporation.*

cessing speeds even further. In 1982, Japan announced a goal of producing a computer 1000 times faster than the fastest computer then available (the Cray 1).

In the future, as in the past, faster information processing will come from a combination of technological advances. The availability of large memory units with faster access times speeds up processing time. The use of laser optics for storage and for communication of data is also an important advance. Nevertheless, the development of faster computer processors is considered a necessity for improved performance in the future.

In the 1970s and 1980s, increases in the speeds at which computer processors operated were achieved by packing more and more electronic circuits on tiny semiconductor chips. In 1987, IBM reported that its scientists had designed an integrated chip 16 times more densely packed than any chip then available. A single prototype chip held 16 million bits of information. Japanese computer manufacturers, as well as IBM, are investigating ways to create a 256-million-bit memory chip that would incorporate circuit lines only several hundred atoms wide. Manufacturers will continue to work out ways of producing semiconductor chips that contain even more circuits. This, however, is only one way of improving processing time. By the mid-1980s, computer manufacturers were seeking completely new ways of improving the operating speeds of computer processors. Several of these appear very promising.

Increasing Speed by Parallel Processing. Until the early 1980s, computers were designed to do only **serial processing.** In serial processing, a computer is equipped with a single processor. The processor carries out (or executes) one instruction at a time. Though a single processor may be designed to execute instructions at very high speeds, the limitation of executing a single instruction at a time hinders the achievement of faster processing.

Computer scientists have increased processing speeds by a technique called **parallel processing.** In parallel processing, a computer is equipped with more than one processor. Multiple processors allow a computer to handle a number of instructions at the same time.

Although a few microcomputers have been designed for parallel processing, initial attention has been focused on larger parallel processors. Among the early commercial computers designed for parallel processing was a machine known as the **Connection Machine.** Introduced in 1986, the machine was invented by Danny Hillis, 29 years old at the time and founder of the Thinking Machine Corporation. Before the Connection

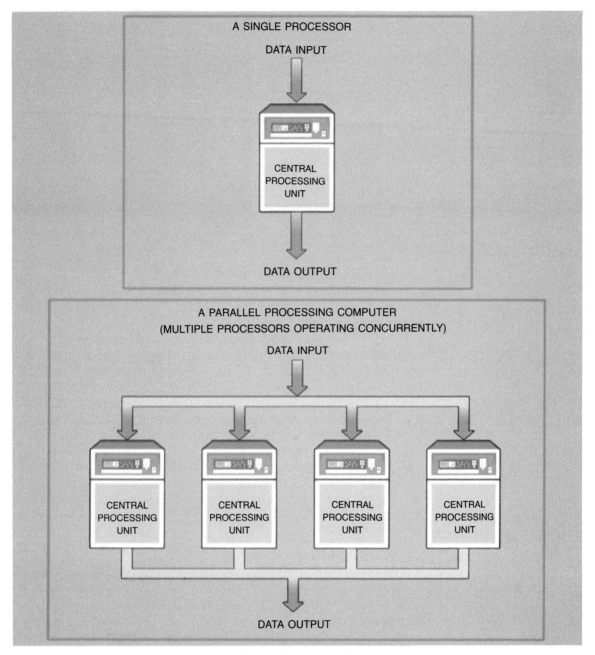

A COMPARISON: SERIAL PROCESSING AND PARALLEL PROCESSING.

Machine was made available, parallel processing computers incorporated only several hundred processors in one machine. The Connection Machine contains as many as 64,000 processors, linked together, with all processors capable of doing calculations simultaneously. The machine can execute between 1 bil-

THE CONNECTION MA-CHINE. The Connection Machine, developed by Daniel Hillis, was one of the first large parallel processing computers. *Courtesy Thinking Machine Corporation.*

lion and 7 billion instructions per second, depending on the kind of application being processed.

By 1987, several other manufacturers in this country were designing computers containing as many as 250,000 processors operating in parallel. At that time, the Japanese planned to incorporate as many as 1 million processors in a fifth generation of computers designed in that country. However, one problem in parallel processing still to be solved is the lack of adequate software for the new machines. Software languages used to program serial computers, such as BASIC, COBOL, and FORTRAN, do not efficiently meet the needs of parallel processors. Nevertheless, computer experts are excited about the potential of parallel processing architecture for improving information processing speeds.

Increasing Speed by Superconductive Technology. Scientists are also seeking to improve processing time by using radically new technologies in computer hardware. One promising approach is to use circuitry made of superconductor materials rather than semiconductors in computer processors. **Superconductive circuits** operate at extremely low temperatures, at which little or no resistance to the flow of an electric current exists. One type of superconductive switching device is known as a **Josephson junction.** It is named after Brian Josephson, a British scientist credited with developing the technology. The Josephson switch permits information to be transferred within a computer at much faster speeds than can be achieved in computers made with semiconductor switches.

SUPERCONDUCTIVE CIR-CUITRY. In superconductive wires, such as the thread-like ceramic wires illustrated, there is little resistance to the flow of electric currents. Computers made with superconductive circuitry can thus operate at faster speeds. *Courtesy Digital Equipment Corporation.*

It is believed that computers built of superconductive circuits will operate 50 times faster than the fastest computer available today at probably no greater cost. For example, instead of machine cycles of 50 *nanoseconds* (50 billionths of a second), a superconducting computer would have machine cycles as short as 6 *picoseconds* (6 trillionths of a second).

Increasing Speed by Optics Technology. Other scientists believe an even more radical approach to computer design should be taken. Instead of computers that use electrical components, they envision computers that run on light. An **optical computer** would process data by means of tiny beams of laser light, instead of electric currents.

In 1986 researchers at Bell Laboratories in New Jersey developed a switch that turns light on and off the way a transistor switches electric current on and off. These optical switches, known as **transphasors,** are the key to the development of optical computers. There are many advantages to computing with light. Since light can travel through a computer at 186,000 miles per second, the transfer speeds in an optical computer would be far faster than those in a computer dependent on the flow of electricity. Scientists are now talking about transfer speeds as high as 50 femtoseconds (a **femtosecond** is one quadrillionth of a second).

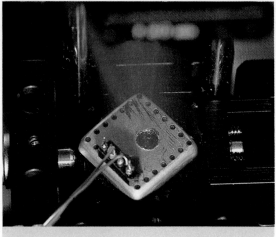

OPTICAL SWITCHES. This switch, developed by Alan Huang of AT&T Bell Laboratories, is an example of the technology that will make computers faster and more efficient to run in the future. *Copyright by Ken Kerbs, 1986.*

Another advantage of optical computers is that the switches might be able to operate in more states than the "on" and "off" of electronic transistors, which, as you have read, represent the binary numbers "1" and "0," or bits. If this is possible, then the binary logic that has controlled computer design since the outset would no longer be used. Instead, a new type of numbering system, more flexible than the binary system, could become the basis of computer operations.

Although some experts doubt that optical computers can ever be built, scientists at Bell Laboratories (where the transistor, the device that marked the second generation of computers, was invented) are optimistic. They believe they will be able to develop an optical computer by the mid-1990s.

The development of faster computer processors is important for several reasons. First, they will make it possible to do faster number crunching—that is, to perform calculations or other operations at increased speeds. More important, faster processors will open the doors to new computing applications, such as the modeling of atmospheric and other environmental conditions on a global scale. This is not possible to do now, given the limitations of processing speeds in presently available computers. High-speed processing is a necessary prerequisite for the development of "smarter" computers.

DEVELOPMENT OF SMARTER COMPUTERS

Ever since the first computer was invented, scientists have argued about the possibility of developing a computer smart enough to be taught to act and think as a human. We have computers now that can beat you in a game of tic-tac-toe, beat almost everyone in chess, and solve equations and problems that could not be done in a lifetime of manual calculations. These skills require a computer to have the ability to "think" in the sense that it must select the most appropriate alternative actions to solve the problems. Of course, in these cases a human (computer programmer) has instructed the computer how to select the best alternative. The question remains whether humans will ever be able to build a computer that can reason, actually learn, and improve its level of performance without human intervention.

Researchers in a field of technology called **artificial intelligence,** also known as AI, are trying to develop computers and software smarter than those we have today. They work in laboratories around the world. The Japanese government has established as a major research goal the development of a computer that can learn and reason. There are many different aspects of the AI research efforts now under way. In fact, two phases of the research work are already producing products that are being used: so-called expert systems and systems for processing natural languages.

Expert Systems for Problem Solving.   One of the first successful products of artificial-intelligence research has been the development of **expert systems** for problem solving. An expert system is a computer program (a software package) that makes it possible for a computer to provide answers to questions in a specialized area as capably as a human can. An expert system program incorporates a body of knowledge provided by a group

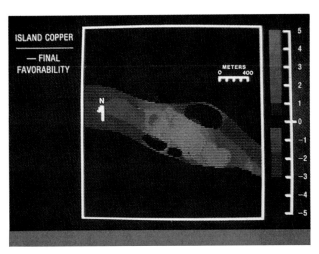
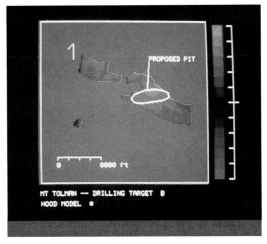

AI EXPERT SYSTEM. Artificial intelligence expert systems are used for problem solving in specialized areas. Shown here is the output produced from an expert system designed to predict the best potential places to find mineral deposits. *Courtesy SRI International.*

of experts in the particular field. For example, there are expert systems for medical diagnosis, including one for diagnosing lung diseases. Directed by this program, a computer will ask a patient the same questions that leading specialists in lung diseases would ask. The computer program reviews this data and reaches conclusions about the nature of a patient's illness, following the same reasoning and intuitive judgment processes followed by the expert specialists.

Expert systems are available for problem solving in many different fields, including business management and finance, government, science, engineering, education, and medicine. There are several investment programs designed to provide expert advice to individuals interested in selecting the best stocks to invest in. These systems attempt to anticipate stock market trends and identify specific stocks that usually move positively in relation to particular trends. Another type of expert system is available to counsel high school students by determining which colleges are appropriate to a student's interests and academic achievements and then advising the student on how to apply to these colleges. Mining companies have successfully used expert systems to predict the presence of particular mineral deposits in which they are interested.

Systems for Processing Natural Languages.

A second active area of artificial intelligence research attempts to extend our understanding of written and spoken languages, including English, Spanish, French, Russian, Japanese, and other widely used languages.

A better understanding of written and spoken forms of each language is essential if scientists are to develop smarter computers. At a minimum, a smart computer should be able to summarize news and magazine articles and translate material written in one language into another; for example, an article written in Russian into English, or vice versa. Many computer programs have been written to make summaries (or abstracts) of written copy and to perform translations. As yet, however, none are completely satisfactory.

Scientists are seeking an even more important benefit for computer users from AI research on natural languages. The goal is to make computers completely user-friendly. This goal will be achieved only when computers can understand instructions that are spoken to it in the natural language of the user, like English, French, or Spanish.

In Chapter 4 you read about the status of voice recognition input devices, and Chapter 6 described voice synthesizers that can translate output information into voice responses. At present, both voice input to computers and voice response output

A USER-FRIENDLY COMPUTER. In the future, people and their computers will have a friendlier working relationship. *Courtesy AT&T Laboratories.*

THE GOAL. The goal is to make computers that will understand spoken commands.

are limited in application, although a few natural-language programs for microcomputers are already available. For example, users can access some of the information in the Dow Jones News-Retrieval Service by spoken commands. On the other hand, it is not generally possible for a sales manager to find out how a particular salesperson is doing with respect to product sales by simply asking a computer a question such as: How many of our new computer display terminals has Joan sold in the state of California? The ideal is to have machines that can exchange conversation with humans as did Captain Kirk's computer in the TV series and movies of "Star Trek."

Chapter 14: Trends in Information Technology   357

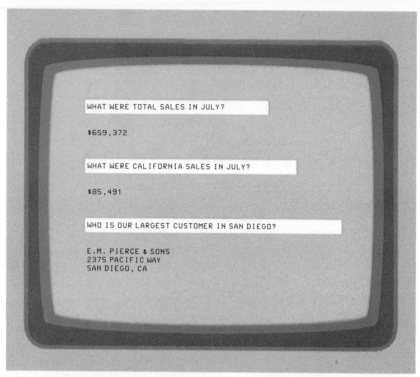

WHAT WERE TOTAL SALES IN JULY?

$659,372

WHAT WERE CALIFORNIA SALES IN JULY?

$85,491

WHO IS OUR LARGEST CUSTOMER IN SAN DIEGO?

E.M. PIERCE & SONS
2375 PACIFIC WAY
SAN DIEGO, CA

NATURAL LANGUAGE INQUIRY SYSTEM. With a natural language inquiry system, a user enters an inquiry into the computer in simple words the computer can interpret and act upon.

CHECK YOURSELF

Match each phrase with the word or term that best defines it.

1. A computer that can execute more than one instruction at a time.
2. A computer that processes data by means of light beams.
3. Research to develop smarter computers.
4. A computer program that can solve problems.
5. One trillionth of a second.
6. One quadrillionth of a second.
7. The name for an optical switch.
8. A computer that can execute only one instruction at a time.
9. Circuits that operate at extremely low temperatures.

a. Serial processing computer
b. Parallel processing computer
c. Expert system
d. Superconductive circuitry
e. Artificial intelligence
f. Femtosecond
g. Microsecond
h. Picosecond
i. Optical computer

DEVELOPMENT OF INTELLIGENT ROBOTS

Closely associated with research efforts to develop smarter computers is the work being done to develop intelligent robots that are computer-controlled. As you read in Chapter 8, industrial robots are now being used in Japan, the United States, and other countries to perform repetitive assembly-line work and many tasks too dangerous for humans. An example is the handling of radioactive materials. A large bank in New York also uses a robot to handle mail service within its office building. The robot follows a designated path on each floor, stopping at preassigned stations to pick up and deliver mail. Automobile manufacturers use many robots to weld parts together, lift heavy parts, and paint entire car bodies.

More intelligent robots incorporate various sensing devices operating under the control of microprocessors. A robot that has the ability to see uses a computerized system that converts signals from a video camera into dot images, which the computer analyzes. This makes it possible for the robot to identify its position relative to other objects around it. Additional sensors can give a robot a sense of touch—that is, the ability to distinguish the size, shape, temperature, and degree of hardness of an object. Still other sensors can provide robots with a hearing capacity that can exceed that of a human; for example, ultrasounds that no human can hear can be detected by robots. The Voyager spacecraft sent out to explore various planets in the solar system is piloted by robots. The spacecraft has many different types of sensors and cameras that can gather information and send it back to earth. The Mars Lander had a robot arm and an automated chemical analysis laboratory built into it. The arm could be commanded by computer control from Earth to scoop up Martian soil and place it in the chemical analysis devices on board. The chemical makeup of the soil and atmosphere was determined and the information was sent back to Earth.

Researchers expect that by the early 1990s, highly intelligent robots will be available. They have already successfully tested robots that can locate and pick up an egg without breaking it, sort and process fruits and vegetables, pluck a chicken, and even shave the wool off a sheep. Scientists predict that before

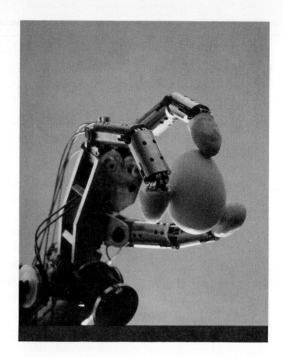

INTELLIGENT ROBOTS. Various sensing devices give the intelligent robot the ability to see and hear and a sense of touch. The robotic hand, with a sensative touch, can pick up an egg without breaking it. *Courtesy Hitachi.*

the end of the century, robots will be examining ocean floors, flying airplanes and navigating ships, removing minerals from underground mines too dangerous for human workers, and performing a wide variety of assembly and inspection jobs in manufacturing plants.

TOMORROW'S PERSONAL COMPUTERS

When the first assembled microcomputer, the Apple II, was introduced in the late 1970s, many computer professionals who were used to working with mainframe computers regarded it as a toy. They thought it would never play an important role in business information processing. Indeed, there was some justification for their position. The original Apple computer had limited processing power and main memory capacity. The only form of auxiliary storage was floppy disks, and output information could be displayed only in text or numerical form or printed in rather poor quality print as compared with today's standards.

By the mid-1980s, vast improvements had been made in microcomputers for business and for the home. For just about the same price as the original microcomputers of the late 1970s, users were able to purchase systems that had much faster processors, much larger main memory capacities, and much more auxiliary memory on hard disks. A wide array of high-quality printers was available. Graphic display and printing capabilities were available on many systems. By 1986, annual sales of personal computers in the United States reached almost 8 mil-

All models include integrated display support, 256-color graphics capability, clock/calendar, and ports for serial, parallel and pointing devices. All systems use a common IBM enhanced keyboard and accept any IBM Personal System/2 monochrome or color display. All models accept the 200MB IBM 3363 Optical Disk Drive option.

	Model 30	Model 50	Model 60	Model 80
Microprocessor	8086	80286	80286	80386
Potential system throughput	Up to 2½ times PC XT	Up to 2 times PC AT	Up to 2 times PC AT	Up to 3½ times PC AT
Standard memory	640KB	1MB	1MB	Up to 2MB
Expandable to		7MB	15MB	16MB
Diskette size and capacity	3.5 inch 720KB	3.5 inch 1.44MB	3.5 inch 1:44MB	3.5 inch 1.44MB
Fixed disk	20MB	20MB	44, 70MB	44, 70, 115MB
Additonal options			44, 70, 115MB	44, 70, 115MB
Maximum configuration	20MB	20MB	185MB	230MB
Expansion slots	3	3	7	7
Operating system(s)	PC DOS 3.3	PC DOS 3.3 and Operating System/2	PC DOS 3.3 and Operating System/2	PC DOS 3.3 and Operating System/2

A NEW GENERATION OF PERSONAL COMPUTERS. In 1987, IBM introduced its series of Personal System/2 Computers. *Courtesy IBM Corporation.*

lion units. Worldwide, more than 15 million personal computers were sold that year.

Computer manufacturers expect the sales of personal computers to continue to increase into the 1990s. In 1986 scientists in the computer science department at Carnegie-Mellon University predicted that by the early 1990s a new generation of personal computers would be available. They forecasted that the new personal computers would cost no more than the 1986 machines, but that these new computers would be 5 to 10 times as powerful and able to process 3 million instructions per second. In addition, the personal computers of tomorrow will have 10 to 20 times as much useful memory. Main memories of four, and even eight, million bytes (four to eight megabytes) will be common. Hard disks will be the standard form of auxiliary storage; they will provide an additional 30 to 100 megabytes of storage. The machines will also be equipped to handle optical data storage.

The personal computers of tomorrow may not look much different from the way they do now, but the components will be crammed into smaller cases. The image on the display screen will be sharper and more detailed, and the screen will be able to hold a full page of text and an illustration. You can expect that in the future every personal computer will be equipped with the advanced graphics capabilities now found only on more expensive systems.

Some experts believe users will not have to work with text-driven software or learn any programming language, such as BASIC, to use the next generation of personal computers. Instead, all software will be graphically oriented. The user will manipulate a mouse or a joystick to move an arrow among familiar names and symbols on the screen, much as the Macintosh user does today. The symbols will become standard among manufacturers and software suppliers so that a user can move from a machine of one manufacturer to another and from one software package to another without spending days to learn a new system. Voice-operated personal computers will also be common by the mid-1990s.

TECHNOLOGICAL ADVANCES BRING MIXED BLESSINGS

Throughout this book you have read about the impact that computers have had on information processing. Since computers were introduced in the 1950s, the ways in which work is performed in business and government have changed markedly. In the decades to come, new technological advances, such as those discussed earlier in this chapter, will change the ways in which office and industrial work is performed. Perhaps more startling will be the influences the new technologies will have on life styles.

When used properly, computers provide many benefits to society. The computer is now so firmly embedded in the operations of banks, stores, offices, manufacturing plants, government agencies, hospitals, and schools that it is hard to imagine how this country could get along if our computers were to stop working. Nevertheless, social critics often wonder whether the computer and other technological advances, such as the automobile, airplane, and television, have actually improved the quality of our lives. The debate over whether we are better off with the technological advances will continue. This is because some unavoidable and undesirable side effects accompany technological advances. Think of the automobile. Most of us would agree that the technology that led to the development of automobiles has brought many benefits to our lives. Yet, the automobile causes air pollution, traffic jams, and, if misused, harm to innocent people. A car that runs out of control when driven at 80 miles per hour may injure or kill innocent bystanders.

Computer technology, if misused, can also cause harm. You should be aware of some of the ways in which computers may be misused and of the negative impact that some believe computers and robots may have on society.

COMPUTERS AND INDIVIDUAL PRIVACY

You have read about the advantage of storing data electronically in **databases.** Information recorded in a database file can be easily retrieved by a computer. Many databases called data banks contain records that have information about hundreds of thousands, even millions, of individuals.

INTERNAL REVENUE SERVICE	Increasingly, the IRS is exchanging data with state and local tax authorities to check the accuracy of tax returns
SOCIAL SECURITY ADMINISTRATION	Your Social Security number—the code that third parties need to tap into computerized information on you—is available to at least 125 government and private agencies
MOTOR VEHICLE DEPARTMENTS	About 40 states will sell direct-mail firms the information you provide when registering a vehicle or applying for a license. This reveals your age, sex, Social Security number—even, through deduction, your income range
FBI	Its National Crime Information Center has more than 10 million centrally stored records of criminal histories—all available to state and local authorities
COURTS	Some states are computerizing their court documents—making it easier to monitor everything from eviction to criminal proceedings
CREDIT BUREAUS	The five largest credit reporting companies control records on more than 150 million individuals
BANKS	Most banks are allowed by law to give out information on customers' accounts and credit histories to state government investigators
LIFE INSURANCE COMPANIES	By tapping a central database run by a company called the Medical Information Bureau, they can find out details about your medical history from claims information provided by insurers
DIRECT-MAIL COMPANIES	By combing through some of the above records and other information, they churn out lists of specific individuals whom salespeople or political campaigns may want to contact

DATA: BW, *PRIVACY JOURNAL*, GOVERNMENT REPORTS

EXAMPLES OF DATA BANKS. *Reprinted from Feb. 9, 1987 issue of Business Week by special permission. Copyright © 1987 by McGraw-Hill, Inc.*

DATA BANK INFORMATION. Information that is given by a customer filling out a loan application in a bank or finance agency is stored in a data bank. Such information may be made available to law enforcement agencies. *Courtesy Hewlett-Packard Company.*

Without electronic databases, business and government could not use computers effectively. Banks, finance and credit agencies, insurance companies, and retail stores are only some of the business organizations that maintain files of data (or data banks) about the individuals who are their customers. Government agencies have even larger data banks for recording information about individuals. The U.S. Census Bureau, the Internal Revenue Service, the Social Security and Veterans Administrations, the FBI, and the Department of Justice are some of the federal agencies that maintain data banks on individuals. State and local governments also maintain data banks.

There are several risks associated with the maintenance of data banks, either by private businesses or by government. First, there is the danger that information stored in the computer records may fall into the hands of someone who is not authorized to have access to it. If an unauthorized person is able to get access to a data bank which contains information about you, such as the amounts that you owe to others, it can be said that there has been an *invasion of privacy*—yours.

The opportunities to invade individual privacy are growing because the number of data banks is increasing. Many people are concerned about the potential for the invasion of privacy that exists with the new **electronic funds transfer** (EFT) systems used in banking. EFT systems provide the means of achieving a *cashless society.* In a cashless society, you do not receive payment for work in cash or by check, nor do you pay for purchases in cash or by check. The amount of your paycheck is transferred electronically from your employer's bank account into your bank account. Using a debit card, you can then authorize your bank to pay for any purchase you make, whether at a supermarket or a department store. The amount of the purchase is immediately deducted from your bank account and added to that of the seller.

With an EFT system, a bank has a full record of the income and the spending habits of millions of individuals recorded in a data bank. Some people worry that government agencies, private businesses, or even individuals might try to get access to this information when they are not authorized to do so.

There is still another potential harm in data banks. This is that a data bank may contain erroneous information about an individual. It is always possible that an error in data input or in processing the input may occur. For example, a credit agency might record in its file that you have not paid a particular bill that you have in fact paid. Such a record could negatively affect the willingness of a store to let you open a charge account. For this reason, you should be allowed to know what information is recorded in your file. If you find that the information is incorrect, you need assurance that it will be corrected.

Concern about the risks just described has led to actions to protect the personal privacy of each individual with respect to information in data banks. Federal legislation, the *Privacy Act of 1974*, grants each individual the right to become aware of all the information about him or her in the files of federal government agencies. This law also provides each individual with the opportunity to correct any false data. In addition, each federal agency is responsible for ensuring that the information it has stored is not misused.

Additional federal legislation provides students and parents with the right to see and to challenge educational records. It also provides that the disclosure of school records will be limited. Other federal laws limit the type of information that credit bureaus can collect. These laws also provide you with the right both to know what is in your records and to have the data corrected, if necessary. More recent legislation regulates the way in which information in EFT databases can be used. Some states have passed similar laws to protect the privacy of information maintained by state agencies and private organizations.

COMPUTERS AND CRIME

As the numbers of computers and computer networks have grown, so have the opportunities for criminal misuse of the facilities. Businesses and governments have often installed computer systems without proper consideration of how to safeguard the systems. Individuals who are highly skilled in system and program design have found ways to steal money, property,

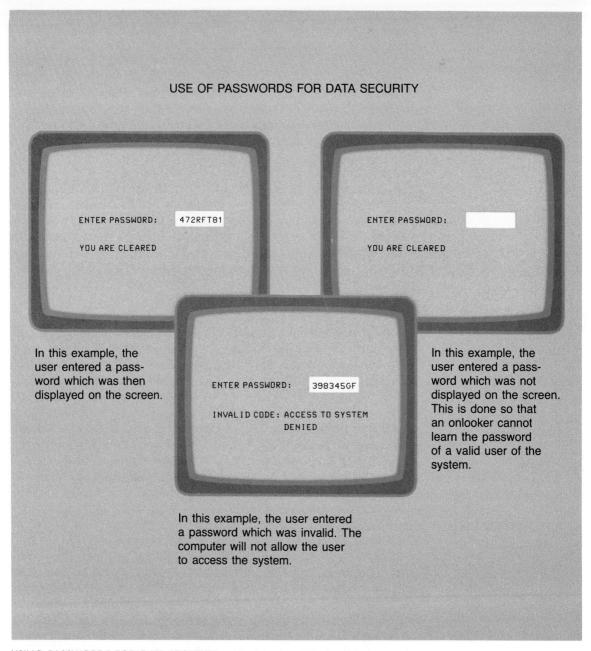

USE OF PASSWORDS FOR DATA SECURITY

ENTER PASSWORD: 472RFT81

YOU ARE CLEARED

ENTER PASSWORD:

YOU ARE CLEARED

ENTER PASSWORD: 398345GF

INVALID CODE: ACCESS TO SYSTEM
DENIED

In this example, the user entered a password which was then displayed on the screen.

In this example, the user entered a password which was not displayed on the screen. This is done so that an onlooker cannot learn the password of a valid user of the system.

In this example, the user entered a password which was invalid. The computer will not allow the user to access the system.

USING PASSWORDS FOR DATA SECURITY.

or information by breaking into and manipulating computer systems and programs.

A California bank was robbed of more than $10 million by a computer specialist. He was completely familiar with the bank's computer system, through which millions of dollars were transferred to other banks each day. The computer specialist first

SECURITY PROTECTION.
Passkeys and secret
access codes offer
security protection to
computer centers.
Courtesy Honeywell, Inc.

falsely established a bank account under his own name in the bank's database. By terminal input, he then arranged to transfer funds from other accounts to his account. Eventually the crime was detected, and the stolen money was recovered.

Other criminals have used their computer expertise to falsify medical claims or Social Security records and to direct payments to themselves. Customer order and inventory systems have been manipulated by criminals who order merchandise to be shipped to their own homes but billed to another name. Sometimes individuals using computer terminals try to steal information, such as new product information, from a database or electronic mail system of a competing business. Even students have attempted to raise their grade averages that are stored in a school's database.

On-line database systems that are accessible by computer terminals through telephone dial-up or communications networks are special targets for computer criminals. Management tries to limit terminal access to a computerized database by means of **passwords** and other identification codes. A user of the system must identify himself or herself to the computer with a valid password and identification code. If an individual attempts to use the system without valid identification, the computer will lock up, or disconnect the telephone line, preventing access to the system. It also may notify management or a security guard of the unauthorized attempt to gain access. Too often, however, passwords and identification code numbers may be stolen or are easy for others to guess. Illegal break-ins to a system may be reduced by changing passwords and identification codes frequently. New methods for establishing access identification codes give more assurance that no unauthorized person will be able to break into a system.

Unfortunately, misguided students using personal computers and telephone lines have considered it a challenge to break into important business databases or critical government networks. Sometimes, they have destroyed valuable information or extracted it from the files. The word **hacker,** which originally described a programming enthusiast, now refers to an illegal computer trespasser. Initially, the illegal breaking into a computer by a hacker was considered more of a prank than a crime. However, the 1986 Computer Fraud and Abuse Act subjects a hacker to the same penalties that face other computer criminals. It is now a federal crime for anyone to access network databases, electronic mail, and electronic bulletin board systems without authorization.

COMPUTER TECHNOLOGY AND EMPLOYMENT OPPORTUNITIES

The mixed blessings of technological advances are well illustrated by the impact of these advances on employment opportunities. Typically, some jobs are eliminated as a result of new technologies in an industry. *Job displacement,* as this impact is called, occurred when the car replaced the horse and buggy as the means of personal travel. As automobile plants were built, the demand for people skilled in the manufacture of buggies decreased.

Advances in information technology have also resulted in job displacement. At the beginning of this century many individuals skilled in hand-posted bookkeeping methods were employed by many businesses. By mid-century, such skills were no longer in great demand. Instead, businesses sought individuals who could operate accounting and punched-card machines. Today, individuals experienced only in accounting or punched-card machine operation would have difficulty finding an employer who could use their skills.

Since their introduction, computers have eliminated the need for many clerical jobs in which people performed repetitive types of calculating, sorting, typing, and other routine operations. In industrial plants, robots have displaced assembly-line

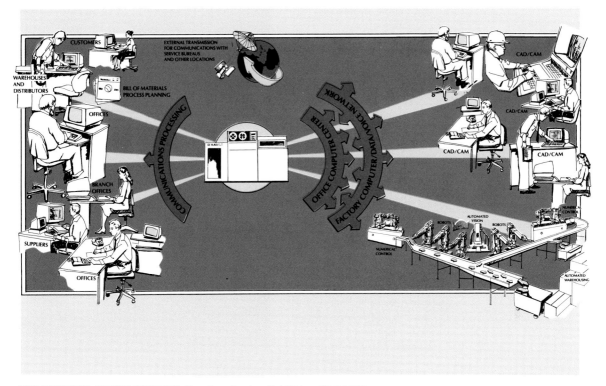

THE FACTORY OF TOMORROW. *Courtesy Penton Publishing Company.*

workers who welded parts together or hand-painted automobile bodies. Computer-controlled robots have also displaced some skilled machinists. In the future, we can expect even more types of clerical and industrial work to be performed by computers and robots.

On the other hand, think of all the new employment opportunities that have been created by computer and robot technologies. People are needed to design, manufacture, sell, repair, and use the new equipment and services. Chapters 12 and 13 described many of the new jobs that have come into being because of technological advances in information processing.

So far, there appear to be more jobs created than displaced by computers and robots. Interestingly, those countries using the greatest number of robots in 1986 were among those with the lowest unemployment rates. However, no one knows with certainty what will happen to employment opportunities when the smarter computers and more intelligent robots described earlier in this chapter become available.

The U.S. Department of Labor estimates that by 1995 there will be 10 times more computers in use than there were in 1986. It predicts an incredible 97 percent growth in employ-

COMPUTERIZED MAP DISPLAY. Automobiles of the future will have computerized maps that will display the driver's location and the surrounding roads and highways. *Courtesy Chrysler Corporation.*

ment of computer operators and technicians to handle this growth. This means we must find better ways of retraining individuals whose jobs will be displaced by computers or robots. Displaced workers in offices and industrial plants should have a chance to participate in the new employment opportunities that will be created by future technological advances.

CHANGING THE WAY IN WHICH YOU WILL WORK AND LIVE

Whether you work in an office, store, bank, industrial plant, laboratory, hospital, or school, you will probably have access to a personal computer connected to a larger computer network. Mail will be delivered to you via your computer screen, and your written communications will be prepared on the computer and delivered via a telecommunications network. If your work involves the preparation of data for computer processing or the use of computer output or reference information, your terminal will serve as the communications link between you and computerized databases. Even if you do not choose a career in computer operations or in systems and programming, you will have many opportunities to work with computers. As a salesperson, doctor, nurse, lawyer, research scientist, librarian, teacher, or business manager, you will need a computer to help you in your work.

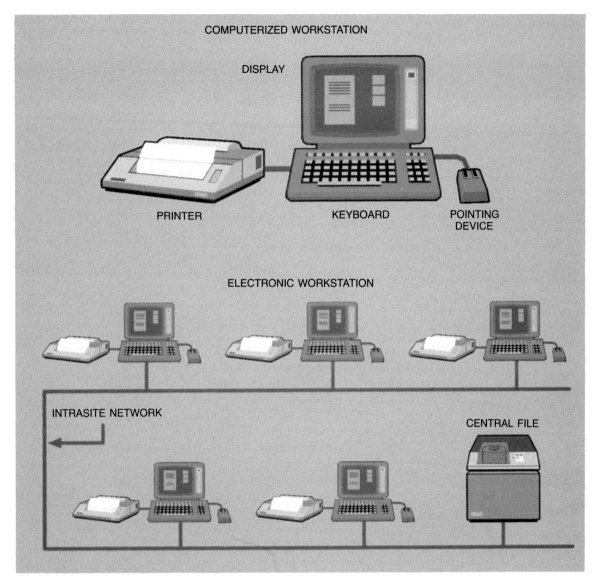

COMPUTERIZED WORKSTATION

DISPLAY

PRINTER   KEYBOARD   POINTING DEVICE

ELECTRONIC WORKSTATION

INTRASITE NETWORK

CENTRAL FILE

THE COMPUTERIZED WORKSTATION. A network links many computerized workstations to one another and to central files.

In your home, the computer will help you shop, bank, keep up with the most recent news, learn new skills, make travel reservations, and communicate with your friends. It will also serve as a family entertainment center. If you are sick, you will receive advice on medical treatment by computer.

In spite of the advances already made, the information (and computer) revolution has a long way to go. You should expect your employers to adopt new technologies and new systems. As a result, your job responsibilities and the ways in which you accomplish work will often change. In addition, to gain the advantages of using personal computers at home, you will have to learn new ways of handling your personal chores, such as shopping or banking.

To remain an active participant in this fast-changing world, you must maintain your computer literacy. The information you have gained from studying this book is only a start. Staying informed about what computers can do involves a lifelong commitment to learning.

CHECK YOURSELF

Supply the missing words:

1. An electronic file containing records about individuals is called a ___?___ .
2. A ___?___ is used to identify an authorized user of a computer system.
3. Unauthorized access to a database is an invasion of ___?___ .
4. One type of illegal computer trespasser is called a ___?___ .
5. An intelligent robot is controlled by a ___?___ .
6. EFT stands for ___?___ ___?___ ___?___ .
7. Maintenance of computer literacy involves ___?___ learning.
8. In a ___?___ society you do not pay for purchases in cash or by check.
9. The U.S. Department of Labor estimates that by 1995 there will be ___?___ times more computers than in 1986.
10. Elimination of jobs through technological advances is called job ___?___ .

Answers: (1) database; (2) password; (3) privacy; (4) hacker; (5) computer; (6) electronic funds transfer; (7) lifelong; (8) cashless; (9) ten; (10) displacement.

REVIEW QUESTIONS

1. Define *technology* and *information processing technology*.
2. Why was Thomas J. Watson's prediction about the demand for computers wrong?
3. Name four areas in which significant technological improvements are expected.
4. Explain the difference between serial and parallel processors.
5. Describe the Connection Machine and its capabilities.
6. What are superconductive circuits, and what advantage do they have over semiconductors?

7. Explain how optical computers will work.
8. Give two reasons why scientists are trying to develop computers that work faster.
9. What is the purpose of artificial intelligence (AI) research?
10. Define the term *expert system* and describe an example of such a system.
11. Give two reasons why the AI work on natural languages is important.
12. Describe the features and capacities of intelligent robots.
13. Describe the features of tomorrow's personal computer.
14. What is a database? Give two examples of databases.
15. Explain what is meant by invasion of privacy.
16. Describe four types of laws that deal with protection of privacy.
17. Give three examples of criminal use of computers.
18. Explain how management attempts to prevent unauthorized use of computer systems.
19. What is a hacker?
20. Define and give an example of *job displacement.*
21. What benefits do technological advances bring?

COMPARING IDEAS

The questions below are designed to help you think about what you have learned in this chapter. They are "thought" questions. There is no one correct answer.

1. Some say that the manufacture of faster and smarter computers may not be good because the machines may replace skilled workers in factories and offices. What do you think about this?
2. What are the arguments for and against the idea that computers can think and act as humans?

INFORMATION PROCESSING ACTIVITIES

Now you can try out the kinds of information processing activities business workers perform. Below is a summary of the work you will do. You will find the actual information and business forms you need in your *Information Processing Work Kit.*

1. You will be asked to review the development of a CD-ROM product.
2. You will prepare a system specifications report on the proposed new project.
3. You will prepare a list of necessary hardware specifications and a marketing plan.

SOFTWARE PROJECT 6

USING INTEGRATED SOFTWARE

As you learned in Part 6, changes in technology promise to change the way we will live and work in the future. Each business will benefit from improved technology in different ways. One trend does appear to be consistent in all businesses. In past years, only a small portion of a company's information was in computer readable form. Today, most large businesses and an increasing number of small businesses maintain the majority of their information on computers. This practice changes the way in which managers make decisions. It is now possible to process business data in ways that would have taken an unreasonable amount of human effort in the past. Sorting data, for example, which is very time consuming using manual methods can be accomplished in seconds using application software.

In this project you will demonstrate the many ways in which existing business data can be changed to meet new information needs at Video-II-Go. The owner hopes that the microcomputer can produce an increased amount of information without a major increase in clerical effort.

Each time a new use for the microcomputer is found, more employee time is spent on the computer. Pat Brown is pleased with the computer uses so far, but wants to make sure that the clerical time is well utilized. Since the most time-consuming step in putting a business application on the computer is inputting information, the owner wants to be sure that data that has been entered once will not have to be reentered for a second application.

INFORMATION PROCESSING PROBLEM

Video-II-Go is growing rapidly. Like many growing businesses, the operation is finding it more and more necessary to communicate with individuals and other businesses on a regular basis. These groups include customers, employees, suppliers, and support agencies such as banks and insurance companies. Pat has found that in preparing letters and documents to each of

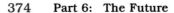

these groups its becomes necessary to gather information from files using several computer application packages. An order to a video tape supplier, for example, might start with a letter prepared using word processing, require a mailing address from one database, a list of video tapes from a second database, and end with a summary of the order prepared on a spreadsheet. The owner would like to be able to combine data from several files in a single report.

INFORMATION PROCESSING SOLUTION

When computer data can be moved from one software application to another without keyboarding the data again, the packages are said to be *integrated*. This is accomplished in two ways.

The first method requires individual software packages that convert data to one or more standard data formats (such as to an ASCII code). Once the data is converted, it is read by another package designed to accept this standard format. This procedure allows a word processing package, for example, to read a mailing label database in a common file format.

The second procedure involves the purchase of an integrated software package which includes the most common applications such as word processing, spreadsheet, database, and graphics. These packages have a built-in capability that passes data from one application to another. Although these packages can be expensive, Pat believes that it will be cost-effective by reducing the amount of data entry required.

Your supervisor will demonstrate the use of an integrated software package to you before you begin the keyboarding activities.

KEYBOARDING ACTIVITIES

1. You will need to retrieve many of the data files you prepared for the previous Video-II-Go software projects before you can complete the following activities.
2. Prepare a letter to one of Video-II-Go's suppliers for the purchase of additional video tapes. The supplier is Command Video Distributors, 1121 Victor Drive, Fort Worth, Texas 76102. Pat Brown would like to purchase one additional copy of the five tapes that have been out of stock the most. Sorting the video tape database file by the No. Out of Stock field produced the report shown below. Compose a letter requesting one copy each of tapes listed in the chart following the opening paragraph of your letter. The chart should be the database file listing the five video tapes hav-

VIDEO-II-GO				RENTAL WORKSHEET
Tape No.	Title	No. of Rentals	Fee	No. Out of Stock
412	Suspicion of Guilt	43	2.00	12
503	The Connection	40	2.00	10
501	Wait for Summer	19	2.00	7
512	Before You Say Goodbye	24	2.00	4
603	Superdome II	23	2.00	4

ing the highest number of out of stock requests. The letter will be signed by Pat Brown, President of Video-II-Go.

Have your supervisor review your letter before going on to the next step. Save the file.

3. If you refer to the Sales Summary Worksheet from Software Project 5 you will note that Marty was the winner of the sales competition for June. Prepare a letter of congratulations to Marty Hays at 66 Sky View Way, Fort Worth, Texas 76105. Include a copy of the graphic report showing June's sales data. If possible, combine the letter and the graphic output on a single page. The letter will inform Marty that the $100 bonus will be added to his next payroll check. The letter will be signed by Pat Brown.

Have your supervisor review your output before going on to the next step. Save the file.

4. Pat Brown has applied for a loan from Central Bank. The loan officer has requested a copy of the previous month's payroll data as part of the loan application. Prepare a letter to the loan officer, Marylou Franks at Central Bank, 2000 Broadway Avenue, Fort Worth, Texas 76100. The letter will be signed by you (as assistant payroll clerk) and will include the spreadsheet data that you prepared in Software Project 3. Indicate that you are providing the information at the request of your employer, Pat Brown.

Have your supervisors review your output before going on to the next step. Save the file.

5. Pat would like to increase rentals of the five least popular video tapes. To identify these tapes you should sort the database prepared in Software Project 4 on the No. of Rentals field in ascending numerical order. Move this data to a word processing file. Prepare a letter for Video-II-Go

customers informing them that rental of these tapes will be half price during the month of August. Pat Brown will sign the letter. Use the customer address file you prepared in Software Project 1 for the names and addresses of all the customers to receive this letter.

Have your supervisor review your output before going on to the next step. Save the file.

6. If you have not already done so, print copies of the four letters you have prepared in this project.

ENRICHMENT ACTIVITY

If you have access to desktop publishing software, prepare a coupon (similar to those used in magazines and newspapers) from Video-II-Go that lists the five least popular tape titles and indicate that the customer will receive "50% OFF THESE TI-TLES." Date the coupon *August 1*, and indicate that it expires in 30 days. If possible, combine the coupon and the text of the letter on a single page. Have your supervisor review your output before printing a sample letter.

INTRODUCTION TO PROGRAMMING

Many business people look at a computer as the ideal worker. It is fast, accurate, and tireless. But to employ this worker, you need to speak its language. One language that many computers understand is BASIC. Like all languages, BASIC has a structure (syntax) and a vocabulary. Because BASIC uses English words, you can learn it quickly. The BASIC projects in this book will show you how to make a computer work for you. Each project consists of instruction, a sample program, sample output, and activities to reinforce the material just covered.

COMMANDS AND PROGRAM STATEMENTS

The NEW Command and the PRINT and END Statements

The computer can be told what to do by typing in certain BASIC words known as *commands.* The command NEW, for example, clears the computer's memory of any program that was there so that it is ready for a new program to be entered. The word READY will appear on the screen or paper.

As you type the word NEW, it will be displayed on the computer screen or paper. Pressing the key marked RETURN (ENTER on some computers) tells the computer that you have finished typing the command and that it should be carried out.

If the computer understands the command, it will be executed. If not, an *error message* will be printed.

For example, if you typed in the word MEW instead of NEW and then pressed the RETURN key, the computer would not know what you meant. It would print an error message and then wait for you to give it another command. You could then repeat the command correctly, and it would be carried out as if you had not made the error.

In order for the computer to do something useful, it must be given a series of instructions which it remembers and then carries out when told to. This list of instructions is called a *program.*

In BASIC, each instruction is made up of a *line number* and a *statement.* The sample program shown uses two common BASIC statements: PRINT and END.

NEW   The NEW command clears the computer's memory and makes it ready to accept a new program.

PRINT The PRINT statement starts with the word PRINT and is followed by letters, numbers, or spaces enclosed within quotation marks.

END   The END statement ends the program. It is the last statement in a program.

SAMPLE PROGRAM

To enter this program into the computer's memory, you would first type the number 10, then the word PRINT, then the word GREETINGS in quotation marks. When you press the RETURN key, the computer reads the line and includes it as part of the program being stored in memory.

The BASIC program consists of two instructions. The first tells the computer to print whatever is between the quotation marks. The second instruction indicates that the program is over and the computer should stop processing it.

```
10 PRINT "GREETINGS"
20 END
```

The line numbers do not have to be consecutive (for example, 1, 2, 3, and so on). Programmers usually number by tens to make the program easy to read and to allow new lines to be added later on. When the RUN command is given, the instructions will be carried out in order of their line numbers, from lowest to highest. The END statement should have the highest line number.

OUTPUT

The RUN and LIST Commands

To cause the computer to *execute,* or carry out, the program, you must give the command RUN. When you do this, the word GREETINGS will appear on the screen or paper because that is what the instructions of the program tell the computer to do. If you make any errors in the program statements you entered, for example, misspelling the word PRINT, the computer will print an error message. The word GREETINGS will not be printed.

Another important BASIC command is LIST. This causes the instructions of the program to be displayed on the screen or printed on paper so that the programmer may examine them.

It is important to be clear about the difference between RUN and LIST.

RUN The RUN command tells the computer to execute, or carry out, the instructions in the program.

LIST The LIST command tells the computer to print the statements, or instructions, that make up the program.

As long as the program remains in memory, you may give the RUN or LIST command as often as you wish. This ability to repeat a task again and again is one of the features of computers that make them so useful. Giving the NEW command erases the program from the computer's memory.

The LIST command will cause the computer to display the program, like this:

```
10 PRINT "GREETINGS"
20 END
```

The RUN command will cause the computer to process the program, and the result will look like this. READY means that the computer is waiting for your next command.

```
GREETINGS
```

KEYBOARDING ACTIVITIES

1. Enter the program shown in the Sample Program section.
2. Use the RUN command to cause the program to be executed, and examine the output.
3. Keyboard the following program line.

```
15 PRINT "TO YOU!"
```

Give the LIST command, and examine the program listing to see that line 15 has been inserted between lines 10 and 20.

4. RUN the new version of the program, and examine the output.
5. Keyboard this program line.

```
15 PRINT "TO EVERYONE!"
```

Now LIST the program. The new line 15 replaced the old line 15. RUN the new version of the program, and examine the new output.

6. Keyboard this line.

```
15
```

That's right, just the line number with no statement after it. LIST the program. Line 15 is now gone. Entering a line number with nothing following it is a way of removing a line from a program. When you RUN the program, the output should be the same as when the original program was RUN.

ENRICHMENT ACTIVITIES

1. Give the NEW command to erase the previous program from the computer's memory, and write a new program telling the computer to print your name, address, age, and school name. LIST and RUN the program.
2. Change the program so that it causes the computer to print out the school address also. LIST and RUN the program.
3. Change the program again so that your age is no longer printed when the program is RUN. LIST and RUN this version of the program.
4. Give the NEW command again, and write a new program to print out any message you wish.

BASIC Project 2

INTRODUCTION TO OUTPUT: MAILING LABELS

All businesses need to store and communicate data. BASIC can help reproduce needed customer information such as mailing addresses.

PROGRAM STATEMENTS

The REMARK and PRINT Statements

BASIC allows you to store and display data in various ways. The REMARK statement is used to identify programs or to store information of interest for future use. The PRINT statement can be used to produce lines and boxes in computer output.

REMARK   The REMARK statement starts with the word RE-MARK (REM for short) and is followed by letters, numbers, special characters, or spaces. REMARK differs from PRINT, since no sign of this statement will appear on the output when the program is RUN.

PRINT   The PRINT statement can be used with special characters such as an asterisk (*) to format or box computer output.

SAMPLE PROGRAM

REMARK statements are commonly used to identify the purpose of and identify specific areas within the program.

The PRINT statement can be used to repeat special characters (*, -, .) to produce lines and boxes in computer output. You will see how special characters can be used to separate data on reports when you enter and RUN the program. Notice that PRINT statements without words in quotation marks (lines 20, 80, 100, 160, 180, and 250) produce blank lines.

```
10 REMARK PRINT OUT THREE MAILING LABELS
20 PRINT
30 PRINT "***********************"
40 PRINT "MS. JUDY R. CASHEO"
50 PRINT "1345 OLYMPIC BLVD."
60 PRINT "SEATTLE, WA 98940"
70 PRINT "***********************"
80 PRINT
90 REMARK START MAILING LABEL 2 ON THE NEXT LINE
100 PRINT
110 PRINT "***********************"
120 PRINT "MR. HALL R. ALEXANDER"
130 PRINT "P.O. BOX 7345"
140 PRINT "OMAHA, NE 68107"
150 PRINT "***********************"
160 PRINT
```

```
170 REMARK START MAILING LABEL 3 ON THE NEXT LINE
180 PRINT
190 PRINT "************************"
200 PRINT "DR. MARION BANDLEY"
210 PRINT "845 SOUTH FRONT ST."
220 PRINT "SUITE 2156"
230 PRINT "SAN DIEGO, CA 90956"
240 PRINT "************************"
250 PRINT
260 END
```

OUTPUT

The program as provided will display three mailing labels if key-boarded and RUN. Notice that the REMARK lines (10, 90, and 170) do not produce output. To display the complete contents of the program, including the REMARK lines, you must type LIST and press the RETURN key.

When the computer program is RUN, the output on the screen or printer should look like this:

```
************************
MS. JUDY R. CASHED
1345 OLYMPIC BLVD.
SEATTLE, WA 98940
************************


************************
MR. HALL R. ALEXANDER
P.O. BOX 7345
OMAHA, NE 68107
************************


************************
DR. MARION BANDLEY
845 SOUTH FRONT ST.
SUITE 2156
SAN DIEGO, CA 90956
************************
```

KEYBOARDING ACTIVITIES

1. Enter and RUN the program given above.
2. Examine the output.

3. LIST the program; compare the listing with the sample RUN.

ENRICHMENT ACTIVITIES

1. Add a REMARK statement indicating the author and the date that the program was written.
2. Write a new program that will prepare an announcement for a grand opening for a bank in your neighborhood. (Use the NEW command to erase the previous program from the computer's memory so that you will have a clean workspace in which to write this new program.)

All the programs you have written for these BASIC projects have been erased from the computer's memory when the NEW command was given or when the computer was turned off. This is not very efficient. Businesses need to use the same programs over and over and cannot enter long and complicated lists of instructions into memory by keyboarding each time they are needed. Programs are saved by being copied from the computer's *main memory* to a *secondary storage device,* such as a *magnetic tape* or *disk.* When a program is needed again, it may be copied from the tape or disk back into the main memory.

Chances are the computer you are using has a *disk drive,* which may be used to store programs on and retrieve them from magnetic disks. An ordinary cassette tape recorder might be used for saving programs on tape.

After you have written a program, a command such as SAVE is used to record it on a tape or disk. When you want to retrieve a program you have saved earlier, you use a command such as LOAD or OLD to copy from the tape or disk into the main memory.

Each computer system works differently, so you will have to ask your instructor or read the manual that comes with the computer in order to learn the correct procedures for the system you are using.

Once you have done this, save the programs you write for each BASIC project so you can go back to them at a later date.

| BASIC Project 3 | FORMATTED OUTPUT: BUSINESS LETTER |

Word processing needs are growing every day in the modern office. Programming can be used to store and retrieve routine correspondence. The following exercise will give you practice in preparing formatted output.

PROGRAM STATEMENTS

The PRINT and PRINT TAB Statements

We will expand upon our use of the PRINT statement in several ways in this exercise. The following program also introduces the PRINT TAB statement, which is used to tell the computer where (on a line) to start printing output. The statement always includes a number enclosed in parentheses. PRINT TAB (25) "HELLO" will cause the computer to print the word HELLO starting at the twenty-fifth space from the left margin.

SAMPLE PROGRAM

```
10 REMARK SAMPLE LETTER
20 PRINT TAB(20)"MAY 11, 19--"
30 REMARK CHANGE THE NEXT FIVE LINES FOR NEW ADDRESS
40 PRINT "MR, ROBERT THOMPSON"
50 PRINT "112 SCOTT STREET"
60 PRINT "SCOTTSDALE, TN 31340"
70 PRINT
80 PRINT "DEAR MR, THOMPSON,"
90 PRINT
100 PRINT "    PLEASE CANCEL OUR MEETING SCHEDULED"
120 PRINT "FOR FRIDAY, MAY 21, I WILL CALL FOR A NEW"
130 PRINT "APPOINTMENT,"
140 PRINT
150 PRINT
160 PRINT TAB(20)"SINCERELY,"
170 PRINT
180 PRINT
190 PRINT TAB(20)"MARTINA JONES"
200 PRINT
999 END
```

The PRINT TAB statement starts with the words PRINT TAB. These words are followed by a number in parentheses and whatever is to be printed within quotation marks. *NOTE:* If your computer system does not have a PRINT TAB command, use the print statement and space bar as shown here:

```
20 PRINT "                          MAY 11"
```

Notice that the date will be printed starting at position 20 on the line. The PRINT TAB statement will also make sure that the date will line up with the close and signature.

OUTPUT

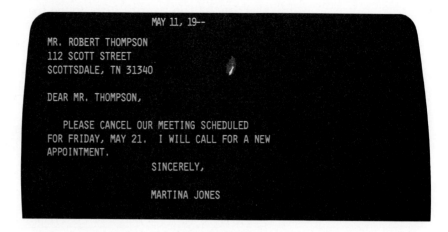

```
                    MAY 11, 19--

MR. ROBERT THOMPSON
112 SCOTT STREET
SCOTTSDALE, TN 31340

DEAR MR. THOMPSON,

   PLEASE CANCEL OUR MEETING SCHEDULED
FOR FRIDAY, MAY 21.  I WILL CALL FOR A NEW
APPOINTMENT.
                    SINCERELY,

                    MARTINA JONES
```

KEYBOARDING ACTIVITIES

1. Enter and RUN the program given above.
2. Examine the output.
3. Modify the program so that the date, close, and signature will start at print position 25.

ENRICHMENT ACTIVITY

Prepare a program that will produce a daily sign-in sheet for all the students in your class or work group. Discuss what will take place when new individuals enter.

BASIC Project 4

COMPUTER RUN CARDS

Many people think of computers as good tools for working with numbers and doing mathematics. The following exercise shows how a computer may also be used with words. It produces a computer job request card while introducing a new BASIC tool; the string variable.

PROGRAM STATEMENTS

The LET and DIM Statements and String Variables

The LET statement allows you to assign the value of a data item to a variable name for the purpose of storage and processing. LET can be used with numbers or strings (also called character strings). A *string* is a series of letters, numbers, punctuation marks, or other symbols. Names, addresses, and telephone numbers are examples of strings.

The result of a LET statement is that an item can be referred to by the name that it was given in a previous BASIC statement. This can eliminate a great deal of data input, which is costly. The item is called a *constant* because its value does not change. The name is called a *variable* because its value changes when the LET statement is used.

For example, both these BASIC programs will produce the same output.

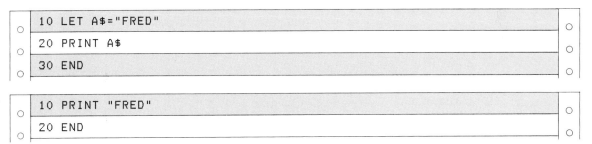

```
10 LET A$="FRED"
20 PRINT A$
30 END
```

```
10 PRINT "FRED"
20 END
```

The following program will print FRED and then print MARY.

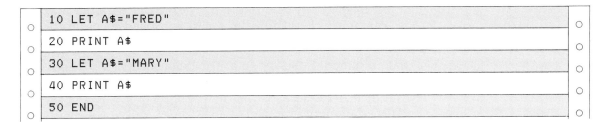

```
10 LET A$="FRED"
20 PRINT A$
30 LET A$="MARY"
40 PRINT A$
50 END
```

The value of A changes, or varies, from FRED to MARY because of the LET statements. The LET statement assigns the value FRED and then the value MARY to the variable called A. The PRINT statements cause the value of the variable to be printed.

Since the computer stores numbers and strings differently in its memory, it must know which type of data will be assigned to a variable by a LET statement. String variable names always end with a dollar sign ($). If there is no dollar sign, the computer assumes that the data will be numeric.

Many versions of BASIC allow you to use words for variable names. This makes it possible to use variable names such as NAME, ADDRESS, and AGE that are descriptive of the type of data to be assigned with LET statements.

The maximum allowable length of variable names varies from one version of BASIC to another, and in some cases, only single letters may be used. Consult the reference manual for your particular system to find out what the limitations are in your version of BASIC.

In this exercise, single letters are used for variable names. Since the data assigned to the variables are strings, each single letter is followed by a dollar sign.

Some versions of BASIC require you to specify the maximum length of a string that could be assigned to a string variable by a LET statement. The DIMENSION (or DIM) statement is used for this purpose.

The following statement means that the length of a string assigned to the string variable A may not exceed 25 characters.

```
100 DIM A$ 25
```

LET The LET statement starts with the word LET. This word is followed by a variable name, for example, A, X, Y, or Z; and a number or a string. A *string* is a series of letters, numbers, punctuation marks, or other symbols. The variable name assigned to a string must end with a dollar sign ($).

DIM The DIM statement starts with the word DIM. This word is followed by the name of the string variable and the maximum length of the string enclosed in parentheses.

DIM statements usually go at the beginning of a program because they must precede any use of the variable name in a LET, PRINT, or other statement. Many versions of BASIC do not use the DIM statement. Instead, a maximum length for strings is assumed. This maximum is generally quite large (often 256 characters), so the programmer need not be concerned about it.

Consult your instructor and reference manual to see if DIM statements are used in your version of BASIC and, if not, what the maximum allowable string length is.

NOTE: Do not confuse this DIM statement with the DIM statement used to dimension *arrays*. Arrays are like lists or tables of related data items. The size of an array must be decided upon before it is used. Arrays are commonly found in most versions of BASIC.

```
110 LET A$="WRITE TAPE FOR J. CROWLEY"
120 LET B$="JAN 12, 19--"
130 LET C$="ACCOUNTING"
140 LET D$="19-142"
150 LET E$="DISKETTE"
160 LET F$="TAPE #953"
170 LET G$="MAIN COMPUTER"
180 LET H$="LINE PRINTER"
190 LET I$="ROOM 152"
200 PRINT
210 PRINT "*************************************************"
220 PRINT
230 PRINT "    JOB REQUEST CARD"
240 PRINT
250 PRINT "JOB NAME:";A$;TAB(40)"DATE:";B$
260 PRINT "DEPARTMENT:";C$;TAB(40)"CHARGE NO.:";D$
270 PRINT "INPUT:";E$
280 PRINT "STORAGE:";F$
290 PRINT "PROCESSING:";G$
300 PRINT "OUTPUT:";H$
310 PRINT
320 PRINT "SPECIAL INSTRUCTIONS----------------------------------"
330 PRINT "----------------------------------------------------"
340 PRINT "----------------------------------------------------"
350 PRINT "ROUTE TO:";I$
360 PRINT
370 PRINT "*************************************************"
999 END
```

SAMPLE PROGRAM

Job request cards are prepared to give specific instructions to computer operators.

You will note that nine assignment or LET statements are made. Each variable is named by a letter (A through I) followed by a $.

The variable names (H$ is equal to LINE PRINTER) can be used in PRINT statements. This can save a great deal of data input and computer storage.

You will also notice in this program that more than one variable can be printed on a single line of output. On line 250, for example, you can see that the job name and the date will be printed on the same line. The TAB (40) will cause the date to be printed starting at space 40 on the line of output.

Notice that semicolons are used to separate the different components of the PRINT statement.

OUTPUT

```
***************************************************
   JOB REQUEST CARD
JOB NAME: WRITE TAPE FOR J. CROWLEY  DATE: JAN 12, 19--
DEPARTMENT: ACCOUNTING              CHARGE NO.: 19-142
INPUT: DISKETTE
STORAGE: TAPE #953
PROCESSING: MAIN COMPUTER
OUTPUT: LINE PRINTER
SPECIAL INSTRUCTIONS-------------------------------------------
------------------------------------------------------------
------------------------------------------------------------
ROUTE TO: ROOM 152
***************************************************
```

KEYBOARDING ACTIVITIES

1. Enter and RUN the program given above.
2. Modify the program to include the following: a second tape, number 407; and a special instruction, "MAKE TWO TAPE COPIES FOR SECURITY"

ENRICHMENT ACTIVITIES

1. Create a computer program that produces a letter of application for part-time employment. In your program use the LET statement and a string variable for the company name. In this way you can send the same letter to a new company simply by changing the contents of the string variable.
2. Produce two applications using your program.

INVENTORY

Computer systems are made up of numerous machine components. In some businesses, computer system components are treated like all other pieces of office equipment, and equipment locations must be accurately recorded and maintained. We can use BASIC to produce an equipment roster that can be easily updated when items are moved.

PROGRAM STATEMENTS

You used string variables (A$, C$, and so on) and set them equal to character strings (characters between quotation marks). We can use BASIC to create numeric variables. Numeric variable names *do not* have a dollar sign at the end. AGE, N, TOTAL, and B2 are examples of numeric variable names in BASIC. (Keep in mind that some versions of BASIC allow only single letters or a letter followed by a digit to be used for numeric variable names. Other versions allow longer names. Check your reference manual to find out what your system requires.) You will notice that the same variable can be given many different values in the same program. This is also true of string variables.

SAMPLE PROGRAM

```
10 REMARK INVENTORY FOR TYPEWRITERS
15 REMARK CHANGE LINES 30,50,70,90,110, WHEN EQUIPMENT MOVES
20 REMARK TO NEW ROOM
30 LET N1=121
40 PRINT "SCRIPTOR MODEL 3R IS IN ROOM";TAB(30);N1
50 LET N2=122
60 PRINT "ADVANCE MODEL 5 IS IN ROOM";TAB(30);N2
70 LET N3=123
80 PRINT "SCRIPTOR MODEL 3S IS IN ROOM";TAB(30);N3
90 LET N4=151
100 PRINT "ADVANCE MODEL 6 IS IN ROOM";TAB(30);N4
110 LET N5=152
120 PRINT "ADVANCE MODEL 7 IS IN ROOM";TAB(30);N5
130 END
```

In this program string variables (N1$, N2$, and so on) could have been used instead of numeric variables because no arithmetic operations were done with the room numbers. In BASIC Project 7 we will see a program where numeric variables are required. Here the programmer may make the choice.

OUTPUT

The room locations will all be printed starting at print location 30 to make the report more readable.

```
SCRIPTOR MODEL 3R IS IN ROOM          121
ADVANCE MODEL 5 IS IN ROOM            122
SCRIPTOR MODEL 3S IS IN ROOM          123
ADVANCE MODEL 6 IS IN ROOM            151
ADVANCE MODEL 7 IS IN ROOM            152
```

KEYBOARDING ACTIVITIES

1. Enter and RUN the program given above.
2. There is a shorter form of the LET statement. Oddly enough, it is formed by simply leaving out the word LET. The BASIC program line 30 N = 121 is the same as 30 LET N = 121. Change lines 30, 50, 70, 90, and 110 of the sample program, leaving out the word LET. Then run the program to verify that the output is the same as before. (The word LET is optional when this statement is used with string variables also.)
3. Modify the program to report the following changes.
   ■ All scriptors are now in Room 123.
   ■ The advance Model 6 has been dropped from inventory.

ENRICHMENT ACTIVITY

Prepare an inventory report for office equipment in your school or agency. Add serial numbers and the date purchased on a second line of print. (Do you need a string variable or a numeric variable for a serial number? What do you need for a date?)

BASIC Project 6   COMPUTER RUN CARDS: ON-LINE

The use of computer languages like BASIC can greatly simplify the development of computer software. Interactive languages make coding and testing much easier. The following exercise improves the program developed in BASIC Project 4 by allowing for on-line data input.

PROGRAM STATEMENTS

The value of a BASIC computer program greatly increases as the program becomes more flexible. In Project 4 we were able to prepare a job request card by changing the values of the string variables stored in the program. The INPUT statement allows us to alter the value of a string variable by keyboarding in data when the program is RUN. This means that values of variables may be changed without altering the program itself.

INPUT The statement starts with the word INPUT. This word is followed by a numeric variable (for example, A) or a string variable (for example, C$). Using the INPUT statement, we can enter a numeric variable (INPUT A) or a string variable (INPUT C$). This statement usually follows a PRINT statement, which explains to the user what kind of input is expected.

The semicolon is used after the PRINT statement to keep the computer from going to the next line. The INPUT statement then causes a question mark to be printed to show that the program is waiting for the user to key in data.

SAMPLE PROGRAM

The program below will wait at nine separate lines for user input (115, 125, 135, 145, 155, 165, 175, 185, 195). When the RUN command is given, the computer will first display the questions shown at the top of page 395.

```
10 REM INTERACTIVE VERSION OF BASIC PROJECT 4
100 REM PRINT JOB CARD FROM STRING VARIABLES
110 PRINT "JOB NAME";
115 INPUT A$
120 PRINT "DATE";
125 INPUT B$
130 PRINT "DEPARTMENT";
135 INPUT C$
140 PRINT "CHARGE NO.";
145 INPUT D$
```

```
150 PRINT "INPUT";
155 INPUT E$
160 PRINT "STORAGE";
165 INPUT F$
170 PRINT "PROCESSING";
175 INPUT G$
180 PRINT "OUTPUT";
185 INPUT H$
190 PRINT "ROUTE TO";
195 INPUT I$
200 PRINT
210 PRINT "*********************************************************"
220 PRINT
230 PRINT "        JOB REQUEST CARD"
240 PRINT
250 PRINT "JOB NAME:"A$;TAB(40)"DATE: ";B$
260 PRINT "DEPARTMENT:"C$;TAB(40)"CHARGE NO.: ";D$
270 PRINT "INPUT:";E$
280 PRINT "STORAGE:";F$
290 PRINT "PROCESSING:";G$
300 PRINT "OUTPUT:";H$
310 PRINT
320 PRINT "SPECIAL INSTRUCTIONS -----------------------------------"
330 PRINT "-------------------------------------------------------"
340 PRINT "-------------------------------------------------------"
350 PRINT "-------------------------------------------------------"
360 PRINT "ROUTE TO:";I$
370 PRINT
380 PRINT "*********************************************************"
999 END
```

The words JOB NAME were printed because of the PRINT statement in line 110. The question mark was produced by the INPUT statement in line 115. The program will not continue to line 120 until data is keyed in. When you type in WRITE TAPE FOR J. CROWLEY and press the RETURN key, the string you

```
JOB NAME?
```

just typed is assigned to the variable A$. The program then continues on to line 120, which causes the word DATE to be printed. Line 125 then causes a question mark to be printed. You will see this on your screen or paper.

```
DATE?
```

If you type in JAN. 12, 19- -, the value of B$ becomes JAN 12, 19- -, just as it would if you included the program line 120 LET B$ = "JAN. 12, 19- -" instead of using the INPUT statement (see Project 4).

The program will continue, waiting for data at each INPUT statement. After the last INPUT statement at line 195, the program continues, printing out the job request card. If you supply the same data that was used in the LET statements of Project 4, the output will be the same.

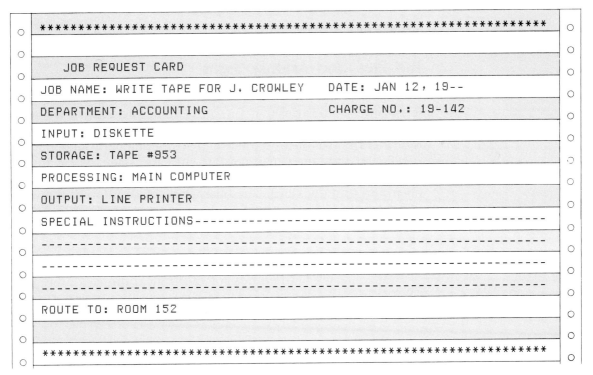

```
**********************************************************************

     JOB REQUEST CARD

 JOB NAME: WRITE TAPE FOR J. CROWLEY     DATE: JAN 12, 19--

 DEPARTMENT: ACCOUNTING                  CHARGE NO.: 19-142

 INPUT: DISKETTE

 STORAGE: TAPE #953

 PROCESSING: MAIN COMPUTER

 OUTPUT: LINE PRINTER

 SPECIAL INSTRUCTIONS------------------------------------------------
 --------------------------------------------------------------------
 --------------------------------------------------------------------
 --------------------------------------------------------------------
 ROUTE TO: ROOM 152

 **********************************************************************
```

KEYBOARDING ACTIVITIES

1. Enter and RUN the program given above.
2. Provide input data for each of the input questions. Use the data from Project 4.

3. RUN the program again, using different data. Compare the two outputs. RUN it a third time with a third set of data.

ENRICHMENT ACTIVITY

Prepare a label-making program that produces an identification label for any user. It should include the name, street address, city, ZIP Code, and phone number. Use a special character such as the asterisk (*) to form a box around your label output.

BASIC Project 7

SAVINGS DEPOSIT

Even the simplest data processing system will include objectives and requirements. The following exercise produces the minimum output for a useful savings deposit information system. It is not the complexity of the calculations that matters, but the value of the information the program produces.

PROGRAM STATEMENTS

The Plus and Asterisk Signs and Parentheses

It is difficult to think of business data processing without thinking of handling financial transactions. Most processing requires the use of fundamental arithmetic operations.

A PRINT statement can contain an expression using any of the four mathematical operations (addition, subtraction, multiplication, and division). The operations of addition and multiplication are indicated by using the symbol + for addition and the asterisk (*) for multiplication.

+ The plus sign stands for addition.
* The asterisk sign stands for multiplication.
( ) Parentheses can be used to tell the computer to perform the arithmetic operation within the parentheses first.

When the computer *evaluates* (figures out the value of) an expression, it does multiplication and division first, then addition and subtraction. The expression $3 + 4^*2$ would be evaluated by first multiplying 4 times 2 to get 8 and then adding 8 to 3 to get 11.

You can change this order by using parentheses. The computer evaluates what is in parentheses first, so $(3 + 4)^*2$ would be evaluated as 14. First 3 is added to 4 to get 7. Then 7 is multiplied by 2 to get 14.

Variables may also be used in expressions, as we will see in the sample program.

```
10 REMARK PROGRAM TO CALCULATE SAVINGS ACCOUNT INFORMATION
20 PRINT "TYPE BEGINNING BALANCE";
30 INPUT B
40 PRINT "TYPE DEPOSIT AMOUNT";
50 INPUT D
60 PRINT "TOTAL NOW IN ACCOUNT IS"; B+D
70 PRINT
80 PRINT "INTEREST (9.5%) IN 1 YEAR WILL BE";(B+D)*.095
90 PRINT
100 END
```

SAMPLE PROGRAM

In this program the user will enter the values for B (balance) and D (deposit). Since the input must be numeric, there is no dollar sign after the variable names.

This program shows that BASIC can be used to print both stored information and the results of an expression that is evaluated in the program.

OUTPUT

The following output would be produced if a balance of 125 (no $, please) and a deposit of 33 were inputted.

```
TYPE BEGINNING BALANCE?125
TYPE DEPOSIT AMOUNT?33
TOTAL NOW IN ACCOUNT IS 158
INTEREST (9.5%) IN 1 YEAR WILL BE 15.01
```

As you RUN this program, you should be aware of the possibility of making an error when data is entered into the program. At line 30, for example, the computer waits for you to type in a value for BALANCE. What if you typed in HARRY? Since BALANCE is a numeric variable (no $ at the end), the string HARRY would not be accepted, and an error message would be printed. You would have to start the program over from the beginning by typing RUN again.

Remember that if a string variable is used, any string of letters, numbers, or other characters may be assigned to the variable. A or LIZ or 128 or AL3-6767 may all be used with string variables; 128 could also be used with a numeric variable.

Also remember that only numeric variables may be used in arithmetic operations.

KEYBOARDING ACTIVITIES

1. Enter and RUN the program given above.
2. Input the following transaction amounts.

BALANCE	DEPOSIT
296	107
380	600
159	10

3. Modify the program to calculate the current savings interest rate in your area.

ENRICHMENT ACTIVITY

Create a savings deposit program that accepts the following input data.

Your name	Beginning balance
Account number	Deposit
Today's Date	Savings rate

Construct this program so that it will display or print two copies of a savings deposit receipt.

NOTE: You can repeat any BASIC statements in a program as long as each use has its own line number. For example, this will print HI twice.

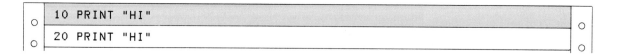

```
10 PRINT "HI"
20 PRINT "HI"
```

| BASIC Project 8 | LOAN PAYMENTS |

Computers are often used to count. Businesses and consumers will find BASIC very useful in performing the kind of arithmetic that is required when buying and selling goods. The following exercise shows all the common arithmetic functions.

PROGRAM STATEMENTS

As in addition and multiplication, symbols are used to represent subtraction and division.

  —   The minus symbol stands for subtraction.
  /   The slash symbol stands for division.

We can now create a BASIC program that uses all four math operations to calculate report data.

SAMPLE PROGRAM

If your version of BASIC allows it, use long descriptive variable names, such as AMOUNT for A, TOTAL for T, and BALANCE for B.

```
10 REMARK CALCULATE LOAN REPAYMENT
20 PRINT "HOW MUCH DO YOU WISH TO BORROW";
30 INPUT A
40 PRINT "AT 16.5% SIMPLE INTEREST, YOUR 4 PAYMENTS WILL BE"
50 T=A+A*.165
60 B=T
70 PRINT "PAYMENT 1";T/4
80 B=B-T/4
90 PRINT "BALANCE IS";B
100 PRINT "PAYMENT 2";T/4
110 B=B-T/4
120 PRINT "BALANCE IS";B
130 PRINT "PAYMENT 3";T/4
140 B=B-T/4
150 PRINT "BALANCE IS";B
160 PRINT "PAYMENT 4";T/4
170 B=B-T/4
180 PRINT "BALANCE IS";B
190 END
```

OUTPUT

The following output would be produced if the amount of $1000 were inputted as the amount to be borrowed.

```
HOW MUCH DO YOU WISH TO BORROW?  1000
AT 16.5% SIMPLE INTEREST, YOUR 4 PAYMENTS WILL BE
PAYMENT 1  291.25
BALANCE IS 873.75
PAYMENT 2  291.25
BALANCE IS 582.5
PAYMENT 3  291.25
BALANCE IS 291.25
PAYMENT 4  291.25
BALANCE IS 0
```

KEYBOARDING ACTIVITIES

1. Enter and RUN the program listed above.
2. Enter the following data.

Amount
1000
1450
600

3. Modify the program to calculate the current loan interest in your area.

ENRICHMENT ACTIVITY

Create a program that will produce a report for any number of payments. *WORKING TIP:* Use the INPUT statement.

SALARY SCHEDULE

Paying employees is a very important function in any business. Computers are used to process payroll data because they are accurate and reliable and because they can perform a variety of processing operations. The following exercise will show how BASIC can be used to calculate daily wages under a variety of working conditions.

PROGRAM STATEMENTS
The IF . . . THEN and GOTO Statements

In previous programs the INPUT statement was used to allow the user to keyboard variable input data as the program was run. The IF . . . THEN statement allows for decision making with respect to processing operations with a BASIC program. An example of an IF . . . THEN statement is 50 IF T = 1 THEN 600. If the value of T is 1 (as the result of an INPUT or LET statement before line 50), the program will *branch*, or jump, to the line number following the word THEN in the statement. If T has a value other than 1, the program will continue at the next line after line 50. The branch is called a *conditional branch* because it occurs only when a certain condition is met; in this case it is that T = 1.

The equals sign (=) is not the only relationship symbol that can be used in an IF statement. Any of the following symbols can be used.

=	Is equal to	>=	Is greater than or equal to
>	Is greater than	<=	Is less than or equal to
<	Is less than	<>	Is not equal to

These relationships make it possible for a program to make decisions about alternative processing operations on the basis of the input data a user provides.

Another type of branch is called an *unconditional branch* because it will always occur. In BASIC, the GOTO statement causes a jump to a specified line number. For example, 10 GOTO 90 will always cause the program to continue at line 90 after line 10. We will see in the sample program how this can be useful.

As the flowchart on page 402 shows, a program may follow one of several paths by using conditional branching.

SAMPLE PROGRAM

For the sample program shown on page 403, at line 70, a value for T is INPUT. The IF . . . THEN statements check this value and then direct the program along the appropriate path.

If T = 1, the IF . . . THEN at line 80 will cause a branch to line 200. If T does not equal 1, the program continues at line 90, where a test is made to see if T = 2. If this condition is met, there is a branch to line 300. Otherwise the program continues at line 100. If T = 3, there is a jump to line 400. If not, line 110 is the next line to be executed.

The GOTO statements are used to branch to the END of the program following a PRINT statement, thus assuring that only

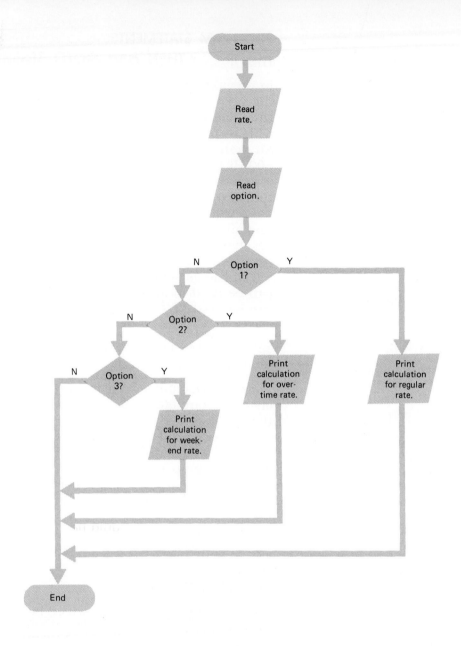

one message is printed for each value of T. Notice that if a value for T other than 1, 2, or 3 is INPUT at line 70, no branching will result from the IF . . . THEN statements in lines 80, 90, and 100. The program will reach line 110, where the GOTO statement will cause a branch to the END without any message having been printed out.

IF . . . THEN statements can compare alphabetic as well as numeric data, but the variable names must follow the rules for string variables. For example, 50 IF NAMES = "JOE" THEN 600 is a perfectly good BASIC program line.

```
10 REMARK CALCULATE DAILY SALARY FOR VARIOUS POSSIBLE SHIFTS
20 PRINT "INPUT WEEKLY WAGE RATE";
30 INPUT R
40 PRINT "TYPE 1 FOR REGULAR TIME"
50 PRINT "     2 FOR OVERTIME"
60 PRINT "     3 FOR WEEKENDS"
70 INPUT T
80 IF T=1 THEN 200
90 IF T=2 THEN 300
100 IF T=3 THEN 400
110 GOTO 410
200 PRINT "DAILY WAGE FOR REGULAR TIME IS";R/5
210 GOTO 410
300 PRINT "DAILY WAGE FOR OVERTIME IS";(R/5)*1.5
310 GOTO 410
400 PRINT "DAILY WAGE FOR WEEKENDS IS";(R/5)*2.0
410 END
```

OUTPUT

The following output would be produced if the amount of 280 were inputted for weekly wages and 1 for type of pay.

```
INPUT WEEKLY WAGE RATE? 280
TYPE 1 FOR REGULAR TIME
     2 FOR OVERTIME
     3 FOR WEEKENDS
?1
DAILY WAGE FOR REGULAR TIME IS 56
```

KEYBOARDING ACTIVITIES

1. Enter and RUN the program listed above.
2. Input the following data.

WAGE	OPTION
250	2
290	1
310	3

3. Modify the program to give *triple time* (3.0) for weekend work.
4. To see clearly how the GOTO statements work in this program, remove them and RUN the program using the same data you used in Activity 2 above. Also, RUN the program again and type in 4 for the option. Examine the output.

ENRICHMENT ACTIVITIES

1. Modify the sample program so that the message INVALID OPTION NUMBER is printed if a number other than 1, 2, or 3 is provided by the user.
2. Modify the sample program so that a string variable (T$) is used instead of T. Instead of numbers, the user would enter the word REGULAR, OVERTIME, or WEEKEND. The IF . . . THEN statements will also have to be changed so that tests are made for the strings instead of for numbers.
3. Create a BASIC program to produce a wage report that includes daily and monthly pay. Assume that the current week's schedule is repeated 4 times to calculate the monthly total.
4. Deduct (subtract) 1 percent of the monthly total for union dues, and show this deduction on the wage report output.

access time The length of time needed to store (or write) data or to retrieve (or read) data from memory.

acoustic coupler A special type of modem that has a cradle with rubber caps designed to hold the handset of a typical telephone.

Ada A general-purpose programming language developed under the direction of the Department of Defense. Ada promotes the development of portable, modifiable programs.

applications package A program that is purchased or leased from software developers or supplied by hardware manufacturers. Sometimes called off-the-shelf or canned programs, such packages are available for a wide variety of business information processing needs.

arithmetic-logic unit (ALU) A part of the central processing unit that performs computations and makes comparisons as instructed.

artificial intelligence (AI) A field of computer technology in which researchers and electronic product developers concentrate on simulating human intelligence with computer applications.

automation Performing work without human effort except that of instructing a machine in the work to be done.

BASIC The acronym for a general-purpose programming language whose full name is **Be**ginner's **A**ll-Purpose **S**ymbolic **I**nstruction **C**ode. Because BASIC is interactive, it is easy to test and debug.

batch processing The term applied to the collection of data for a set period of time for processing as a unit. The data can also be prepared at a different site and sent by mail or transmitted by remote terminal to a central location for processing.

binary system A computer number system based only on 0 and 1. Because this system contains only two digits, it is often called the base-two system.

bits (binary digits) The two values that result from current passing through magnetic cores. Each core is given a value of either "0" or "1," depending on the direction in which it is magnetized.

business modeling A technique that allows a manager or professional to predict the future of a business under a range of conditions.

byte A group of bits used to store a single character. A byte usually consists of eight bits which the computer handles as a unit.

C programming language A general-purpose programming language developed for writing systems software. The C language, which has only 30 or so required words, has flexible commands that allow it to be used with new and developing systems.

central processing unit (CPU) The "brain" of a computer, controlling the execution of processing instructions. A CPU consists of three parts: a control unit, an arithmetic-logic unit, and a storage unit generally referred to as the main memory.

central processor The combination of a computer's control unit and its arithmetic-logic unit.

coding The translation of each flowchart instruction into a programming language instruction.

COBOL The acronym for a programming language long used and still very popular in business. The full name is **CO**mmon **B**usiness-**O**riented **L**anguage.

communications The transmission or distribution of information from one person or place to another. Business information may be exchanged in a variety of forms—manually or electronically.

compiler A special computer program designed to translate a program from a high-level, English-like programming language into a machine-readable binary format such as a machine language.

computer-aided design (CAD) A computer system that permits an engineer to design products, machines, and buildings on a computer screen rather than on paper. The designer can update the drawing electronically as many times as necessary.

computer-aided manufacturing (CAM) A computer system that assists factory management both in producing parts exactly as specified by a CAD system and in scheduling the various manufacturing steps to achieve the required customer delivery dates.

computer-assisted instruction (CAI) The use of computers to help a student learn by working at his or her own pace. It is a system of individualized instruction using a computer programmed to present course work and practice material.

computer graphics specialist This computer professional designs visual displays and presentations for computer output.

computer hardware The physical equipment used for processing information by computer. Such equipment includes the computer which is electronic in operation and made up of individual devices that are interconnected. Besides the computer itself, there are input devices, storage devices, and output devices.

computer-integrated manufacturing (CIM) A computer system that connects and integrates all the manufacturing tasks in a factory to automate and control the process from a central computer.

computer networking The sharing of information among computer devices and their users by means of communications systems.

computer operator An individual who works with programmers and systems analysts on problems of work flow. This operator also works with computer technicians to ensure appropriate maintenance and repairs to prevent and resolve machine failures.

computer-output microfilm (COM) A special computer output device that records information at very high speeds on microfilm and microfiche.

computer program A list of instructions telling the computer what work to perform and how to perform it. A computer program is written in a programming language.

computer programmer The person who writes a computer program, or series of instructions, for the computer.

computer programming The task of preparing instructions for processing.

computer software The list of instructions (programs) and other procedures a computer system uses in information processing.

computer system A specific group of physically attached devices that perform processing operations. Input, central processing, storage, and output devices are generally included.

control unit The part of the central processing unit that interprets the instructions in a computer program. The control unit calls on the input devices, the storage unit, the arithmetic-logic unit, and the output devices as needed to have the instructions carried out.

customized software Software designed and developed to meet the specific requirements of the end user.

data Facts represented by numeric and alphabetic characters and special symbols. This raw data is processed into information by the computer.

database The term for a collection of computerized data organized into records and fields to permit easy access and retrieval.

database management software A program package that can be purchased from computer manufacturers or software service companies. The package consists of a set of standard machine instructions that make it easier for a programmer to write a program for handling the storage, updating, and retrieval of data in a file organized into records and fields.

database management systems (DBMS) The term for computer software designed to organize and maintain the information in databases.

data dictionary A listing (catalog) containing names and structures of all data types.

data entry Keying of input data directly into a computer or recording of data in machine-readable form.

data-entry operator An individual who works full time on input preparation and the keying of input data.

data field An area in the computer's main memory where a data record is stored.

data preparation The term referring to the tasks of collecting, recording, and classifying the data needed to produce the required information.

data processing See information processing.

data sorting The process of arranging paper documents or data records on magnetic disks or tapes in the desired sequence.

decision support system (DSS) A type of computer software program designed to aid management in obtaining and evaluating information. A DSS permits a manager to test the impact that alternative actions might have on the business.

desk debugging A manual self-check of programming code for accuracy and completeness.

desktop publishing The process of creating on a personal computer a document that looks like a professionally designed and printed document. Specialized software for a microcomputer and a laser printer instructs the computer to size and insert photos, graphics, and line drawings into the text copy.

diagnostics Computer-generated error messages that flag mistakes in coding. Such messages are included in the computer output to enable the programmer to correct syntax or other errors before rerunning the program.

direct access The ability to go directly to the storage location for the particular data required for processing, without having to

search through all the records from the beginning of the file.

disk drives Devices used to write (or store) data on disks and to read (or retrieve) data already stored.

distributed data processing (DDP) The term used for dividing (or distributing) computer processing work among two or more computers that are located in physically separated sites but connected by communications lines.

documentation Illustrations, comments, and explanations that must be prepared for each working program. Documentation typically includes flowcharts and written explanations (narratives) of the purpose of the program and each routine in it, sample input and output, and a test run.

electronic bulletin board A communications network that permits the posting of messages by personal computer users for other such users. A message input at a computer terminal is transmitted to the central computer of the electronic subscription service or special interest group (SIG) and placed in a storage unit for bulletin board messages.

electronic mail The name given to a mail system that uses computers and communications lines to transmit messages from one computer user to other users. Messages may be in the form of letters, memos, reports, or graphic displays.

electronic spreadsheet Computer software that allows the user to set up worksheets arranged as a series of rows and columns in a matrix format. A spreadsheet is used for doing calculations such as addition, subtraction, division, and multiplication automatically.

expert system A computer program that makes it possible for a computer to provide answers to questions in a specialized area. An expert system program incorporates a body of knowledge provided by a group of experts in the particular field.

fiber-optics A rapidly growing new technology that is replacing the older twisted-wire and coaxial cable technologies in voice and data communications facilities. A fiber-optic channel transmits voice and data communications by means of laser light beams.

field See data field.

file A collection of records about a particular business activity. Data is stored in a file and retrieved from a file regardless of the type of storage device used.

file maintenance The process of updating records in a file or database so they contain the latest information.

floppy disk A round, record-like object used for storing input data, processing instructions, and output data. These disks are usually 5¼ or 3½ inches in size.

flowchart A diagram showing the step-by-step instructions in a computer program. Such a diagram is prepared before the instructions to the computer are written in a language that can be understood by the computer.

graphics output The term for charts, maps, drawings, newspapers, books, and even movies that are produced on a computer and then displayed as soft copy on a screen and/or printed as hard copy on paper.

hard copy Data recorded in a form readable by human beings. Hard copy can be prepared manually or by machine.

hard disk The name for rigid, metal platters that have many times the storage capacity of floppy disks.

hardware See computer hardware.

information Facts organized in a meaningful way.

information processing The varied activities performed to convert data into useful information.

information processing cycle The full set of operations that take place, from collection of input data to the availability of output data.

input A collection of raw data at the start of the information processing cycle.

input/output (I/O) devices Mechanisms for reading in data to be processed and for reporting the results of processing.

inputting The recording operation, referring to the transfer of data entered at a keyboard or other device into the computer.

integrated circuits Thousands of small circuits etched on a silicon chip. As these circuits became more compact, they were called large-scale integrated (LSI) and very large-scale integrated (VLSI) circuits.

integrated packages The term for computer data that can be moved from one software application to another without keyboarding the data again.

intelligent terminal The name given to a programmable input device with substantial processing capabilities.

interactive graphics Communication between a user and a computer to develop a design or a drawing on a display screen. Architectural drawings are an increasingly popular application employing advanced computer technologies.

interactive processing The type of transaction processing in which a user conducts a dialogue or discussion with the computer through the use of an input device.

laser disk See optical disk.

local area network (LAN) A type of private network that links by communications lines computers, terminals, and other electronic equipment located within a relatively small geographic area. Telephone lines are the usual communications link.

Logo A programming language designed to teach problem-solving to children. Logo provides commands that offer graphics, data processing, and file creation.

mainframe Another name for the central processing unit of a large computer system. This unit includes a control unit and an arithmetic-logic unit.

management information system (MIS) A computer system designed to assist management with the direction, assessment, and planning of business operations.

menu A program's list of user choices or possible actions usually shown on a video display terminal. Choices are usually expressed in English-language statements for ease of use.

microcomputer The name given to a small, low cost computer system with a microprocessor as its "brain." A microcomputer can perform input, processing, storage and retrieval, and output operations rapidly, accurately, automatically, and economically despite its relatively small physical size.

microprocessor A complete central processing unit (the equivalent of the brain) of a computer placed on a single large-scale integrated (LSI) circuit.

microwave communications system A technology that enables a sending station to communicate data (or voice conversations) to a receiving station at another location by broadcasting signals.

minicomputer A computer having a smaller capacity for both primary and secondary storage than medium-size and large-size mainframe computers.

networks Communications systems that connect computers, terminals, and other electronic office equipment to accelerate the exchange of information.

office automation The use of new technology to reduce the human effort involved in performing office functions.

off-line data entry A two-step process that requires first the recording of input data in machine-readable form and then the entering of the recorded data into a computer for processing.

on-line inquiry The type of transaction processing in which an individual may directly request information by terminal from a computer and receive an immediate answer.

on-line terminal An input device with which it is possible to enter data directly into the storage or processing unit of a computer system. The terminal is connected to a computer by cable or by a communications line.

operating system A set of manufacturer-developed programs that perform three functions. They provide coded instructions for certain repetitive operations, they keep track of the running time for each job, and they schedule the sequence of jobs so as to perform the work in the shortest possible time. DOS, MS/

DOS, and ProDOS are examples of popular microcomputer operating systems.

optical disk The name for a storage device with a capacity many times that of a hard disk; that is much more durable than other disks; and that cannot be accidentally erased. Such a device is sometimes called an optical-laser disk.

output Useful information available at the end of the information processing cycle.

output reporting The operation of making the output results available to those who need them. The information that results from the information processing cycle may be reported in many different forms, depending on how the results are to be used.

packaged software Computer programs written for a large number of users with similar needs. Such programs are also known as off-the-shelf software.

parallel processing A technique for significantly increasing information processing speeds by equipping a computer system with multiple processors. Multiple processors allow a computer to handle a number of instructions at the same time.

parallel systems The operation of both the new and the old system at the same time. Management can assess the accuracy and the effectiveness of the new system by comparing its results with the results of the old system.

Pascal A general-purpose programming language that makes it easier than most other languages for a programmer to understand and alter work done by another programmer.

plotter One type of graphics printer used to provide hard copy of graphics output. The output appears in such forms as multicolored charts, graphs, diagrams, and maps.

point-of-sale data-entry system The entering of input data (concerning the product) into a computer at the location of a sale.

problem-solving The term for the process of figuring out the particular requirements for a given system.

processor See central processor.

program A series of instructions the computer is given for processing. The instructions are written by a computer programmer.

program flowchart   See flowchart.

program library   A file of all the programs needed to perform the computer processing work in a business.

programmer   See computer programmer.

programming   The preparation of a comprehensive list of instructions for computer processing.

programming language   The special language used in writing a computer program. The translation of each flowchart instruction into a programming language instruction is known as *coding*.

query languages   A group of programming languages that allow the user to instruct the computer by answering questions or issuing commands provided for by the language.

random-access memory (RAM)   The term for the most common type of main memory because the data contained in each storage address can be directly retrieved without regard for the sequence in which it was stored.

read-only memory (ROM)   The term for the type of main memory with data permanently or semipermanently recorded in it, which can be read only. This means that no new data can be transferred into ROM during processing. ROM is used to store program instructions that the computer always needs to operate.

real-time system   A business system that incorporates transaction processing.

record   The term for a collection of data about a particular individual, object, event, or transaction. Each record is comprised of data fields.

remote terminal   An on-line terminal located at a different site from the computer.

retrieval   The operation of searching for and finding data that is stored.

ring network   A communications system without a central computer. The network is made up of a series of computers and terminals connected by a communications line to permit direct communication from one com-

ponent to another. A ring network is generally used to handle the exchange of information among computer users and facilities within a single organization or group of organizations.

robotics   The use of robots controlled by computer to perform work ordinarily done by humans. Robots usually have computer-controlled arms and hands. A computer-controlled camera placed inside a robot enables the robot to recognize different objects.

satellite transmission   The broadcast of signals from an earth station to an orbiting satellite that amplifies and retransmits the signal to a receiving station on earth, possibly thousands of miles away from the sending station.

scanner   An input device that can accept data from source documents in typed, hand-printed, or machine-printed form. This device, also called a character reader, can be either a magnetic ink character reader (MICR) or an optical-character-recognition (OCR) scanner.

scenario   The term for a paired condition and projected result used in business forecasting.

semiconductor   A primary storage device consisting of small chips of silicon on which memory circuits and support circuits are etched. It is used for primary storage in the most recent computer models.

service bureau   A company that provides computer information processing services for a fee.

shared-logic system   A central processing unit shared by a number of individual workstations, each with a keyboard and video display terminal (VDT) connected by a cable to a large central processing and storage unit.

simulation   One usage means representing the operation of a system in a real-life situation by a computerized model. Another means using a set of test data for which the correct output and responses are known.

software   See computer software.

source document   Business form on which data is recorded as the starting operation in an information processing cycle.

star network A communications system consisting of a central computer to which many terminals and remote computers in different locations are connected by communications lines. A star network is often used in time-sharing systems whose end-users have no need to communicate with one another.

storage The saving of data for future use in information processing. The length of time the data is stored can vary from less than a second to months or even years.

subroutine A set of instructions that are generally used more than once. The instructions are written once, and the main program has statements that call upon the subprogram when it is needed.

supercomputer The name used for the largest, fastest, and most expensive type of computer available. These computers, which are much faster than the largest mainframe computers, can perform hundreds of millions of complex scientific calculations a second.

symbolic form The use of a letter, a number, or some other image to represent an idea to be communicated. The name usually used for programming languages in symbolic form is assembler.

systems analysis This first phase of system development work identifies exactly what a new or revised system is supposed to accomplish and what benefits should come from the system. It is also called problem analysis because it involves problem-solving.

system audit An evaluation process that management uses to examine the extent to which each of the predicted benefits of a new system is taking place.

system checkpoints The term for the checking and control operations that management establishes to ensure the accurate processing of data.

system conversion The process of changing from an old system to a new system.

system design This second phase of system development work identifies exactly how a system will accomplish the objectives specified in the systems analysis stage.

system development The process of creating a new system or of revising an existing system. This process usually requires four steps: systems analysis, system design, system implementation, and system evaluation and maintenance.

system feasibility report A report that summarizes the findings of the systems analysis phase. Its purpose is to compare the suitability of the present system with that of alternative systems.

system flowchart The series of manual and machine steps that make up the particular system being designed.

system implementation The steps that are necessary to install a new system and to put it into operation.

system specifications Documentation that defines the organization of the individual programs that make up the system.

technology The application of scientific knowledge to improve ways of doing things. Information processing technology is the application of science to improve methods of information processing.

teleprinter An input device that provides a printed copy of data as it is keyed into a computer.

terminal intelligence The classification of input devices with respect to their work ability or "intelligence." Classed in this way, there are three groups of terminals: dumb, smart, and intelligent.

telecommunications The transmission of data electronically by telephone circuits, microwave networks, or satellite transmission.

telecomputing A term for computer conferencing that permits interactive discussion between participants at different locations who communicate with each other through personal computer terminals.

teleconference A conference of people at different physical locations who, through communications networks, exchange ideas as though they were meeting in person.

time-sharing The sharing of a particular computer processor by a number of interactive users at one time.

transaction processing The processing of input data for a particular event as the event occurs. The business system that incorporates such processing is often referred to as a real-time system.

utility program A collection of instructions designed to perform common programming functions. Examples of such functions include sorting, copying, editing, deleting, and printing.

video display terminal (VDT) A data-entry unit equipped with a keyboard and TV-like screen. The screen displays characters and lines of text as they are being typed or retrieved. A VDT is sometimes called a CRT (for cathode ray tube) terminal.

videotex A two-way information service sent over a subscriber's telephone line or two-way television channel. A subscriber to a videotex information service can request information by depressing keys on a small hand-held terminal.

volatile memory The term applied to semiconductor memory because all the program instructions and data stored in main memory are lost when the electric current is turned off. The instructions must be stored on an auxiliary memory unit if they are to be used again.

word processing The processing of textual (primarily alphabetic) data to produce letters, reports, manuals, catalogs, newspapers, magazines, books, or other documents.

Index

Jobs, Steven, 38
Josephson, Brian, 356
Josephson junction, *def.*, 356

K

Key-to-disk input, 94–96
Key-to-tape input, 95

L

Laptop computers, 56–57; *def.*, 56
Large-scale integrated (LSI) circuits, 37
Laser disk, 126–127; *def.*, 126
Laser printer, 138–139
Law enforcement information systems, 205–206
Letter-quality printer, 43; *def.*, 133
Light pen, 90, 146
Line printer, 134–135; *def.*, 134
Local area network (LAN), 170–171
Logic operations, 114–115
Logo, 254
Lovelace, Lady Ada Augusta, 30–31

M

Machine language, *def.*, 249
Magnetic-bubble memories, 125–126; *def.*, 125
Magnetic card and tape typewriters, 41
Magnetic-disk storage, 8, 18, 118–122
   disk drives for, 118–119
   disk packs, 121–122
   floppy disks, 119–120
   hard disks, 120–121
   read-write heads for, 118–119
Magnetic-ink character recognition (MICR), 100–101; *def.*, 100
Magnetic-tape cassettes, 56, 60, 123;
Magnetic-tape storage, 96, 122–124
Main memory, 107–111; *def.*, 51
Mainframes, 59–61; *def.*, 59
Management information system (MIS), 195–196, 316–318; *def.*, 195
Manufacturing economy, 307
Mark I, 31–32
Marketing and technical support representative, 332–333
Mass storage devices, 124
Mauchly, John, 33, 34–35

Medical information systems, 202–203
Megabyte, *def.*, 111
Memory address, 107–108
Microcomputers, 19–20, 38, 54–57; *def.*, 19, 37, 55 (*see also* Home personal computers, systems for)
   central processing unit of, 106
   clones of, 56
   desktop, 57
   floppy disk for, 55
   in the future, 364–366
   hard disk for, 55–56
   laptop, 56–57
   magnetic-tape cassette for, 56
Microfiche, 148–149
Microfloppy disk, 120
Microforms, 148–149; *def.*, 148
Microimages, 148–149
Microprocessors, 37–38; *def.*, 37, 106
Microwave communications system, 160–162; *def.*, 161
Minicomputers, 37, 57, 59; *def.*, 57
Modems, 165–167; *def.*, 165–166
Monitor, 53
Monochrome screens, 140
Mouse, 90, 146
Multiplexers, 168

N

Nanosecond, *def.*, 113, 357
Narrowband channels, *def.*, 163
Natural languages, processing, 360–362
Networking, 169–180, 210–211
   distributed data processing, 173–174
   electronic blackboard, 176–177
   electronic mail, 175–176
   local area network (LAN), 170–171
   multiuser systems, 172
   private, 170–172
   ring network, 170
   star network, 169
   teleconferencing, 176–177
Nonimpact printer, 135–139; *def.*, 135
Nonletter-quality print, 133–134; *def.*, 133
Nonreadable copy, 8
Nonvolatile memory, 109
Numeric sorting, 11–12

O

Octal (base 8) number system, 71

Off-line input devices, 92–96; *def.*, 92
   card reader, 94
   entry of data, 96
   key-to-disk shared-processor systems, 95
   punched-card, 93–94
   recording data on magnetic media, 95
Off-the-shelf software, 271–273
Office automation, 45–46; *def.*, 45
On-line input devices, 86–92; *def.*, 86
   display screen characteristics, 87–90
   graphics terminal, 91
   on-line display terminal, 87–91
   printing terminal, 92
   remote terminal, 87
   terminal intelligence, 90–91
On-line inquiry, *def.*, 84–85
On-line inquiry systems, 156–157; *def.*, 156
On-line terminal operator, 334
Operating system, 263–264; *def.*, 263
Operational equipment, *def.*, 232
Optical character readers (scanners), 98–99
Optical character recognition (OCR), 98
Optical computer, 357–358; *def.*, 357
Optical (laser) disk storage, 126–127; *def.*, 126
Optical fiber channel, 160
Optical mark scanner, 98
Optical mark scanners, 98
Optical scanning methods, 98–99, 219–220
Output, *def.*, 6
Output devices, 52–53, 130–151; *def.*, 131 (*see also* Graphics output; Printers)
   display of statistical or text output, 140–141
   microform, 148–149
   punched-card, 150
   storage on disk or tape, 151
   voice-response, 149–150
Output formats, 221–222
Output reporting, 13–14, 156; *def.*, 13

P

Packaged software, 271–273; *def.*, 271
Page printer, 134, 135; *def.*, 134
Parallel processing, 354–356; *def.*, 354